Ælfric

By JAMES HURT

University of Illinois

Twayne Publishers, Inc.   ::   New York

ABOUT THE AUTHOR

James Hurt is an associate professor of English at the University of Illinois, Urbana, Illinois. He received his AB and MA degrees from the University of Kentucky in 1956 and 1957, and his Ph.D. degree from Indiana University in 1965. He has also taught at the University of Alaska, the University of Kentucky, and Indiana University (Kokomo campus). He has published articles in the *Journal of English and Germanic Philology, Modern Drama, Modern Fiction Studies,* and the *Keats-Shelley Journal, English Studies,* and the *Journal of the Folklore Institute.* In addition to his academic duties, he is artistic director of The Depot, an experimental theater in Urbana.

AELFRIC

by James Hurt

Aelfric is a critical survey of the work of the most important writer of English prose before the Norman Conquest. The volume begins with a brief account of the social, political, and intellectual situation of the last half of the tenth century in England, the world in which Aelfric lived and wrote. It goes on to draw together the few facts that are known about his life into the outline of a biography. It then proceeds to a systematic survey of the comparatively voluminous work of Aelfric. Detailed critical descriptions are provided of the two series of *Catholic Homilies*, the *Lives of Saints*, the miscellaneous Bible translations, and the Latin grammar and *Colloquy*. Special attention is given to the underlying unity and coherence of Aelfric's work, as well as to such topics as his relationship to the tradition of medieval biblical interpretation, his narrative techniques, and his theory and practice of translation. A separate chapter is devoted to a study of Aelfric's prose style, the achievement for which he is best known.

The first book-length study of Aelfric to appear in twenty-five years and the first in English in over fifty years, *Aelfric* brings together for the first time the results of a great deal of recent scholarship on this major figure in Old English literature. An annotated bibliography of major scholarly studies of Aelfric is provided for the guidance of the student who wishes to use the book as a guide to further study. But even for the general reader, Aelfric may serve as an introduction to a body of work interesting not only for its early date but for its intrinsic value, as it appears against the background of its own time and from the longer perspective of the present.

Preface

The inclusion of Ælfric in the Twayne English Authors Series might suggest a number of perennial questions about the continuity of English literature and the propriety of maintaining or not maintaining the great gulf that ordinarily separates Old English and later literature. These questions certainly deserve the attention they have received, but I have chosen to ignore them in this brief study of the most accomplished prose writer of the Old English period. I have taken for granted that Ælfric and his works are worth studying for their own sake and that they deserve the attention of anyone interested in good writing, whether he is especially interested in Old English or not.

I do not minimize, however, the problems that confront the non-specialist in approaching the work of a writer so remote from us chronologically and, in some ways, intellectually. I have therefore attempted in the first chapter not only to summarize what is known of Ælfric's life but also to suggest something of his social, political, and intellectual environment. The brevity and superficiality of this survey may offend the specialist, but I have chosen to risk doing so rather than to puzzle other readers by omitting all mention of the conditions which inspired Ælfric's work and guided its course.

In the succeeding chapters, rather than following an all-inclusive, chronological plan, I have selected five aspects of Ælfric's achievement and organized each chapter around one of these topics. Chapter 2 deals with Ælfric as a homilist; Chapter 3, with his work as a hagiographer; Chapter 4, with his Bible translations; and Chapter 5, with his pedagogical texts for Latin instruction. The final chapter abandons this organization by content to consider Ælfric's prose style, the aspect of his work for which he is chiefly remembered.

The problem of quotations has been difficult. It seems very important that such a stylist not be quoted in inevitably lame modern translation, but I realized also that many readers lack a knowledge of Old English. I have therefore quoted Ælfric in Old

English but have included a modern translation immediately following each quotation. These have been included in the text, rather than in the notes, as a matter of the reader's convenience. The translations are for the most part my own, rather than published translations, because I believed it desirable that the modern translations be genuinely modern and reasonably consistent in style. Ælfric's Latin is quoted only in English (S.H. Gem's translations). Although Ælfric's Latin style deserves more attention, I have not considered it necessary to include the Latin texts here.

The texts of the quotations are drawn from the standard editions cited in the Bibliography. Here again I have striven for clarity and consistency. In general, I have followed the principles presented by John Pope in his valuable new edition of the previously unedited homilies. That is, although the "ordinary prose" is printed in the customary way, passages in "rhythmical prose" are arranged in rhythmical lines, whether they are so arranged in the printed texts or not. There are, however, no medial spaces between "half-lines." This method should call attention to the form without suggesting that it is poetic in any sense and should aid the reader in perceiving the correct rhythm. All punctuation has been altered, if necessary, from the printed texts to conform with modern practice, again to make it easier to read the texts easily and accurately. No indications of stress or length have been included, and certain symbols have been silently expanded. (The Old English ampersand, for instance, has always been expanded to "and.") References are identified in the text, rather than the footnotes. The abbreviations are, I believe, self-explanatory, and always refer to the printed texts listed in the Bibliography.

JAMES HURT

University of Illinois

Contents

Chronology

c. 955	Ælfric born, probably somewhere in Wessex.
c. 970	Entered the Old Monastery at Winchester.
c. 985	Ordained as a priest.
987	Went to the newly founded monastery at Cernel.
989	*Catholic Homilies* I.
992	*Catholic Homilies* II.
992–1002	*De Temporibus Anni, Grammar, Glossary, Genesis, Colloquy, Interrogationes, De Falsis Deis, De XII Abusivis, Lives of Saints, Hexameron, Joshua* (in approximately this order, along with miscellaneous other homilies and occasional pieces).
1002–1005	*Numbers, Judges, Admonitio* (probably also a series of forty homilies for the Proper of the Season, called by Clemoes Temporale Homilies I).
1005	Went to the new monastery of Eynsham as abbot; Latin *Letters for Wulfstan; Letter to the Monks of Eynsham.*
1005–c. 1010	*Letter to Sigeweard,* reissue of *Catholic Homilies* I, *Life of Æthelwold,* English *Letters for Wulfstan,* probably another series of homilies (Temporale Homilies II), reissue of *Catholic Homilies* II.
c. 1010	Ælfric died.

CHAPTER 1

Ælfric and the Tenth Century

ABBOT Ælfric of Eynsham was born about the middle of the tenth century, and his life spanned the last half of that century, a period of great political, social, and intellectual activity. He saw during his lifetime a renaissance of English culture that rivaled and in some ways surpassed the earlier "golden age" of intellectual and artistic activity in eighth-century Northumbria. He also lived to see what England had dreaded above all else, the renewal of attacks by the Danes, whose depredations during the preceding century had been halted by King Alfred. They descended again during his lifetime, "like wolves," Ælfric said, and threw England into a political and economic chaos ended only by the conquest of the island by William the Conqueror, several decades after Ælfric's death.

Ælfric's life and work were intimately related to his age. He led a quiet life and participated, as far as we know, in none of the great political events of his time. We do not know how well known he was during his own lifetime, but in retrospect, it seems that his work so well reflects the quality of his age that we may speak of the late tenth century as the Age of Ælfric, as we speak of the eighth century as the Age of Bede or the ninth century as the Age of Alfred.

I *England 950–1000*

The birth of Ælfric at mid-century happened to coincide with the end of a long and tortuous process of political reunification of England after the assaults of the Danes in the ninth century.[1] The Danes had attacked Lindisfarne in 793; over the first half of the ninth century, their incursions grew in size and ferocity until it was clear by 850 that they intended to conquer the whole island. In 865, the Great Army of the Danes landed in East Anglia; it was led by the Viking chieftains Ivar the Boneless and Halfdan, both sons of the famous Ragnar Lothbrok. Over the next fifteen years, this army methodically pushed across England, taking violent possession of area after area. They held virtual possession of Northumbria,

Mercia, and East Anglia by 871, when Alfred became king of Wessex in the middle of a sustained Danish attack against his kingdom.

Alfred bought peace from the Danes and thereby gained five years respite from their attacks, during which he struggled to amass the force necessary to repel them. In 875, when they returned to attack Wessex again, Alfred was able to fend them off; but they returned again in 878. Alfred was forced to fall back to a small fortification at Athelney in the midst of the marshes southwest of Selwood. From this base, he conducted raids against the invaders, and finally engaged the enemy at Edington and defeated him. Alfred proceeded to fortify southern England, and he advanced in 886 to London and occupied it.

The occupation of London was decisive; it was followed by a treaty between Alfred and the Danish king Guthrum, by which England was divided between them. Alfred kept control of London and southern England; Guthrum was given possession of the Danelaw, the area north of a line running roughly northwest from London to Chester. Wessex remained English, and Alfred was able to devote the last years of his life to the restoration of English learning and culture, which had been virtually destroyed by the Danes.

When Alfred died in 899, he was succeeded in turn by his son, Edward the Elder, and by his grandsons Athelstan, Edmund, and Eadred, whose reigns stretched from 899 to 955. The controlling purpose that ran through their reigns was the recovery of the Danelaw. In 910, Edward defeated a large Danish force in Staffordshire; by 924, the year of his death, he held all England south of the Humber, the traditional boundary of the southern English. His successor, Athelstan, pushed the line ever farther north and engaged combined Scandinavian, British, and Scottish forces in a battle in 937 at Brunanburh (exact location now unknown), where he won a victory celebrated in heroic verse reminiscent in style of the old epics.

Brunanburh did not mark the end of English struggles with the Danes; but to Athelstan's contemporaries, as to posterity, it seemed to mark a pivotal point in history. The England that the Danes' Great Army had invaded in 867 had been an island fragmented into separate kingdoms, with political dominance passing among them according to the chances of war and politics. The England that emerged from Brunanburh was a nation, forged in the fire of the Danish wars and united under the crown of Alfred's Wessex.

The Danes would return and the throne would be contested, but England would never return to the old political order. Brunanburh symbolized this significant transformation; the unification of England became complete in 954, during the reign of King Eadred, when Eric Bloodaxe, last of the Scandinavian kings of York, was expelled from his throne and all Northumbria was once more in English hands.

England in 955 was a country of perhaps a million people who lived in a few fair-sized towns and many small villages. London was even then the largest of the towns; estimates of its tenth-century population, and of Winchester's, vary greatly because neither city was included in the eleventh-century Domesday Survey, our main source of such statistics. But York, which was about the size of Winchester and considerably smaller than London, numbered about eight thousand inhabitants in the tenth century. Norwich and Lincoln had about five thousand inhabitants each, and a few other sizable towns—Thetford, Oxford, Colchester, Cambridge, and Ipswich—had populations between a thousand and four thousand.

Between the towns, much of the countryside was wild and desolate. Three great forest areas, the Weald, the Essex-Chiltern belt, and the Bruneswald, covered about half of the southern part of the island. Farther north, the country was less heavily wooded, though sizable forests were found here and there, notably a chain of forest lands between the Trent and Severn rivers in the western midlands. Massive stretches of marshland also isolated the separate parts of England. A large fen region covered much of East Anglia, and another, the Humber fen, formed a boundary between the northern and southern kingdoms. Despite these obstacles, travel and communication were made somewhat easier by a basic network of roads that crisscrossed the island, survivals from Roman times. Other reminders of Roman days remained here and there: abandoned towns, deserted fortresses, temples, and bridges on which the Old English tended to look with awe as "the work of giants."[2]

The center of administration of the government was London; the treasury was at Winchester. In these two cities, and on several royal estates, the king presided over a court known for its splendor and cosmopolitan character. Even in pagan days, the kings of England had surrounded themselves with wealth and material splendor; the recently excavated ship tomb of a seventh-century East Anglian king at Sutton Hoo, Suffolk, contained objects of great

richness and beauty.[3] In the mid-tenth century, the greater sway of
the king of all the English encouraged yet greater pomp and display:
magnificent buildings, gold-inwrought tapestries, cups and other
ornaments in precious metals, treasures from abroad. This age was
one in which the king came to be regarded not merely as a leader of
men but as God's particular agent. The king was elected by the
royal council or *witan;* but, once consecrated to the throne, the
king ruled not merely by the sanction of man but "by the grace of
God." The elaborate coronation of King Edgar at Bath in 973,
presided over by Archbishop Dunstan, is a key event in the development of the idea of English kingship: it demonstrates, in its ceremon-
iousness, its dignity, and its pomp, the degree to which the sanctity
of the king was shown outwardly in material splendor.[4]

The political stability achieved in England by mid-century made
possible the second and last period of high cultural achievement
in Anglo-Saxon history. The first such period had been the late
seventh and eighth centuries, when the separate kingdoms had
reached an approximate balance of power and men could turn from
war to art and learning. This period had been dominated culturally
by Northumbria and its great figures had been Bede and Alcuin of
York. Now, in the second half of the tenth century, a similar respite
from political turmoil brought about a second period of cultural
development, one centered, however, in the south and east midlands.
Its leaders were the Benedictine monastic reformers Dunstan,
Æthelwold, and Oswald; and its chief literary figure was Ælfric.

The throne of England was occupied during this half-century by
Eadwig (955–959), Edgar (959–975), Edward (975–978), and
Æthelred (978–1016). The events of their reigns formed a dramatic
reversal, a succession of prosperity by disaster that suggests tragedy.
This tragic sequence left a deep mark upon those who lived through
it; its lessons formed a major theme of Ælfric and his fellow homilist
Wulfstan at the end of the century.

The climax of Edgar's reign, during which art and learning
flourished in an England at peace, was his coronation. Edgar was
crowned when he had already reigned for fourteen years. (The
coronation was perhaps delayed so long in order to hold it when
Edgar reached the age of thirty, the minimum age for ordination to
the priesthood.) A kind of tragic irony marked the course of the
English throne in the years immediately following the coronation.
Edgar died two years later, in 975; and his successor, his son Edward,
was brutally murdered in the third year of his reign. The long reign

of his successor Æthelred was so marked by disaster and incompetent leadership in meeting it that Æthelred was forever known by an epithet which is a bitter pun: *Æthelræd Unræd.* (*Æthelræd* meant "noble counsel"; *unræd* meant "no counsel.")

The Danes returned soon after the ten-year-old Æthelred took the throne; and, as a hundred years before, their raids rapidly grew in frequency and ferocity. But Æthelred was no Alfred, and he was surrounded by men of wavering allegiance at best. The nation's leaders adopted the fatal policy of trying to buy off the Danes and so levied a "Danegeld": a tax to raise tribute money. Six times in Æthelred's reign the tribute was paid, growing gradually heavier, as blackmail payments do. The tax drained the country; and, as the Danes grew more demanding, England grew poorer, weaker, and less able to defend herself.

Against the intricate tapestry of blackmail, deceit, and treachery that forms the political history of late tenth-century England, one episode stands out that temporarily reminded the demoralized people of their heroic past. In 991, a small English force commanded by Ealdorman Brihtnoth met a larger Viking force at Maldon. Conducting themselves by the same code that Beowulf followed, they gave the enemy the advantage and then engaged him with epic determination. A contemporary poet wove an old-fashioned heroic poem out of the result: the entire force, refusing to leave the field alive, fell beside its leader.[5]

But weakness of national leadership in England and the legendary fighting powers of the trained and disciplined Vikings from Jomsborg determined the issue. The Danish commander Swein Forkbeard launched an all-out attack against England in 1013; Æthelred fled to Normandy. This time a dramatic reversal like the one Alfred had brought about never came. After a period of additional chaos, the Dane Cnut became king of England in 1016. Danish kings held the throne until 1042, when Edward the Confessor restored the old line of Wessex. His successor, Harold, was to be the last Anglo-Saxon king; on September 28, 1066, William of Normandy disembarked with a Norman army on the shores of England.

II *The Benedictine Revival*

Against the grim chronicle of tenth-century political events must be set the story of the religious and intellectual life of Ælfric's day. For, though Ælfric's work was marked by the disasters of politics and war, the work was made possible by a general revival of cultural pursuits that flourished through the darkest hours of the close of the century. This revival was nurtured by the English monasteries under the leadership of three remarkable men: Dunstan, Æthelwold, and Oswald.[6]

Monasticism had always played an important role in English Christianity. The Celtic church had been organized around its monasteries, within each of which might be several bishops, who had no fixed dioceses, but who traveled about freely, preaching and ministering to the people. The Synod of Whitby, in 663, had spelled the end of the Celtic practice, replacing it with the diocesan organization of the Roman church. But, within the diocesan framework, monasteries continued to flourish. St. Augustine himself had founded the monastery of St. Peter and St. Paul at Canterbury; in the two hundred years after his arrival in 597, fifty or so monasteries were founded around England, if we count only those whose names survive.

The monasteries had played a dominant role in the eighth-century cultural flowering in the north. The earliest of these northern monasteries was Lindisfarne, founded by Aidan, the first missionary to Northumbria, on the island of Lindisfarne, just off the coast of Northumbria. Other early northern monasteries were at Gilling, Melrose, Tynemouth, Gateshead, and Lastingham. There were "double monasteries," with communities of both priests and nuns, at Hartlepool, Whitby, and Coldingham. Other notable monasteries were the twin houses of St. Peter at Monkwearmouth and St. Paul at Jarrow, founded in 674 and 681, respectively, by the learned Benedict Biscop. Jarrow holds a special place in the history of early English monasticism because it was the monastery where Bede spent his life.

The Danish invasions put an end to this first period of monastic glory. Lindisfarne, on its exposed, unprotected island, had borne the brunt of one of the first Danish attacks in 793. The raiders had sacked the monastery and forced the monks to take to the road, carrying the relics of their saint, Cuthbert, for a long period of wandering; and Bede's Jarrow was sacked the following year. As the Danes swept across the country, monastery after monastery fell, libraries were burned, and monks were slaughtered. When Alfred came to the throne, little was left of the monastic movement. The extent of the ruin is indicated by Alfred's famous remarks about the situation when he became king in the preface to his English translation of Gregory's *Pastoral Care:*

Swiðe feawa wæron behionan Humbre ðe hiora ðeninga cuðen understondan on Englisc, oððe furðum an ærendgewrit of Lædene on Englisc areccean; and ic wene ðæt noht monige begiondan Humbre næren. Swæ feawa hiora wæron ðæt ic furðum anne anlepne ne mæg geðencean besuðan Temese ða ða ic to rice feng . . . . Ða ic þa ðis eall gemunde ða gemunde ic eac hu ic geseah, ærþæmþe hit eall forheregod wære and forbærned, hu þa cirican geond eall Angelkynn stodon maðma and boca gefylda.

(There were very few on this side of the Humber who could understand their service-books in English, or even translate a letter from Latin into English; and I believe that there were not many beyond the Humber. So few there were that I cannot remember a single one south of the Thames when I came to the throne. . . . When I remembered all this, I remembered also how I had seen, before it had all been ravaged and burned, the churches around all England standing filled with treasures and books.)[7]

Alfred, of course, labored to restore the church and the educational system. He gathered scholars around him: Werferth, Bishop of Worcester; Plegmund, Archbishop of Canterbury; Asser, Alfred's earliest biographer. He encouraged the study of Latin; and, for those unable to read Latin, he translated or had translated a small library of indispensable books: Gregory's *Pastoral Care* and *Dialogues,* Orosius's *Universal History,* Bede's *History,* Boethius's *Consolation of Philosophy,* and part of St. Augustine's *Soliloquies.* In the marshes of Athelney, in the place from which he had organized his counterattack on the Danes, he built a new monastery, as a sign of thanksgiving. At Shaftesbury, he built a nunnery, and his daughter Æthelgifu became its abbess.

But these efforts bore little fruit in Alfred's lifetime or in the lifetimes of his immediate successors on the throne, his son Edward and his grandsons Athelstan, Edmund, and Eadred. Edward completed the New Minster his father had planned for Winchester, and he laid Alfred's body there. Alfred's widow founded a nunnery, also at Winchester. The real restoration of the monasteries, however, was to be the work of the reign of King Edgar. The leaders in this work were the three great monastic bishops: Dunstan, Bishop of Worcester and Archbishop of Canterbury; Æthelwold of Winchester; and Oswald, Archbishop of York and Dunstan's successor as Bishop of Worcester. The characters of these three men were very different;

yet they were united in the common goal of restoring English monasticism to the high place it had once held in the life of the country.

Dunstan, who was born about 909 in Somerset,[8] was of a family of high rank and was distantly related to King Edward. Dunstan spent his childhood at Glastonbury, the most ancient monastery in England, connected by tradition to Joseph of Arimathea and to King Arthur. Here he was educated and eventually became one of the brethren, though he did not yet enter into genuine monastic life. In 923, Dunstan's uncle, Athelm, became Archbishop of Canterbury; and Dunstan visited him at Canterbury and came to know the court, including the young king, Athelstan. After 926, when Athelm died, Dunstan was regularly in attendance at court, where he eventually had trouble because of the envy and distrust of some of his companions. The young Dunstan was brilliant and learned and had a wide range of interests. He was skilled in music and art and was particularly interested, it seems, in secular poetry and in the songs and legends of his people. But a strong thread of otherworldliness and mysticism ran through his character, and perhaps he was rather tactless. At any rate, it came to be rumored that he studied heathen magic and spells; after a time, when the gossip had reached the king, Dunstan was dismissed from court. Some of his enemies followed him, fell upon him, beat him, and left him in a muddy bog. Dunstan went to the house of a second episcopal uncle, Ælfheah of Winchester. Here, at the age of twenty-six, as he recovered from his experience at court and as he talked with his uncle, he began to acquire the sense of a great mission for his life: the restoration of English monasticism.

The decline of English monasticism in the ninth century had not been an isolated phenomenon; it had been matched by a parallel decline on the Continent. But, in 935, a strong reform movement had been working for twenty-five years to restore the monasteries. The form which this movement took was a return to the observance of the Benedictine Rule, the directions laid down by the founder of the order for the regulation of monastic life, or the development of these directions in the ninth century by Benedict of Aniane. The *Capitulare Monasticum* of Benedict of Aniane required uniformity in all monasteries concerning the daily schedule of prayers, the rules of conduct, even the amounts of food served. Monks were to keep silence, to avoid any but the most necessary contacts with the world, to observe the strictest obedience to spiritual guardians, and to follow a rigorous daily routine of worship and prayer.

Opposed to this demanding way of life was the tradition formulated by the eighth-century St. Chrodegang of Metz, by which monasteries could be formed of clergymen who lived together under rule but who were unbound by the Benedictine vows and who could own property and even live apart from the monastery. These permissive practices had spread widely, not only in France but also in England.

The beginning of reform on the Continent had been the establishment of a monastery at Cluny in Burgundy in 910. From this center, the reform movement spread to other monasteries: notably Fleury on the Loire and Ghent and St. Omer in Flanders. It is uncertain how much influence these Continental reforms had upon the young Dunstan; but, under the guidance of Ælfheah of Winchester, he began to formulate ambitions for similar reforms in England. The prospect of renouncing secular life was at first daunting to him; but, after a critical illness, he decided to become a monk and to labor to restore regular monasticism in England. This decision was taken about 936. He took up residence at Glastonbury and began to gather around him other monks who would follow the Benedictine Rule.

King Athelstan died in 939 and was succeeded by his brother Edmund, a great friend of Dunstan. The new king immediately revoked Dunstan's banishment and recalled him to court. But again the old gossip of dark learning was circulated and Edmund banished Dunstan, as his brother had done before him. This time, however, something happened in which Dunstan's early biographers were to see the hand of God. Edmund, on a hunting trip, in a wild chase after a stag, narrowly escaped being carried to his death over a precipice. In the moments before his horse jerked to a stop, he thought of Dunstan and of the injustice he himself had done him. Returning from the hunt, he summoned Dunstan, took him to Glastonbury, and installed him there as abbot; Dunstan was at last in a position to put into practice his plans for the revival of the monasteries.

In the forty-five years that remained of his life, Dunstan labored to carry out his purpose, first as abbot of Glastonbury for thirteen years; then—after a year of exile as the result of personal friction with King Eadwig and his advisers—as Bishop of Worcester and London for three years; and finally as Archbishop of Canterbury for twenty-eight years.

The second key figure in the monastic movement was Æthelwold, Bishop of Winchester from 963 until 984.[9] Æthelwold, who was born in Winchester, came under the influence of Ælfheah at about the same time Dunstan did; as a matter of fact, they were consecrated to the priesthood by Ælfheah on the same day. Æthelwold entered the cloister at Glastonbury while Dunstan was abbot there and learned the Benedictine life. In 954, he requested permission to go abroad to study Benedictine practices more thoroughly; in order to persuade him to stay in England, King Eadred made him abbot of a small and poor monastery at Abingdon. Here he plunged into the labor of restoring the ruined buildings, of building a new church, and of instituting strict obedience to the Rule of St. Benedict. In the years that followed, Æthelwold, as abbot of Abingdon, and after 963, as Bishop of Winchester, strove to extend even farther the work of Dunstan.

Archbishop Oswald, the third of the leaders of the reform, received, as Dunstan and Æthelwold had, the initial impulse toward his mission at Winchester, though by the time Oswald arrived there Ælfheah was dead and Æthelwold had not yet arrived to install regular monks in place of the secular clerks who led an easy life there.[10] Growing dissatisfied with his life at Winchester, Oswald left England and went to Fleury, where he enthusiastically embraced the study of the Rule. In 961, soon after his return to England, he became Dunstan's successor as Bishop of Worcester and continued his work of restoration and reform.

The prominence of Dunstan, Æthelwold, and Oswald in the history of the tenth-century monastic reform is perhaps due to the circumstance that each was the subject of a biography written soon after his death. Undoubtedly, many others led in the movement, for it was a widespread and lasting activity. But we know something of what each of these men did, for each left the mark of a strong personality upon the history of his time. The character of Dunstan emerges clearly from the record of his deeds and from the pages of his first biography. If the repeated incidents of antagonism and envy toward him indicate a certain austerity and perhaps tactlessness in his personality, another side of his character emerges in the biographer's accounts of his dreams, visions, and prophecies. He seems to have been a man to whom the line between this world and the next was very thin, for dreams and reality were, to him, inextricably mixed. Perhaps the repeated accusations of witchcraft stem from this quality. As a reformer, Dunstan's policy was temperate; he apparently did not attempt to bring about sudden changes in practice. At Worcester and later at the abbey at Canterbury, secular clerks continued to serve. But, as opportunity arose, he filled their posts with men who would carry on the work of reform. Glastonbury was his particular care; from the monastery there, monks went out, with his encouragement, to rebuild and reinvigorate monastic life throughout southern England.

Eleanor Duckett has characterized Æthelwold as "a man full of rushing energy, impetuous, driven by a single purpose, unencumbered by scruple of policies to be weighed and balanced."[11] If Dunstan was the man of visions of the reform, Æthelwold was the man of action. His character appears clearly in the story of his reform of the Old Minster at Winchester. When Æthelwold arrived as bishop in 963, he found the choir filled with secular clerks, many married, many given to gluttony and drunkenness (according to Ælfric's account). After he had given them some time to reform their manner of living, Æthelwold's patience ended. Appearing before the door of the cathedral one Sunday morning, he ordered those who would to take the monastic vows and those who would not to leave. The furious clerks stormed out and appealed to King Edgar, who referred the matter to Dunstan, who agreed with Æthelwold; the order remained; the clerks did not return.

But Æthelwold's influence was not merely negative; he was a great builder and a patron of art and learning. From Winchester, his influence went out to restore and rebuild monastery after ruined monastery: at Milton in Dorset, at Chertsey in Surrey, and especially in the eastern fen country: Medeshamstede, Ely, and Thorney.

But, if Dunstan supplied a quiet leadership from Canterbury and Æthelwold supplied fervor and aggressiveness to the movement, Oswald brought persistence and practicality. It was he who carried forward the restoration of Worcester that Dunstan had begun. He brought scholars from France to teach the discipline to English monks, he worked out methods for the use of monastic lands that later served as models, and he worked to record and systematize his work and that of his fellow reformers. Like Æthelwold, he established many monasteries and saw that they prospered: Winchcombe, Pershore, Evesham, Crowland, and others.

If the work of the monastic reformers had been merely the alteration of monastic routine, their labors would have had little long-range impact. But their aim was higher, their achievement greater. In the environment that they created, old books could be studied again and new ones written. Art was cultivated, most notably in the work of the "Winchester School" and in the architecture of the newly rebuilt monasteries. Alongside Latin, English prose came to be valued, not only in the works of Ælfric, but also in those of Wulfstan and others. The reformers reached outside the monasteries to reform English life itself, and they succeeded in making England once again, for a while, a place where art and learning could flourish.

III *The Intellectual Temper*

Also important in reading tenth-century literature is some knowledge of the intellectual temper of the times. It is impossible to deal with this subject adequately in a few paragraphs; but, at the risk of oversimplification, we may describe briefly three clusters of ideas and values which, in various forms, pervaded and shaped Anglo-Saxon life on all levels and which were still very much alive in the tenth century. These are the pagan Germanic heritage, the Classical heritage, and the Christian heritage.

We know little about the scope of pagan ideas and traditions in Anglo-Saxon life,[12] but it must have been greater than the surviving ecclesiastical documents suggest. The Anglo-Saxons, we know, never lost their sense of kinship with their Germanic kinsmen on the Continent; as a matter of fact, this sense of kinship led to the very early and fairly extensive missionary efforts from English Christians to the Germanic tribes. And intellectual leaders in England from Bede to Dunstan, we are told, took an interest in the songs and legends of the pagan past. Even through the clerical filters, we can see pagan traditions and beliefs persisting throughout the Old English period, especially among the common people. A charm for making one's land fertile invokes Erce, mother of earth; Bede mentions a midwinter festival called the "night of the mothers"; the boar-emblems on the helmets in *Beowulf* recall that the boar was sacred to the pagan god Freyr. Place-names in England even today recall the names of Germanic gods: Woden (Woodnesborough, Wednesbury, etc.), Thunor (Thunderfield, Thurstable), and Tiw (Tysoe, Tuesley). As late as Ælfric, preachers felt the need to attack from the pulpit charms, fortune-telling, and other superstitions of a pagan coloring.[13] The pagan gods were sometimes preserved into Christian literature as devils and ogres, like the monstrous creatures in *Beowulf*. And perhaps a vestige of pagan religion lingers in the ambiguous "fate," so often referred to in Old English poetry; though it is hard to find a particular use of the term which is irreconcilable with Christianity.

Ultimately more important than these random vestiges of paganism is the persistence through the Old English period of a pattern of social relationships and ethical values derived from pagan Germanic society. This has been called the "heroic code," or the "*comitatus* ideal." This cluster of ideas, sometimes merged with analogous Christian ideas, was an important element in Anglo-Saxon life. At the center of the code was the ideal of loyalty, which found its fullest expression in heroic society in the relationship between a man and his lord. Each lord was surrounded by a band of followers: the *gesithas*, "companions." These followers were favored by the lord in time of peace with gifts and "hall-joy"; they repaid these favors in time of war by a fierce loyalty which extended to giving their lives to protect or avenge the lord. This loyalty was primarily a personal one, not a generalized "patriotism."

The chief virtue of the lord, in heroic terms, was liberality or munificence. In the heroic poems, gifts are frequently given spontaneously or as a token of gratitude for unusual service. Thus, after Beowulf vanquishes Grendel, Hrothgar ceremoniously presents him with a golden standard and a banner, armor, a famous treasure-sword, and eight horses; the grandeur of the gifts is described in lingering detail by the poet. More prosaic was the lord's gift of armor and horses to a new follower; such a gift came to be a legal obligation, known as the *heriot* and governed by specific rules. For example, the *heriot* was to be repaid to the lord on the man's death, unless he fell in battle. Such gifts were apparently felt to be symbolic of more substantial favors: gifts of land and the bestowal of personal protection.

The follower, in return, owed his lord absolute loyalty to the death. If the lord fell in battle, his survivors were to fight, no matter what the odds, until they fell beside him. Similarly, the "companions" were to be prepared to follow their lord into exile, if need be; or, if he were killed, they were to exact complete vengeance upon his killers. No action was regarded with more abhorrence than disloyalty or betrayal of a lord to whom one owed allegiance.

The bonds of loyalty between a man and his lord were paralleled by those which bound a man to his kinsmen. Throughout Germanic society, the ties of blood relationship were held very dear. To a kinsman, a man owed many obligations; it was his responsibility to arrange for the marriage of the unmarried women of his family, to set the terms of marriage agreements, and to continue to protect the wife's interests even after the marriage. He was to provide for the rearing of young orphaned kinsmen and to see that kinsmen accused of crimes not only came forward to answer the charges but also received justice at the hands of the law. The chief recorded expression of these ties, however, was the code of vengeance, by which a man exacted payment—in blood or in money—for the murder of a kinsman. The vendetta was in the nature of a sacred obligation; it transcended personal feelings and was regulated by exact conventions and agreements. If vengeance was originally a spontaneous and unregulated action, by the time of our earliest knowledge of it, it had become surrounded by carefully detailed legal conventions. Payment in money or property could be accepted in lieu of blood vengeance; in the laws of Alfred, the amounts of such payments were carefully fixed as *wergilds*.

The heroic codes of the *comitatus* and of blood vengeance find frequent expression in the older poetry. *Beowulf*, for example, may be seen as the expression of an intricate series of interlocking patterns of heroic loyalties: between Beowulf and Hrothgar and Hygelac, between Beowulf the young warrior and his "companions," between Beowulf the aged king and his people, and so on. The ancient poem *Widsith* is a roll-call of heroic names and deeds celebrating, through the voice of a fictitious wandering minstrel, the munificence of great kings and the deeds by which their followers repay them. The lament of "The Wanderer" is for the loss of the lord and the sorrow of the breaking of heroic ties.

But these codes were by no means moribund in the tenth century, neither in poetry nor in practice. The poem of *Maldon* tells how the followers of Brihtnoth fought the Danes, against hopeless odds, to fall beside their leader. The various tales of cowardice and treachery in the reign of King Æthelred were particularly abhorrent because of the general consciousness of the heroic ideal, against which such deeds stood out in horrid contrast. *Maldon* provided by no means the only example of the heroic code in action from the late tenth century, for Streonwold's men chose the same course in Devon in 988, and the men of the East Angles met a similar fate in 1004.

Old English life may be thought of, then, as set in a matrix of ancient pagan belief which found expression in persistent superstition and perhaps even worship and in the pervasive influence of traditional codes of behavior. Christianity, inevitably, modified the pagan traditions; but it seldom succeeded in erasing them. For the most part, it did not even attempt to do so. Paganism and Christianity came to stand in a complex relationship in Anglo-Saxon England, an interweaving so intricate that the fabric cannot be separated.[14]

Just as Pope Gregory suggested that Christian churches be built on sites where pagans were accustomed to worship, so the church for the most part transmuted and accommodated the heroic structure of social relationships and beliefs rather than attempting to eradicate it. The loyalty which man owes to God is often referred to in terms of the old heroic code, but this loyalty does not replace man's loyalty owed also to earthly lords. The church added its spiritual power to the oaths of allegiance, and even condoned deeds of violence undertaken in defense of a lord or in vengeance for him. Alcuin, in 801, praises, for example, a man who had "boldly avenged his lord"; and Ælfric's contemporary, Archbishop Wulfstan, in 1014 condemns betraying a lord's soul as being even worse than betraying one's military oaths to him.

Christian teaching is everywhere fitted into the heroic frame of reference. Christ is the great lord; the disciples, his thanes. The sin of Judas, then, takes on the loathsome coloring of heroic disloyalty. Man is bound to God by the ties of the heroic code; God dispenses favors like a Germanic lord and demands in return faithful service. Heaven is like the hall of the lord; the bliss of the saints, the "hall-joy" of heroes. All men are brothers and are bound by ties like those which bind blood-kinsmen.

The code of vengeance was harder to reconcile with Christianity than the code of loyalty. The church seems to have encouraged settlements of feuds by payment of *wergilds* rather than by bloodshed and to have invoked heavy penances on those who resolved feuds by violence. At the same time, it was careful to establish *wergilds* for its own members; these *wergilds* were to be paid to the monasteries and were enforced by royal power. Moreover, even the social structure of the Old English church seems to have owed something to the heroic patterns, in its groupings of priests and monks around bishops and abbots, from whom they received protection and to whom they owed loyalty.

All these interpenetrations of paganism and Christianity resulted in a Christianity in England of a peculiarly native coloring which gained strength from its roots in racial and tribal traditions. These roots also ran back, of course, to Celtic culture, the inheritance of the church from its British and Irish sides. The victory at the Synod of Whitby in 663 for Roman usages did not end the influence upon the church of Irish Christianity, with its unrestrained and often exotic mysticism; its tendencies toward extreme asceticism; its emphasis upon simplicity, poverty, and humility. It is hard to gauge the continuing influence of this aspect of the church, but it is often recognizable in the legends of saints and in the vision literature of the period.[15]

The view that Western culture is a product of the fusion of Germanic and Roman cultures has been thoroughly developed by Christopher Dawson.[16] Rome did not contribute only Roman Christianity to Northern culture of the Dark Ages; it also transmitted to England, as to all of Northern Europe, the heritage of secular Classical culture. Historians of the last fifty years have uncovered more and more evidence of cultural ties between England and the Mediterranean world, ties reaching back to the Stone and Bronze Ages. Evidence of very early ties with the Aegean world and the East is to be found in the art forms and techniques of both the British and the Anglo-Saxons. The designs of the treasures from Sutton Hoo, for instance, have been linked not only with Sweden, but also with Byzantium and the eastern Mediterranean. Traffic with the Mediterranean world seems to have been heavy and steady throughout the Anglo-Saxon period. The older view of an island completely de-Romanized by the time of the Augustinian mission in 597 has been largely replaced by a belief that Roman influence must have been still fairly strong in England in the sixth century. This influence was renewed by a new wave of missionaries late in the seventh century: Theodore, Hadrian, and others, who quickly brought Classical learning to such a point in England that Aldhelm could boast that England surpassed Ireland in learning. In this environment appeared Bede, who has been called "one of the greatest 'classic' minds of the Middle Ages." Even the author of *Beowulf* may have been indebted to Virgil's *Aeneid*.

The most eloquent description of the characteristic Anglo-Saxon fusion of Northern heroic, barbarian culture, and Roman

Christianity and Classicism has been made by Clinton Albertson. His summary deserves quotation: "The Anglo-Saxons' literature is then, like their culture, an amalgam, but a rich, vibrant, fascinating amalgam, like the pages of the Lindisfarne Gospels. It is the autobiography of the heroic northern mind becoming Roman and western. It is not the case of an old northern tradition revised by western monks . . . . The best of Anglo-Saxon literature is a new *creation*, a oneness resultant upon this cultural fusion, not just the jointed work of later pious revisers."[17]

As we shall see, Ælfric's homilies, in their way, express this oneness brought out of multiplicity, as *Beowulf* does in its way. His constant interpretation of biblical and Christian material in terms of local culture, his moral fervor, his love of clarity and common sense, his eminent practicality—all reflect the mingled intellectual traditions of his England.

IV *Ælfric's Birth and Childhood*

Only the broad outlines of Ælfric's life are visible to us after the passage of a millennium. We know about when he was born, about when he died, and a few general things about the way he spent his life and the order in which he composed the works for which we remember him. And even these few bits of information are the result of fairly recent scholarly inquiry; for centuries, the very identity of Ælfric was unknown, even while his works were the subject of antiquarian and scholarly dispute. It should be remembered, however, that Ælfric's biography, scanty as it is, is more complete than that of many a more prominent man of the centuries before the modern practice of keeping voluminous records began. For Cynewulf, we have only a name; and we lack even that for the *Beowulf* poet. We know at least enough of Ælfric's life to establish a loose chronology of his works and the key events of his life.[18]

Ælfric seems to have been born about the middle of the 950s, perhaps in 955. We know that he was sent to the monastery of Cernel in 987 and that he was a priest at the time. If we assume ordination at the customary age of thirty and a lapse of about two years before his departure for Cernel, we can date his ordination in 985 and his birth in 955. It is fairly certain that he was a native of Wessex, for the consistently West-Saxon forms of his language betray no trace of another origin.

The circumstances of his life indicate that his family was of the middle class. He remained a simple priest until the age of fifty, when he became an abbot. His advancement would probably have been more rapid if he had been of aristocratic birth, for the Anglo-Saxon church liked to place men in positions of authority who could deal with their secular counterparts on a fairly equal social basis. For the same reason, it is unlikely that he was from a family of the lower class; for, if he had been, he probably would never have become an abbot. His tone of address to men of power and position (to Ealdorman Æthelmær, for example) has the modest confidence of one who respects but is unawed by high rank. Such confidence might come, of course, from a sense of his intellectual and ecclesiastical dignity alone, but the impression given is otherwise.

Like most medieval writers, Ælfric tells us nothing of himself personally except occasionally to illustrate some objective point. The only comment he makes on his early life appears in the preface to Genesis, in which, to illustrate the low state of Latin learning prevailing in England, he cites the priest with whom he began the study of Latin. The man could understand "a little Latin," Ælfric says, but he did not understand even the difference between the Old Law of the Old Testament and the New Law (Crawford, 76).

A middle-class boyhood in Wessex in the mid-tenth century, with some beginning instruction in Latin: beyond this general idea of Ælfric's early life, we can only move into the realm of speculation. Marguerite-Marie Dubois points out that the Latin tutor, the Wessex setting, and the probably upper-middle-class status suggest certain kinds of positions for Ælfric's father.[19] He might have been a member of the king's personal retinue, what Bede called the *comites* and Alfred called the *gesith*. Or he might have been a merchant. Dubois also points out that Ælfric is almost certain to have had brothers, since it was not the practice of Anglo-Saxon parents to end the family line by consecrating only sons to the church. But such castings of probability, reasonable as they may be, are unverifiable and lead nowhere.

V *Ælfric at Winchester*

Whatever the circumstances of Ælfric's early life, sometime in the early 970s he entered the monastic school at Winchester. The date is unknown; Ælfric says in his *Letter to the Monks of Eynsham* that he lived in Æthelwold's school "many years." Since Æthelwold died in 984, Ælfric may have been at Winchester by 970 or shortly thereafter.

Æthelwold had come to Winchester as bishop from his notable successes at Abingdon in 963. After his sensational expulsion of the secular clergy, he had set forth upon a characteristically vigorous program of reform. Æthelgar, one of his disciples, was established as abbot of the monastery, and here, as well as in the nunnery, the Benedictine discipline was quickly established. Æthelwold himself planned and oversaw the building of a magnificent new church, which was completed and dedicated with great ceremony in 971. The consecration was attended by King Edgar and Archbishop Dunstan; the high point of the proceedings was the removal of the bones of St. Swithun from their grave outside the church to a new tomb by the high altar of the new church. (Swithun had been Bishop of Winchester in the mid-ninth century.) The disinterment of his relics had been accompanied by miraculous events and healings, many of which Ælfric later described in his saint's life of Swithun (*LS* XXI).

By the time Ælfric entered the monastic school there, Winchester had become the intellectual center of the reform movement. Æthelwold himself, though he had many other obligations at court and in the other monasteries whose progress he supervised, apparently took an active role in the work of the school. In his Latin life of the bishop, Ælfric says that Æthelwold took particular pleasure in teaching personally the students at Winchester and in "exhorting them with pleasant words to better things" (*V. Æ.,* 223). The scriptorium had been founded by Swithun himself; now, under Æthelwold's leadership, it was reinvigorated and craftsmen gathered here to produce a series of notable examples of the bookmaker's art. Shortly before Ælfric's arrival, Godemann, one of the most accomplished of the Winchester artists, had produced the Benedictional which still survives, bearing Æthelwold's name. Here, too, somewhat later, was produced the Tropary of Æthelred, compiled for use with the new organ of the cathedral.[20]

For the monks, life under the Rule at Winchester was firmly oriented around the liturgy, around the service of God by prayer and ceremony.[21] The exact schedule followed by the medieval monastery is hard to reconstruct, for the surviving *horaria* or timetables do not indicate "clock time" but merely the sequence of exercises.[22] Also, there were three timetables according to the season: winter, summer, and Lent. Here is an example of a typical monastic day, based on the Regularis Concordia for the winter season:

2:00 A.M.	Monks go to choir for prayer and psalms, followed by Lauds (or Matins) and Lauds of All Saints and of the dead.
Dawn	Prime, followed by psalms and prayers.
6:45	Reading in the cloister; private masses for those who were priests.
8:00	Monks return to the dormitory to wash and dress, then go back to the church for Terce and the "morning Mass."
9:00	Chapter, which might include a spiritual conference and the confession of faults.
9:45–12:30	Work.
12:30	Sext, followed by the sung High Mass and None.
2:00	Dinner (the only meal of the day).
3:00	Reading.
5:00	Vespers, Matins of the dead. A drink was served in the refectory, followed by a short public reading in choir, and Compline.
7:00	Monks retire for the night.

These times are all approximate, for the monks lived by "sun time"; and their day lengthened and shortened according to the season. During the summer, there was a second period of sleep between the night office and Prime, and two meals were served rather than one, the second about 6 P.M. Such was the daily routine followed by Ælfric from early youth through the rest of his life.

The monastic school at Winchester was basically a school for the training of monks.[23] Child oblation—the dedication of a young child to the monastic life—was common, and it was necessary to train these children in reading, the recitation of the offices, singing, and the other necessary monastic skills. In addition, despite occasional opposition, most monastic schools like Winchester accepted as pupils local children not destined for the monastic life, especially the sons of the nobility.

The curriculum was based upon the *trivium* (grammar, rhetoric, and dialectic) and the *quadrivium* (arithmetic, geometry, music, and astronomy), though in a weakened form, oriented for the most part toward the practical needs of monastic life. The first and most basic study was grammar, which meant the study of the Latin language and its literature. The first four years or so of a student's career was devoted to learning to read and write Latin, with some attention perhaps to metrics and the elements of rhetoric. This groundwork was followed by reading in Latin literature of the church, especially lives of saints, patristic biblical commentaries, and ecclesiastical history. Of the *quadrivium*, the subjects stressed were arithmetic and astronomy (or cosmography), especially in their application to the calendar and the computation of feast-days. Music, of course, was the study of plain-song, for use in the services.

Ælfric's education, of course, went far beyond the basic curriculum. The extent of his literary study is clear from the sources of his works, particularly his homilies; he was probably the best-educated man in the England of his day. But, as a monastic student and later as a teacher, his work was oriented toward the simple outlines of the monastic curriculum.

After about ten years of study, Ælfric, as a candidate for the priesthood, would have embarked on studies more specifically directed toward ordination, further study of theology and study of priestly duties. If he followed the typical pattern, he would have taken minor orders in adolescence, become a deacon at about twenty-five, and been ordained a priest at the canonical age of thirty.

VI *Ælfric at Cernel*

The first date in Ælfric's life which can be established with any certainty is 987, when he left the monastery at Winchester to go to a new monastery at Cernel (now Cerne Abbas), in Dorset. The foundation charter of this abbey is still preserved.[24] It was begun during King Edgar's reign, when so much development in monasticism took place; it was to be a memorial to the hermit Eadwold, the pious brother of King Edmund of East Anglia, who had been martyred by the Danes in 870. Eadwold's hermitage was thought to have been near the spot where the new monastery was to stand.

The founder of the new monastery was Æthelmær, a prominent nobleman who came to have great influence over the course of

Ælfric's later life. Æthelmær's father was Æthelweard, ealdorman of the province which included present-day Devon, Somerset, and Dorset. The office of ealdorman was a high one; he was the king's representative in the area; and, in a country as yet only loosely unified, he had power which sometimes rivaled that of the king himself. Æthelweard, a powerful patron of learning and the monastic movement, was something of a scholar himself: he contributed to the Anglo-Saxon Chronicle and wrote a Latin chronicle of his own, based upon Bede, Isidore, and the Anglo-Saxon Chronicle.[25] He was also apparently the patron of the restoration of Pershore Abbey in Worcestershire during Edgar's reign. Æthelweard died around the turn of the century, perhaps in 1002; until his death, he and his son Æthelmær were a continual influence on Ælfric, suggesting scholarly work for him and encouraging him in it.

It seems probable that Ælfric was sent to Cernel in order to teach the new monks there the Benedictine Rule and to organize the teaching program there. It was the custom to extend the reform into new monasteries in this way; Oswald brought the scholarly monk Abbo to Ramsey from Fleury, a center of the Continental reform, for a similar purpose. Ælfric was to remain at Cernel as a scholar-teacher for eighteen years. When he left, in 1005, it was to become abbot of yet another new monastery, also founded by Æthelmær, at Eynsham. The main body of Ælfric's writing was done at Cernel, and it grew directly out of his teaching young boys in the monastic school, older monks the Rule and more advanced studies, and laymen in the parish church on Æthelmær's estates.

Recent students of Ælfric's work have come to see that it reflects a consistent and long-range plan.[26] In the preface to his first collection of homilies, he suggests something of the origins of this plan. It occurred to him, he says, to translate this material from Latin into English because he had seen and heard many errors in the existing English books, which might lead unlearned men astray (CH I, p. 2). At Cernel, we may believe, as elsewhere in England, there was great need for learning in both English and Latin. Knowledge of Latin had declined until many priests themselves could not read the material they needed. This situation needed to be remedied; but, in the interim, it was essential that fundamental material be made available in clear, accurate, English translation.

Therefore, Ælfric embarked on a program of composition, adaptation, and translation on a very large scale; but the work was conjoined by a few simple aims. First, he set about presenting in a clear form the basic teachings of the church in such a way that lay-men could understand them. Second, he presented in a similarly clear form other material useful to priests and monks in carrying out their work. And third, he produced material to be used in the teaching of Latin soundly and effectively to the students of the monastic school, so the next generation of clerics would not have to rely on English translations.

The doctrine that Ælfric presented amounted to a survey of universal history. He set forth the central facts of the Old Testament and of the "Old Law," the facts of Christ's Incarnation and the "New Law," and the essential stages in the spread of Christianity throughout the world, first by the apostles and then by the martyrs and confessors. The conclusion of this Augustinian world historical view was the Day of Judgment. Other works amplified this plan by giving accounts of the physical world, instructing parish priests in their duties, and teaching monks how to live in the monastic way.

Ælfric's plan inevitably suggests comparison with King Alfred's, of the previous century. Like Ælfric's, Alfred's plan was intended to counter the widespread decline in learning of his day, the after-math of the Danish depredations. Alfred aimed, like Ælfric, at providing in English, for those ignorant of Latin, texts which set forth knowledge basic to faith. His works, too, fit into a consistent, overall plan which includes material about the physical world (Orosius's *History*), about the rise of Christianity in England (Bede's *History*), and about basic moral and philosophical teachings (Gregory's *Pastoral Care,* Boethius's *Consolation of Philosophy,* and Augustine's *Soliloquies*). Ælfric knew Alfred's work, of course, and no doubt drew general inspiration from it. But his plan differs from Alfred's in being of far greater scope and in being designed directly for particular groups: monastic students, monks and priests, and laymen.

It is possible that Ælfric had conceived his plan and had begun to carry it out even before he left Winchester, for he appears to have completed his first volume of homilies in 989, only two years after he went to Cernel. This volume, the first series of *Catholic Homilies,* consists of forty homilies arranged according to the church year. A second series, completed in 992, adds forty more homilies arranged according to the same plan. Ælfric suggests, in the Latin preface to the first series, that the two volumes be kept separate, one being read in church one year, the other the next. But he gives his permission for homilies from the two series to be combined, if anyone wishes to do so (*CH* II, p. 2). Taken together, the eighty homilies of the two volumes of *Catholic Homilies* constitute a fairly comprehensive survey of Christian world history, from Creation to the final Judgment. The first piece in the double series, "On the Beginning of Creation" (*CH* I. I), is not assigned to a particular day but is to be preached "when you wish"; and it stands as a kind of general introduction to the two volumes. It gives an account of the events in Genesis, the life of Christ, and the Last Judgment, thus presenting, in brief form, the essentials of both the Old Law and the New.

Ælfric next turned, it seems (though it is impossible to be sure of exact chronology), to a subject which was a basic part of the medieval curriculum: cosmography. The practical application of the study of astronomy and the solar year was the calculation of church festivals and especially Easter. The computation of Easter was a matter of controversy for centuries; it was, among other things, the chief specific point of difference between the Celtic church and the Roman one. Ælfric's modest treatise on the subject, *De Temporibus Anni,* treats the divisions of time and of the solar year, the basic principles of astronomy, and the phenomenon of the atmosphere. Ælfric's sources are Bede's astronomical works, but he adapts them very freely and adds some material not found in Bede.

About 995, Ælfric produced another group of works with a clear relevance to his general plan: his *Grammar,* a Latin-English *Glossary,* and a textbook in the form of a Latin dialogue, the *Colloquy.* Ælfric's sense of the close relation between the *Grammar* and his other translations is clear from his preface, in which he says he decided to translate Priscian's Latin grammar after he had translated the two volumes of homilies, because grammar is "seo cæg, ðe ðæra boca andgit unlic" (the key which unlocks the meaning of those books) (Zupitza, 2). Ælfric's *Glossary* is appended to about half of the fifteen manuscripts of the *Grammar.* The items are arranged according to subject, beginning with words having to do with God and Creation, continuing with the names of "members"— of the body, of society, and of the family—and ending with lists of birds, fish, animals, etc. The little Latin dialogue, the *Colloquy,* has attracted wide interest not only because it is one of the only pieces in a semidramatic form from the Old English period but because of its rare series of miniatures describing the daily lives of common people. A master asks questions of students, who assume the roles of representatives of various occupations. The result is a vivid, though brief, panorama of Anglo-Saxon life.

Ælfric's next book was a major work, which, like the *Catholic Homilies* and the Latin instructional material, requires closer examination later. This work was the *Lives of Saints*, another collection of forty pieces. This compilation, according to the English preface which heads it, was made at the specific request of Æthelweard and Æthelmær, but it obviously fits closely into Ælfric's larger purposes. In the same preface, Ælfric distinguishes sharply between this volume and the two volumes of homilies which preceded it. The saints' lives in the volumes of homilies celebrate saints whose feast-days are honored by the laity. These new lives deal with saints whose days are celebrated only by the monks (*LS* p. 4). Furthermore, these new pieces are for the most part not homilies, written to be read aloud in church, but are designed to be read privately, though in form they are similar and obviously might furnish material for homilies. Thirty-one of the pieces are of this kind; six others are homilies (*LS* I, XII, XIII, and XVI–XVIII), and three items at the end seem separate from the rest: the *Interrogationes, De Falsis Deis,* and *De XII Abusivis.* Again, one item seems intended to serve as a general introduction to the whole series: number XVI, "The Memory of the Saints," which outlines the types of saints and speaks in general of their significance. One of the items appended to the *Lives* deserves particular notice: the *Interrogationes Sigewulfi in Genesin,* an English translation of a handbook on Genesis written by the eighth-century English scholar Alcuin in the form of catechetical questions and answers on Genesis and dedicated to his pupil Sigewulf.

Another group of works which belongs primarily to the period at Cernel is the Bible translations and adaptations. These translations give Ælfric a permanent place in the history of the Bible in English, and seem clearly to fit into his broad plan of instruction. Nevertheless, he seems to have felt considerable reluctance to undertake such work. In the Old English preface to Genesis (Crawford, 76), Ælfric addresses Æthelweard, reminding him of his requests for a translation of Genesis. The task seemed burdensome and uncongenial to him, Ælfric says; but Æthelweard had told him that he needed to translate only as far as Isaac since someone else had translated the rest. In the texts that survive, it

appears that Ælfric did translate only as far as Chapter xxiv, though
later editors added the rest of Genesis by the other translator and
versions of Exodus, Leviticus, and Deuteronomy to his Genesis
translation, a section of Numbers that he had translated, and his
epitomes of Joshua and Judges to produce the so-called *Old English
Heptateuch*. Ælfric, of course, had translated a number of biblical
passages in the course of composing his homilies; and he had made
free versions, mostly highly condensed, of the books of Kings
(*LS* XVIII), the Maccabees (*LS* XXV), Esther (Assmann VIII),
and Judith (Assmann IX). The homiletic paraphrase of Job (*CH* II.
XXXV) is sometimes spoken of as a translation as well.

This list of Ælfric's works while at Cernel may be concluded with
the *Hexameron,* the *Admonitio,* and the *Letter for Wulfsige.* The
Hexameron is a very free treatment of St. Basil's *Hexameron,* or
"account of the week of Creation." Ælfric also includes in this work
material drawn from Bede's commentaries on Genesis. The
Admonitio is an English version of St. Basil's *Admonitio ad Filium
Spiritualem,* and it seems intended for the instruction of new monks.
In a series of short chapters, it presents commentaries on the
virtues of faithful monks, such as chastity, love of God and
of one's neighbor, and the avoidance of worldliness and avarice.
The *Letter for Wulfsige* was written at the request of the Bishop of
Sherborne, who wanted a pastoral letter on the duties of the
clergy to be sent to all clergymen in his diocese. Ælfric begins with
a short personal letter to Wulfsige, and then divides the main
body of the letter into two parts, the first consisting of thirty-five
short sections; the second, of two longer sections. The subjects
covered in the first part include the need for celibacy, the division
of the orders, and the behavior of a good priest. Most of the second
part is devoted to instructions about the Eucharist. An interesting
detail of the work is the warning in Section xxxv against funerals
because of the "heathenism which is there committed."

In addition to these and a few smaller works, Ælfric, during his
time at Cernel, continued to revise and develop his homilies for the
church year. Peter Clemoes has meticulously reconstructed the
general outlines of these revisions and expansions.[27] Ælfric, it
appears, expanded his series of homilies in two stages, which
Clemoes chooses to call Temporale Homilies I and II. Temporale
Homilies I, which must have consisted of about forty items (Ælfric's
customary number), was a series of homilies, using many from the
two series of *Catholic Homilies,* from the Proper of the Season to

the Sunday after Pentecost. Temporale Homilies II must have been a two-volume series of approximately eighty homilies, which extended the series through the entire year. The second volume survives in an imperfect form (Trinity College, Cambridge, B.15.34); the first, which perhaps contained prefaces, is lost. Altogether, Clemoes lists over a hundred extant homilies of Ælfric; some others must have been lost; but Ælfric's work was circulated so much that probably most of his homilies do survive.

By the time Ælfric left Cernel in 1005, his overall plan of education was generally complete. For laymen, he had written several series of homilies which set forth clearly and gracefully the central elements of the Christian faith. He had also translated into English selections from the Bible that he believed most important in understanding the preparation under the Old Law for the New. For monks and priests he had compiled a reading book of texts which told of their outstanding predecessors in the dissemination of the faith, and he had written a simple handbook of clerical duties and responsibilities. For the boys in the monastic school, he had provided Latin texts that would lead them into an elementary knowledge sounder than that he had received from his first teacher.

VII *Ælfric at Eynsham*

In 1005, or possibly the year before, Ælfric moved to Eynsham, in present-day Oxfordshire, as abbot of a new monastery there. The foundation charter of Eynsham still survives and is of considerable interest to students of Ælfric. It is even possible that Ælfric wrote the charter himself, for it is in the clear, graceful Latin of Ælfric's other Latin works.[28] The charter indicates that the monastery was built by the Æthelmær who had built Cernel and who had been Ælfric's patron there. Æthelweard had died, probably in 1002; and Æthelmær himself was now of an age to begin thinking of a quiet retirement. According to the charter, Æthelmær himself was to live in the monastery, "like a father to the monks." Ælfric is mentioned in the charter, though not by name: "And I desire that he who is now the superior may continue to hold that office as long as he lives, and after his death that the brethren may choose one from their own number according as the rule prescribes, and I myself will live with them, and enjoy the endowment as long as life lasts." Ælfric himself witnessed the charter, along with fifteen other abbots.

After eighteen years of teaching and writing at Cernel, then,

Ælfric became an abbot himself, carrying on in a new role the work of the reform. The main structure of his work was complete now; the works that he wrote during this last period of his life were principally amplifications of that structure and "occasional pieces" written in his capacity as a well-known scholar-cleric.

An important group of these occasional pieces is the letters. A letter in Latin, *Letter to the Monks of Eynsham,* survives which was written as he began his abbacy. Another, in English, is the *Letter to Wulfgeat.* Wulfgeat of Ylmandun, a prominent landowner in the vicinity of Eynsham, was the son of Leofsige, ealdorman of the West Saxons; his name appears on a number of charters between 986 and 1005. In 1006, he was stripped, for some reason, of his honors and estates by a royal judgment. Ælfric refers in the brief introductory lines of the *Letter* to the English writings he had lent to Wulfgeat and to his promise to send more. In the first half of the *Letter,* which consists of a brief summary of basic Christian doctrine, Ælfric begins by describing the Trinity and then presents the Christian world-view from the Creation and the Fall of Man, through the Incarnation, to the Day of Judgment. The second half is a commentary, derived from Augustine, on the text, "Agree with thine adversary quickly, whiles thou art with him in the way" (Matthew 5:25).

The tone of Ælfric's lines to Wulfgeat suggests the position that Ælfric now had among the prominent laymen of the area. Similar in this respect is the *Letter to Sigeweard* that Ælfric wrote at the request of another prominent thane, Sigeweard of Easthealon. Sigeweard was one of those who had signed the Eynsham charter; Ælfric had visited his estate, as we know from a passage near the end of the work addressed to him. Ælfric says:

Ðu woldest me laðian, þa ic wæs mid þe, þæt ic swiðor drunce swilce for blisse ofer minum gewunan: ac wite þu, leof man, þæt se þe oðerne neadað ofer his mihte to drincenne, þæt se mot aberan begra gilt, gif him ænig hearm of þam drence becymð. Ure Hælend Crist on his halgan godspelle forbead þone oferdrenc eallum gelyfdeum mannum: healde se ðe wille his gesetnysse.

(When I was at your house you urged me to drink more than I was accustomed. You ought to know, dear friend, that if any one compels another to drink more than is good for him, and any harm result, the blame is upon him who caused it. Our Savior Christ in His gospel has forbidden believers to drink more than is necessary. Let him who will, keep the law of Christ.)

(Crawford, 14–15)

The *Letter to Sigeweard* is interesting both as one of the fullest of Ælfric's several summaries of Christian doctrine, as he saw it, and as one of the few works which is basically original with him, though he did draw incidentally upon Augustine's *De Doctrina Christiana* and upon Isidore of Seville's *In Libros Veteris ac Novi Testamenti Proemia.* Caroline L. White characterizes the *Letter* as a "practical, historical introduction to the Holy Scriptures."[29] As Ælfric surveys the books of the Bible, he emphasizes the continuity of Scripture and the way that each book fits into sacred history. Beginning with the creation of the world, the fall of the angels, and the fall of man, he progresses through the history of Israel, the wisdom books, and the major and minor prophets. The second part of the book takes up the New Law: the gospels and epistles, the Acts, and the Revelation of John.

The *Letter to Sigefyrð* seems to be addressed to a local person, also. A Sigefyrð signed the Eynsham charter; perhaps he is the same thane to whom the *Letter* is addressed. The occasion which elicited the *Letter* is specified in the introduction:

> *Ælfric abbod gret Sigefyrð freondlice!*
> *Me is gesæd, þæt þu sædest be me,*
> *þæt ic oðer tæhte on Engliscum gewritum,*
> *oðer eower ancor æt ham mid eow tæhð,*
> *forþan þe he swutelice sægð, þæt hit sy alyfed,*
> *þæt mæssepreostas wel moton wifian,*
> *and mine gewritu wiðcweðað þysum.*

> (*Ælfric, abbot, sends friendly greetings to Sigefyrð!*
> *It was told to me that you said of me,*
> *that I taught one thing in my English writings,*
> *and the anchorite on your manor teaches another,*
> *for he says openly that it is allowed*
> *for priests to marry,*
> *and my writings deny this.*)

(Assmann, 13)

There follows a straightforward and detailed presentation of the argument for clerical chastity. Christ chose a maiden to be His mother, both He and His apostles lived chastely, as did the holy confessors of more recent times: Martin, Gregory, Augustine, Basil, Cuthbert, Bede, Jerome, and the desert fathers. Ælfric later revised this *Letter,* dropping the address to Sigefyrð and greatly expanding the discourse on chastity to make it a full homily (*De Virginitate* in CCCC 419).

The *Letters for Wulfstan* were written in response to a specific request from Ælfric's fellow homilist, Archbishop Wulfstan of York. Wulfstan was also Bishop of Worcester, near Ælfric's new monastery at Eynsham. About 1005, he asked Ælfric to write two letters in Latin on clerical duties to be used among the secular clergy; a year later, he asked him to translate these letters into English. The letters take up some of the same subjects as the similar letter which Wulfsige had commissioned from Ælfric a few years earlier. The first letter summarizes the Christian ages of the world, a familiar theme in Ælfric, as we have seen: the ages before the Law, under the Law, and under God's grace. He then describes the early church, the Roman persecutions, and the work of the synods. A list of the seven orders of the ministry follows, and the letter ends with a brief treatment of a priest's duties and obligations.

The second letter seems intended for use at an annual gathering of the clergy for the distribution of holy oil. It begins,

> *Eala ge mæssepreostas, mine gebroðra!*
> *We secgað eow nu þæt we ær ne sædon.*
> *Forþon þe we todæg sceol dalan urne ele,*
> *on þreo wisan gehalgodne, swa swa us gewisað seo boc . . . .*
> *halige ele, oþer his crisma and seocra manna ele.*

> (*O ye priests, my brothers!*
> *We say to you now what we have not said before.*
> *For today we are to divide our oil,*
> *hallowed in three ways, as the book tells us . . . .*
> *holy oil, chrism, and sick men's oil.*)

(Fehr, 147)

The letter that follows gives directions for the administration of the Lord's Supper; the celebration of Passion Week, including Ash Wednesday and Palm Sunday; and the celebration of the Mass on other occasions. The letter also includes expositions of the Ten Commandments and the eight deadly sins. One version of this second English letter for Wulfstan is of particular interest, because it is Wulfstan's rewriting of Ælfric's work. Comparison of Wulfstan's version with Ælfric's original demonstrates very vividly the difference in their styles.

Finally, we may include among these "occasional pieces" Ælfric's Latin *Life of Æthelwold*. This *Life* was completed in 1006, for it is dedicated to Bishop Kenulph, who became Bishop of Winchester in 1006 and died the same year. The preface to the *Life* begins, "Ælfric abbot, an alumnus of Winchester, desires for the honorable Bishop Kenulph and the brethren of Winchester salvation in Christ. It seems to me worthy now at last to call to mind some of the deeds of our father and great teacher, Æthelwold, for twenty years have passed since his departure. With my narrative, brief indeed and unadorned, I gather into this writing those things which I have learned either from you or from other faithful ones, lest perchance they pass into utter oblivion for want of writers" (*V.Æ.,* 253).

The *Life of Æthelwold* was formerly generally thought to be an original work; it now appears to be a characteristically Ælfrician reworking of an earlier life by Wulfstan, a monk of Winchester.[30] This perhaps explains the almost complete absence of any personal reminiscences of Æthelwold and the highly conventional tone of the whole *Life*. (The preface itself, which does not mention any source specifically, is little more than a pastiche of the rhetorical clichés for the opening of a saint's life, such as the declaration that the knowledge of the saint is in danger of being lost, the assertion of personal knowledge, and the claim of a "rustic" style. It therefore proves little about the actual circumstances of composition.)

Through these active years as abbot, Ælfric not only responded to requests for works, he also continued to revise and augment his major work, his series of homilies. According to Clemoes's reconstruction of the chronology, the completion of the second series of Temporale Homilies belongs to these years, earlier works were reworked and reissued, and *Catholic Homilies* II, there is reason to believe, was revised and issued again. Separate pieces include the largely unpublished *De Creatore et Creature* and *De Sex Aetatibus Mundi,* which together present an "epitome of world history . . . which is very close to the main theme of Ælfric's total plan."[31]

The date of Ælfric's death is unknown. It used to be often given as about 1020, but on very scanty evidence; no documentary evidence exists to prove that Ælfric must have been alive in any given year after 1006. Clemoes suggests a date as early as 1010, on the basis of Ælfric's known works and the assumption of "an output at the same rate after 1006 as before it."[32] If he died then, he was about fifty-five years old.

CHAPTER 2

Catholic Homilies

WITH the following words, Ælfric, about 989, dedicated his first major work, *Catholic Homilies,* a volume of forty sermons freely translated from Latin into English prose:

> I, Ælfric, scholar of Æthelwold, the benevolent and venerable Superior, send greeting of good wishes to his Lordship Archbishop Sigeric in the Lord. However rashly or presumptuously undertaken, I have nevertheless formed this book out of Latin writers and from Holy Scripture, translating into our ordinary speech, for the edification of the simple, who know only this language both for reading and for hearing; and for that reason I have used no difficult words, but only plain English; so that our message might the more readily reach the hearts of those who read or hear, to the profit of the souls of those who cannot be taught in any other tongue than that to which they were born. (*CH* I, p. 1)

Later in this Latin preface, he states his intentions of supplying some of the omissions of "sermons or histories" in this first volume by issuing a second volume, already under preparation. This second series of homilies appeared in 992, again with a dedication to the Archbishop: "Inasmuch as you have only too amply praised the result of my study, and have willingly accepted that translation, I have hastened to form this following book, according as the grace of God has guided me (*CH* II, p. 1).

The Latin prefaces to the *Catholic Homilies* make very explicit Ælfric's immediate purpose in preparing these two volumes of sermons. He is first of all concerned to provide for the "unlearned of our race" knowledge for the salvation of their souls. He therefore has written in English, "avoiding garrulous verbosity and strange expressions, and seeking rather with pure and plain words, in the language of their nation, to be of use to my hearers, by simple speech, than to be praised for the composition of skillful discourse, which my simplicity has never acquired" (*CH* II, p. 1). At the same time, he is concerned that the doctrine, though understandable to the laity, be sound and orthodox. He lists his major authorities—

Augustine, Jerome, Bede, Gregory the Great, Smaragdus, and Haymo—and points out that "the authority of these writers is willingly accepted by all Catholics." He has, he says, "carefully avoided falling into errors that might lead astray," and he admonishes any who are dissatisfied with his work to make their own and not to "pervert my translation, which I trust by the grace of God, and not from vainglory, I have been able to work out by careful study." Lastly, as Clemoes has pointed out,[1] the prefaces indicate that Ælfric thought of his work as a "consciously 'literary' act." No doubt much of his work had been written to meet his own day-to-day needs as teacher and preacher, but these volumes are not random compilations of occasional pieces. They are the product of systematic thought and were offered to his superior and to the church as finished works. They may, therefore, be studied as unified wholes.

I *Contents and Arrangement*

The manuscripts of the two sets of Ælfric's homilies all bear the title *Sermones Catholici*. The title *Catholic Homilies* was assigned them by the seventeenth-century scholar Abraham Wheloc,[2] because they were intended for general, not merely monastic, use. In some respects, the manuscript label is more appropriate; for, strictly speaking, a "homily" is an exposition or a commentary on a scriptural text, a "sermon," a general discourse on a dogmatic or moral theme. About two-thirds of the items in the two volumes are homiletic, in the strict sense; the rest are narratives, topical discourses, or simple expansions of scriptural texts.

The first volume of *Catholic Homilies* contains, as Ælfric indicates in the preface, forty homilies that are arranged according to the feast-days of the church year, beginning with Christmas and ending with the second Sunday of Advent. The second volume, however, despite Ælfric's declaration in the preface to that volume, appears to contain forty-five homilies. This apparent contradiction has been resolved by Kenneth Sisam,[3] who has pointed out that *Catholic Homilies* II.XXIV and II.XXVII (here, as below, Benjamin Thorpe's numbering) are "pendants" to preceding sermons, and furthermore that the sermons numbered by Thorpe one through thirty-nine cover only thirty-four feast-days. The last six sermons are not assigned to specific days, but are for general use ("on the nativity of one apostle" and "on the dedication of a church"). The total

number, reckoned by feast-days, is then the forty promised by
Ælfric.

We have, therefore, eighty-five separate items: six general sermons for topical use, two "pendants," one sermon to be preached
"whenever you will" and which serves as a general introduction to
the two series (*CH* I.I), and seventy-six sermons arranged in two
series which cover the major feast-days of the church year as
observed by the English church. Ælfric says in his preface to the
first volume that the division into two series is intended as a guard
against tedium; and he suggests, as we have observed, that one
series bé read in church one year, the other the next. But he gives
his permission for the two series to be combined into one, if anyone
wishes to do so (*CH* I, p. 2). As a matter of fact, the earliest manuscripts of the homilies preserve Ælfric's division; later ones combine
the sermons in both volumes into one sequence; and eventually, in
other collections, the original integrity of the series is lost since the
sermons are mixed indiscriminately with those of other authors.

The subjects of these sermons are as varied as their types. According to Smetana's reckoning,[4] of the eighty-five items, fifty-six are
homiletic in the narrow sense; that is, they are commentaries on
scriptural texts and are indebted to the Church Fathers. Seventeen
others are saints' lives, and the remaining twelve are topical sermons,
expansions of scriptural narrative, and so forth.

Partly because of Ælfric's free method of adaptation and partly
because of the conventional nature of his material, the study of
his sources for the sermons is a rather complicated matter.[5] The
starting point is his own list of his major sources in his preface to
Volume I: Augustine, Jerome, Bede, Gregory, Smaragdus, and Haymo. But relatively seldom does Ælfric produce a straightforward
translation of a single text; almost invariably he weaves together,
according to his own purposes, material from several sources,
expanding and compressing source material and adding transitions
and commentary of his own. For example, *Catholic Homilies* I.II
draws on six separate homilies by Gregory, Smaragdus, and
Bede; I.V and I.XXVII draw on five sources each; and II.III and II.V
draw on four each.[6]

Ælfric's heaviest debts are to Gregory the Great, Bede, and
Augustine, reflecting thereby his aim to make his homilies reflect
the orthodox authority "willingly accepted by all Catholics." By a
rough reckoning, Gregory is a major source for about thirty-three

of the eighty-five items in the two volumes; Bede for about twenty-three; and Augustine for about fourteen. All three are used incidentally and for short passages here and there throughout other homilies as well; thus, the total work is permeated with the thought of these three Fathers. Although no other sources are used as pervasively as these three, many others are used: besides Jerome, Smaragdus, and Haymo (named in the preface), Severianus, Fulgentius, Ratramus, Origen, Sulpicius Severus, and various anonymous writers contribute major parts of one or more sermons.

A recent study of Ælfric's sources by Father Cyril Smetana has not only revealed some interesting facts about Ælfric's methods but indirectly provided some additional insight into his conceptions of his work.[7] Ælfric, he proves, used as his primary immediate source for the *Catholic Homilies* an already existing homiliary collected by Paul the Deacon. Paul the Deacon (720–799?) was a monk of Monte Cassino who spent some time at the court of Charlemagne, seeking the release of his brother who had been taken prisoner by the Frankish king. At Charlemagne's request, he compiled and edited an authoritative collection of nearly two hundred and fifty homilies for use in the Carolingian lands. This homiliary was regarded in its day as a masterpiece of critical scholarship and acquired enormous prestige. Versions and modifications of it remained in use for centuries, and its influence is still to be seen in the present calendar of feasts.

The list of items which comprise the original version of Paul's collection has been reconstructed by F. Wiegand.[8] On the basis of this list, Smetana has discovered that Ælfric was clearly heavily indebted to this homiliary. For the fifty-six exegetical homilies in Ælfric's collection, eighty-six patristic sources were used. Sixty-five of these appeared in the original version of Paul the Deacon's collection; most of the rest of them were in later versions of the work. It seems, therefore, that Ælfric had before him a version of the homiliary of Paul the Deacon very much like the original but varying from it in some respects.

Ælfric's use of Paul the Deacon not only underscores his emphasis on orthodoxy and authority in the prefaces but also tells us something of the way he conceived his task. Clemoes has pointed out the similarities in Paul's and Ælfric's projects.[9] Paul had compiled his collection in order to provide the basis for sound preaching in Charlemagne's realm. Ælfric had a similar aim for his own collection,

which was written for use in an English church badly in need
of learning and a sense of order. Paul's collection was requested by
Charlemagne and received his approval; Ælfric similarly sought
the official approval of Archbishop Sigeric, head of the English
church, for his collection. In one important respect, however,
Ælfric's aims went beyond those of Paul the Deacon. Whereas
Paul had merely assembled patristic homilies in Latin, Ælfric
reshaped his sources and put them into the language of his own
country. The result was a carefully organized summary of the
religious learning of his day, but Ælfric made it thoroughly English
and at the same time Catholic in its authority and orthodoxy.

Paul the Deacon's collection was not the only source of this kind
used by Ælfric, though it was the major one. He also drew upon collections by two other Carolingians, Smaragdus and Haymo of
Auxerre, both specifically mentioned by Ælfric in his preface.[10]
Smaragdus was the compiler of a series of brief excerpts from the
works of the Fathers; Haymo, upon whose work Ælfric drew more
heavily, had compiled a homiliary similar to Paul the Deacon's,
though smaller in scope. Over twenty-five of the *Catholic Homilies*
are indebted to some degree to Haymo's compilation. A fourth
compilation, perhaps not really comparable, upon which Ælfric
drew, was one he had made himself, a collection of items he apparently began to assemble even before he left Winchester and which
survives in an eleventh-century copy now at Boulogne.[11] At least one
item in this "commonplace book," a digest of Julian of Toledo's
Prognosticon, furnished some details for the first volume of the
Catholic Homilies.

Ælfric, as we shall see, handled his sources very freely. He often
combined parts of several homilies and added material of his own to
produce, in effect, a new work; but he always did so with a keen
respect for the spirit of his authorities. But much of his attitude toward his work is suggested by his very selection of sources. His
collection of homilies was not a random assemblage of occasional
pieces; it was grounded upon a systematic selection of sources
sanctioned not only by the authority of their authors but also by the
approval of previous editors.

II *Ælfric's Methods of Interpretation*

Fifty-six, or approximately two-thirds, of the eighty-five sermons in the *Catholic Homilies* are exegetical: methodical expositions and commentaries on scriptural texts. In these homilies, Ælfric expounded his texts in accordance with a long, well-established tradition of exegesis. His translations of his sources are seldom mechanical or literal—he translated, he says, not "word for word" but "sense for sense"—but for the most part he adopts his sources' interpretations of scriptural texts without substantial alteration. In this fidelity to authority, he reflects, of course, his general intention of providing a body of orthodox doctrine in accessible form.

The basis of this exegetical method was the theory of allegory or multiple levels of meaning: the so-called fourfold (sometimes threefold) method of interpretation.[12] Apparently, this critical method is derived ultimately from Jewish haggadic exegesis, as adapted by Alexandrian philosophers and theologians in their effort to reconcile Christianity and Platonic philosophy. The most notable early figure in the tradition was the Alexandrian Neo-platonist Philo (c. 20 B.C.—c. 50 A.D.), who attempted to prove that Greek philosophical ideas underlay the story of the Old Testament. Philo drew not only upon Jewish traditions of allegory but also upon the Stoics' allegorical readings of Homer to construct a critical theory of multiple senses.

Philo's methods were taken over and refined by the third-century Christian theologian Origen. Origen fixed the outlines of the allegorical method for Christian writers, and his methods were followed, with some variations, to the end of the Middle Ages. Origen used a three-level system of interpretation: literal, moral, and spiritual. Essentially, this meant that any scriptural text could be interpreted as a literal statement, as a guide to morality, and as an allegorical allusion to the spiritual world. St. Augustine (354–430) used an adaptation of this scheme, which he explained in his *Of Christian Doctrine*. It incorporated four levels: historical (the literal level), etiological (consideration of causes), analogical (consideration of the relationship between the Old and New Testaments), and allegorical (a figurative level).

Ælfric's chief authority, Gregory the Great (c. 540–604), used a threefold method, much like Origen's, which Gregory explained in his dedication to his lectures on the Book of Job: "First we lay the foundations in history; then by following a symbolical sense, we erect an intellectual edifice to be a stronghold of faith; and lastly, by the grace of moral instruction, we as it were paint the fabric in fair colors . . . . For the word of God both exercises the understanding of the wise by its deep mysteries, and also by its superficial lessons nurses the simple-minded. It presents openly that wherewith the little ones may be fed; it keeps in secret that whereby men of loftier range may be rapt in admiration."[13] These three levels— literal, allegorical, and moral—with a fourth, the anagogical (dealing with the other world, the spiritual dimension, and Heaven and Hell) frequently added, became the standard model for the patristic exegetes; and it is followed by Ælfric.[14]

In practice, three kinds of figurative interpretations may be identified—allegory (in the strict sense), symbolism, and typology. Allegorical interpretations are usually *ad hoc* figurative readings of texts; symbolism, in contrast, is highly conventional and depends upon a body of traditional lore concerning the proper interpretation of, for example, numbers, animals, and plants. Each number in the Bible had a "deeper meaning." Key numbers, of course, were one (for the unity of God), three (for the Trinity), four (for the Evangelists), seven (for the sevenfold gifts of the Holy Spirit, the seven last words of Christ, the seven joys of Mary), and twelve (for the twelve tribes of Israel, the twelve disciples). But other numbers were also interpreted (two, for the love of God for man; five, for the Pentateuch), and the digits of a number were often added to provide additional material for interpretation. In the other large bodies of conventional symbolism, ones dealing with plants and animals, the lamb symbolized purity; the ram, power; the goat, lust; and the dove, meekness. The wolf was the devil. The palm, of course, indicated victory; the red rose, death; and the white lily, purity.

Typology was the interpretation of the Old Testament in the light of the New. The persons and events of the Old Testament were presumed to "prefigure" the life of Christ and the history and doctrines of the Catholic Church. Christ himself was "prefigured" in, among others, Adam, Noah, Moses, and Samson. Noah's ark, Eve, and the tabernacle all were types of the Church, while the Pharaoh was one of several types of the devil.

Ælfric took over from his models these arts of interpretation and bodies of lore, although he used them critically and with considerable sensitivity to the needs and capacities of his audience.

Of Christ's miracles, for example, he wrote in the sermon for Shrove Sunday,

Þeahhwæðere þa wundra þe Crist worhte, oðer ðing hi æteowdon þurh mihte, and oðre ðing hi getacnodon þurh geryno. He worhte þa wundra soðlice þurh godcunde mihte, and mid þam wundrum þæs folces geleafan getrymde; ac hwæðre þær was oðer ðing dingle on ðam wundrum, æfter gastlicum andgite.

(But the miracles which Christ wrought demonstrated one thing through power and another thing they betokened through mystery. He wrought these miracles truly through divine power, and with these miracles confirmed the people's faith; but yet there was another thing in those miracles, in a spiritual sense.)   (*CH* I.X, 154)

This contrast between the literal and the spiritual senses Ælfric often expressed as between the "lichamlic" or "flæsclic" and the "gastlic." He uses a small number of other formulas to introduce allegorical interpretations. A typical example is the following from the sermon for Midlent Sunday:

Ac we willaþ eow secgan þæt gastlic andgit þyssera ealdra gesetnyssa, forþan þe seo ealde æ is mid gastlicum andgyte afylled. . . .

(But we will say to you the spiritual sense of these old institutes, for the old law is filled with spiritual meaning. . . .)   (*CH* II.XII, 198)

The potentialities for excess in the use of the allegorical method are obvious. Ælfric, who often declines to follow his sources into the most strained interpretations, either merely omits them silently or gives as his reason the limitations of his hearers:

Þises godspelles traht sprecð gyt menigfealdlicor ymb ðas wæter-fatu and heora getacnungum, ac we ondraedað us þæt ge ðas foresædan getacnunga to gymeleaste doð, gif we eow swiðor be ðam gereccað.

(The exposition of this gospel speaks yet more fully about these water-vessels and their meanings, but we fear that you will neglect the meanings already given, if we relate to you further about them.)   (*CH* II.IV, 70)

Professor Schelp cites an amusing example of Ælfric's conservatism of interpretation of numbers.[15] Gregory, in his Homily 24, grapples with the fact that Peter is said to have caught 153 fish (John 21:11). This is the number of the elect, Gregory says, and is the product of adding the Ten Commandments to the Sevenfold Gifts and multiplying twice by the Trinity ($10 + 7 \times 3 \times 3 = 153$). This, apparently, is too much for Ælfric, and he omits it, remarking merely:

Ða getel þæra fixa hæfþ maran getacnunge þonne ge understandan magon.

(The number of the fishes has a greater tokening than you can understand.) (*CH* II.XVII, 292)

Allegorical interpretation is, of course, not the only method used by Ælfric. He also frequently uses classification, for example, and he is a master of the exemplum, or illustrative story. He is a critical follower of tradition, also, in the larger structural patterns of his homilies. He regularly uses the method called "continuous gloss": the arrangement of text and gloss consecutively, as opposed to placing the gloss in the margin or between the lines of the text. Thus a homily often consists of a biblical text, followed by a section of doctrine, in which the text is thoroughly glossed, and finally a moral section which points the lesson for the audience.[16]

Ælfric's use of traditional methods of exegesis and his critical conservatism in following his sources, like his selection of the sources themselves, indicate his desire to build a body of preaching materials for the laity which would be beyond reproach in their permanent relevance and authority.

III *Homiletic Exegesis: Midlent Sunday*

The twelfth sermon of the first series, for Midlent Sunday, may serve to illustrate Ælfric's customary method of developing an exegetical sermon. Not one of his most inspired sermons, it is however, fairly typical of this kind of sermon; furthermore, it contains some interesting remarks on the art of interpretation itself. Ælfric's text is Matthew's account of the miracles of the loaves and the fishes. He begins with a graceful English translation of the text itself, telling how Christ went to the sea of Galilee and to a mountain with his disciples ("leorning-cnihta") and was followed by five thousand people. Calling for a little boy's five barley loaves and two fishes, he blessed them and divided them among the five thousand and "hi ealle genoh hæfdon" (they all had enough). And what was left over filled twelve baskets. Having set forth the text, Ælfric proceeds to interpret it line by line, drawing upon various arts of interpretation. The sea is interpreted allegorically as the world, and Christ's passing over it reminds us that Christ came into this world as a man. He ascended the mountain and sat with His disciples as He ascended to heaven and sits now with the saints. The sea is an appropriate figure for this world, Ælfric says, because of its variety and changeable nature.

Christ's lifting up His eyes and seeing the multitude coming is also interpreted allegorically as His receiving those who come to Him spiritually. He will feed these with "gastlicum fodan" (spiritual food) as He fed the multitude with the loaves and the fishes. Ælfric now comes to the miracle itself, and he inserts some characteristic comments on miracles. Although Ælfric does not minimize the miraculous either in his homilies or in his saints' lives, he nevertheless often reveals a certain wariness about emphasizing them too much and takes pains to equate them with the normal order of things. Thus, here:

Fela wundra worhte God, and dæghwamlice wyrcð; ac ða wundra sind swiðe awacode on manna gesihðe, forðon ðe hi sind swiðe gewunelice. Mare wundor is þæt God Ælmihtig ælce dæg fet ealne middangeard, and gewissað þa godan, þonne þæt wundor wære, þæt he þa gefylde fif ðusend manna mid fif hlafum: ac ðæs wundredon men, na forði þæt hit mare wundor wære, ac forði þæt hit wæs ungewunelic.

(God has wrought many miracles and daily works; but these miracles are much weakened in the sight of men, because they are very common. A greater miracle it is that God Almighty every day feeds all the world, and directs the good, than that miracle was, that he filled five thousand men with five loaves: but men wondered at this, not because it was a greater miracle, but because it was unusual.) (*CH* I.XII, 184)

Ælfric then indicates the necessity of interpretation of written texts. With a picture, it is enough to see it and praise it, but a story is often "deope on getacnungum" (deep in its significations):

Swa is eac on ðam wundre þe God worhte mid þam fif hlafum: ne bið na genoh þæt we þæs tacnes wundrian, oþþe þurh þæt God herian, buton we eac þæt gastlice andgit understandon.

(So also it is with regard to the miracle which God wrought with the five loaves: it is not enough that we wonder at the miracle, or praise God on account of it, without also understanding its spiritual sense.)

(CH I.XII, 186)

Ælfric uses allegory and plant and number symbolism to set forth the "spiritual sense" of the miracle. The loaves and fishes stand for Christ's teaching, and He gives the food to His disciples to distribute, just as He sent them later into the world to teach His doctrine. The leftover scraps suggest the deeper doctrines which the laity cannot understand and which the clergy must gather and preserve. The boy who brought the bread and fish, because he did not taste it himself, suggests the Jewish people who did not understand their scriptures until Christ revealed their meaning.

Each number has its significance, in conformity with tradition and with the general interpretation of the text. The five loaves are the five books of the Pentateuch, but the two fishes symbolize the Psalms and the Prophets. There were five thousand men in the crowd to correspond to the five loaves; and, because a thousand is a "perfect number," it suggests the perfection of those fed by Christ's teachings. The twelve baskets into which the fragments were gathered stand for the twelve disciples, who received those doctrines of Christ which were too difficult for the laity. Plant symbolism is used to gloss the detail that the multitude sat upon the grass. Since "all flesh is grass," grass conventionally means "fleshly desire"; and those fed by Christ must trample and press down fleshly desires as the multitude sat upon the grass.

His doctrinal section completed, with the text thoroughly glossed, Ælfric concludes his tripartite structure with a moral section of admonition to his audience. The multitude declared Jesus to be a prophet after seeing his miracle; we will be blessed if, not having seen, we still believe:

We cweðað nu, mid fullum geleafan, þæt Crist is soð witega, and ealra witegena Witega, and þæt he is soðlice ðæs Ælmihtigan Godes Sunu, ealswa mihtig swa his Fæder, mid ðam he leofað and rixað on annysse ðæs Halgan Gastes, a buton ende on ecnysse. Amen.

(We say now, with full belief, that Christ was a true prophet, and prophet of all prophets, and that he is truly Son of the Almighty God, as mighty as his Father, with whom he lives and reigns in unity of the Holy Ghost, ever without end to eternity. Amen.)

(CH I. XII, 190, 192)

The Midlent homily is based on two homilies by Augustine and Bede, and the interpretation of the miracle of the loaves and the fishes is thoroughly traditional. If it seems strained and pedantic to a modern reader, it is because we have lost the medieval perception of the world as suffused with the mystery of God and of sacred literature as a pleasingly enigmatic store of layered meaning. Ælfric, of course, shared these perceptions with his authorities; he uses their interpretation of the miracle and then weaves it into a clear and graceful presentation of his own, appropriate to his audience.

IV *Homiletic Narrative: The Vision of Drihthelm*

About seventeen of the items in the *Catholic Homilies* are saints' lives as Ælfric promised in the Latin preface to the first series; "And I have not only explained the writings of the Evangelists in this work, but have also set forth the life and passions of saints, for the benefit of the unlearned of our race" (*CH* I, p. 1). In the first series appear lives of St. Stephen (III), St. John (IV), St. Clement the Martyr (XXXVII), and St. Andrew (XXXVIII). In the second series appear St. Stephen again (II); St. Gregory the Great (IX); St. Cuthbert (X); St. Benedict (XI); SS. Philip and James (XVIII); SS. Alexander, Eventius, and Theodolus (XX); St. Fursey (XXII); the Vision of Drihthelm (XXIII); St. James the Apostle (XXXI); the Seven Sleepers (XXXII); St. Matthew (XXXVII); SS. Simon and Jude (XXXVIII); and St. Martin (XXXIX).

Ælfric's sources for these hagiological sermons are varied. Some are taken over from already existing sermon treatments, as are the sermons on St. Stephen; others are adapted from longer accounts, such as Sulpicius Severus's Life of St. Martin; while still others are based on non-hagiological works, like the sermons on the vision of Drihthelm and the story of Ymma, which are drawn from Bede's *Ecclesiastical History*.[17]

The homiletic saints' lives in the *Catholic Homilies* celebrate saints commemorated by the whole Church. The *Lives of Saints* collection was to deal with the saints which the monks commemorated among themselves, and it was apparently intended primarily for private reading rather than for liturgical use. This distinction, as we shall see, is a rather fine one; and the items in the *Lives of Saints* are similar in form to those in the *Catholic Homilies*. But it is worthwhile to look briefly at one of the earlier narratives which was intended directly for homiletic presentation to a lay audience. And a good example for this purpose is Ælfric's treatment of "The Vision of Drihthelm," both because of its intrinsic interest and because it typifies Ælfric's ordinary practice in adapting a narrative to homiletic use. The "Vision" (*CH* II.XXIII) is very closely based on Bede's *Ecclesiastical History* (V.12), as Ælfric acknowledges in the opening lines of the homily:

Beda, ure lareow, awrat, on ðære bec þe is gehaten "Historia Anglorum," be sumes mannes æriste, on ðisum iglande, þisum wordum writende:

(Bede, our doctor, has written, in the book which is called "Historia Anglorum," of a certain man's resurrection in this island, in these words writing:)   (*CH* II. XXIII, 348)

The item is headed *Alia Visio* (Another Vision), and its selection was obviously suggested by the preceding item, an adaptation of the anonymous "Life of Fursey." Fursey was a Scottish priest who twice visited the underworld and had angels and devils war over possession of his soul. He remained unharmed except for a burn on the shoulder and face, a reminder of a minor misdeed; and, after his second return, he spent twelve years going around Britain, telling his story, and exhibiting his burn.

The stories of Fursey and Drihthelm are, of course, chiefly interesting today as specimens of the popular medieval literary form, the visit to the underworld, a form which serves as the basis of Dante's *The Divine Comedy*. The "Vision of Drihthelm," though much shorter and simpler than Fursey's vision, shares many of its characteristics: the presence of a heavenly guide, a fiery vision, and comments on the transformed later life of the visionary. Drihthelm is said to have been a pious Northumbrian who rose from his deathbed the morning after his death. He divided his property among his wife, his children, and the poor and entered the monastery at Melrose.

The bulk of the story is Drihthelm's own account of his experience. He was led by a shining angel to a vast, burning pit where he saw lost souls being tormented; among them were five new arrivals, including a priest, a layman, and a woman. He was then led eastward to a beautiful, flowery place, which he was told was Heaven, and then returned to his body. After his return, he led a life of great asceticism, often praying while standing up to his neck in an icy stream:

Ðaða hine man axode hu he mihte ðone micclan cyle forberan, he andwyrde, "Maran cyle ic geseah, and wyrsan." Eft, ðaða hi axoden hu he
mihte swa stearce forhæfednysse healdan, he andwyrde, "Stiðran and
wyrsan ic geseah."

(When any one asked him how he could bear that great cold, he answered,
"I have seen a greater and worse cold." Again, when they asked him how
he could observe such rigid abstinence, he answered, "I have seen a more
rigid and worse.")

(*CH* II.XXIII, 254)

Bede's treatment of the story of Drihthelm is of an appropriate
length for a homily, and Ælfric translates it fairly straightforwardly
with few omissions and no expansions. He does omit Bede's circum-
stantial details of Drihthelm's home and of Melrose and his
historically-minded account of his authority for the story, a monk
named Hæmgils who had known Drihthelm. He also alters the
sequence of Bede's narrative to provide a dramatic situation for
Drihthelm's account of his vision. Bede mentions near the end of the
account that King Aldfrith used to visit Drihthelm; Ælfric introduces this episode earlier and makes the vision a dramatic speech
to Aldfrith and "certain pious men."

But these are minor changes. Ælfric also adds a brief conclusion,
citing a similar vision in Gregory's *Dialogues* and pointing the
obvious lessons: that we must live piously and seek to help those
in hell-torment through our prayers. The homily is interesting not
because of its striking interpretations or any particular originality in
treatment but because it exemplifies Ælfric's keen sense of his
audience's attention, his perception of homiletic possibilities in a
non-homiletic source, and the clarity and economy of his handling
of narrative. We also see these characteristics illustrated in the
narratives of the *Lives of Saints*.

V *Moral Instruction: On the Greater Litany*

To the categories of exegetical homilies and saints' lives in the
Catholic Homilies, we may add a third, rather loose category of
sermons of general moral instruction. All the sermons, of course, are
filled with moral applications of doctrine; and Ælfric's customary
sermon structure calls for a section of direct moral counsel at the
conclusion. But a few of the sermons are not tied to a particular

text or devoted to a narrative; they are devoted wholly to moral instruction. Such a sermon is the twenty-first item in the second series: "On the greater litany."

This sermon apparently is largely original with Ælfric.[18] Although various details may have been derived from his reading, the structure and organization seem to be his own. He begins with a characteristic statement that teachers have an obligation to transmit holy knowledge to those who are not learned, in order that men should not err through ignorance. He then quotes Christ's "highest commandment":

Lufa ðinne Drihten mid ealre ðinre heortan, and mid eallum mode: þis is þæt mæste bebod. Is eft oðer bebod ðisum swiðe gelic, Lufa ðinne nextan swa swa ðe sylfne: þas twa bebodu belucað ealle bec.

(Love thy Lord with all thine heart, and with all thy mind: this is the greatest commandment. There is again another commandment very like unto this, Love thy neighbor as thyself: these two commandments comprise all the books.)
(*CH* II. XXI, 314)

The first half of the sermon is built around an exposition of this text. Ælfric proceeds by defining key words; first comes an examination of the meaning of "love." Christ and John are quoted to the effect that love is proved by good works, and the love of God and the love of man are contrasted and compared; then "neighbor" is examined, and Christ is quoted on the universal brotherhood of man. Through this first section of the sermon, Ælfric characteristically continually provides exempla, parables, and homely illustrations of his abstract points. On the presence of the Holy Trinity in men's hearts, he says:

Menn dæftað heora hus, and wel gedreoglæcað, gif hi sumne freond onfon willað to him, þæt nan unðaeslicnys him ne ðurfe derian; and we sceolon us clænsian fram unclænum dædum, þæt se Mihtiga God on urum mode wunige, seðe ænne gehwilcne þurh his Gast geneosað.

(Men put their houses in order, and are well content, if they desire to receive a friend to them, that no impropriety may offend him; and we should cleanse ourselves from unclean deeds, that the Mighty God may dwell in our mind, who visits every one through his Spirit.)
(*CH* II.XVI, 316)

In the second part of the sermon, Ælfric turns to separate consideration of the moral obligations of the various classes of men from kings downward. The key virtues for kings are righteousness and wisdom, for they must first direct themselves and then their people. Bishops, priests, and judges are admonished to use their authority wisely and justly and to live in such a way as to exemplify their own teachings. The duties of wives and husbands, parents and children are the subject of a long section in which Ælfric takes up his favorite theme of chastity. The purpose of sexual intercourse is procreation, and lust is wrong, even within wedlock:

God forgeaf gescead menniscum gesceafte, and ungesceadwisum nytenum setne timan, þæt men sceoldon lybban heora lif mid gesceade, swa swa þa clænan nytenu cepað heora timan. Se mann is gesceapen to his Scyppendes anlicnysse, and soðlice ða nytenu sindon sawullease. Nu bið mannum sceamu þæt hi mislybban sceolon, and ða nytenu healdað heora gesetnysse.

God gave reason to the human creation, and to the irrational animals a fixed time, so that men might live their lives with reason, as the clean animals observe their times. Man is created in his Creator's likeness, and truly animals are soulless. Now it is a shame to men that they should mislive, and the animals observe their established law.)

(CH II. XXI, 324)

Parents are enjoined to correct their children and they in turn are to honor their parents, and a cautionary tale is told of a child who was recklessly nurtured. He cursed God, without parental reproof, until devils carried him off as he cried, "My father! My father!" Brief counsel is also given to servants and masters, to the rich and the poor, which leads Ælfric into a concluding section in which he generally considers the problem of the distribution of happiness and misery in the world. His conclusion is highly orthodox:

Menigfealde beoð þæs Metodan Drihtnes egsan and swingla ofer scyldigum mannum, þæt ða sceortan witu ðises geswincfullan lifes foryttan ða toweardan, þe næfre ne ateoriað.

Manifold are the Lord Creator's terrors and scourges over guilty men, in order that the short punishments of this painful life may prevent those to come, which will never fail.)

(CH II. XXI, 328)

VI *Ælfric as a Homilist*

As the comments on particular homilies have indicated, the eighty
five items in the two series of *Catholic Homilies* are varied in subject
matter and in structure. Yet, it is possible to make some general
comments on Ælfric's practices as a writer of homilies and thus to
indicate something of the nature of his achievement in this area
First of all, the doctrine expressed in the homilies is highly orthodox
and it consists of the basic teachings of the church. In many respects
it is summarized in the first sermon in the double series, "On the
Beginning of Creation," to be preached "whenever you will,"
which serves as a general introduction to the collection. This sermon
begins by summarizing Genesis and then tells of the coming of
Christ, His sacrifice, and His resurrection. The end of the homily
extends the story to the last judgment, when "He shall come at the
end of the world with great majesty, in clouds" (*CH* I. I, 28).

This Christian view of history contains the basic elements of
Ælfric's doctrines, which are those of the church as a whole. He
returns over and over to the same themes: God the Creator, the
Trinity, the life and works of Christ, and man's sin and redemption
His moral teaching is similarly straightforward and orthodox
Favorite topics are the duties of priests and teachers to spread the
word of God and those of priests and laymen alike to pursue the
ideal of chastity, spiritual as well as fleshly. Taken as a whole, the
two series of homilies amply fulfill Ælfric's promise in the Latin
preface to the first series to provide knowledge "which I thought
might be enough for simple persons, for the amendment of their
lives, inasmuch as laymen cannot take in all things, though they
may learn them from the mouth of the learned" (*CH* I, p. 1).

The treatment of this material is equally orthodox. As we have
seen, Ælfric took care to select as his sources those writers universally
approved by the church; not only in the prefaces but also within the
individual sermons, he continually points out that his work is derived
from established authority: "the wise Augustine," "the doctor
Haymo," "Gregory the expounder." He follows their methods of
interpretation—allegorical, typological, symbolic—and adopts, for
the most part, their readings of the texts. Although his treatment
of his sources would hardly be called "translation" today but "free
adaptation," he preserves through his reorderings the interpretation
of his authorities.

Although Ælfric's English prose style is considered in some detail in Chapter 6, we may note that the *Catholic Homilies,* though for the most part not in the fully developed rhythmic style of Ælfric's later works, are written in a style notable for its clarity and movement—one eminently suited to oral delivery. Indeed, perhaps the most notable feature of Ælfric's manner as a homilist is his continual sense of his audience's needs and capacities. His sources are extremely varied in style, length, and degree of complexity; but Ælfric transmutes each of them into a piece suited to the comprehension of his listeners. We are often reminded of this intent by the direct addresses to the listeners. In the sermon on the "Octaves and Circumcision of Our Lord," for example, he interrupts his exposition to say, "It is probable that some of you do not know what circumcision is" (*CH* I.VI, 92). And he then explains the meaning of the word, with comments on its history and spiritual significance. Or, when he feels it necessary to develop a theme at some length, he will insert a word of encouragement: "This is very wearisome for you to hear; if we had dared to pass it silently, we should not have said it to you" (*CH* II.XXI, 324).

But the real concern of Ælfric for his audience comes less from such direct comments as these than from the overall design of the series and Ælfric's control of that design. Structured inevitably around two progressions through the church calendar, the homilies present a comprehensive view of Christian history in a form both acceptable to the learned and accessible to the humble. In the care with which they are composed and in the larger purposes which they achieve, they go beyond their first purpose of supplying the immediate needs of a preacher to take on the qualities, in Clemoes's words, of a "consciously 'literary' act."

CHAPTER 3

Lives of Saints

ÆLFRIC introduced his *Lives of Saints,* a third collection of translations written about 998, with these words. (The dedication to Æthelweard is the chief evidence for the date, but since Æthelweard did not die until 1002, the collection may be that late.)

Ælfric gret eadmodlice Æþelwerd ealdorman, and ic secge þe, leof, þæt ic hæbbe nu gegaderod on þyssere bec þæra halgena þrowunga þe me to onhagode on englisc to awendene, for þan þe ðu, leof, swiðost, and Æðelmær, swylcera gewrita me bædon, and of handum gelæhton eowerne geleafan to getrymmenne mid þære gerecednysse þe ge on eowrum gereorde næfdon ær. Ðu wast, leof, þæt we awendon on þam twam ærrum bocum þæra halgena þrowunga and lif þe angelecynn mid freols-dagum wurþað. Nu gewearð us þæt we þas boc be þæra halgena ðrowungum and life gedihton þe mynstermenn mid heora þenungum betwux him wurðiað.

(Ælfric greets humbly Æthelweard ealdorman, and I say to you, sir, that I have now gathered into this book such passions of the saints as I have had leisure to translate into English, because you, sir, and Æthelmær have most earnestly asked me for such writings, and from my hands you have already received, for the strengthening of your faith, writings which you never had before in your language. You know, sir, that we translated in the two earlier books the passions and lives of those saints which the English people honor with feast-days. Now it has seemed good to us to write this book about the passions and lives of those saints whom the monks celebrate among themselves.)

(*LS*, English Preface, 4)

In the six to ten years since the second series of *Catholic Homilies* had appeared, Ælfric had probably been at work on other pieces, including the *Grammar,* the *De Temporibus Anni,* and his Bible translations. There is a suggestion in the preface that Ælfric had been giving single lives to Æthelweard to read for some time before he gathered them into a set.

Much the best surviving manuscript of the *Lives* is the British Museum manuscript (Cotton Julius E. vii), from which W. W. Skeat

printed his edition. Skeat numbered the separate items in his edition
of this manuscript I through XXXVI. Four of these items have
been shown to be not by Ælfric (XXIII, XXIIIB, XXX, and
XXXIII),[1] and eight others are not saints' lives, but discourses on
general subjects (I, XII, XIII, XV, XVI, XVII, XVIII, and XXV).
Nevertheless, the headings in the manuscript are somewhat ambiguous
and do not correspond exactly to Skeat's; and it seems that if the
four non-Ælfrician items were dropped and the numbering altered,
we would have a collection of forty items, parallel in this respect
to each volume of the *Catholic Homilies*.[2] Despite Ælfric's statement
in the preface and the general tenor of the collection, there is no
reason to believe that the non-hagiological items were not originally
part of the set.

The *Lives* have commonly been referred to as a third set of "homilies." It is true that they are comparable to the earlier series in
form and arrangement; indeed, the two *Catholic Homilies* contain
some hagiological homilies, as we have seen. However, as Clemoes
has pointed out,[3] the *Lives* appear to be intended for private reading,
not for liturgical use. The homilies regularly include oral formulas
(such as "we will relate to you . . .") which are missing in the *Lives*.
Furthermore, the items in the *Lives* are more varied in length and
do not seem to be tied to the time requirements of preaching, as the
homilies are (however loosely). Also, the *Lives* are explicitly intended for monastic use, and there is some question as to whether
preaching would have been done in the vernacular to a monastic
congregation at this time. The distinction may not be an important
one. Obviously, the *Homilies* might be read privately; and the
Lives might serve, and undoubtedly often did serve, as the bases
of sermons.

The selection of material and the sources used in the *Lives of
Saints* demonstrate aims similar to those for the *Catholic Homilies*.
In the *Lives,* as in the *Homilies,* Ælfric is clearly pursuing his plan to
provide a sound, systematic body of Christian literature for his
country. The separate items are widely varied, but collectively they
constitute a broad survey of the major individual saints and kinds
of saints honored by the faithful. Two of the items, for example,
are lives of apostles—number XV, on St. Mark, and number
XXXVI, on St. Thomas the Apostle. The other apostles had been
treated in the *Catholic Homilies;* Ælfric's comprehensive aims are
clear by his inclusion of the last two in the *Lives*.

Of the eight items in the series that are not hagiographic, one—
"The Memory of the Saints"—seems intended as a kind of general
introduction to the series; it was perhaps originally placed first
in the collection, though it is number XVI in Skeat's edition of the
Cotton manuscript. Other non-hagiographic items include biblical
material (XVIII, on the Book of Kings; XXV, on the Maccabees)
and general discourses, such as XII, on Ash Wednesday, and XVII,
"On Auguries."

The Roman martyrs constitute the subjects of the largest single
group of lives. There are accounts of the "passions" of St. Julian
(IV), St. Sebastian (V), the Forty Soldiers (XI), St. George (XIV),
and half a dozen more. A particular kind of Roman martyr—the
virgin martyr—is the subject of several of these lives. Another notable
group deals with the lives of native English saints. Ælfric himself
obviously was particularly interested in providing his audience
with accounts of British saints; and he drew upon Bede and upon
Latin hagiographers of his own day for lives of St. Alban (XIX),
St. Æthelthryth (XX), St. Swithun (XXI), St. Oswald (XXVI), and
St. Edmund (XXXII). Another large group consists of lives of
famous "confessors," bishops and abbots who had attained saint-
hood not through martyrdom but through ecclesiastical service.
Among these lives are those of St. Basilius (III); St. Maurus, missionary from St. Benedict to the Franks (VI); and St. Martin (XXXI).

The sources of the *Lives of Saints* cannot be described as easily as
those of the *Catholic Homilies*. [4] No one writer is so dominant among
them as Gregory is among the authorities for the *Homilies,* and
the range of sources is very wide. As in the *Homilies,* though,
Ælfric shows in *Lives of Saints* a careful concern for textual matters;
and he selects the "standard" life of each saint for his translation.
He uses, for instance, Ambrose's lives of St. Sebastian and St.
Agnes, Sulpicius Severus's life of St. Martin, and Bede's accounts
of the earlier English saints. A number of the lives are based upon
versions of anonymous lives now gathered in the *Acta Sanctorum.*

However, despite the apparent intention in the *Lives* to represent
the whole range of Latin hagiography and to draw upon standard
sources, Ælfric does not include a number of lives that would seem
to have been obvious choices: Jerome's life of Paul the Hermit,
for example, and Athanasius's life of St. Anthony, which was widely
known in the translation into Latin by Evagrius. Indeed, none of
the lives of the "desert fathers" appears in the series. An explanation,

of sorts, for this omission appears in the Latin preface to the *Lives:*
"I hold my peace as to the book called *Vitae Patrum,* wherein are
contained many subtle points which ought not to be laid open to
the laity, nor indeed are we ourselves quite able to fathom them"
(*LS,* Latin Preface, 2). What exactly Ælfric regarded as inappropriate for the laity in the *Vitae Patrum,* he does not explain.
His comment is even more puzzling since he has just said that the
book is intended for monks, not the laity; furthermore, it appears
that he did draw upon some version of the *Vitae Patrum,* despite
his apparent disclaimer.[5]

I *English Saints' Lives Before Ælfric*

Ælfric was by no means the first to write saints' lives in English;
such pieces had been written in England at least as early as the
latter part of the eighth century.[6] The great body of Latin hagiography had been introduced into England very soon after the conversion in 597 by missionaries eager to reinforce their teachings by
providing their new converts with a spiritual substitute for the
heroic legends of their pagan past. According to Bede, Gregory
the Great sent relics to England; and, very early, churches were
named after prominent saints. By the early eighth century, enough
saints' lives were available in England for Bede to make an important
contribution to the tradition by composing the first historical
martyrology, one that gave not only names and dates but also a
brief narrative of the circumstances of each martyr's death. Bede
also wrote other hagiographic pieces, including two lives of St.
Cuthbert, the *Lives of the Abbots,* and the many saints' lives embedded in the *Ecclesiastical History of the English Church and People.*
Other writers, too, were at work on saints' lives at about the same
time: an anonymous monk of Whitby had written a life of Cuthbert,
and a monk of Lindisfarne had written the earliest life of Gregory
the Great.

Bede and his contemporaries wrote their saints' lives in Latin;
the first lives in English—at least among those that survive—seem
to have been written in Mercia toward the end of the eighth century.
There are six of these lives, in alliterative English verse: *Elene,
Juliana, Fates of the Apostles, Andreas,* and two poems on St.
Guthlac. (*Andreas* may not be Mercian in origin, but may be evidence of a Northumbrian school of English hagiographic verse.)

Of these poems, *Elene*, *Juliana*, and the *Fates of the Apostles* are the work of Cynewulf, on the evidence of runic "signatures" bearing his name. All of these poems are derived from Latin originals. Even the Guthlac poems, the only ones concerning a native saint, are based on an anonymous eighth-century Latin life of Guthlac. *Elene*, derived from the Latin *Acta Cyriaci*, concerns the discovery by Helena, the mother of Constantine, of the true cross. *Juliana*, a typical tale of the martyrdom of a virgin saint, is perhaps even more extravagantly told than its Latin source is. The brief, sub-literary *Fates of the Apostles* is a simple list of the ways the twelve apostles met their deaths. *Andreas* is a romantic tale of the adventures of St. Andrew and St. Matthew among the cannibal Anthropophagites, and the Guthlac poems are poetic treatments of episodes from the life of the English hermit. It is very likely that these six surviving poems are only a small part of the hagiographic material produced in England in the eighth century. There may well have been other poems of this kind, and it is almost certain that legends of the saints, especially local ones, must have been in oral circulation when Bede gathered the materials for his *History*.[7]

The works produced in Wessex in the late ninth century under the supervision of King Alfred did not include saints' lives, unless we may so term the *Dialogues* of Gregory the Great, translated by Bishop Werferth of Worcester. The second book of the *Dialogues* consists of a life of St. Benedict, and the fourth contains a number of legends of saints' visits to heaven and hell. A few scattered pieces suggest, however, that the writing of saints' lives in the vernacular did continue through this period. The ninth-century *Life of St. Chad*, written in Mercia, and the *Blickling Homilies*, probably written slightly earlier than Ælfric's, include several saints' lives. The *Life of Chad* and the *Blickling Homilies* are written in a heightened style, indebted to poetic practice; and they thus anticipate, in a general way, Ælfric's stylistic methods.

In short, enough vernacular saints' lives survive from the Old English period to suggest that, at least in the eighth and tenth centuries, many such lives must have been written, the bulk of which are now lost. Even on the basis of the surviving texts alone, Rosemary Woolf points out that "the hagiographic form was the dominant narrative kind in the Old English period."[8] There is nothing surprising in this fact; in some ways, the saint's life came to fill in a Christianized society the function that the epic or lay had had in pagan society; and we may see the epic manner appearing in many ways in the Cynewulfian saints' lives not only in diction but also in characterization and tone. The lurid sensationalism of *Juliana*, for example, must have had something of the same popular appeal as pagan tales of adventure had; and *Andreas* is very self-consciously indebted to *Beowulf*. A precedent already existed for the treatment of saints' lives in such secular and "literary" manners in the work of the fourth-century Prudentius, whose *Peristephanon* consists of verse accounts of the passions of fourteen martyrs.

Bede's hagiographic writings, the *Life of Chad*, and the *Blickling Homilies*, are most specifically religious in purpose. Bede wrote in Latin for the edification of a monastic audience; the *Life of Chad* and the *Blickling Homilies* are didactic in purpose, but they are in English and were probably intended for a lay audience. Their authors, like Ælfric, wrote to provide materials for sermons for the common people. In many ways, Ælfric's *Lives of Saints* is the epitome of several tendencies in Old English hagiography. Like the earlier vernacular homiletic saints' lives, his lives are intended to instruct; and, like the eighth-century hagiographic poems, they please by recalling the diction and the style of the heroic poems of the past, so that the Christian saints seem to be genuine heirs of the heroes of Germanic legend.

II   *"The Memory of the Saints"*

Peter Clemoes has pointed out that number XVI in the *Lives of Saints* was probably originally intended to stand at the head of the collection as a sort of general introduction.[9] Like the *Lives of Saints*, both series of *Catholic Homilies* begin their sermons for specific dates with Christmas Day, the beginning of the church year. But the *Homilies* have an item outside this scheme which seems to serve as an introduction: "On the Beginning of Creation," to be preached "whenever you wish." "The Memory of the Saints" (XVI), which was probably intended to occupy a similar place in the *Lives of Saints*, is also marked "Spel loca hwænne mann wille" (to be preached when you will).

"The Memory of the Saints" is also closely parallel to "On the Beginning of Creation" in its form and method, and thus illuminates not only Ælfric's intentions in the *Lives* but also the relationship the series bears to the *Catholic Homilies* in Ælfric's overall plan.

Like "On the Beginning of Creation," the piece is a broad account of universal history. But whereas "On the Beginning of Creation" turns around the pivotal events in Christian history—the Creation, the Incarnation, the Last Judgment—"The Memory of the Saints" is appropriately built around the pivotal characters in the history. The *Lives of Saints*, it is suggested, is to deal with the same material as the *Catholic Homilies*; but the intent is to present this material through the lives of individual men.

The structure of the homily is based upon two of Ælfric's most frequently used rhetorical devices: classification and enumeration. The first half consists of a chronological roll-call of the categories of saints. We must take care to live piously, Ælfric says, and

> *We magon niman gode bysne,*
> *ærest, be ðam halgum heah-fæderum,*
> *hu hi on heora life gode gecwemdon,*
> *and eac æt þam halgum þe þam hælende folgodon.*

> *(We may take good examples,*
> *first, from the holy patriarchs,*
> *how they in their lives pleased God,*
> *and also from the Saints who followed the Savior.)*

(*LS* XVI.9–12)

There follows a list of holy men—patriarchs, prophets, etc.—from the Old Testament, from Abel and Enoch through Noah and Abraham down to David, Elias, and Daniel. No attempt is made to tell of their lives, but each receives a brief, lyrical comment. So of David Ælfric writes,

> *Dauid for his man-wyrnysse and mild-heortnysse*
> *wearð gode gecweme and to cynincge gecoren,*
> *swa þæt god sylf cwæð pus be him,*
> *"Ic afunde me dauid, iessan sunu, æfter minre heortan,*
> *seðe minne willan mid weorcum gefremð."*

> *(David for his meekness and mildheartedness*
> *was pleasing to God and was chosen king,*
> *so that God Himself spoke thus concerning him,*
> *"I have found David, Jesse's son, after my own heart,*
> *who shall perform my will by his works.")*

(*LS* XVI.55–59)

The apex of this sequence is, of course, the life of Christ Himself, which Ælfric summarizes in eighty-two lines, emphasizing the piety and devotion of those men who followed Him, the apostles and disciples. The first half of the sermon is then brought to an end with a survey of the major groups of saints who have lived since Christ, during the age of the dissemination of the faith. There are the holy martyrs,

> *swa micclum onbryrde*
> *þæt hi sweltan woldon ærðan þe hi wiðsocon gode,*
> *and heora lif aleton ærðan þe heora geleafan,*
> *and wurdon ofslagene for ðam soðan geleafan.*

> *(so greatly inspired*
> *that they chose rather to die than to deny God,*
> *and laid down their lives rather than their faith,*
> *and were slain for the true faith.)*   (*LS* XVI.191–94)

Others, too:

> *Þa wæron halige bisceopas gehealtsume on þeawum,*
> *and wise mæssepreostas þe wunodon on clænnysse,*
> *and manega munecas on mycelre drohtnunge,*
> *and clæne mædenu þe criste þeowodon*
> *on gastlicre drohtnunge, for heora drihtnes lufan.*

> *(Then were holy bishops, frugal in their manners,*
> *and wise mass-priests who lived in chastity,*
> *and many monks of excellent conduct,*
> *and pure maidens who served Christ*
> *in spiritual service, for their Lord's love.)*
>   (*LS* XVI.212–16)

The classifications clearly correspond to those of the saints' lives in the series itself and suggest the comprehensive historical sweep of the saints' lives Ælfric selected.

Enumeration is the main structural device of the second half of the sermon, also. Here Ælfric turns to the virtues we can learn from the saints and the vices which they teach us to avoid. We live, he says, in the latter days of the world and the devil is especially eager to snare us,

> *forðan þe he wat geare þæt þysre worulde geendung*
> *is swylce gehende, and he on-et forði.*

*(because he knows well that this world's ending is
very nigh at hand, and therefore he makes haste.)*

(*LS* XVI.226–27)

The "three chief virtues" are, of course, faith, hope, and charity. The "eight chief sins" are gluttony, fornication, avarice, anger, sorrow, sloth, vain boasting, and pride. These are countered by the "eight chief virtues": temperance, purity, liberality, patience, spiritual joy, perseverence, love of God, and humility. The sermon ends with a call to the congregation to fight against the sins with the virtues, as did the saints, to their glory.

"The Memory of the Saints," considered as an introduction to the *Lives of Saints,* provides guidance in several ways to reading the series. Most obviously, it establishes the categories of saints which are to be followed in the collection. The lives are arranged, of course, according to the calendar of feasts, not by "categories"; but Ælfric picked and chose among the possible saints, and a general desire to offer a more or less representative selection of the types seems to underlie his particular choices.

Second, the sermon makes clear the relationship of this book of hagiographical readings to the two preceding volumes of sermons. Ælfric's general framework remains the Augustinian view of history: that human history has been guided by the power of God and that it turns around the three key events of the Fall, the Incarnation, and the Last Judgment. The Old Testament saints, Christ and His apostles, and the martyrs and confessors of the period since the Crucifixion epitomize in their lives the travails of the pious in these three ages. The *Lives of Saints* are thus as firmly grounded on the Christian view of universal history as are the *Catholic Homilies.*

Finally, the yoking in the sermon of biography and direct moralizing—the successive listings of saints and of their vices and virtues—suggests the spirit in which we should read the individual lives. The modern reader is tempted to read medieval saints' lives as crude and undeveloped biography. Often tacitly committed to evolutionary theories of literary history and preferring the realistic modes, he is likely to see the medieval saints' lives as somehow "culminating" in, say, William Roper's *Life of More,* which is comparatively "modern" in its use of historical and biographical fact. There is, of course, some truth in such a view, but it illuminates modern biography more than it does the saint's life. Ælfric and his predecessors and contemporaries did not conceive of the saint's life as bound by the same standards of historical accuracy to which they often showed themselves to be sensitive in other works. (We may compare, for example, Bede's use of the miraculous in the hagiographic and the non-hagiographic portions of the *Ecclesiastical History*.)

The saint's life was a highly conventionalized, thoroughly didactic form: as Rosemary Woolf has noted, it is "part panegyric, part epic, part romance, part sermon."[10] Its concern was less with historical fact than with spiritual truth, and its often sensational or garish action was designed to reveal a truth usually masked by the confused surface of ordinary life. The intent is not to defend the saint's life as a major literary form; for, to quote Miss Woolf again, "Though so important, the saint's life was extremely limited by its conventions. There was in it by definition a combination of simplicity and artificiality which precluded it from transcending the bounds of minor forms of literature."[11] Nevertheless, if we are to read saints' lives at all, we should approach them as highly conventionalized, didactic pieces, not as crude attempts at realistic biography.

Clearly, the second half of "The Memory of the Saints" specifies the virtues which Ælfric aims to inculcate through his *Lives* and the vices personified by the saints' antagonists. The virgin martyrs teach us purity; the confessors teach us humility and the love of God; and such saints as Chrysanthus, liberality and spiritual joy. It would, of course, be going too far to make one-to-one correlations between the individual saints and the virtues listed in the sermon; but the virtues are never far from Ælfric's mind, and he sometimes changes the tenor of a source to point a particular lesson, as when he makes St. Edmund, the martyr king, an exemplar not of chastity, but of the liberality, humility, and love of God of the Christian king. In several ways, then, "The Memory of the Saints" is a fitting and illuminating introduction to the *Lives of Saints*.

III *The Passions of Martyrs*

The saints of the Old Testament appear in the *Lives of Saints* primarily in the Bible translations—the Book of Kings (XVIII) and the Maccabees (XXV)—and may most conveniently be considered elsewhere. The next group of saints in the chronological sequence of "The Memory of the Saints" is the martyrs. A highly conventionalized pattern existed for the "passion," or account of the circumstances leading to a martyr's death.[12] Well over half of the hagiographic items in the *Lives of Saints* are passions and follow the conventional form in varying degrees. There are a number of passions of well-known Roman martyrs—St. Julian (IV), St. Sebastian (V), the Forty Soldiers (XI), and several others—and some of the lives of other saints, such as St. Edmund (XXXII), draw upon the conventions of the passion also.

The world presented by the typical passion is a highly stylized one. Although the setting is historical, it is distorted and simplified in order to magnify the hero and to emphasize the theme of perseverance and devotion. The passion often begins with an account of the saint's good works, and it often includes the circumstances of his conversion. The conflict is introduced by describing a persecution of Christians being carried out by a wicked emperor and by an equally wicked local governor. Eventually the saint is arrested and brought to a confrontation with his persecutors. One convention for the development of this section is a formal, theological debate between the saint and his judge; another is a "contest" of miracles arranged between the saint and the pagan priests. The saint, of course, remains steadfast, refusing to recant; and he is imprisoned. Conventionally, his courageous deportment in prison leads to conversions among his fellow prisoners and even among his jailers. A lengthy description of tortures and sufferings usually follows, for the persecutors attempt to break the saint's will. Often this section is handled quite sensationally; considerable ingenuity is used in devising elaborate and sometimes grotesque tortures. Finally, the saint is killed, often by beheading; his body is disposed of and sometimes an account of his posthumous miracles ends the passion.

The possibilities for extravagance in this form are obvious, and many passions, particularly the later ones, become exaggerated and grotesque. The villainy of the persecutors and the piety of the saint, the savagery of the tortures and the superhuman endurance of the saint pass all reasonable bounds. Ælfric accepts the conventions of the form; he makes no attempt to rationalize the miracles or to soften the sharp distinctions between good and evil in the narratives. But, as Dorothy Bethurum has pointed out,[13] his adaptations are notable for their restraint in handling the more lurid elements in the passions. For one thing, he avoids translating some of the more harrowing passions, though among them were some of the ones best known in Anglo-Saxon England, judging from the Old English martyrology.[14] In those Ælfric did select, he often omitted gruesome or merely sadistic passages, such as several in the life of St. Sebastian (sections IV and V) and in the life of St. Eugenia (section XIII).

In the handling of specific conventions, Ælfric, in general, follows the tradition; but his critical temperament leads to alterations here and there. His persecuting emperors—Diocletian, Claudius, Decius, Domitian—are wholly evil; he uses a few stock phrases over and over to describe them: "the wicked tormenter" ("St. Julian," IV. 104) and "the devil's worshipper" ("St. Sebastian," V. 10). The piety of the saint is equally absolute, as manifested not only by his miracles and his mass conversions. The passions of St. Julian and of the Forty Soldiers are particularly full of miracles. Among other wonders, Julian heals a blind man (IV.149 ff.) and restores a dead man to life (IV.268 ff.). Stones thrown at the Forty Soldiers miraculously turn back against the throwers (XI.100 ff.), and a frozen lake upon which they are exposed miraculously thaws (XI.95 ff.).

Most of the miracle stories which Ælfric includes from his sources are the types most common in medieval hagiography—miracles of healing, miraculous preservations from harm, and such miraculous signs of blessedness as heavenly lights and sweet odors.[15] In only three of his passions does he use the miraculous as a "test" in the conventional motif of the contest between the saint and a pagan priest. St. Julian engages in a healing contest with idol worshippers to heal a blind man (IV.149 ff.), Sebastian miraculously discovers a concealed astrological device (V.250 ff.), and St. George drinks poison safely in a contest with the sorcerer Athanasius (XIV.67 ff.).

Ælfric is similarly restrained in his use of the conventional debate between the saint and his judge, apparently to avoid boring his audience. These wholly unbelievable and often dryly theological exchanges sometimes ran to great length in early passions. Ælfric includes such passages rarely and, when he does, he often cuts them short. In "St. Julian," for example, Martianus engages in a long debate with the saint over the relative merits of the Christian and pagan gods. Ælfric abbreviates it with the words,

> Þeos race is swiðe lang-sum fullice to gereccenne,
> ac we hit sæcgað eow on þa scortostan wisan.
>
> *(This story is very tedious, to tell it all,*
> *but we tell it to you in the briefest way.)*   (*LS* IV.139–40)

He has different compunctions about the conventional descriptions of tortures and death; here the danger is not of boring the audience but of allowing such gruesome scenes to usurp the main emphasis of the narrative. So again Ælfric abbreviates many passages and, for the most part, sticks to the more stylized and conventional torments: torture on the rack, starvation, beating, etc. An exception is the passion of St. Chrysanthus (XXXV); he is, among other torments, drenched in "ealdum miggan" (old urine) and sewed in an ox hide and placed in the sun (XXXV.158 ff.). But such grotesqueries are rare in Ælfric.

A sharp division occurs between the earlier passions and the later, more conventionalized ones, in their treatment of torture. In the earlier lives the saint feels pain and endures it through his devout perseverance. In the later lives, as the torments become more exaggerated, the convention is for the saint to be miraculously preserved from pain; and he endures in comfort the most horrendous tortures. There is, of course, a fundamental illogic here. If the saint is immune to pain, his achievement of martyrdom becomes less praiseworthy, though such immunity may testify to his general blessedness. There is also an implicit suggestion in such narratives that the blessed do not suffer in this world. This doubtless unintentional implication is clearly false, as even the example of Christ on the cross testifies.

Ælfric for the most part follows his sources in having his martyrs immune from pain. When St. George, for example, is put into a cauldron of boiling lead,

> *þæt lead wearð acolod þurh godes mihte*
> *and georius sæt gesund on ðam hwere.*

> *(the lead was cooled through God's might*
> *and George sat sound in the cauldron.)*   (*LS* XIV.115–16)

A noteworthy exception, however, to this general practice is in the life of St. Vincent (XXXVII), in which perhaps the most graphic and sadistic descriptions of tortures occur. Vincent is starved, put on the rack, beaten with rods, burned with torches and hot irons, and put in a prison cell full of sharp, broken tiles. His sufferings are somewhat tempered by God's grace—angels minister to him in the prison—but he does suffer pain and eventually dies of his

wounds. (In most passions, beheading is the only way the persecutors can kill the saints.)

A subtype of the martyr's passion is that which deals with the
suffering and death of virgins. As we would expect from Ælfric's
general interest in the theme of chastity, a number of passions of
this type appear in the *Lives of Saints*: St. Eugenia (II), St. Agnes
(VII), St. Agatha (VIII), St. Lucy (IX), and St. Cecilia (XXXIV).
The story of St. Æthelthryth (XX), the story of Felicula in "The
Chair of St. Peter" (X), and the stories of Basilissa and Daria, the
chaste wives of St. Julian and St. Chrysanthus (IV and XXXV) also
draw upon the conventions of this type.

One such convention appears in lives of women saints who are
persecuted, suffer, and die in much the fashion of other martyrs,
but who are also distinguished in the days before their martyrdom
for their chastity. In such stories, a wedding-night scene often
appears in which the bride and groom decline to consummate the
marriage and pledge themselves to perpetual chastity. Thus St.
Cecilia (XXXIV) converts her husband Valerian, and thus St.
Julian (IV) converts his wife Basilissa. A similar scene appears in
"The Passion of Chrysanthus and Daria" (XXXV), in which
Chrysanthus converts Daria, who had been sent to seduce him;
and, though they are afterward married, they live celibate lives. In
the other major kind of virgin-martyr passion, the martyr is brought
to grief through refusing the suit of a wooer. Thus St. Agatha (VII)
refuses the attentions of the son of Sempronius, the prefect, and
indignantly declares that she is wedded to Christ. When she also
refuses to sacrifice to Vesta, she is placed in a house of harlots,
where her virginity is miraculously preserved; but she is also finally
tortured and beheaded. A number of these conventions appear in
perhaps the most romantic of the virgin-martyr stories, the life of
St. Eugenia (II). Eugenia disguises herself as a man and, in this
disguise, eventually becomes the abbot of a monastery. Accused of
attempting to seduce a wealthy widow, Eugenia clears her name
by dramatically baring her breast in the courtroom.

The martyr's passion in the early Middle Ages was a form alien
to modern sensibilities. It was part history, part sermon, and part
fairy-tale; and modern readers are tempted to reject it as an un-
palatable hybrid and as interesting only as a precursor of serious,
factual history or of the romances of the High Middle Ages. To
Ælfric, however, its stylized world of pagan persecution and

Christian triumph was a means of representing the permanent conflicts that underlie the confusion and chaos of ordinary life. In his versions of these popular pieces, he worked within the conventions of the form; but he also tempered their potential extravagancies with taste and reverence.

IV *The Lives of Confessors*

The earliest-acknowledged, non-biblical saints were, of course, the martyrs. But, as Christianity triumphed in Western Europe and the persecutions ceased, another group came to be recognized as saintly. These were the "confessors," men and women whose sanctity was manifested not by martyrdom but by lives of great piety and service to God, usually, though not necessarily, within the church:

> *halige bisceopas, gehealtsume on þeawum, and wise*
> *mæsse-preostas þe wunodon on clænnysse, and manega*
> *munecas on mycelre drohtnunge, and clæne mædenu þe*
> *criste þeowodon on gastlicre drohtnunge for geora drihtnes*
> *lufan.*
>
> *(holy bishops, frugal in their manners, and wise mass-*
> *priests who lived in chastity, and many monks of excellent*
> *conduct, and pure maidens who served Christ in spiritual*
> *service, for their Lord's love.)*

(LS XVI.212–16)

The form of the confessor's life came to be as rigidly conventionalized as that of the martyr's passion.[16] Many of the conventions of the form were established and disseminated by a small group of hagiographic works which were widely known and imitated throughout Europe. Perhaps the most important of these was the *Life of St. Antony* by St. Athanasius, as translated from Greek into Latin by Bishop Evagrius of Antioch in the late fourth century; but other influential models for the confessor's life were Jerome's *Life of Paul the Hermit*, Sulpicius Severus's *Life of St. Martin*, and the *Dialogues* of Pope Gregory the Great. The form of the *Life of St. Antony* was so widely imitated that we can speak of certain conventions that pervade European hagiography as "Antonian." Some of these conventions are: (1) a prologue, in which the author professes to write at the urgent request of others and declares that he writes on good authority, either as an eye-witness or as one who has spoken to eyewitnesses; (2) an initial description of the saint's early days, including early miraculous signs of special sanctity and the circumstances of his religious vocation; (3) an account of the saint's mature career, either as a hermit, struggling against the forces of evil in isolation, or as a holy cleric; (4) a description of the heights of the saint's blessedness, often including the powers of prophecy and of healing and some-times a sermon from the saint; (5) an account of a divine warning of death, a farewell address to disciples, and a blissful death; and, finally, (6) an account of posthumous miracles around the saint's grave or shrine. There were also conventional elements which appeared over and over in various sections of this narrative pattern: conventional statements in the prologue, conventional miracles such as lights from heaven, sweet odors around the saint, and the like, and conventional motifs for the presentation of the saint's death.

St. Antony was, of course, a hermit, whose blessedness was achieved in isolation. But the pattern of the *Life of St. Antony* could also be adapted to the life of a holy churchman. The vocation of the hermit was not to go into the desert but into the church, and the sanctity of the saint's middle life was achieved not in lonely struggles against devils but in the active life of a churchman. Thus the Antonian life could furnish a model for almost any kind of saint's life, and its simple chronological skeleton could be fleshed out with a selection of the conventional details most appropriate to the subject. Many of Ælfric's sources were modeled on the *Life of Antony*, and he preserves in his adaptations not only the basic structure but also a great many of the stock elements which func-tioned as Antonian conventions. He usually compresses and ab-breviates the form, however, since he is usually adapting longer works into homiletic pieces.

One of the fullest and best of Ælfric's lives of confessors and one which demonstrates the Antonian pattern very clearly is the life of St. Basilius (III). St. Basil the Great (329–379) was bishop of Caesarea; Ælfric's homily for January 1, the day of his death, is based on an anonymous Latin life of the saint.[17] Like all Antonian lives, the life of Basil is arranged roughly in three parts: his early life and vocation, the sanctity of the saint's mature life, and the circumstances of his death. Basil, as a youth, studies pagan philos-ophy in Athens under Eubolus, the philosopher, along with

Julian, later to become emperor, and Gregory, later to become bishop. God leads Basil to turn to Christian learning, and he converts his old teacher, the two going together to be baptized in the Jordan. At his baptism, fire descends from heaven, and the Holy Spirit appears as a dove from the fire.

Basil is consecrated bishop in Caesarea; and, in response to his prayer for guidance, Christ and His apostles appear in his church to bless him. The middle section of the life, then, is dedicated to a lengthy enumeration of Basil's miracles and good works, from writing the Greek liturgy to performing miracles of healing. Many of the other miracles in this section are uncharacteristically romantic for Ælfric, who tended to minimize miracles outside the conventional types established by scriptural and early hagiographic precedent. We have a lengthy account, for example, of a young man who, Faust-like, sells his soul to the devil in return for the love of a beautiful maiden. He confesses his sin to Basil, who contends with a devil and regains the contract, telling the youth,

> Ne hoga þu embe þæt;
> ure hælend is swiþe wel-wyllende, and wyle þe eft under-fon,
> gif þu mid soðre dædbote gecyrst eft to him.

> (Do not be anxious about that;
> our Saviour is very gracious, and will receive you again,
> if you with true repentance will turn again to Him.)

(LS III.416–18)

The concluding section of the homily, which deals with the saint's last illness and death, is very full and detailed and accounts for the last hundred lines or so of the 670-line homily. When Basil is warned by a pagan leech, Joseph, that he will die shortly, Basil, eager to convert the leech, gets him to say that Basil cannot possibly live through the day. He then prays that he may live until noon of the next day. He does, and the leech is converted with all his household. Miraculously, too, a woman who had written her sins on a piece of paper finds them blotted out through Basil's deathbed prayers.

The great virtue of the St. Basil life is that Ælfric, without departing from his source, is able to present a selection from it that gives a vivid sense of his subject's character. Basil's learning and wit are clear in the homily, and even the miracle stories, though

unusually extravagant, present a consistent portrait of a vigorous
man contending with his intellect against a predominantly pagan
society in the early days of Christianity. His adversaries can be
virtuous, though pagan—as are Eubolus and Joseph—and he converts them, as Ælfric remarks, through his great learning (III.
666).

The life of St. Maur (VI) follows the same pattern, but it is only
about half as long as the life of Basil. Based on a Latin life by Faus-
tus (acknowledged by Ælfric, 1. 366), it tells the story of the holy
abbot of the Franks. More ambitious in scope is the life of St.
Martin (XXXI), another version of whose life Ælfric had included
in the *Catholic Homilies* II (XXXIX). Both pieces are based primarily on the widely known life by Sulpicius Severus, but the second
treatment in the *Lives of Saints* is over twice as long as the first, running to 1495 lines, about the length of Sulpicius's original. St. Martin
was bishop of Tours from 371 to 397, the year of his death; Sulpicius was his contemporary and wrote from personal knowledge
of him.

The existence of two adaptations by Ælfric of the same substantial works allows us an interesting glance into Ælfric's methods in
making his adaptations.[18] In neither version does he stick to his
main source; he interweaves with it other material concerning
Martin drawn from Sulpicius's *Letters* and his *Dialogues* and from
the *Historia Francorum* of Gregory of Tours. Ælfric's critical
temperament and his conscientiousness are clear from the way he
knits together material from all his sources into a clear narrative.

Ælfric's second version of the *Life of Martin* was probably not
written specifically for the *Lives of Saints*, but was perhaps included
to fill out the volume. Far longer than most of the *Lives*, this life
is divided into fifty-five brief chapters in the manuscript. Too,
although the *Lives of Saints* was probably intended for private
reading, most of the items could be more easily adapted to homiletic
use than could the long *Life of Martin*. Ælfric's expansions consist
mainly of additional material from Sulpicius, dropped in the shorter
version, and of new material concerning Martin's death from Gregory of Tours's *De virtutibus S. Martini,* a book he had probably
encountered after writing the first version.

V The English Saints

It is not surprising that Ælfric took particular care to include several English saints in the *Lives*. Nationalistic feeling aside, the *Lives*, as a grand survey of Christian history told through the lives of its saints, would not be complete unless it were shown that God's power and grace continued to inspire men and women to saintly deeds in Ælfric's age and place. Five items, therefore, consist of lives of English saints: St. Alban, the British proto-martyr (XIX); St. Æthelthryth, the virgin queen (XX); St. Swithun, the saint of Ælfric's own Winchester (XXI); and SS. Oswald and Edmund, martyr-kings (XXVI and XXXII). These lives have always been of particular interest to readers of Ælfric and include the most frequently anthologized pieces. That they were also especially interesting to Ælfric is evident not only from the care he devoted to them but also from an eloquent passage at the end of the life of Edmund:

> *Nis angel-cynn bedæled drihtnes halgena,*
> *þonne on engla-landa licgaþ swilce halgan*
> *swylce þæs halga cyning is, and cuþberht se eadiga,*
> *and sancte æpeldryð on elig, and eac hire swustor,*
> *ansunde on lichaman, geleafan to trymminge.*

> *(The English nation is not deprived of the Lord's saints,*
> *since in English land lie such saints*
> *as this holy king, and the blessed Cuthbert,*
> *and Saint Æthelthryth in Ely, and also her sister,*
> *incorrupt in body, for the confirmation of the faith.)*
>   (*LS* XXXII.259–63)

Ælfric drew heavily upon Bede for his material on native saints. Three of the lives—those of Alban, Æthelthryth, and Oswald— are adapted from Bede's *Ecclesiastical History*. The lives of Swithun and Edmund are based on Latin lives of those saints by Lantfred, "the foreigner," and by Abbo of Fleury.[19] The life of Swithun is of particular interest because Ælfric adds to Lantfred's account some of his own memories of the veneration of Swithun at Winchester. Swithun, who was bishop of Winchester, died in 862, and in the century after his death a vigorous cult had sprung up around his relics. Little was known of his life. Lantfred's work covers merely the *Translatio et Miracula S. Swithuni*, and Ælfric remarks reproachfully on the carelessness of his contemporaries who failed to record the facts of his life:

> Þæt wæs þæra gymeleast þe on life hine cuþon
> þæt hi noldon awritan his weorc and drohtnunge
> þam towerdum mannum ðe his mihte ne cuðon.

> *(Such was their carelessness who knew him in life*
> *that they would not write down his works and conversation*
> *for future generations who did not know his power.)*

(*LS* XXI.9–11)

Ælfric's account, then, consists of a description of how Swithun appeared some years after his death to a faithful smith (1. 24) to tell him to carry word to the authorities that he desired that his body be exhumed and moved into the new church of St. Peter. After several miracles had testified to the validity of this vision, the body was moved; the rest of the work consists of an enumeration of the ensuing miracles, mostly miracles of healing. One miracle related to Ælfric's personal experience is the appearance of Swithun in a vision to reproach the monks who had become careless in performing their duty to sing the Te Deum each time a healing occurred. The monks corrected their error, and Ælfric remembers,

> Hi hit heoldon þa syððan symle on ge-wunon,
> swa swa we gesawon sylfe for oft,
> and þone sang we sungon unseldon mid heom.

> *(From then on they always observed this custom,*
> *as we ourselves have very often seen,*
> *and have not seldom sung this hymn with them.)*

(*LS* XXI.262–64)

Ælfric is also apparently writing from his personal memories of Winchester near the end of the life when he describes (11. 432 ff.) how the walls of the church at Winchester were hung full of the crutches and stools of cripples who had been healed by Swithun. The last lines of the life are also notable for the mixture of nostalgia and bitterness when Ælfric, writing in the dark days of Æthelred's reign and the Danish assaults, recalls the peace and order of the days of his youth:

We habbað nu gesæd be swiðune þus sceortlice,
and we secgað to soðan þæt se tima wæs gesælig
and wynsum on angel-cynne, þaða eadgar cynincg
þone cristen-dom ge-fyrðrode, and fela munuclifa arærde,
and his cynerice wæs wunigende on sibbe,
swa þæt man ne gehyrde gif ænig scyp-here wære,
buton agenre leode þe ðis land heoldon.

(We have now spoken thus briefly of Swithun,
and we say of a truth that the time was blessed
and winsome in England, when King Edgar
furthered Christianity, and built many monasteries,
and his kingdom still continued in peace,
so that no fleet was heard of,
save that of the people themselves who held this land.)

(*LS* XXI.434–49)

The most elaborate of the lives of English saints, and in some
ways the finest achievement of Ælfric's work in the saint's-life
form, is the life of King Edmund (XXXII). King Edmund was a
fairly obscure East Anglian king who was killed by the Danes in
870. In the century after his death, a cult sprang up around his
burial place; and, in time, his legend came to be one of the most
extensive bodies of English hagiographic material; for it gathered
accretions from folk tale and eventually assumed the character
of medieval romance.[20] Ælfric added little to the legend as it came
to him through the *Passio Sancti Eadmundi* of Abbo of Fleury,
but his treatment of the material is notable for the way he subtly
reinterprets the character of Edmund by drawing upon both hagiographic conventions and those of Germanic epic. The result is a
brief, but effective "Christian epic" in which the ideals of heroic
pagan society and those of Christianity merge.

Abbo professed to write from a source directly connected to
Edmund's death. Edmund's sword-bearer, who witnessed the
martyrdom, was said to have described it to Archbishop Dunstan
when Dunstan was a young man at the court of King Æthelstan;
Dunstan, just before his death, passed the story on to Abbo; and
it was thus transmitted orally across a hundred years or so by only
three informants. Ælfric, who begins his account by summarizing
these facts in ordinary prose, changes to his heightened poetic-
prose style for the legend itself. Edmund ruled over the East Angles
until the Danes landed under the command of Hingwar and Hubba.

After ravaging the land, the Danes arrive in East Anglia and send Edmund a threatening message, demanding that he surrender. Edmund, who sends back a brave and eloquent reply, refuses either to submit or flee; he will receive the Danes without weapons as Christ would have done (11. 103–04). The Danes seize him, tie him to a tree, shoot him full of arrows, and then behead him. When the Danes have departed and when Edmund's people seek his body, they find his head guarded by a great gray wolf and miraculously calling to guide the searchers. They bury the head and body and raise a church on the spot, where many miracles are performed.

Ælfric follows Abbo very closely in the outlines of this simple tale; his major change is that he greatly compresses the story, making his version less than half as long as Abbo's. But, in the process of compression, he changes the whole tone and spirit of the legend. Abbo makes Edmund a wholly unbelievable stereotype who rather complacently seeks martyrdom knowing he will be rewarded in Heaven. His reply to the Danes is in highly ornate Latin prose and is heavily theological in content. Ælfric takes particular care in recasting the whole exchange between Edmund and the Danes. Behind Edmund's simple and forthright reply lies the whole tradition of Germanic epic heroism, one strangely transmuted by the spirit of Christian charity:

> Þæs ic gewilnige and gewisce mid mode,
> þæt ic ana ne belife æfter minum leofum þegnum,
> þe on heora bedde wurdon mid bearnum, and wifum,
> færlice ofslægene fram þysum flot-mannum.
> Næs me næfre gewunelic þæt ic worhte fleames,
> ac ic wolde swiðor sweltan, gif ic þorfte,
> for minum agenum earde; and se ælmihtiga god wat
> þæt ic nelle abugan fram his biggengum æfre,
> ne fram his soþan lufe, swelte ic lybbe ic.
>
> (This I desire and wish in my mind,
> that I should not be left alone after my dear thanes,
> who in their beds, with children and wives,
> have suddenly been slain by these seamen.
> It was never my way to take to flight,
> but I would rather die, if I must,
> for my own land; and the almighty God knows
> that I will never turn aside from His worship,
> nor from His true love, whether I die or live.)   (LS XXXII.74–82)

Ælfric presents Edmund as a heroic Christian king, the product
of the English blending of the traditions of kingship inherited from
pagan Germanic culture on one side and Christian doctrine on the
other. The warrior-kings of the Germanic tribes were first among
equals; they wielded their weapons alongside their men, seeking
fame in battle and accepting the obligation of giving protection
to those who served them. To the Christian, the kingly office came
to be equated with the priesthood; the king was God's vicar, and
he took oaths not only to his people but to God Himself. The coronation of King Edgar, which took place late in his reign—delayed
probably until Edgar had reached the canonical age for ordination
to the priesthood—was presided over by Archbishop Dunstan.
Edgar's prayers and oaths, his anointing, and the ecclesiastical
flavor of the whole ceremony indicated that he was a king who
ruled "by the grace of God." A similar synthesis underlies Ælf-
fric's characterization of King Edmund—king and martyr.

Much of what we have said in Chapter 3 about Ælfric's achievement as a homilist may also be applied to his work as a hagiographer.
In the *Lives of Saints*, as in the *Catholic Homilies*, his selection of
material, his interpretations, and his doctrine are highly orthodox;
his style is lucid and eloquent; and his attitude toward his audience
is sensitive and sympathetic without being condescending. Taken
individually, a number of the lives—those of St. Basilius, St. Martin,
and St. Edmund, for example—are among the high points of Old
English prose. Considered as a whole, the individual parts of the
Lives of Saints are unified by the large design indicated in the introductory "Memory of the Saints." And, considered as part of the
general educational plan that underlies all Ælfric's literary work,
the *Lives* occupies a place very near the center of that plan.

Reading the *Lives* in the twentieth century, we are continually
tempted to emphasize elements in them which were probably pe-
ripheral to Ælfric's major purposes. The saints' lives are only incidentally precursors of realistic biography, revelations of Old English
life, reminiscences of epic, or anticipations of romance. Their central
purpose, as Ælfric suggests in "The Memory of the Saints," was
identical to that of the *Catholic Homilies*: to reveal the spiritual truth
of the great divine pattern that underlay the bewildering variety
of historical fact. But, whereas the *Catholic Homilies* had dealt

directly with the power of God as it moves through human history, *Lives of Saints* deals with that power as it had been revealed in the long series of holy men from the Old Testament saints through Christ and His apostles, the martyrs of the early Christian era, and the confessors of more recent times. If we have lost this perspective, we may value the *Lives* for the eloquence of their prose, for the vigor of their narrative style, for the charm of their stylized portraiture; but we should remember that they draw their life from the high purpose which inspired them.

CHAPTER 4

Bible Translations

ACCOUNTS of the history of the translation of the Bible into English generally credit Ælfric with being the first important translator. If this claim is to be substantiated, a rather broad interpretation of "translation" must be adopted. As we have seen, a number of Ælfric's homilies are scriptural and the summaries of several biblical books appear in his collections; but these are hardly translations in the ordinary sense. Perhaps his closest approach to strict translation is his version of the first part of Genesis, which appears in the so-called *Old English Heptateuch;* and he undertook even this work with strong misgivings, which he expressed in the preface to Genesis.

He had expressed similar misgivings much earlier, of course, about treating holy matters in the native tongue and thus running the risk of exposing them to the contempt of the ignorant and vicious. In an epilogue to the second series of *Catholic Homilies,* he had written,

Ic cweðe nu þæt ic næfre heononforð ne awende godspel oþþe godspeltrahtas of Ledene on Englisc.

(I say now that henceforth I will never turn gospel or gospel-exposition from Latin into English.)   (*CH* II, 594)

Again, in the Latin preface to the *Lives of Saints*, he expressed qualms about writing homilies in English:

I do not promise, however, to write very many in this tongue, because it is not fitting that many should be translated into our language, lest peradventure the pearls of Christ be had in disrespect. (*LS*, Latin Preface, 3)

And at the end of the preface to Genesis, written about 997, he wrote,

Ic cweðe nu ðæt ic ne dearr ne ic nelle nane boc æfter ðisre of Ledene on Englisc awendan.

(I say now that I neither dare to nor will translate any book hereafter from Latin into English.)   (Crawford, 80)

Ælfric apparently overcame, to some degree, his reservations about translating Holy Writ later in life, for in the *Letter to Sigeweard* he expresses no doubts about the propriety of translating the books he mentions. Nevertheless, he remains something of a biblical translator *malgré lui*.

A survey of Ælfric's biblical translations should begin with the numerous, though scattered, passages of Scripture which appear in the homilies. The *lectiones*, plus the scriptural passages which appear in the bodies of the homilies, amount to a considerable body of work; and separate consideration might be given to *Catholic Homilies* II.XXXV, which is a homiletic epitome of the Book of Job. A second category of biblical pieces is the summaries of Old Testament books: Kings, the Maccabees, Judges, Esther, and Judith. Peter Clemoes has suggested a rationale for these summaries in relation to Ælfric's general plan. Ælfric had expounded much of the typology of the significant events of the Old Testament in the *Catholic Homilies*. He had also drawn upon the Old Testament for moral exempla, but had not treated it systematically on the level of moral interpretation. "And so, as an appendix to his homilies, he provided summary narratives of certain Old Testament books, narratives that with very little elucidation made the point that obedience to God is best."[1] Kings and the Maccabees were included in the *Lives of Saints* (XVIII and XXV). The others which followed—Judges, Esther, and Judith—suggested particular moral lessons, as Ælfric explained in the *Letter to Sigeweard*.

Ælfric's contribution to the so-called *Old English Heptateuch* completes his work in biblical translation. This editorial compilation of Old English translations of the first seven books of the Bible was formerly assigned principally to Ælfric, but it now appears certain that the only Ælfrician translations which appear in it are the first part of Genesis, the last part of Numbers, Joshua, and the version of Judges mentioned above.

I *Old English Bible Translation before Ælfric*

Ælfric's varied pieces of Bible translation amount to a larger body of work than any other Old English Bible translations; nevertheless, some tradition of Bible translation did exist when he began his work,[2] although the first steps in the direction of an English version of the Bible had been taken rather slowly. There is no mention of any attempts in this direction during the first century after Christianity was introduced into England in 597. The work of Cædmon, the unlettered Whitby cowherd whose story is told by Bede, and the "Cædmonian" Old English poems on Genesis, Exodus, Daniel, and Judith can hardly be called translations; but such "Christian epics" seem to have taken the place of any attempt to produce a native version of the Bible until the tenth century.

There was a long-standing tradition that Bede had translated large portions of the Bible into English, but the only contemporary evidence of this is the passage in Cuthbert's *Life of Bede* in which he describes how Bede dictated the final words of a translation of the Gospel of St. John with his dying breath. If there ever was such a translation, it has perished, along with any other Bible translations Bede may have made. Other traditions, similarly doubtful, credit Aldhelm, the seventh-century abbot of Malmesbury, with a translation of at least the Psalms and perhaps even more, and King Alfred with extensive translating projects.

Such legends aside, the surviving texts which, along with the Cædmonian poems, anticipate Ælfric are mostly glosses. Such insertions of Old English translations between the lines of a Latin text are fairly numerous. The earliest surviving example appears to be a text of the Psalms, known as the Vespasian Psalter, which dates from about 825. At least ten other glossed Psalters of later dates also survive. The Gospels were the other portion of the Bible most frequently glossed. The Lindisfarne Gospels, one of the most beautiful of Old English books, was glossed in the Northumbrian dialect about 950, and a North Mercian gloss was inserted in the Rushworth Gospels somewhat later. Although these glosses generally give an equivalent for every word in the text, they can hardly be called independent translations; for they follow the Latin word order and make no attempt to capture English idiom.

The most ambitious project, however, and one which may be called a genuine translation, was a version of the four Gospels in West Saxon about the middle of the tenth century. Four manuscripts from the eleventh century and two more from the twelfth century have been preserved of this work, testifying to some fairly widespread and continuing interest in it. These "West Saxon Gospels" are very competent translations, and they reveal a good command both of Latin and of English idiom. They are generally held to be the work of three translators, one who did Matthew, another who did Mark and Luke, and a third who did John. Arthur H. Abel, however, has recently argued that all four Gospels should be attributed to Ælfric.[3] The evidence for such an attribution, attractive as it may be, is very slight and subjective, as Abel himself admits. Whoever the author or authors might have been, the Gospels are the product of the same monastic revival of which Ælfric was a part; he probably knew them; and his own concentration upon the Old Testament may have been based upon a wish to supplement this already existing selection from the New Testament.

The work of the Old English Bible translators before Ælfric was not extensive, and the political chaos of the eleventh century was to dash any prospect that it would have culminated in a complete Old English version of the Bible. But it was notable for its high points—the Cædmonian poetic paraphrases and the West Saxon Gospels—and for its early date: England was one of the earliest of European countries to produce even this much of a vernacular Bible. Ælfric did not benefit notably from it; he wrote primarily to supply a pressing need rather than to contribute to an already existing tradition. But his forerunners did supply a precedent for his work, and perhaps we may see in the styles of the old poetic renderings and of the West Saxon Gospels general inspirations for Ælfric's rhythmic manner and his own clarity and simplicity.

II *Ælfric's Theory of Translation*

Ælfric's method of free translation—sometimes rendering fairly exactly and sometimes condensing, paraphrasing, or elaborating—is reminiscent of the famous metaphor which appears in the preface to King Alfred's translation of St. Augustine's *Soliloquies,* in which Alfred defended his own freedom of selection and arrangement:

Gaderode me þonne kigclas, and stuþansceaftas, and lohsceaftas, ond hylfa to ælcum þara tola þe ic mid wircan cuðe; and bohtimbru and bolt-timbru to ælcum þara weorca þe ic wyrcan cuðe, þa wlitegostan treowo be þam dele ðe ic aberan meihte. Ne com ic naþer mid anre byrðene ham, þe me ne lyste ealne þane wude ham brengan, gif ic hyne ealne aberan meihte. On ælcum treowe ic geseah hwæthwugu þæs þe ic æt ham beþorfte. Forþam ic lære ælcne ðara þe maga si ond manigne wæn hæbbe, þæt he menige to þam ilcan wuda þar ic ðas stuðansceaftas cearf, fetige hym þar ma, and gefeðrige hys wænas mid fegrum gerdum, þat he mage windan manigne smicerne wah, and manig ænlic hus settan and fegerne tun timbrian þara, and þær murge and softe mid mæge oneardian ægðer ge wintras ge sumeras, swa swa ic nu gyt ne dyde.

(I gathered for myself staves, and stud-shafts, and cross-beams, and handles for each of the tools that I could work with; and bow-timbers and bolt-timbers for every work that I could do, as many as I could carry of the comeliest trees. Neither did I come home with a burden, for it pleased me not to bring all the wood home, even if I could bear it. In each tree I saw something that I needed at home; therefore I advise every one who is able, and who has many wagons, to direct his steps to the same wood where I cut the stud-shafts. Let him there obtain more for himself, and load his wagons with fair twigs, so that he may build many a neat wall, and many a rare house, and a fair enclosure, and live in it in joy and comfort both winter and summer, as I have not yet done.[4]

Ælfric himself commented often on his methods in the prefaces to his own translations. Almost invariably, except in the preface to Genesis, such comments appear in the Latin prefaces rather than the English ones. They thus seem to be addressed, unlike the translations themselves, to learned readers who might oppose both translation into the vernacular in general and Ælfric's methods in particular. As early as the preface to the first series of *Catholic Homilies,* Ælfric made explicit a philosophy of translation which he repeated in later prefaces and to which, despite the development of his style, he remained faithful in practice through the rest of his career. First of all, he translates sense for sense, not word for word. (A similar opposition had been expressed in the Proem to the Old English translation of Boethius's *Consolation of Philosophy.* King Alfred, the author said, had translated this work sometimes word for word; sometimes sense for sense.)[5] Second, the style is to be simple and unadorned, the better to reach the hearts of the un-tutored for whom the works are intended. He eschews rhetorical ornament in favor of "the pure and open words of the language of this people" (*CH* I, Latin Preface, 1).

The Latin prefaces to the *Lives of Saints* and the *Grammar* express substantially the same intentions. Ælfric repeats that his method is to translate sense for sense and that he has willingly abbreviated and epitomized in order to avoid boring his listeners. The *Grammar* is for "tender youths" and he has therefore simplified his explanations, though he knows that words may be interpreted in many ways. If Ælfric seems somewhat on the defensive concerning his methods of translation in the *Homilies* and the *Lives of Saints*, he was doubly so when he came to biblical translation. Those who opposed translation of the Fathers into the vernacular would have certainly objected to translation, especially a free one, of the Scriptures. Ælfric is likely to have known the strictures that St. Jerome had laid upon biblical translation. Jerome, translator of the Vulgate Bible, had expressed his own theory of translation most fully in his *Preface to Eusebius* and *Epistle to Pammachius*. In the *Preface to Eusebius*, he recommends strongly giving sense for sense, rather than word for word, "except in the case of the Holy Scriptures where even the order of words is a mystery."[6]

St. Jerome's comments, and the natural diffidence that Ælfric felt in attempting scriptural translation, explain why the English preface to Genesis contains a particularly full explanation and defense of his methods. The task, Ælfric says, is a dangerous one:

Nu þincð me, leof, þæt þæt weorc is swiðe þleolic me oððe ænigum men to underbeginnenne, for þan þe ic ondræde, gif sum dysig man þas boc ræt oððe rædan gehyrþ, þæt he wille wenan, þæt he mote lybban nu on þære niwan æ, swa swa þa ealdan fæderas leofodon þa on þære tide, ær þan þe seo ealde æ gesett wære, oþþe swa swa men leofodon under Moyses æ.

(Now it seems to me, sir, that this work is very dangerous for me or anyone else to undertake, for I fear that, if some foolish man should read this book or hear it read, he would think that he could live now, under the New Law, just as the Patriarchs lived in that time, before the Old Law was established, or as men lived under the law of Moses.)

(Crawford, 76)

Ælfric warns the reader that he will confine himself to setting forth the bare text and will avoid interpretation:

We secgað eac foran to þæt seo boc is swiþe deop gastlice to understandenne, and we writaþ na mare buton þa nacedan gerecednisse. Þonne þincþ þam ungelæredum þæt eall þæt andgit beo belocen on þære anfealdan gerecednisse, ac hit ys swiþe feor þam.

(I say in advance that this book has a very deep spiritual meaning, and I write no more than the naked facts. The unlearned will think that all the meaning is contained in the simple narrative, but this is far from true.)
(Crawford,77)

Ælfric has clearly wrestled with Jerome's admonition that even the word order is sacred in Holy Scripture, and has attempted to reconcile it with his own conviction that a faithful translation must be true to the nature of the new language:

We ne durron na mare awritan on Englisc þonne ðæt Leden hæfð, ne ða endebyrdnysse awendan, buton ðam anum, ðæt ðæt Leden and ðæt Englisc nabbað na ane wisan on ðære spræce fadunge: æfre se ðe awent oððe se ðe tæcð of Ledene on Englisc, æfre he sceal gefadian hit swa ðæt ðæt Englisc hæbbe his agene wisan, elles hit bið swyðe gedwolsum to rædenne ðam ðe ðæs Ledenes wise ne can.

(I dare write no more in English than the Latin has, nor change the word order, except insofar as Latin and English differ in their idioms. Whoever translates or teaches from Latin into English must always arrange it so that the English is idiomatic, else it is very misleading to one who does not know the Latin idiom.)
(Crawford, 79–80)

Through all Ælfric's prefaces, and especially in the English preface to Genesis, he reveals that his translation methods were the result of careful consideration and deliberate choice. Well aware that other learned men may object to his practices, he has adopted them nonetheless for particular purposes and to meet specific needs. He is, however, eager to overcome possible objections from his contemporaries and to attempt to reconcile his methods with the recommendations of patristic authority. For, in the matter of translation, as in his choice of texts and his methods of interpretation, he wants his work to express the best thought of his day and to win the approval of the faithful and learned.[7]

III *The* Letter to Sigeweard

Shortly after Ælfric became Abbot of Eynsham in 1005, he wrote a piece variously known as the *Letter to Sigeweard* and *On the Old And New Testaments*. The *Letter* is a brief, popular exposition of the Bible, original with Ælfric, though he is indebted to such works as St. Augustine's *De Doctrina Christiana*. It may usefully be considered along with Ælfric's Bible translations not only because it provides an interesting summary of his interpretations of biblical material but also because, throughout the *Letter,* Ælfric alludes to his own English versions of various books of the Bible.

Little is known of the Sigeweard to whom the *Letter* is addressed. A Sigeweard signed the Eynsham charter, and the *Letter* itself establishes that Sigeweard had entertained Ælfric at his estate and had often asked him for his books. At the end of the *Letter,* Ælfric mildly rebukes Sigeweard for having pressed him to drink more than was desirable when he visited him, and points out that "over-drinking" destroys both a man's soul and his safety. Earlier in the *Letter,* however, Ælfric specifically praises Sigeweard for his "godan weorc," and later he inserts a few words on the theme of Christ's injunction, "If ye love me, keep my commandments." Christ, Ælfric says, loves the deed more than the smooth word (Crawford, 57–58), possibly an additional allusion to Sigeweard's virtue.

The *Letter,* which surveys in order the books of the Bible, classifies them, summarizes most of them very briefly, and comments on the place of each in the scriptural canon. Ælfric seems to make a particular point of mentioning his own English treatments of biblical material in the appropriate places, possibly in response to a particular request of Sigeweard, who had asked Ælfric for his English writings (Crawford, 16). He makes thirteen such allusions, some of them very specific, as when he refers to his homily on the sevenfold gifts (Crawford, 18), and some general, as when he mentions his many homilies on the Gospels (Crawford, 56). The *Letter* is thus invaluable in the study of Ælfric's canon as well as for its reflection of Ælfric's overall view of the Bible.

Throughout the *Letter,* Ælfric emphasizes, as he repeatedly did elsewhere, the unity and coherence of sacred history. As in *De Initio Creaturae* (CH.I.I), in *De Creatore et Creatura,* and in its sequel *De Sex Aetatibus Mundi,* he stresses the pattern of Creation-Fall-Redemption-Judgment that lies behind the variety of history and of biblical literature. Thus, throughout his progression through the books of the Bible, he is careful to show how each fits into the design of God's plan, and thus, at the end of the work, he provides a retrospective view of the "six ages of the world" as another way of showing the unity of universal history.

Ælfric's brief passages of interpretation are primarily typological and moral. He reminds Sigeweard that "each holy father by words and deeds clearly gives testimony to our Savior and His coming" (Crawford, 24). He does not, of course, provide exhaustive typological interpretations of the Old Testament in his short introduction, but he does mention the most important points: Adam, created on the sixth day, prefigures Christ, whose birth began the sixth age of the world; Eve betokens the Church; Abel's murder prefigures the Crucifixion, and so on. Moral instruction is similarly brief, though pointed. Of the Book of Judges, Ælfric says,

> Ic þohte þæt ge woldon þurh wundorlican race
> eower mod awendan to Godes willan on eornost.

> *(I thought that you would, through this wonderful history,*
> *turn your mind to God's will in earnest.)*   (Crawford, 34)

The books of Judith and the Maccabees are made to yield a topical moral: that the English should defend their land against foreign armies (Crawford, 48). A number of moral interpretations appear, but the major moral point which Ælfric makes in the treatise, and one to which he returns several times, is that works are more valuable than words. The *Letter* begins with a statement of this idea, an appropriate one in a work addressed to a pious but not particularly learned layman:

> Ic secge þe to soðan,
> þæt se bið swiþe wis, se þe mid weorcum spricð,
> and se hæfð forþgang for Gode and for worulde,
> se ðe mid godum weorcum hine sylfne geglengð.

> *(I tell you truly*
> *that he is very wise, who speaks with works,*
> *and he proceeds well with both God and the world,*
> *who furnishes himself with good works.)*

(Crawford, 15)

Sigeweard himself is praised for his good works, and man's justifiable pride in his good deeds is equated with God's pride in His own works. The Maccabees did not fight "with fair words only," but with "victorious deeds" (Crawford, 49). Similar observations appear throughout the *Letter,* and Ælfric ends, just before the final personal note on drinking, with this comment:

Nu miht þu wel witan, þæt weorc sprecað swiþor
þonne þa nacodan word, þe nabbað nane fremminge.
Is swa þeah god weorc on þam godan wordum,
þonne man oðerne lærð and to geleafan getrimð
mid þære soþan lare, and þonne mann wisdom sprecð
manegum to þearfe and to rihtinge, þæt God se geherod, seþe a rixað. Amen.

(Now you may well understand, that works speak more
than naked words which achieve nothing.
Yet there is good work in good words,
as when a man teaches another and leads him to faith
with true knowledge, and when a man speaks wisdom
to many for their needs and their guidance, to the praise of God,
who reigns forever. Amen.   (Crawford, 74)

This distrust of "good words," qualified though it is, may appear to be a rather surprising moral lesson to derive from a summary account of Holy Scripture. But it is thoroughly in keeping with Ælfric's practical temperament and points up the nature of his own translations, summaries, and adaptations of Scripture. He is never centrally concerned with learning for its own sake, but always has a particular moral purpose in mind in producing an English version of Scripture, always strives to bring about "good work in good words."

IV *Bible Translations in the* Catholic Homilies

Ælfric translated a considerable body of biblical material while composing the *Catholic Homilies*.[8] The *lectiones* are all translated, short biblical passages are frequently cited illustratively, and certain homilies are principally concerned with the retelling of biblical narratives. A serious difficulty in studying his methods in making these translations—and his other Bible translations as well— is that we do not know the exact recension of the Latin Bible from which he worked. The textual history of the Vulgate Bible in the Middle Ages is very complicated,[9] and our knowledge of the versions current in Ælfric's day is too limited to permit any reliable observations on his translations of specific verses. All comments must be based on the assumption that he used a "standard" recension of the Vulgate—one close to the modern authorized Vulgate— and must correspondingly be taken as tentative.

Despite Ælfric's expressed sensitivity to the special responsibilities of the Bible translator, no obvious differences in method separate his Bible translations from his others. As in his translations and adaptations of the Fathers, he is constantly and perhaps centrally concerned with the needs of his audience. His changes are, therefore, of two kinds. First, he strives to simplify and clarify narrative and exposition so the work may be easily grasped when presented orally to simple, uneducated people. Second, he tries to make the moral content of the material as clear and unambiguous as possible. He sometimes adds a comment which draws an explicit moral; at other times he silently omits details which might obscure the moral lesson or which might be misunderstood by his hearers.

One way of simplifying his material was to omit anything that might seem confusing, irrelevant, or repetitious. In *Catholic Homilies* I.XXII, he translates the account of the Day of Pentecost found in the second chapter of Acts. Although he follows the order of the account fairly closely, he makes a number of small omissions, the reasons for which we can probably deduce. Verses 9–11 are largely dropped, apparently because they contain a number of unfamiliar and unnecessary proper names. Small redundancies are eliminated, as when *stupebant autem omnes,* which begins both verses 7 and 12, is rendered only once as *"ða wearð seo menigu swiðe ablicged"* (1. 60).

Sometimes omissions seem to be motivated by a general desire for conciseness and economical expression, rather than by any particular objection to the omitted material. Thus in the same homily, in translating Acts 2:14–35, he omits parts of verses 17, 19, 33, and 34, and all of verses 18 and 20 through 31; and the result, a speech of Peter's, is pointed and effective, gaining power through its relative brevity. Another kind of alteration Ælfric makes fairly freely is the rearrangement of material. Again, he seems to be motivated in these changes by a desire for clarity and consistency. In *Catholic Homilies* I.VI, on "The Octaves and Circumcision of Our Lord" (11. 16–35), he translates the passage on the covenant of circumcision from Genesis, chapter 17; and he arranges the verses quite freely to clarify the sequence of events. Verse 5 is changed to a place before verse 15 to bring together the references to God's changing the names of Abram and Sarai to Abraham and Sarah, and verse 3 is moved to follow verse 7 to divide God's speech into two clear parts, separated by Abraham's falling on his knees.

This kind of transposition and rearrangement sometimes results, as it also does in the non-biblical translations, in a new narrative constructed of details drawn from widely separated sources. In *Catholic Homilies* I.XXI, Ælfric translates the account of the Ascension from Acts 1:1–15, in which it is said that the apostles returned to Jerusalem from the Mount of Olives without any preparatory reference to their having left Jerusalem. Ælfric supplies this lack by drawing upon the parallel section in Luke, and the result is this kind of an interweaving of the two Gospels:

> And he lædde hi ða ut of ðære byrig up [from Luke 20.51]
> to anre dune ðe is gecweden mons Oliveti [from Acts 1.12],
> and hi gebletsode up-ahafenum handum [from Luke 20.50].
> þa mid þære bletsunge ferde he [from Luke 20.51].

> (And He led them out of the city [from Luke 20.51]
> to a hill which is called the Mount of Olives [from Acts 1.12],
> and blessed them with hands uplifted [from Luke 20.50].
> Then with the blessing he departed [from Luke 20.51].)
>
> (*CH* II.XXI, 18–20)

An even more striking composite of biblical material is Ælfric's account of the laying of Christ's body in the sepulchre and of His resurrection in *Catholic Homilies* I.XV. His principal source is Matthew, but he draws upon all three of the other Gospels as well. He translates about a third of the verses he uses exactly, alters the rest of them slightly, and provides a few short passages of transition of his own where necessary.

A final kind of change Ælfric makes in his translations of biblical material in the *Catholic Homilies* is additions of interpretative comment. Many examples of such additions could be cited; Charles R. Davis has pointed out an interesting one in *Catholic Homilies* I.III, on the Passion of St. Stephen. Ælfric's source, in Acts, does not mention that Stephen's persecutors are Jews. But Ælfric, at least four times, explicitly identifies them as Jews (11. 17, 23, 50, and 56). Conversely, Ælfric consistently adds to Stephen's name the epithets "se eadiga" (the blessed) or "se halga" (the holy) (11. 13, 30–31, 52, and 61–62). Davis concludes that "Ælfric deliberately stresses the guilt of the Jews and . . . is ever careful to preserve in his hearers the desired attitude both toward the Jews and toward his subject, Stephen."[10]

V *The Homily on Job*

The most extended rendering of the Bible in the *Catholic Homilies*
is *Catholic Homilies* II.XXXV, a homiletic epitome of the Book of
Job. It is difficult to decide whether to call this piece a paraphrase
or a translation: the treatment is certainly very free, and yet over
half the lines in the homily are very direct translations of the biblical
book. Ælfric never produced a careless or mechanical translation,
but few better examples can be given of his great attention to detail
in reshaping a source for his intended audience.[11]

After a short preface, Ælfric begins the homily with a translation
of the first eight verses of Job. These verses are very closely translated except for verses 4 and 5, where Ælfric omits a reference
which might suggest that Job's sons engaged in dissipation, and
another to burnt offerings. In the first case, Ælfric seemingly wishes
to avoid suggesting that Job's sons, who afterward appear guiltless,
were guilty of any wrongdoing; and, in the second, he seems to
want to avoid reminding his hearers of pagan practices of worship.
He therefore translates *holocausta* (burnt offerings) as "seofonfealde
lac" (sevenfold gifts).

These eight verses are followed by a passage added by Ælfric
explaining Satan's helplessness in the presence of God; for Ælfric
is again anticipating his listeners' lack of sophistication and their
possible confusion over Satan's being allowed to appear before
God. Ælfric next inserts a translation of a series of verses from
chapters 29 (verses 12–16) and 31 (verses 20, 16–17, 25, 29, and 32–
42). In these verses, Job describes his own virtuous ways of life.
The result is a short "character" of the ideal rich man: benevolent
to the poor and the unfortunate and ever ready to confess his sins.
Ælfric then continues with a translation of the rest of the first
chapter, omitting only verse 13, another reference to Job's sons'
eating and drinking. He concludes this first section with a brief
passage of commentary, denouncing Satan and praising Job.

The second chapter is translated relatively closely, with only
small and insignificant omissions. Additions and alterations are
also minor: short interpretative comments after verses 6 and 10
explain why Job was tried and draw an analogy with Adam's temptation through Eve in the Garden. Interestingly, the "comforters"
are described as "þry cyninges" (three kings) and "gesibbe" (kinsmen), apparently in an attempt to exalt Job even more. Ælfric's

most radical compression of his source comes in the middle section, where chapters 3–41, the long poetic debate between Job and his comforters, is summarized in a few lines. This passage ends with a dramatic expression of Job's faith in God, taken from chapter 19 (verses 25–27). The homily ends with a fairly close translation of Job 42:7–16 and a brief final passage of original explanation and interpretation.

Ælfric's version of Job is not an equivalent of the biblical text, nor was it meant to be. It was intended for a particular use: oral delivery before an unsophisticated audience in need of moral instruction. Ælfric's changes serve two purposes, one narrative and one moral. He is concerned to reduce the length of the book to make it suitable for delivery as a homily and to make the narrative line so clear that it could be immediately grasped upon one hearing, even by the ignorant. He is also concerned that the moral lesson be just as clear and unambiguous to the same audience. Ælfric's Job is a simplified and idealized portrait of the virtuous rich man in good fortune and in bad. As such a portrait, the homily is eminently successful.

VI *Epitomes of Old Testament Books*

Another group of works that may be regarded as free Bible translations may be surveyed briefly as a group. These are a series of paraphrases of the Old Testament books of Kings, the Maccabees, Esther, Judith, Judges, and Joshua. As we have already mentioned, Clemoes has pointed out that these books have in common the moral lesson that "obedience to God is best." They were probably intended as an "appendix to the homilies," which had expounded the typology of the Old Testament comparatively thoroughly but had not given systematic treatment to its moral interpretation.

The paraphrases of Kings and the Maccabees appear in the *Lives of Saints* as numbers XVIII and XXV. Both are presented frankly as reading pieces; neither has a homiletic introduction and neither seems to be restricted in length by the limits of homiletic presentation. Ælfric mentions his English versions of both books in the *Letter to Sigeweard*: Kings, in lines 507–508; and the books of the Maccabees, in lines 836–38:

> *Ic awende hig on Englisc*
> *and rædon gif ge wyllað eow sylfum to ræde.*

(I have translated them into English;
read them if you wish for your own instruction.)   (Crawford, 51)

How compressed a version of Kings Ælfric wrote may be judged
by the fact that in 481 lines he covers the major episodes of both 1
and 2 Kings as well as some other material from 1 Samuel. Essentially, Ælfric has selected passages which describe the major figures
in this section of the Bible and has strung them together to suggest
the sequence of Hebrew kings. He begins with passages from 1
Samuel, chapters 13, 16, and 17, which describe Saul and David.
He then picks up the story with Ahab, from 1 Kings, chapter 17.
The life of Solomon is silently omitted, perhaps because of his
spectacular marital career, about which Ælfric elsewhere expressed
fears that it might mislead the unsophisticated. The last two hundred
and fifty lines or so cover 2 Samuel in the biblical sequence but with
many omissions.

The moral lesson of the Book of Kings is made explicit by Ælfric
both in the *Letter to Sigeweard* and at the end of his paraphrase.
Some of the kings were righteous, he says in the *Letter* (11. 508 ff.),
while others were evil and fared very badly. At the end of the paraphrase, he is equally pointed:

> *se þe synnum gehyrsumað*
> *and godes beboda forsyhð, nu þæs godspelles timan,*
> *þæt he bið þam cynincgum gelic ðe gecuron deofolgild,*
> *and heora scyppend forsawon.*

> *(he who obeys sins*
> *and despises God's commands, now in the gospel's age,*
> *is like the kings who chose idolatry,*
> *and despised their Creator.)*

(*LS* XVIII.475–79)

The Maccabees is also radically compressed in Ælfric's summary.
Passages from both books are woven together to summarize, in
811 lines, the story of the battles of Judas Maccabeus. The passages
selected are translated fairly closely, but Ælfric knits them together
with original passages of transition and explanations of things
likely to be unfamiliar to his audience. Thus there are digressions
on Old Testament dietary laws (11. 37–84), on angels appearing on
horseback (11. 508–13), and on elephants (11. 564–73):

> *Sumum menn wile þincan syllic þis to gehyrenne,*
> *for þan þe ylpas ne comon næfre on engla lande.*
> *Ylp is ormæte nyten, mare þonne sum hus,*
> *eall mid banum befangen, binnan þam felle,*
> *butan æt ðam nauelan, and he næfre ne lið.*

> *(To some men it will seem strange to hear this,*
> *because elephants never come to England.*
> *An elephant is an immense beast, greater than a house,*
> *all surrounded with bones, within the skin,*
> *except at the navel, and he never lies down.)*

> (*LS* XXV.564–68)

Ælfric's choice of the Maccabees for extended treatment seems to have been motivated by a more specific intention than the inculcation of the general lesson that service to God is best. Judas Maccabeus led a heroic revolt against his people's oppressors; England, suffering under the Danish attacks, needed a Judas Maccabeus, too. That lesson is, indeed, drawn explicitly by Ælfric at the end of his paraphrase:

> Secgað swa-þeah lareowas þæt synd feower cynna gefeoht;
> *iustum*, þæt is, rihtlic; *iniustum*, unrihtlic;
> *ciuile*, betwux ceaster-gewarum; *Plusquam ciuile*, betwux siblingum.
> *Iustum bellum* is rihtlic gefeoht wið ða reðan flot-menn,
> oþþe wið oðre þeoda þe eard willað fordon.

> (Nevertheless teachers say that there are four kinds of war;
> *justum*, that is, just; *injustum*, that is, unjust;
> *civile*, between citizens; *Plusquam civile*, between relatives.
> *Justum bellum* is just war against the cruel seamen,
> or against other peoples that wish to destroy [our] land.)

> (*LS* XXV.705–09)

The summarized translation of Joshua which appears in the *Heptateuch* also deals with the subject of "just war." Nothing is known of the circumstances of its composition, except that Ælfric mentions in the *Letter to Sigeweard* that it was written at the request of Æthelweard (Crawford, 32). Moreover, the paraphrases of Judges, Esther, and Judith emphasize substantially the same point. All three tell stories of just wars waged by God's chosen people against their enemies. Of Judges, Ælfric says in the *Letter to Sige-*

weard, that it tells how the Hebrew nation, when it forsook God, was oppressed by "hæðenum leodum" (heathen peoples). But when they called upon God with true repentance, he sent them aid and they were delivered. In commenting on Esther and Judith in the *Letter,* he is even more explicit:

> *Seo ys eac on Englisc on ure wisan gesett*
> *eow mannum to bysne, þæt ge eowerne eard*
> *mid wæpnum bewerian wið onwinnendne here.*
>
> *(It has also been put in English, in our manner,*
> *for your instruction, so that you may defend your land*
> *with weapons against a foreign army.)*   (Crawford, 48)

Dubois points out that Judith appears to be particularly addressed to a feminine audience, either nuns or widows who had taken a vow of chastity.[12] In praising Judith's chastity, he digresses to attack incontinency among nuns (1. 429); and, at one point, he directs his words to a female audience:

Ic wylle eac secgan, min swustor, þæt . . . clænnys micele mihte hæfþ.

(I also wish to say, my sister, that . . . purity has great power.)

(Assmann, 115)

Of the method employed in these epitomes, little need be said. Ælfric follows here the technique employed in his other paraphrases; he translates selected passages closely and connects them with original passages of summary, explanation and commentary. Dubois provides tables demonstrating, in some detail, the relationships between Ælfric's versions and the Vulgate text.[13]

VII *The Old English Pentateuch*

We come last to Ælfric's one venture into sustained translation in the generally accepted sense, as opposed to the rendering of incidental passages or to the making of paraphrases: his contribution to the so-called Old English Pentateuch. The circumstances under which Ælfric undertook this project are described in the preface to Genesis, one of the lengthiest and most interesting of Ælfric's English prefaces. The preface is addressed to Æthelweard, who had requested that he complete an already existing partial translation of Genesis:

Þu bæde me, leof, þæt ic sceold ðe awendan of Lydene on Englisc þa boc Genesis: ða þuhte me hefigtime þe to tiþienne þæs, and þu cwæde þa þæt ic ne þorfte na mare awendan þære bec buton Isaace, Abrahames suna, for þam þe sum oðer man þe hæfde awend fram Isaace þa boc oþ ende.

(You requested, sir, that I should translate from Latin into English the book of Genesis: I thought it burdensome to undertake this, and you told me that I need translate only to Isaac, Abraham's son, for someone else had translated from Isaac to the end of the book.) (Crawford, 76)

Ælfric then discusses in the preface the danger, in translating the Old Testament, that ignorant men will think that they can live now as the Patriarchs lived under the "Old Law." He also comments on the proper ways of interpreting the Old Testament and remarks on his techniques of translation.

Ælfric's translation of the first part of Genesis was incorporated, apparently in the eleventh century, into a compilation of Old English translations of the Pentateuch which was printed, in the seventeenth century, along with Ælfric's versions of Joshua and Judges, as the "Old English Heptateuch." This title is retained by its modern editor, S. J. Crawford, for his Early English Text Society edition of the works. Just how much of this composite translation of the Pentateuch is Ælfric's work is somewhat in doubt.[14] Most, if not all, of the translation was formerly attributed to him, but it now appears that the only portions by Ælfric are Genesis, chaps. 1–24 (with the exceptions of chapters 4–5 and 10–11), and Numbers, 13–26. Ælfric apparently did no more than fulfill his agreement to translate "as far as Isaac" in the Book of Genesis, but there is some evidence that he made minor revisions in the other man's translation of the rest of the book. As for the passage from Numbers, it appears to be part of a homily by Ælfric incorporated into the composite translation by the eleventh-century editor.

The Book of Genesis, with its account of the Creation and Fall, was of course one of the central parts of the Bible to Ælfric, as it is to all Christians; and he treated its contents in many forms. *De Temporibus Anni* and the *Hexameron* cover the Creation, relating it to the facts of the physical world; and the homiletic accounts of universal history, especially *De Initio Creaturae* (*CH* I. I), lay particular stress upon the Creation. There is reason to believe that Ælfric's translation of Alcuin's handbook on Genesis, the *Interrogationes Sigewulfi,* was written after the Genesis translation in order to supply the need for interpretation mentioned in the Genesis preface.[15]

In the translation itself, however, Ælfric confines himself for the most part to the aim he expresses in the preface:

We secgað eac foran to þæt seo boc is swiþe deop gastlic to understandenne, and we ne writaþ na mare butan þa nacedan gerecednisse.

(I say also in advance that the book is very deep in its spiritual meaning, and I write no more than the naked narrative.)   (Crawford, 77)

He translates somewhat more closely and literally than he does in his other biblical versions. Within the twenty-four chapters he translated, the major omissions are chapters 4–5 and 10–11. Chapters 4–5 include the story of Cain and Abel, and chapters 10–11 the story of the Tower of Babel; but, for the most part, they consist of genealogies and apparently were regarded as expendable by Ælfric. These omissions have been supplied in the surviving manuscripts by other translators.

In addition to these large omissions, a number of smaller omissions and compressions of material occur. The list of Nahor's twelve sons is omitted, with a note that their names are in the Latin version: "let him who wishes read them there" (Crawford, 143). The same formula is used to pass over the account of Isaac's wife in Genesis 24:11–60. At another point he refuses to translate objectionable material:

Se leodscipe wæs swa bysmorful þæt hi woldon fullice ongean gecynd heora galnysse gefyllan, na mid wimmannum ac swa fullice þæt us sceamað hyt openlice to secgenne.

(The nation was so corrupt that they would foully satisfy their lust against nature, not with women but so foully that we are ashamed to say it openly.)   (Crawford, 132)

The style of the translation up to chapter 19 is non-rhythmical, but the rhythmical style does begin to appear in it and is used consistently from chapter 22 on.

In general, the reservations Ælfric expressed in the preface about translating the Bible are implicit in the translation itself. Ælfric did his job conscientiously and thoughtfully, but he was too conscious of how the "naked narrative" could be misunderstood to translate freely and fully the Book of Genesis.

Ælfric's work as a Bible translator is full of paradoxes. On the one hand, he constantly expressed fears that his work would cause "the pearls of Christ to be held in disrespect"; on the other, he produced the largest, most impressive body of Bible translation in Old English. He apparently shared Jerome's conviction that even the individual word is sacred in Holy Scripture; and yet, he translated so freely that much of his work could be regarded as loose paraphrase. Although he says that he "dared write no more in English than the Latin has," he frequently adds passages in which he draws explicit morals from the biblical materials.

These paradoxes do not exactly amount to contradictions. They stem rather from difficulties inherent in the translation of sacred texts and from the very fact that Ælfric was too sophisticated and self-conscious a stylist to believe that a direct and literal-minded approach would resolve these difficulties. Like King Alfred, he knew that he had to "gather his own tools and his own timber" and to build the best house he could. The result was a series of clear, eloquent, and useful fragments; but Ælfric's own misgivings were too strong for it to be more.

CHAPTER 5

The Grammar *and the* Colloquy

A LL of Ælfric's works may be regarded as teaching pieces, in the broad sense of the word, addressed to the laity, as were the *Catholic Homilies,* or to the clergy, as were the *Lives of Saints,* the *Pastoral Letters,* and the *Life of Æthelwold.* But there is also a small group of works that Ælfric wrote specifically in his function as master of oblates at Eynsham for the instruction of his pupils: these include *De Temporibus Anni,* his treatise on chronology and astronomy; the *Grammar* and *Glossary;* and the *Colloquy.* These last works are closely related and perhaps deserve special emphasis for their intrinsic as well as their historical interest.

I *The* Grammar

Ælfric's *Grammar,* as its English preface indicates, followed soon after the *Catholic Homilies,* perhaps in 993–95. He issued it, as he did each volume of the *Catholic Homilies,* with a set of English and Latin prefaces; and he regarded it as closely related to his other works in his overall plan. Thus his English preface begins,

Ic Ælfric wolde þas lytlan boc awendan to engliscum gereorde of ðam stæfcræfte, þe is gehaten *grammatica,* syððan ic ða twa bec awende on hundeahtatigum spellum, forðan ðe stæfcræft is seo cæg, ðe ðæra boca andgit unlicð.

(I, Ælfric, wished to translate into English this little book of grammar, which is called *grammatica,* after I had translated two books of eighty sermons, because grammar is the key which unlocks the meaning of those books.)

(Zupitza, 2)

The product of this work is of considerable historical interest because it is the first grammar of any language to be written in English. Apparently the work was fairly widely used, for it survives in fifteen manuscripts from scattered points of origin.[1] The *Grammar* not only provides some insights into Ælfric's pedagogic methods but also illuminates his understanding of the Latin language, his conception of its relations to English, and thus his principles of translation. It is also interesting linguistically because it contains one of the largest examples of a specialized technical vocabulary in Old English. Ælfric follows his sources rather closely in the content and arrangement of the books, and his chief original contribution is the invention of a complete set of English equivalents for the traditional terms of the Greek and Roman grammarians. Although, for historical reasons, his terminology did not become established as standard in later English grammar, his coinages demonstrate, as the theological terms of earlier Old English do also, the resources of Old English and its capacity for adaptation to a specialized use.

II *The Grammatical Tradition*

The study of grammar (by which was meant, of course, Latin grammar) was of fundamental importance in the Old English monastic school.[2] It formed the first subject in the so-called "trivium," and it was studied immediately after such preliminaries as learning the letters of the alphabet and the words of the *credo* and the *paternoster*. Only after the fundamentals of the Latin language were learned could the pupils proceed to rhetoric and dialectic and ultimately to the "quadrivium": music, arithmetic, geometry, and astronomy. In theory, at least, the pupils, after reaching a certain early stage, were supposed to speak only Latin, both in and out of school. We have no reason to believe that this rule was strictly enforced in tenth-century English schools, but Ælfric, in his instructional materials, emphasizes the vocabulary of everyday life and seems thereby to imply such an ideal. Despite his vernacular translations, Ælfric never questioned the necessity for a thorough grounding in Latin. His English translations, eloquent though they were, were to supply an immediate need, as had those of King Alfred; and Ælfric labored to insure that the next generation of the clergy would be able to read Latin texts better than his generation could. Grammar was the "key that unlocks the meaning of the books."

Ælfric inherited a double tradition of grammatical study: the "scientific" tradition of the Classical period and the pedagogical tradition of the more recent past.[3] Grammar had once implied the broad study of language in all its aspects, thereby encroaching upon the territories of metrics and the arts of poetry, rhetoric, and dialectics. Grammar had been the invention of the Greeks. Plato and Aristotle had both made contributions to grammatical theory: Plato had divided words into nouns and verbs, and sounds into vowels and consonants; and Aristotle had distinguished four parts of speech and remarked upon the tenses of verbs and the cases of nouns. Grammar was raised to the status of a methodical and important science, however, by the Stoic grammarians: Zeno of Citium (364–263 B.C.), Cleanthes of Assos (331–232 B.C.), and Chrysippus (280–208 B.C.). They established the major outlines of the study and, with the Alexandrian grammarians, the principal terminology. Greek grammar, in the version set forth by the major Alexandrian grammarian, Dionysius Thrax (born c. 166 B.C.), was adapted to the Latin language by M. Terentius Varro (116–27 B.C.); his *De Lingua Latina* established the main outlines of Latin grammar for centuries.

The grammars of the major Greek and Roman grammarians were not primarily pedagogical grammars. For the most part, they were written for native speakers of the language and were objective investigations of the nature and structure of language. The other grammatical tradition, the medieval pedagogical tradition, was a result of the extension of Latin geographically as the international language of learned discourse. Medieval grammars were written primarily to teach students a second language; therefore, they usually had a strongly practical, pedagogical emphasis.

The most influential figures in the shaping of medieval Latin grammar were Donatus and Priscian. Aelius Donatus, who lived in the fourth century, was the author of the *Ars Grammatica* and the *Ars Minor*. These grammars—the "greater Donatus" and the "lesser Donatus"—were the most widely used textbooks of the Middle Ages. To a great extent, they established the form of the Latin grammar studied throughout the Middle Ages and dictated the terminology of the grammars of most of the vernacular languages of Western Europe. Only slightly less prominent as a source of medieval grammar was Priscian (early sixth century), whose *Institutiones Grammaticae* was regarded as the standard advanced textbook to which the student progressed after mastering the more elementary Donatus. The popularity and wide dissemination of Priscian's

Institutes are suggested by the fact that it survives in more than a thousand widely distributed manuscripts. It continued to be used in schools through the Renaissance. Both Donatus and Priscian were in circulation in England very soon after the conversion.

The distinction of being the first English grammarian does not belong to Ælfric, although his is the first grammar in English. Bede, Tatwine, Boniface, and Alcuin had all written grammars of Latin for the instruction of English monastic pupils.[4] Bede's grammar, which survives in only fragmentary form, is brief and elementary; and it was probably intended as a first textbook for beginning students. Tatwine (d. 734), the author of Latin riddles, wrote a grammar which amounts to an expansion of Donatus's *Ars Minor*. Boniface (675–754), the Anglo-Saxon missionary to Germany, wrote a text called *De Partibus Orationis*, based like Tatwine's on Donatus. It includes model paradigms and long lists of examples which amount to glossaries embedded in the text. But the most interesting of early English grammars is the *De Grammatica* of Alcuin (735–804). Although brief, it is a witty, imaginative work which anticipates Ælfric's *Colloquy* as well as his *Grammar* in that it consists of a dialogue between a master and two students: Franco, a fourteen-year-old French boy, and Saxo, his fifteen-year-old English schoolmate. There are some elementary characterizations and entertaining asides in the little dialogue. For the grammatical content, Alcuin drew upon both Donatus and Priscian.

Ælfric's *Grammar* is a much more substantial production than any of these works by his English predecessors. His is a thoroughly practical, pedagogical text in the tradition of Donatus and Priscian; and it neither recalls the "scientific" tradition of the Classical grammarians nor anticipates the inclusive, anthologizing tendencies of later medieval grammarians. Ælfric's carefully composed work effectively adapts Donatus and Priscian to the needs and capacities of contemporary English pupils.

III *The Content and Arrangement of the* Grammar

Ælfric's *Grammar* is frankly based on both Donatus and Priscian. In the Latin preface, he writes, "I have endeavored to translate into your language these extracts from the Greater and Lesser Priscian for you, tender youths, so that, after reading through the eight parts of Donatus in this little book of mine, you can im-

plant in your tender selves both languages, Latin and English, until
you come to more advanced studies" (Zupitza, 1).

In general, the *Grammar* is organized on the plan of the *Ars
Minor* of Donatus, but the major content, the definitions and examples, are drawn mainly from Priscian's *Institutes*. The "eight parts
of Donatus" are, of course, the eight parts of speech, around which
the *Grammar* is organized, following the *Ars Minor*. But Ælfric
apparently conceives of his book as comparable in scope and difficulty to Priscian's, for which he expresses great admiration. Priscian, Ælfric declares, "is known as the ornament of all Latinity."

Despite the extent to which Ælfric draws upon Priscian and
Donatus the *Grammar* is, by no means a mere pastiche of its sources.
Ælfric strives throughout to clarify and simplify the material,
to choose appropriate examples familiar to his English pupils,
and to compare and contrast Latin with English. [5]

He also elaborates the fundamental plan of the book with "handbook" information and summaries that make it more useful.
After the Latin and English prefaces, he begins with a series of
brief explanations of basic terms—"voice," "letter," "syllable,"
and "diphthong" (4–8). He then includes a brief summary and
definition of the parts of speech (8–11). This section is original
with him and seems intended as an aid to beginning students who
need a brief introductory overview of the subject before the detailed
presentation begins. The definitions in this section are brief and
informal, in contrast to the formal definitions later in the book,
and are original with Ælfric. "Noun," for example, is defined as
"the name by which we name everything, whether unique or common" (8). The examples given are from everyday English life,
"Edgar" and "Æthelwold," for example, being used to illustrate
proper nouns.

After these preliminaries, Ælfric begins the major section of the
Grammar, a systematic presentation of the eight parts of speech
(11–280). Beginning with the noun and progressing through the
pronoun, verb, adverb, participle, conjunction, preposition, and
interjection, he follows an orderly method of presentation. He first
defines the part of speech carefully, giving an English equivalent
for the Latin term. He then discusses subdivisions and subcategories
of the part, and he finally treats its properties in some detail. In
this central section of the book, Ælfric moves between Donatus
and Priscian, sometimes acknowledging his source, more often

not. An indication of his freedom in borrowing from both is his Latin definitions of the parts of speech. Donatus is drawn upon for the definitions of the verb, participle, and interjection, while Priscian contributes those of the pronoun and adverb. Ælfric writes original definitions of the conjunction and preposition, drawing upon both his sources. The book ends with three brief appendices of "useful facts": a list of the names of numerals; one of the "thirty divisions of grammatical art" from "voice" and "letter" to "fable" and "history"; and a brief postscript on money measures ("*Libra* on Leden is pund on Englisc," etc.).

Throughout the *Grammar*, Ælfric demonstrates a vivid sense of the needs, the capacities, and the interests of the "tender youths" to whom the book is addressed. He constantly simplifies and clarifies the material, but he does not compromise his aim of writing a fairly thorough text on about the level of Priscian's *Institutes*. His opening, simple summary and the clarity of his overall organization exemplify this intent, as does his practice of compressing or omitting material from Priscian of secondary importance. Thus he omits long sections of unnecessary examples in Priscian with a comment such as this:

Ða naman . . . synd *denominativa* gecwedene, and ðara ys fornean ungerim.

(Names . . . are called *denominativa,* and they are almost numberless.)
(Zupitza, 18)

And thus he ends his section on the verb with,

Nelle we na swyðor her be ðam worde sprecan. Wel, gif ðis aht fremað.

(We will not speak any further here of the verb. It is well, if this benefits anything.) (Zupitza, 222)

Ælfric also freely substitutes his own examples for those of Donatus and Priscian. Sometimes he contributes examples that would be familiar to his students. Such schoolboy phrases as "ic write, wel he writ, yfele we raedað" (I write, he wrote well, we read badly), for example, are used to illustrate the adverb. In other cases, he chooses new examples in the interest of piety: saints' names, holy objects, or scriptural quotations. Names that end in *-eus* are illustrated by "Matheus se godspellere," for instance. Lawrence

Shook calls attention to an interesting treatment of Priscian's examples by Ælfric in the section on jurative adverbs (227).[6] Ælfric refuses either to use Priscian's Roman oaths (*Hercle* and *Mediusfidius*) or to substitute Christian ones. He briefly treats the preposition *per* as a jurative adverb in such phrases as *juro per deum* and *per meum caput,* quotes Christ's injunction to "Let your speech be yea, yea; no, no," and concludes,

Na syndon swergendlice *adverbia*, ac hwæt sceolon hi gesæde, nu we swerian ne moton?

(There are more swearing *adverbia*, but why say anything of them, since we must not swear?)

(Zupitza, 227)

Ælfric also goes beyond his sources in the attention he pays to English grammar and its relation to Latin. In the Latin preface, he hopes that his book will help his students "in both languages, namely Latin and English" (1); and, in the English preface, he similarly says that the book will be "sum angyn to ægðrum gereorde" (an introduction to both languages) (3). Throughout the work, he makes comments on English, which, though they do not amount to anything like a systematic grammar, do demonstrate his absorbing interest in his own language. Most of these comments center on the similarities and differences between the two languages. In discussing the letters of the alphabet, for example, he remarks that in addition to the vowels *a, e, i, o,* and *u,* the letter *y* is often used in names taken from Greek and that "this same *y* is very common in English" (5). He comments that the eight parts of speech apply to English as well as to Latin (11), that Latin does not have patronymic names, as English does (14–15), and that each language has its own untranslatable interjections (279–80).

IV *Ælfric's Grammatical Terminology*

One of the most interesting of Ælfric's original contributions to the *Grammar* is his creation of a complete set of grammatical terms in English.[7] The technical vocabulary of grammar is, of course, highly abstract and difficult to translate. Ælfric's English equivalents to the Latin terms illustrate not only the capacity of Old English to create new words to express involved concepts but also his own ingenuity and his mastery of both Latin and English. Throughout the *Grammar,* each time a new term is introduced, Ælfric translates it into English, usually thereby coining a new word: "*Pronomen* is ðæs namen speliend" (The *pronomen* is the noun substitute) (8), "*Nominativus* ys nemniendlic" (*Nominativus* is naming) (22), and so on. It is sometimes assumed that Ælfric meant to propose these English terms as replacements for the Latin terms, but he seems to have had no such intention. In only a few instances does he himself use the English term consistently in his subsequent discussions; more often he alternates between the Latin and English terms, even using the Latin terms somewhat more frequently. The English terms seem, in most cases, to be explanations of the Latin terms of the kind that a good teacher would provide to help his students understand and remember the new terms, not replacements for them.

Whatever Ælfric's intentions were, he did create a comprehensive set of English grammatical terms in the course of his translation. Probably some of these were already conventional in the classroom practice of his day; they seem inevitable and are probably not original with Ælfric. Most, however, reflect a consistent method and are undoubtedly Ælfric's inventions. A few are taken directly from Latin, such as "case" (Latin *casus*) and "part" (Latin *pars*). A much larger group simply employs already existing English words in new meanings: "had," "cynn," "tid," "name," and "word," for Latin *persona, genus, tempus, nomen,* and *verbum,* for instance.

Another large group of terms employs combinations of native words to render the meaning of the Latin terms. *Vocales,* for instance, is rendered "clypiendlice" (speakings) and *semivocales* is "healfclypiendlice" (half-speakings). Sometimes the product is a compound word or phrase. *Syllaba* becomes "stæfgefeg" (letter-combination), and *pronomen* becomes "naman speliend" (noun substitute). Often such compounds result from analysis and literal translation of each morpheme in the Latin terms. Thus *participium* (*parti* + *cip* =, from *capere,* "to take") is rendered "dæl nimend" (part-taking). The English term thus derived is usually precise, but is occasionally impossibly clumsy. *Interjectio,* for instance, is analytically translated "betwuxaworpennys" (between-throwing), an accurate enough rendering but a tongue twister, like "underðeo-dendlic" (under-joining) for *subjunctivus.*

Ælfric could hardly have meant to propose the regular adoption of such terms; they are explanatory renderings of the Latin terms, for teaching purposes. The only English terms that he himself uses regularly in preference to the Latin ones are such simple and natural substitutions as "tid" for *tempus,* "cynn" for *genus,* "word" for *verbum,* and "stæf" for *littera.*

Ælfric's vernacular grammatical vocabulary was one of the first such vocabularies for any European language. It did not, however, become established as the permanent English grammatical vocabulary. The Norman Conquest effectively ended the continuity of English scholarship; and, when the study of grammar in English was resumed centuries later, new translations of the Latin terms were made, which ultimately became standard. Thus we speak today of "letters" rather than "staffs," of "tense" rather than "tide," and of "gender" rather than "kind." Nevertheless, Ælfric's grammatical vocabulary provides a valuable insight into the resources of Old English as well as of his own as linguist and teacher.

V *The* Glossary

Appended to seven of the fifteen extant manuscripts of the *Grammar* is a Latin-English *Glossary* of several hundred words. This *Glossary,* probably by Ælfric and intended to accompany the *Grammar,* is not arranged alphabetically but by topics. There are eight sections. The first begins with *deus omnipotens* and gives the words for the major parts of God's creation: Heaven, the angels, the earth, the sea, and man. The second section—*Nomina membrorum*—names the "members" of the body, of society, and of the family. The last six sections take up the names of birds, fish, animals, plants, trees, and domestic items. The *Glossary* is of considerable value, of course, in the study of the Old English vocabulary; but it is not otherwise remarkable. Its contents and arrangement follow a familiar pattern in medieval texts; if Ælfric had any specific source, it was probably the *Etymologies* of Isidore of Seville.[8]

It does bear some relationship to both the *Grammar* and the *Colloquy.* The emphasis in the *Glossary* is strongly upon "everyday" words, ones that pupils would be likely to need in everyday life around a monastery, rather than words that would be needed in translating academic texts. It therefore shares the practical goals of the *Grammar* and suggests that Ælfric aimed at his pupils' mastery of Latin as an everyday, spoken language. The same goal is suggested by the earthy little *Colloquy,* the vocabulary of which is partially contained in the *Glossary*. The fact that some of the Latin terms in the *Colloquy* do not appear in the *Glossary* has led to the suggestion that Ælfric probably had several such lists and that he used the *Colloquy* in conjunction with another *Glossary* that was slightly different from the one that has been preserved.

VI *The Background of the* Colloquy

Ælfric's *Colloquy* is perhaps the most frequently reprinted and widely known of any of his works, rather paradoxically so since it is a slight piece, obviously dashed off to satisfy a pedagogical need. A short dialogue between a teacher and his pupils, it has the modest aim of offering practice in the Latin needed for use in everyday situations in a monastic school. There are good reasons for modern interest in it, however. For one, the Old English gloss offers a sample, admittedly little more than tantalizing, of Old English used in a sustained piece of dialogue. Old English literature has no drama; and, even in the narrative prose and poetry, dialogue is much rarer than it is in, say, the Icelandic saga literature, The *Colloquy* hardly offers anything approaching a genuinely creative, dramatic dialogue—its purpose is too limited and the gloss is too much bound by the Latin for that—but it does suggest, here and there, the movement of a genuine, conversational exchange, despite the classroom setting.

Its very humbleness of purpose gives the *Colloquy* an interest for us that Ælfric and the anonymous glossator of his work could hardly have anticipated. Its concentration on subjects and characters from everyday experience gives us a rare glimpse, brief as it is, of life in and around a tenth-century monastery—the everyday life that never enters the more exalted worlds of the Maldon poem or Ælfric's own passions of Roman martyrs. But, beyond these extrinsic considerations, the *Colloquy*'s "charm" (an overused word that, nevertheless, seems the right one) stems in large part from the skill and wit with which Ælfric executed his task. The little details of monastic life that appear in the dialogue and the pithiness of some of the exchanges reveal clearly a side of Ælfric's character that is partially suppressed in his larger works, though it crops out here and there: his earthiness, his common sense, and his sympathetic concern for the humbler members of society.

Ælfric's Latin text of the *Colloquy* is preserved, either in part or complete, in four manuscripts.[9] The best of these (British Museum, Cotton MS Tiberius A.iii) contains a continuous interlinear gloss in Old English. This gloss is not complete; at the beginning, each word is glossed; but, toward the end, words and phrases which have appeared before are left unglossed. Some attempt is made to use Old English word order, especially in short phrases; but the Latin word order naturally dominates the gloss. It was formerly believed that this text was only partially by Ælfric and that it had been amplified by one Ælfric Bata. There is no good reason, however, to suppose that the Latin portion of the Cottonian manuscript is not entirely by Ælfric. The confusion apparently arose because another manuscript (St. John's College, Oxford, Codex No. 154) contains an expanded version of the *Colloquy* with a rubric in which Ælfric Bata attributes the *Colloquy* to "my master Abbot Ælfric" and says that he himself has expanded it. This Ælfric Bata seems to have been a prolific writer of colloquies; the Oxford manuscript contains three more by him—and all, like his expansions of Ælfric's, are repetitive and pedantic. Nothing else is known of him except for a reference in Osbern's *Life of Dunstan* to an Ælfric Bata "who had tried to disinherit the Church of God." G. N. Garmonsway suggests that the nickname "Bata" may mean he was shortsighted, "whether literally or figuratively."[10]

The authorship of the Old English gloss is another matter. On the face of it, it would seem unlikely that Ælfric wrote it. The gloss of such a teaching piece would be only for the use of the teacher, and we can hardly imagine a Latinist of Ælfric's skill needing a gloss; but it is possible, of course, that it was circulated for the use of other teachers and that Ælfric provided an English gloss in the same way that he provided both Latin and English prefaces for his other books. The gloss is, however, by no means a model of the kind we would expect Ælfric to produce if this were his intention. Not only is it incomplete, it contains a number of errors and mistranslations. Furthermore, a number of words are glossed with Old English words different from those used in the *Glossary* to define the same words. *Sacerdos,* for example, is "sacred" in the *Glossary,* but "mæsse-preost" in the *Colloquy,* and *murenas* is "merenæddre" in the *Glossary*, but "lampredan" in the *Colloquy*. Neither of these arguments is conclusive; Ælfric may have made mistakes himself, and he may have glossed the same word differently at different times. As Garmonsway points out,[11] the *Glossary* is for the child; the

Colloquy, for the master. But the general implication of the admittedly imperfect evidence is that Ælfric did not write the gloss.

The fact that the pupils in the *Colloquy* introduce themselves as plowmen, herdsmen, merchants, etc., has sometimes led to misunderstanding. This introduction tells us, in fact, nothing of the "diffusion of education among all classes"; the pupils are merely assuming roles for the purpose of introducing certain kinds of vocabulary, closely related to the categories of the *Glossary*. Nor is the master a "secular," in spite of his apparent ignorance of monastic life; this pretense is also adopted so certain terms related to monastic life can be introduced. The classroom procedure was probably for the master to ask a series of questions like those in the *Colloquy* which encouraged the students to adopt a series of roles and to compose extemporaneous answers which employed a certain vocabulary. Ælfric may have had several such sets of questions; our text may be one which he wrote down and offered as a model. At early stages of instruction, the teacher may have provided specimen answers; the answers in the *Colloquy* may be intended in this way, or they may even, as Garmonsway suggests, be some of the best of his pupils' replies, which Ælfric himself edited.

This sensible and practical method of instruction was not original with Ælfric. A number of monastic colloquies survive from the Old English period, though Ælfric's is much the most readable of them. A number of them have been collected and edited by W. H. Stevenson.[12] These colloquies derive not from the superficially similar dialogues of Classical literature, but from the most popular Greek textbook of the Middle Ages, the *Hermeneumata Pseudo-Dositheana,* a compilation built around the *Ars Grammatica Dosithei Magistri,* a fourth-century grammar expanded by later writers with vocabulary lists, "readers," and, most relevant to our purposes, little Greek-Latin dialogues on homely subjects. These dialogues vary from manuscript to manuscript; apparently it was common practice for teachers to compose their own colloquies to use along with the grammar. At least two of the colloquies printed by Stevenson follow the colloquies of the *Hermeneumata* closely in content and arrangement.

It is perhaps unfair to evaluate such modest pieces by the standards of art, but the besetting defects of most of them are prolixity and dullness. Garmonsway has indicated some lively scenes in Bata's colloquies;[13] but, for the most part, the characters and their questions are the slightest of pretexts for the introduction of the long word lists which are sometimes clogged with recondite words which seem to serve no purpose but to demonstrate the authors' learning. The great virtues of Ælfric's *Colloquy* are its selectivity and economy. It introduces a good deal of vocabulary, but the word lists never swamp the characters and the simple situation. The conversation is given a dramatic quality in the differences of opinion that emerge, in the shifts in groupings of characters, in the liveliness of some of the thumbnail portraits, and in the unifying effect of a dominant theme.

VII *The* Colloquy

The setting of the *Colloquy* is a classroom, and the participants are a master and his pupils. The first two-thirds of the piece consists of a series of questions and answers concerning various occupations. The Cottonian manuscript contains few indications of speaker—none before the cook (1.194)—but it is never unclear who is speaking. The students begin by asking the master to teach them to speak Latin correctly:

We cildra biddaþ þe, eala lareow, þæt þu tæce us sprecan forþam un-gelærede we syndon and gewæmmodlice we sprecaþ.

(We children beg you, O master, to teach us to speak [Latin correctly] for we are unlearned and speak badly.)   (11. 1–3)

The first speaker, who assumes the role of a monk, tells something of his daily routine: he sings seven services a day and is otherwise occupied with reading and singing (11. 13–16). He introduces his fellow pupils, who will impersonate plowmen, shepherds, oxherds, hunters, fishermen, fowlers, merchants, shoemakers, salt-workers, and bakers.

The pupils, who then assume these roles in this order, are cate-chized about their lives. The result is a gallery of miniatures of characters from contemporary life; a comparison is inevitable with Chaucer's far more ambitious and complex gallery in the Prologue to the *Canterbury Tales*. Although most of the conversations are very brief—the longest are those of the hunter and the fisherman, which run to thirty-six lines each—most of them go beyond

the immediate purpose of introducing vocabulary to suggest the
motivations and the attitudes of the speakers. The plowman fears
his master so much that he plows his acre a day even in a storm
(11. 24–27); the shepherd has to work almost as hard in order to
be faithful to his lord (11. 36–42).

The king's hunter also stresses his relation to his master, but
with a somewhat different emphasis. After describing his methods
of hunting with nets and hounds, he is asked what he does with his
game; and he replies:

Ic sylle cynce swa hwæt swa ic gefo, forþam ic eom hunta hys.

(I give the king whatever I take, for I am his hunter.)   (11. 81–82)

The king, in return, clothes and feeds him well, and sometimes
gives him a horse or a ring, "so that I may pursue my craft more
willingly" (11.84–85).

The dialogues of the fisherman and the merchant are used as an
occasion to introduce lists of terms from the *Glossary* of the names
of fish and of various wares, but such lists never become overwhelming. (In the Oxford text, Bata has expanded these lists and introduced new ones, which do become tedious, of animals, birds, trees,
and plants.) Rather, the vocabulary is introduced easily and naturally
in the course of the short interviews which emphasize not only
the speaker's craft but also his personal attitudes. The plowman's
wretchedness and servility are contrasted with the hunter's rather
complacent recital of his skill and the rewards he receives for it.
The fisherman is not above revealing a healthy respect for the sea
and its dangers:

Wylt þu fon sumne hwæl?
Nic.
Forhþi?
Forþam plyhtlic þinge hit ys gefon hwæl. Gebeorhlicre ys me
faran to ea mid scype mynan, þænne faran mid manegum scypum
on huntunge hranes.

(Would you like to catch a whale?
Not I.
Why not?

Because it is a dangerous thing to catch a whale. It is
safer for me to go to the river with my ship than to go
with many ships to hunt whales.)   (11. 109–14)

Most of the speakers are proud of their crafts, and several insist
rather strongly on their importance to society. The shoemaker
insists that "not one of you could pass the winter were it not for my
trade" (1. 174), and the cook, too, regards himself as indispensable
(11. 200–202). The merchant, the most prosperous of the speakers,
is also the most vehement in insisting on his value to society:

Hwæt sægst þu, mancgere?
Ic secge þæt behefe ic eom cingce and ealdormannum and
weligum and eallum follce.

(What say you, merchant?
I say that I am useful to the king and to ealdormen and to
the wealthy and to all people.)
                                                          (11. 149–51)

The merchant then enumerates the goods he imports, emphasizing
the risks and perils he undergoes. "Do you sell them here at the
same price you bought them there?" asks the master (1. 162). "I
do not," the merchant firmly replies, "What would I achieve by
my labors then?" Eric Colledge has pointed out the prominence
of this theme of just reward for labor in the *Colloquy*.[14] The hunter,
the fisherman, the fowler, all emphasize the profit they seek by their
labors. The fowler even describes how he frees his hawks in the
spring and trains new ones in the fall in order to avoid the expense
of feeding idle hawks through the summer. In this theme of profit,
Ælfric is probably echoing Augustine's lively defense of commerce
and profit in a similar dialogue in his commentary on Psalm 70:
15. The subject was, of course, much debated throughout the Middle
Ages; and it received its fullest treatment in English literature in the
fourteenth-century *Piers Plowman*.

The other thematic thread that runs through all the interviews
is the defense that each speaker makes of the value of his craft to
society, and this theme finally provides the major "dramatic action"
of the *Colloquy* when a "wise counsellor" is introduced (1. 208).
The master asks the counsellor, "Which of these trades seems to you
the greatest?" The counsellor replies that the service to God is

the greatest; and when pressed to name the greatest secular occupation, replies, "Eorþtilþ, forþam se yrþling us ealle fett" (Agriculture, because the farmer feeds us all) (1. 219). This reply immediately provokes an outburst from the smith, the fisherman, and the carpenter, who defend their own crafts, until the counsellor quiets them with a long speech which concludes,

Swa hwæðer þu sy, swa mæsseprest, swa munuc, swa ceorl, swa kempa, bega oþþe behwyrf þe sylfne on þisum, and beo þæt þu eart; forþam micel hynð and sceamu hyt is menn nellan wesan þæt þæt he ys and þæt he wesan sceal.

(Whatever you are, whether priest, or monk, or peasant, or soldier, practice yourself in this, and be what you are; because it is a great disgrace and shame for a man not to be willing to be that which he is, and that which he ought to be.)   (11. 240–43)

The quarrel thus resolved, the *Colloquy* ends with a short interrogation of one of the pupils about his own routine. The pupil tells what he does during the day, what he eats and drinks, and where he sleeps. Ælfric permits himself a small schoolmasterish joke at the expense of the convention in the colloquies of introducing long lists when the master asks the pupil what he eats. The pupil replies with a list of foods (11. 288–89). "You are very greedy, to eat all that," the master replies; and the serious-minded pupil explains that he does not eat all this food at one meal. The master concludes with a short speech admonishing the pupils to be diligent and virtuous (11. 308–15).

It is easy to exaggerate the merits of the *Colloquy*. It remains a modest teaching-piece, despite the appeal of its little glimpses into humble life and its toying with lofty themes. But, in its combination of warmth and liveliness, it reveals very clearly a side of Ælfric's personality which we are likely to miss in his more formal works. Appropriately enough, as the most popular piece in elementary Old English readers, it is still, almost nine centuries later, being used regularly to help students learn a language.

CHAPTER 6

Ælfric's Style

HOMILIST, hagiographer, translator, linguist: Ælfric's work in all these roles reflects his mastery of English prose, and it is as a prose stylist that he is chiefly known. Modern study of Old English literature has quite naturally focused heavily upon the poetry, for the prose of the period is less clearly literary and has more often attracted the attention of historians than of literary students. Nevertheless, recent studies have made clear not only the considerable intrinsic interest of the best Old English prose but also its relevance to the later history of English literature.

The apex of the Old English poetic tradition, judging from the texts that survive, was the eighth century; it is probably correct to see a certain decline in the few later poems, as in *Maldon,* for example. But Old English prose was later in developing; it was not until the late ninth and tenth centuries that the language, in the hands of a few writers, became a medium capable of expressing complex ideas forcefully and clearly in sustained prose. The Norman Conquest, of course, abruptly ended most English writing in either poetry or prose; but the Old English prose masters apparently continued to exercise an influence still felt when English again became a literary medium. Thus we can speak of a "continuity of English prose" with more confidence than of a "continuity of English poetry," despite such phenomena as the fourteenth-century alliterative poems.[1]

Ælfric is the central figure in this blooming—comparatively late in the Old English period—of literary prose. Artificial as it may be, then, to consider style largely apart from content, Ælfric's prose style deserves particular emphasis and even separate consideration in a survey of his achievement; though we should perhaps speak instead of Ælfric's prose styles. Ælfric is best known for the "rhythmical style" of the *Lives of Saints* and later works, but a large part of his literary production—notably most of the *Catholic Homilies*—is in ordinary, non-rhythmical prose. This prose is very accomplished; and, though Ælfric seems to have gradually abandoned it in favor

120

of the highly personal rhythmical prose of his later works, it may usefully be examined separately.

Ælfric seems to have adopted the rhythmical style at some point in the second series of *Catholic Homilies*. The early works—the first series of *Catholic Homilies, De Temporibus Anni*, the *Grammar*, the *Interrogationes*, and most of *Genesis*—are in ordinary prose. (In *Genesis*, the rhythmical style begins to appear in chapter 19 and becomes consistent in chapter 22.) Seven pieces in *Catholic Homilies* II are predominantly rhythmical: X (St. Cuthbert), XIV (The Passion of Our Lord), XVIII (SS. Philip and James), XIX (The Invention of the Cross), XX (SS. Alexander, Eventius, and Theodolus), XXI (On the Greater Litany), and XXXIX (St. Martin). Four others (XI, XII, XXVII, and XXXV) have rhythmical passages of various lengths. All of the saints' lives in *Lives of Saints* are rhythmical, though some of the supplementary pieces are not. After the *Lives*, Ælfric seems to have written exclusively in the rhythmical style, though since the style itself has been used often as chronological evidence, we are not certain of this.

I *Ælfric's "Ordinary Prose"*

All Ælfric's prose, rhythmical or not, is marked by certain characteristics: clarity, balance, and a carefully controlled variety of syntactic patterns. He expressed his stylistic ideal very clearly in the Latin preface to the second series of *Catholic Homilies:* "I have hastened to form this following book, according as the grace of God has guided me. I have tried to do this avoiding garrulous verbosity and strange expressions, and seeking rather with pure and plain words, in the language of their nation, to be of use to my hearers, by simple speech, than to be praised for the composition of skillful discourse, which my simplicity has never acquired" (*CH* II, p. 1).

This declaration need not be taken completely at face value, for it is a commonplace of early medieval rhetoric. Ælfric follows his predecessors in conceiving of style in terms of a contrast between *simplex locution* (simple speech) and *artificiosus sermo* (artificial discourse). He describes his own style as simple and disclaims any ambition to achieve an artificial elegance. In this respect, he follows, ultimately, St. Augustine, whose *De Doctrina Christiana* renounced the Sophistic rhetorical tradition to create a new, Christian rhetoric, based on Cicero and designed for preaching the word of God.[2] Ælfric, in describing his own stylistic goals, seems to echo such passages in *De Doctrina Christiana* as this: "He who teaches will rather avoid all words that do not teach. If he can find correct words that are understood, he will choose those; if he cannot, whether because they do not exist or because they do not occur to him at the time, he will use even words that are less correct, provided only the thing itself be taught and learned correctly."[3]

That such simplicity did not imply a sterile asceticism is elsewhere made clear by Augustine. The task of the preacher, like that of the Ciceronian orator, is *docere, delectare, movere* (to inform, to please, and to move). The preacher must instruct, but he must also charm and arouse the emotions. There is room, therefore, within the general framework of simplicity for a gradation of styles: *genus submissum, genus temperatum,* and *genus grande* (the plain, the middle, and the grand style), corresponding to the three tasks of the orator. The good preacher must move from one style to another, not to display his own skill, but to instruct, charm, and finally move his listeners with a grave and restrained eloquence. "I think I have accomplished something not when I hear them applauding, but when I see them weeping" (*De Doctrina Christiana,* XXIV).

We need not assume that Ælfric was consciously following Augustine's counsels in his own homiletic theory and practice. They had become part of the patristic rhetorical tradition, sometimes appearing as perfunctory commonplaces in the work of writers whose own styles were anything but Augustinian in spirit. (We may, for example, read Abbo of Fleury's remarks in the preface to his *Historia Sancti Eadmundi,* one of Ælfric's sources.) Ælfric's acknowledgment of the Augustinian ideal was, however, anything but perfunctory. His own style is marked by the clarity and restraint Augustine recommends, but it also has the resources to rise to the eloquence of the middle and grand styles when the subject and the purpose demand it.

These qualities are apparent in Ælfric's earliest prose, even before he turned to the rhythmical prose for which he is best known. As an example, we may take the following paragraph from the first homily in the first series of *Catholic Homilies,* "De Initio Creaturae." It will be remembered that this piece serves as a kind of general introduction to the double series and consists of a sweeping survey of universal history. Beginning with a lofty passage in praise of God (ll. 1–18), Ælfric continues with a summary of the

Book of Genesis (ll. 18–27). He then proceeds to the next
pivotal events in Christian history: the life of Christ (ll. 279–315),
the Crucifixion and Resurrection (ll. 316–44), and the Judgment to
come (11. 344–52). In this particular passage, he is describing, with
great brevity, the life of Christ. It is naturally therefore something
of a set piece, and the entire homily is a particularly eloquent one,
but it is not so elevated as to be atypical of Ælfric's prose at this time:

He wæs *buton synnum* acenned, and his lif was *buton synnum*. Ne *worhte*
he þeah nane *wundra* openlice ær þan þe he wæs þrihtigwintre on þære
menniscnysse; *þa siþþan geceas* he him leorningcnihtas; ærest twelf, þe we
hataþ "apostolas," *þæt sind "ærendracan."* *Siþþan he geceas* twa and
hundseofontig, þa sind genemnede "discipuli," *þæt sind "leorningcnihtas."*
þa *worhte* he fela *wundra*, þæt men mihton *gelyfan* þæt he wæs Godes
bearn. He awende wæter to wine, and eode ofter sæ mid drium fotum, and
he gestilde windas mid his hæse, and he forgeaf blindum mannum gesihþe,
and healtum and lamum rihtne gang, and hreoflium smeþnysse, and *hælu*
heora lichaman; dumbum he forgeaf getingnysse, and deafum heorcnunge;
deofolseocum and wodum he sealde gewitt, and þa deoflu todræfde, and
ælce untrumnysse he *gehælde;* deade men he arærde of heora byrgenum
to life; and lærde þæt folc þe he to com mid micclum wisdome; and cwæþ
þæt nan man ne mæg beon gehealden, buton he rihtlice on God *gelyfe,*
and he beo gefullod, and geleafan mid godum weorcum geglenge; he
onscunode ælc unriht and ealle leasunga, and tæhte rihtwisnysse and
soþfæstnysse.

(He was born without sins, and his life was all without sins. He worked
no wonders openly, though, until he had been thirty years in the human
state. Then he chose followers for himself; first twelve, whom we call
apostolas, that is, "messengers." Then he chose one hundred and seventy-
two, who are called *discipuli,* that is, "students." Then he worked many
wonders, so that men might believe that he was God's son. He turned water
into wine, and went over the sea with dry feet, and he stilled winds with
his command, and he gave blind men sight, and the halt and lame good
movement, and the leprous smoothness of skin, and health of their bodies;
to the dumb he gave speech and to the deaf hearing; to the devil-possessed
and the demented he gave sanity, and drove out the devils, and he healed
all sickness; dead men he raised from their graves to life; and taught the
people he met with great wisdom; and said that no man could be healed,
unless he truly believed in God, and he be fulfilled and his faith adorned
with good works; he shunned all evil and all falsehood, and taught righteousness and truthfulness.)

(*CH* I.I, 295–315)

This prose may justly be described as simple, but it is far from naive or uncontrolled. Ælfric's purpose is not, of course, to summarize the life of Christ: he is writing a panegyric, brief enough to fit into the overall plan of the homily. He chooses, therefore, to focus on the miracles; and the general movement of the passage is that of a list of parallel items. The structure of the passage is thus easy to follow, even when delivered orally. The style, too, with its short clauses, its parallelism, and its pronounced rhythms, is eminently suited to oral delivery.

The chief patterning device is repetition. The above italicized words demonstrate how close the pattern of verbal repetition is in the passage; it serves to create an effect of unity and coherence purely as sound, beyond its reinforcement of logical parallels. The first sentence employs the phrase "buton synnum" in successive clauses, which are, however, varied in construction. "Ne worhte he þeah nane wundra" (1. 296) is echoed a few lines later in "þa worhte he fela wundra" (1. 301). In other cases, key words are repeated in variously inflected forms: "Gelyfan," "gelyfe," and "geleafan," and "hælu," "gehælde," and "gehealden."

A fair amount of alliteration of a clearly deliberate kind also appears, though it is not worked into a regular pattern. Most often it is found within a single phrase, rather than in successive phrases as a link between them: "Ne worhte he þeah nane wundra," "awende wæter to wine," "wodum he sealde gewitt," etc. Such uses of alliteration serve to reinforce what is perhaps the most prominent stylistic characteristic of the passage: the tendency of the prose to fall into pairs of short phrases or clauses balanced off against each other. It would be possible to arrange the passage to demonstrate this:

He wæs buton synnum acenned / and his life wæs eal buton synnum. he onscunode ælc unriht and ealle leasunga / and tæhte rihtwisnysse and soþfæstnysse.

But such balancing is almost wholly syntactical; no such devices as alliteration or regular stress are consistently used to bind the pairs together. Nor are all the groups simple pairs; groups of three are introduced:

deofolseocum and wodum he sealde gewitt,/
and þa deoflu todræfde, /
and ælce untrumnysse he gehealde.

The balance and parallelism of the passage, then, have nothing distinctive about them. They are used very skillfully, but not essentially differently from the way they are often employed in good prose of any language.

This one passage cannot fairly suggest the range of Ælfric's early style. The contents of the first series of *Catholic Homilies* run from methodical exposition of scriptural texts through straightforward narrative to such lofty and almost incantatory passages as the opening of the sermon quoted here, and Ælfric adjusts throughout his style to the task at hand. But, throughout its range, his style is marked by its clarity, the flexibility and consistency of its syntactic patterns, and its use of repetition, controlled rhythm, and frequent, though unpatterned, alliterative effects.

II *The "Rhythmical Style"*

The origins of Ælfric's rhythmical style have been the subject of much study. His models, both English and Latin; his purposes in adopting the style; and the principles upon which it is organized—all have attracted the attention of scholars. We may initially define his prose style as one built on a succession of two-stress phrases arranged in pairs linked by alliteration. It suggests the form of Old English alliterative verse, but it differs from the verse in that the rhythms of its two-stress phrases are much looser than those of the half-lines of verse, its use of alliteration is less strictly ordered, and its diction and tone are not those of verse.

We are clearly justified in regarding the rhythmical style as a prose style rather than a poetic style, though the tendency of early students of Old English was to regard it as debased poetry and thus as evidence of a presumed decadence in late Old English literature.[4] Furthermore, the style is not a particularly florid or mannered one, despite its comparative regularity and its capacity for intensification into an exalted eloquence where required. Ælfric's ideal remains the Augustinian one of "pure and plain words" and "simple speech" in his rhythmical as in his ordinary prose.

As we have seen, the rhythmical style begins to appear in certain items in the second series of *Catholic Homilies*. No sharp dividing line separates the rhythmical from the non-rhythmical style; there are transitional passages and to a certain extent the new style represents a development and a regularization of elements in Ælfric's earliest prose: the tendency toward paired phrases and the frequent alliteration. It has been suggested that, in adopting his rhythmical style, Ælfric was carrying a step farther his purpose, one implicit in his earliest works, of developing an English style comparable to good Latin prose. G.H. Gerould has suggested that the immediate inspiration for the rhythmical style was the highly artificial Latin "rhymed prose" of a number of Ælfric's sources, including Augustine, Jerome, Ambrose, Sulpicius Severus, Gregory of Tours, and Bede.[5] This "rhymed prose" was characterized by a heavy use of rhyme, parallelism, antithesis, alliteration, and, especially, rhythmical final clauses. The *cursus*, as the rhythmical final clause was called, had three major types, each involving two stresses and a set number of unstressed syllables: *cursus planus* (/ x x / x), *cursus tardus* (/ x x / x x), and *cursus velox* (/ x x \ x / x). Gerould believes that Ælfric imitated the *cursus* as it appeared in his sources very closely: "These rhythmic endings, along with the alliteration, explain why Ælfric's sentences have a flow that has hitherto been usually taken for the flow of verse. The cadence is wholly a matter of the endings, I believe."[6] He regards Ælfric's alliteration as an attempt to capture with a native substitute the effect of rhyme in his sources.

Gerould does not insist upon his belief that Ælfric's stylistic devices are so closely modeled upon Latin ones. He is chiefly concerned, he says, "to point out that Ælfric was writing prose of a studied sort rather than clumsy and formless verse." This point is a valuable one, as is the general one that Ælfric was accustomed to a heightened, semipoetic prose in his sources and may well have consciously sought to produce similar effects in his own language.

Dorothy Bethurum,[7] though generally agreeing with Gerould's treatment of Ælfric's style as ordered prose, opposes his conclusion that Latin rhymed prose was its principal inspiration. She believes his major models to be English: "Although Ælfric's lines are not the lines of classical Old English poetry and can not be scanned by its rules, they are composed under its aura, and their rhythm approximates that of the heroic poetry more closely than it approximates anything else. . . . He was undoubtedly inspired by the Latin rhymed prose, was sensitive to its effects, and tried to produce in English something comparable to them. But his rhythm was an English rhythm, arrived at in an English fashion and not in a Latin." The question has implications beyond the limits of style, for Miss Bethurum believes that Ælfric's prose was so reminiscent of heroic verse that it would have suggested to his audience a connection between his Christian saints and the old Germanic heroes.

We are probably safe in concluding, with Miss Bethurum, that Ælfric wanted to create an English prose comparable in effect to the heightened Latin of many of his sources and that, to do so, he drew upon the poetic devices of his own language. Gerould's correspondences between the Latin devices and Ælfric's are not very exact, and Ælfric was probably too conscious that every language has its "agene wisan" to attempt any such literal imitation as Gerould suggests.

Ælfric was not alone in seeking a heightened English prose style: we may add to Latin rhymed prose and Old English heroic verse, as models for his style, earlier English prose, especially homiletic prose.[8] The Blickling homilies and those of the Vercelli Book have passages which make heavy use of rhythm and alliteration. The anonymous Life of St. Chad, which its most recent editor dates about 850, similarly anticipates Ælfric in its poetic effects, as does the so-called Old English Martyrology, from about the same time. Even the Alfredian translations (except, perhaps, the Orosius) are highly alliterative in certain passages. The sermons of Wulfstan continue the tradition after Ælfric.

Nevertheless, Ælfric's rhythmical style, while comparable to the styles of earlier homilists and to Wulfstan's, differs from all of them. He uses his own kind of two-stress word-groups and alliteration much more regularly and consistently than any of his predecessors, as nearly as we can judge from the extant texts; and his practice differs radically from Wulfstan's, whose basic unit is the single two-stress word-group rather than the linked pairs of word-groups Ælfric uses. His style is, indeed, so distinctive that its appearance in a text is almost certain evidence of his authorship.

The principles of the style have recently been clarified by a number of scholars, including Angus McIntosh, J. C. Pope, and Peter Clemoes;[9] and the comments that follow are closely based upon their conclusions. The first appearance of rhythmical prose in Ælfric's work should suggest his reasons for adopting it, but the items in *Catholic Homilies* II in which it is first used do not seem clearly different from those in the ordinary style. Peter Clemoes has tentatively suggested that he may have begun to use it for material which demanded an unusually elevated style, such as the narrative of the Passion (*CH* II.XIV).[10] In its formal patterns, the style suggested the order and universality of his themes: "The rhythmical style is the language of the spirit. It is transcendental. The unity of its interrelated, regular sound is the artistic counterpart of the unity of an interrelated, regular universe."[11] Some such intention must have led Ælfric to adopt the rhythmical style initially; but it is interesting to note that, once he adopted it, he apparently used it for all purposes and for all kinds of material. Not only sermons and saints' lives but private letters and occasional pieces are in the rhythmical style. Of course, the works that have survived, even the "private" letters, are of a rather formal character. And, as McIntosh comments in connection with Wulfstan's apparently habitual use of his own rhythmical style, in an age in which even private reading was done aloud, there was no occasion for which a strongly oral, rhythmical style would have been inappropriate.[12]

Of the first works in the rhythmical style, the homily on Cuthbert (*CH* II.X) is one of the most interesting, not only for its subject but because its rather hesitant and inconsistent style suggests that it may be one of Ælfric's first attempts in the new rhythmical form. The following passage tells of Cuthbert's decision to leave the monastery at Lindisfarne and to retreat into seclusion on the tiny island of Farne:[13]

> *Cuþberhtus se halga   siþþan gefremode*
> *mihtiglice wundra   on þam mynstre wunigende.*
> *Begann þa on mode   micclum smeagan,*
> *hu he þæs folces lof   forflean mihte,*
> *þy læs þe he wurde   to hlisful on worulde,*
> *and þæs heofenlican lofes   fremde wære.*
> *Wolde þa anstandende   ancerlif adreogan,*
> *and on digelnysse   eallunge drohtnian:*
> *ferde þa to Farne,   on flowendre yþe.*
> *Þæt igland is   eal beworpen*
> *mid sealtum brymme,   on sæ middan,*
> *þæt wiþinnan eall   ær þam fyrste*
> *mid sweartum gastum   swiþe was afylled,*
> *swa þæt men ne mihton   þa moldan bugian*
> *for þeowracan   sweartra deofla*
> *ac hi ealle   þa endemes flugon,*
> *and þæt igland   eallunge rymdon*
> *þam æþelan cempan,   and he þær ana wunode,*
> *orsorh heora andan   þurh ælmihtigne God.*

(Cuthbert the holy   afterward worked
mighty wonders   living in the minster.
Then he began   often to meditate
how he might flee   from those people's praise
lest he become   too famous in the world
and be estranged   from heavenly praise.
He wished to take up   an anchorite's life
and in solitude   solely to live;
he fared then to Farne   in the flowing waves.
That island is   all surrounded
with salty surf,   in the midst of the sea,
and within, it was all   from long ago
completely inhabited   by dark spirits,
so that men could not   live on the land
for dread   of the dark devils;
but they all   fled together,
and gave up   the island completely
to the noble champion   and he lived there alone,
safe from their anger   through almighty God.)

(*CH* II.X,142)

The general principles upon which the passage is organized are fairly obvious upon even a cursory inspection, although the details of their application may present some problems. The sentences tend to fall into short phrases, usually with two stresses each. The syntax establishes these phrases, which resemble the half-lines of alliterative verse. They are, however, much less rigorously controlled than the half-lines of verse; an indeterminate number of unaccented syllables may appear in any position around the two major stresses. Secondary stresses may appear also, as in "ancerlif adreogan" (1. 7). In this brief passage, the number of syllables in each phrase ranges from four (as in "þæt igland is") to eight (as in "on þam mynstre wunigende"). The average for these thirty-eight phrases is almost six. McIntosh has found an average of seven syllables per phrase in the Life of St. Oswald (XXVI),[14] and Pope reports that this average is accurate for most of Ælfric's later prose.[15] The early pieces in the rhythmical style, however, tend to use shorter phrases. Even so, however, Ælfric's phrases are longer than the half-lines of the poets: *Beowulf*'s half-lines average less than five syllables. The range is greater, too; the range from four to eight in this passage is typical, though Pope reports a few lines of three syllables and a few of eleven or twelve.

The two-stress groups are linked in pairs by syntax and by alliteration, again in much the manner of alliterative verse. There need not be a caesura between the members of a pair, and often there is not; a pause is more likely to come after a pair, at the end of a full "line." The variety in the number of syllables in the two-stress phrases, combined with this tendency toward end-stopped lines with light medial caesuras, if any, might suggest that Ælfric's basic unit is the full, four-stress "line," rather than the two-stress phrase. But, though it is true that a sense of the full line is stronger in Ælfric than in most of the verse, the syntactic groups are clear enough, even without caesura, to establish the two-stress phrase as the basic unit.

The basic pattern of alliteration is similar to that used by the poets; but, like the rhythmic pattern, it is much looser. Brandeis has found that about two-thirds of Ælfric's lines alliterate according to the standards of Old English verse.[16] That is, with one alliterative sound, they alliterate *aa:ax, ax:ay,* or *xa:ay.* With two, they alliterate *ab:ab* or *ab:ba.* The other third, however, vary widely, from lines with no alliteration at all to lines in which all four stresses participate in the alliteration. The Cuthbert passage offers examples of some of the more common patterns:

> *aa:ax*
> *f*erde þa to *F*arne,   on *f*lowendre yþe
> *ax:ay*
> mid *s*ealtum brymme,   on *s*æ middan
> *xa:ay*
> Begann þa on *m*ode   *m*icclum smeagan
> *ab:ab*
> *m*ihtiglice *w*undra   on þam *m*ynstre *w*unigende

Three lines (1, 6, and 15) lack alliteration. Brandeis estimates that about ten percent of Ælfric's lines are not alliterative, though Pope points out that, if we admit alliteration of minor syllables, the figure may be reduced to about three per cent.[17]

The phonetic conventions of Ælfric's alliteration are similar to those of the poets. All vowels may alliterate with one another; consonants generally demand exact correspondence. Ælfric deviates from the practice of the poets chiefly in allowing *s, sc, sp,* and *st* to alliterate with one another and in allowing *hl* to alliterate with either *h* or *l.* As in *Beowulf, hr* may alliterate with either *h* or *r.* (In line 5, above, "læs" alliterates with "hlisful.") Other conventions peculiar to Ælfric have been suggested by Schipper and Brandeis, but Pope points out that evidence for them is not conclusive.[18]

The rhythms and the alliterative patterns are, then, much like those of Old English verse, though considerably freer. That the passage clearly has the effect of prose rather than verse is the result not only of the looser patterning, but also of the essentially prosaic tone and diction. Ælfric draws upon the highly developed body of Old English poetic diction very rarely and then only for carefully controlled effects, as when, in line 18 of this passage, he suggests with the poetic formula "þam æþelan cempan" the conventional Christian imagery of the "warrior of Christ." His prose frequently rises in tone to poetic effects, but it usually does so through a tightening of the regular controls into greater rhythmic and alliterative regularity, as in line 9, "ferde þa to Farne, on flowendre yþe," which uses no "poeticisms" but forms two regular poetic half-lines.

Attention to the rhythmical elements should not obscure the extent to which the prose continues to use devices of unity and coherence prominent in the earlier prose: repetition, parallelism, and balance over larger sections than the two-stress phrase. These devices are less prominent in such narrative passages as the Cuthbert piece than in expository passages, but even here the sentence beginning with line 3 is formed around the antithesis of "folces lof" and "heofenlican lofes." Line 10 is closely echoed in line 17, and lines 13 and 15 use repetition with slight variation in "sweartum gastum" and "sweartra deofla." The entire passage, which forms a small unit, begins and ends with brief summarizing statements.

It is difficult to reconstruct the effect of such a style, so imperfect is our knowledge not only of the sounds and stress patterns of Old English but also of the contemporary connotations of such devices as alliteration. But it seems clear that Ælfric's style is a remarkable combination of freedom and restraint; that it is capable of clear, ordered exposition and narrative; and that it is flexible enough to rise easily and naturally to greater eloquence.

III *The Style of the "Passion of Saint Edmund"*

The full range of Ælfric's style can be demonstrated by an examination of one of his most polished works, the "Passion of Saint

Edmund, King and Martyr" (*LS* XXXII). This piece, it will be remembered, is a radical adaptation of a Latin life by Abbo of Fleury and seems, perhaps more than any other of Ælfric's works, to exploit reminiscences of Germanic epic in order to present Edmund's life as the material for a "Christian epic." The exact date of its composition is unknown, but Clemoes suggests that it must be one of the early *Lives* because Ælfric says he wrote it "within a few years" of 985, when Abbo and Dunstan met.[19] Whatever its date, its style shows the full development of the rhythmical form with which Ælfric seemed to be experimenting in the life of Cuthbert. It is also interesting in the range of styles it uses, from formal panegyric to straightforward narrative and exposition to impassioned exhortation.

The "Passion of Saint Edmund" begins with a prefatory note in non-rhythmical prose in which Ælfric explains the transmission of the story of Edmund's martyrdom from his sword-bearer, a witness, to King Æthelstan and Dunstan to Abbo of Fleury. With line 13, however, as he begins the life itself, he adopts his highest manner for an opening panegyric:

> *Eadmund se eadiga,   eastengla cynincg,*
> *wæs snotor and wurðfull   and worðode symble,*
> *mid æpelum peawum,   pone ælmihtigan god.*
>
> *(Edmund the blessed,   king of the East Angles,*
> *was wise and honorable   and ever glorified,*
> *by his noble ways,   almighty God.*
>
> (*LS* XXXII.13–15)

This passage, which extends to line 25, comes very close to alliterative verse in the regularity of its rhythms and its alliterative patterns. All six of the two-stress phrases quoted conform rhythmically to poetic practice; they could be classified according to the Sievers types or analyzed, in modern terms, as dactylic feet. The alliteration is equally regular; of these thirteen lines, four alliterate *xa:ay;* three, *ax:ay;* and two, *aa:ay.* The other four have double alliteration: three, *ab:ba;* one, *ab:ab.* The syntactic structure of the passage is highly formal; three parallel sentences recite Edmund's virtues:

> *Eadmund se eadiga,   eastengla cynincg,*
> *wæs snotor and wurðfull . . .*
> *He wæs ead-mod and geþungen . . .*
>
> *(He was humble and devout . . .)*

(*LS* XXXII.16)

> *He wæs cystig wædlum and wydewum swa swa fæder.*
>
> *(He was bountiful to the poor and to widows like a father.)*

(*LS* XXXII.22)

With line 26, Ælfric's manner changes abruptly as he begins the narrative portion of the life. The arrival of the Danes, the exchange of messages between Hingwar and Hubba and Edmund, the martyrdom of the king, the miraculous recovery of his severed head, and his posthumous miracles are all described in a rhythmical, but less exalted, style. The rhythm and alliteration are still comparatively regular, but the stiffness of the opening rhetoric is relaxed and the two-stress phrases are looser in their syllabic structure:

> *Hinguar þa becom   to east-englum, rowende,*
> *on þam geare þe Ælfred æðelincg   an and twentig geare wæs,*
> *se þe west-sexena cynincg   siþþan wearð mære.*
>
> *(Hingwar then came   to East Anglia, rowing,*
> *in the year that the noble Alfred   was twenty-one years old,*
> *he who later became   the great West-Saxon king.)*

(*LS* XXXII.36–38)

Ælfric follows his usual practice of telling the story in strict chronological order, separating it into short episodes, each introduced by "þa" (then).

The style rises within this middle section of narrative most notably in the series of set speeches by Edmund and Hingwar's messenger (11. 43–93). Edmund's reply to his bishop who counsels submission deserves quotation:

> *Þæs ic gewilnige   and gewisce mid mode,*
> *þæt ic ana ne belife   æfter minum leofum þegnum,*
> *þe on heora bedde, wurdon   mid bearnum and wifum,*
> *færlice ofslægene   fram þysum flot-mannum.*
> *Næs me næfre gewunelic   þæt ic worhte fleames,*

> *ac ic wolde swiðor   sweltan, gif ic þorfte,*
> *for minum agenum earde,   and se ælmihtiga god wat*
> *þæt ic nelle abugan   fram his biggengum æfre*
> *ne fram his soþan lufe,   swelte ic lybbe ic.*

> *(This I desire   and wish in my mind,*
> *that I should not be left alone   after my dear thanes,*
> *who in their beds,   with children and wives,*
> *have suddenly been slain   by these seamen.*
> *It was never my way   to take to flight,*
> *but I would rather die,   if I must,*
> *for my own land,   and the almighty God knows*
> *that I will never turn aside   from his worship*
> *nor from his true love, whether I die or live.)*

(*LS* XXXII.74–82)

This eloquent epic speech achieves its effect not through an abrupt change of style or through the employment of traditional heroic verbal formulas, but through the tightening and intensification of the controls operating through the less exalted prose. The two-stress phrases become slightly more regular and economical in their syllabic content, the alliteration is handled with great care, and logical and syntactic groups are balanced off against each other rather more strictly than usual.

The style is similarly elevated at the end of the life (ll. 250–76) when Ælfric matches the opening praise of Edmund with a panegyric of all the English saints (the passage quoted in chapter 4). The life of Edmund is not thoroughly representative of Ælfric's mature rhythmical style because of its unusual eloquence. Much of Ælfric's rhythmical writing was more prosaic, but the life does exhibit very clearly the general characteristics of the style and its capacity for elevation. It is unusual only in its exceptional regularity. Pope [20] has analyzed its alliterative patterns in detail and found that of the 262 rhythmical lines (after the prefatory note), 246 alliterate regularly on the principal stressed syllables. A good number of them follow the strict practices of the "classical" Old English poets. Of the remaining sixteen lines, only two (151 and 193) lack any link between halves, and one of these is an exceptional line which imitates the cries of Edmund's head guiding the searchers:

> *Her, her, her;   and swa gelome clypode*
>
> *(Here! here! here!   and so it often cried out.)*
>
> (1. 151)

It is difficult to be certain about the reasons Ælfric adopted the rhythmical style, his own conception of it, or the impression it made on the contemporary audience. But its general effect and its relation to Ælfric's ideas and attitudes seem clear. It is analogous artistically to the graphic arts of his time: the drawings in such a work as the Benedictional of St. Æthelwold, executed during Ælfric's lifetime at his own monastery at Winchester, have something in common with his style. They are simple and symmetrical in design, often partly or wholly in outline. They make no attempt at literal, realistic representation; the lively and meticulously executed detail with which the basic designs are elaborated is ornamental, not realistic. The effect is that of a serene, generalizing art in which the individual detail is subordinated to the general purpose of presenting universal subjects with a lightly ornamented simplicity.

Ælfric's prose is like these drawings in its highly patterned clarity and simplicity. Its patterns are not so rigid as to be constricting, and it is capable of emotional effects, as we have seen. But it functions as a distancing device; its orderliness is a continual reminder of the universal order of which Ælfric writes, and the particular detail, the individual subject, is always seen from a universal perspective through the generalizing effect of the style.

In Ælfric's style, the major elements of tenth-century English culture meet: the clarity and serenity of the Classical tradition as it was transmitted to him through his Latin sources, the universal vision of his Christianity, and the native strength of the Germanic heritage. In this sense, Ælfric's style perfectly reflects the general qualities of his personality and his art. It is difficult for the modern reader, even if he is fluent in Old English, to penetrate the barriers which the passage of time and the shifts in assumptions and values have raised between Ælfric's time and ours and to gain a sense of the man himself. Compared with other Old English writers, he left a remarkably large body of work; but the nature of that work, the conventions of his time, and, we may suspect, Ælfric's own disposition made his work largely impersonal; the man himself is revealed only occasionally and only indirectly.

The keynote of Ælfric's work is didacticism, though in the very highest sense of that often pejorative word. Ælfric was above all a teacher—most immediately of the young students in the monastic school, then of the congregations to whom he preached, and finally of the English nation itself. His entire work is unified by its educational purposes. Beginning with a broad survey, in the *Catholic Homilies* and in the *Lives of Saints,* of the basic teachings of the church most necessary for laymen, he went on to provide, in the pastoral letters and other works, the knowledge priests and monks needed to carry out their work, and in the materials for Latin instruction, the means for raising the level of learning in the next generation. He seems to have been very conscious of the coherence of his work as a whole and was fond of listing his books in his prefaces and letters and of reorganizing and revising earlier pieces, such as the *Catholic Homilies*.

This desire to lead others to knowledge informs not only his work as a whole but each of its parts as well. The good teacher's desire always to be understood, for example, led Ælfric to his persistent striving for absolute clarity. Although most of his writings were translations and adaptations, we can see his mind at work behind each of them as he prunes, rearranges, and explains in order to make the material perfectly clear to his audience. His pedagogical sense of his audience's interests and needs led him also to his constant awareness of the time and place in which they lived. This concern found expression not only in such things as his rendering of Old Testament terms into homely contemporary equivalents and as his emphasizing English saints in the *Lives,* but more importantly, in the way such contemporary facts as the Danish invasions, the series of crises in leadership, and the efforts of the monastic leaders to revive learning shaped Ælfric's choices and emphases in his material. He seldom mentions contemporary events, but such themes as the righteousness of a "just war" of self-defense, the qualities of the Christian king, and the strength that God lends his people in their time of need recur again and again in his work. The teacher's sense of responsibility for the accuracy and authority of his material, too, lies behind Ælfric's care in selecting his sources, his regular practice of seeking the endorsement of his superiors, and his attempts to prevent later writers from distorting his work or destroying its integrity.

Although it is as a stylist—as the first major writer of English prose—that Ælfric is chiefly remembered, his commitment to the service of God through the teaching of his countrymen gave his prose its power and purpose. Its variety, its clarity, and its rhythmic strength are the perfect expression of the quiet devotion and the gentle humanity of its author.

Notes and References

Chapter One

1. There are a number of general histories and surveys of the Old English period. The fullest and most authoritative is Sir Frank Stenton, *Anglo-Saxon England,* Vol. II of the *Oxford History of England* (2nd ed., Oxford, 1947). Briefer are Peter Hunter Blair, *An Introduction to Anglo-Saxon England* (Cambridge, 1956) and D. P. Kirby, *The Making of Early England* (New York, 1968). Dorothy Whitelock, *The Beginnings of English Society* (Penguin, 1952) is sound, readable, and available in paperback. Her *Changing Currents in Anglo-Saxon Studies* (Cambridge, 1958) is a helpful supplement.

2. For a full account of the Romans in Britain, see R. G. Collingwood and J. N. L. Myres, *Roman Britain and the English Settlements,* Vol. I of the *Oxford History of England* (2nd ed., Oxford, 1937).

3. This important excavation is described and illustrated in C. Green, *Sutton Hoo: The Excavation of a Royal Ship Burial* (London, 1963).

4. See P. E. Schramm, *A History of the English Coronation* (Oxford, 1937), and H. R. Loyn, "The King and the Structure of Society in Late Anglo-Saxon England," *History,* XLII (1957), 87–100.

5. The poem has been edited by E. V. Gordon for Methuen's Old English Library (London, 1937). A good study of the background of the battle is E. D. Laborde, *Byrhtnoth and Maldon* (London, 1936).

6. In addition to the general works cited in Note 1, see, on the monastic reform, Dom David Knowles, *The Monastic Order in England* (2nd ed., Cambridge, 1949), M. Deanesly, *Sidelights on the Anglo-Saxon Church* (London, 1962), and R. R. Darlington, "Ecclesiastical Reform in the Late Old English Period," *English Historical Review,* LI (1936), 385–428.

7. *King Alfred's West-Saxon Version of Gregory's Pastoral Care.* Ed. and trans. Henry Sweet. Early English Text Society, OS 45 and 50 (London, 1871–1872), pp. 3–4.

8. See, on Dunstan, J. A. Robinson, *The Times of St. Dunstan* (Oxford, 1923) and E. S. Duckett, *St. Dunstan of Canterbury* (London, 1955).

9. For Æthelwold, see, in addition to the titles cited in Notes 6 and 8, H. W. Heim, "Æthelwold und die Mönchreform in England," *Anglia,* XLI (1917), 405–43.

10. Chapter 6 of Duckett, *St. Dunstan of Canterbury,* is devoted to Oswald.

11. *St. Dunstan of Canterbury,* p. 111.

12. Two useful summary treatments of the subject are Wilfrid Bonser, "Survivals of Paganism in Anglo-Saxon England," *Transactions of the Birmingham Archaeological Society,* LVI (1939), 37–70, and F. P. Magoun, Jr., "On Some Survivals of Pagan Belief in Anglo-Saxon England," *Harvard Theological Review,* XL (1947), 33–46.

13. See the sermon "On Auguries" (*LS,* XVII).

14. Useful general studies of Anglo-Saxon Christianity are M. Deanesly, *The Pre-Conquest Church in England* (2nd ed., London, 1963), and John Godfrey, *The Church in Anglo-Saxon England* (Cambridge, 1962).

15. See J. Ryan, *Irish Monasticism* (Dublin, 1931).

16. Christopher Dawson, *Religion and the Rise of Western Culture* (New York, 1950).

17. Clinton Albertson, "Anglo-Saxon Literature and Western Culture," *Thought,* XXXIII (1958), 111–12.

18. The identity of Ælfric and the basic chronology of his life and works were first set forth by Edward F. Dietrich in Neidner's *Zeitschrift für die Historische Theologie,* XXV (1855), 487–594, and XXVI (1856), 163–256. The other basic accounts are Caroline L. White, *Ælfric: A New Study of His Life and Writings,* Yale Studies in English, II (New Haven, Conn., 1898) and Marguerite-Marie Dubois, *Ælfric: Sermonnaire, Docteur et Grammairien* (Paris, 1943). A recent authoritative reconsideration of the chronology is Peter Clemoes, "The Chronology of Ælfric's Works," in *The Anglo-Saxons: Studies in some Aspects of their History and Culture Presented to Bruce Dickens* Ed. Peter Clemoes (London, 1959), pp. 212–47. The account here given is based closely on these studies.

19. Dubois, *Ælfric,* p. 32.

20. See Francis Wormald, *English Drawings of the Tenth and Eleventh Centuries* (London, 1952). Wormald has also prepared a facsimile edition of *The Benedictional of St. Ethelwold* (London, 1959).

21. On Anglo-Saxon monastic life, see Knowles, *The Monastic Order in England,* and John C. Dickinson, *Monastic Life in Medieval England* (New York, 1962).

22. See Knowles, *The Monastic Order in England,* pp. 448 ff., upon which the timetable below is based.

23. On monastic schools, see in addition to the books cited in Note 21, A. F. Leach, *The Schools of Medieval England* (London, 1915), pp. 31–95.

24. J. Kemble, *Codex Diplomaticus Aevi Saxonici.* 6 vols. (London, 1839–1848), item 656. See also P. H. Sawyer, *Anglo-Saxon Charters* (London, 1968), item 1217.

25. *The Chronicle of Æthelweard.* Ed. and trans. A. Campbell (London, 1962).

26. See, for the best expression of this view, Peter Clemoes, "Ælfric," in *Continuations and Beginnings: Studies in Old English Literature.* Ed. E. G. Stanley (London, 1966), pp. 182ff.

27. "The Chronology of Ælfric's Works." (See Note 18.)

28. Kemble, *Codex Diplomaticus,* item 714. See also Sawyer, *Anglo-Saxon Charters,* item 911.

29. White, *Ælfric: A New Study,* p. 152.

30. D. J. V. Fisher, "The Early Biographers of St. Ethelwold," *English Historical Review,* LXVII (1952), 381–91.

31. Clemoes, "The Chronology of Ælfric's Works," p. 242.

32. Clemoes, "The Chronology of Ælfric's Works," p. 245.

Chapter Two

1. Peter Clemoes, "Ælfric," in *Continuations and Beginnings: Studies in Old English Literature.* Ed. E. G. Stanley (London, 1966), p. 182.

2. Abraham Wheloc, *Historiae Ecclesiasticae Gentis Anglorum,* Libri V. a venerabili Beda . . . Scripti. (Cambridge, 1643).

3. Kenneth Sisam, *Studies in the History of Old English Literature* (Oxford, 1953), pp. 164–65.

4. Cyril L. Smetana, "Ælfric and the Early Medieval Homiliary," *Traditio,* XV (1959), 180–81.

5. On the sources, see, in addition to Smetana, James E. Cross, "Ælfric and the Medieval Homiliary—Objection and Contribution," *Scripta Minora: Kungl. Humanistiska Vetenskapssamfundet i Lund,* 1961–1962; James E. Cross, "Bundles for Burning—A Theme in Two of Ælfric's *Catholic Homilies*—With Other Sources," *Anglia,* LXXXI (1963), 335–46; James E. Cross, "A Source for One of Ælfric's Catholic Homilies," *Englische Studien,* XXXIX (1958), 248–51; and Charles R. Davis, "Two New Sources for Ælfric's *Catholic Homilies,*" *Journal of English and Germanic Philology,* XLI (1942), 510–13. The earliest extensive studies, still valuable, are Max Förster, *Ueber die Quellen von Ælfrics Homiliae Catholicae, I: Legenden* (Berlin, 1895), and "Ueber die Quellen von Ælfrics exegetische Homiliae Catholicae," *Anglia,* XVI (1894), 1–61.

6. See Smetana, "Ælfric and the Early Medieval Homiliary," p. 180, n. 4.

7. See Note 4.

8. F. Wiegand, "Das Homiliarium Karls des Grossen auf seine ursprüngliche Gestalt hin untersucht," *Studien zur Geschichte der Theologie und der Kirche,* I (1897). Wiegand's reconstructed table of contents has been reprinted, with modifications, by J. Leclercq, "Tables pour l'inventaire des homiliaires manuscrits," *Scriptorium,* II (1948), 205–14.

9. Clemoes, "Ælfric," p. 183.

10. See Cyril L. Smetana, "Ælfric and the Homiliary of Haymo of Halberstadt," *Traditio,* XVII (1961), 457–69. (The Haymo referred to is actually Haymo of Auxerre.)

11. Enid M. Raynes, "MS Boulogne-sur-Mer 63 and Ælfric," *Medium Aevum,* XXVI (1957), 65–73.

12. For a brief introductory treatment of this subject, see Harry Caplan, "The Four Senses of Scriptural Interpretation and the Medieval Theory of Preaching," *Speculum*, IV (1929), 282–90.

13. Quoted by Caplan, p. 284.

14. See Hanspeter Schelp, "Die Deutungstradition in Ælfrics Homiliae Catholicae," *Archiv*, CXCVI (1960), 273–95.

15. Schelp, "Die Deutungstradition . . . ," p. 280.

16. See Clemoes, "Ælfric," p. 191.

17. See Smetana, "Ælfric and the Early Medieval Homiliary," p. 188.

18. Förster, *Anglia*, XVI (1894), 58.

Chapter Three

1. Peter Clemoes, "The Chronology of Ælfric's Works," in *The Anglo-Saxons: Studies in some Aspects of their History and Culture*. Ed. Peter Clemoes (London, 1959), p. 219.

2. See, however, A. A. Prins, "Some Remarks on Ælfric's *Lives of Saints* and His Translations from the Old Testament," *Neophilologus*, XXV (1940), 112–22. Prins points out that Dietrich and Maclean both arrived at the number forty, but by different means, both questionable. Prins believes the extant manuscript contains only thirty-eight items and thinks the paraphrases of Judges and Esther must have originally been part of the set.

3. "The Chronology of Ælfric's Works," p. 220.

4. See J. H. Ott, *Ueber die Quellen der Heiligenleben in Ælfrics Lives of Saints* I (Halle, 1892), and C. Grant Loomis, "Further Sources of Ælfric's Saints' Lives," *Harvard Studies and Notes in Philosophy and Literature*, XIII (1931), 1–8.

5. See Constance L. Rosenthal, *The 'Vitae Patrum' in Old and Middle English Literature* (Philadelphia, 1936).

6. The fullest and most recent treatment is T. Wolpers, *Die englische Heiligenlegende des Mittelalters* (Tübingen, 1964). Still useful are G. H. Gerould, *Saints' Legends* (Boston, 1916); C. W. Jones, *Saints' Lives and Chronicles in Early England* (Ithaca, N.Y., 1947); and Bertram Colgrave, "The Earliest Saints' Lives Written in England," *Proceedings of the British Academy*, XLIV (1958), 35–60.

7. See C. E. Wright, *The Cultivation of Saga in Anglo-Saxon England* (London, 1939), pp. 40–51.

8. Rosemary Woolf, "Saints' Lives," in *Continuations and Beginnings: Studies in Old English Literature*. Ed. E. G. Stanley (London, 1966), p. 64.

9. Clemoes, "The Chronology of Ælfric's Works," p. 222.

10. "Saints' Lives," p. 40.

11. "Saints' Lives," pp. 64–65.

12. See Woolf, "Saints' Lives," pp. 43–44.

13. Dorothy Bethurum, "The Form of Ælfric's *Lives of Saints*," *Studies in Philology*, XXIX (1932), 522–23.

14. *An Old English Martyrology*, ed. G. Herzfeld. Early English Text Society, 116 (London, 1900).

15. See C. Grant Loomis, *White Magic* (Cambridge, Mass., 1948).

16. A good account of the Antonian life is Benjamin R. Kurtz, "From St. Antony to St. Guthlac: a study in biography," *University of California Studies in Modern Philology*, XII (1926), 104–46.

17. See Ott, *Ueber die Quellen . . .*, p. 58.

18. G. H. Gerould, "Ælfric's Lives of St. Martin of Tours," *Journal of English and Germanic Philology*, XXIV (1925), 206–10.

19. See Ott, *Ueber die Quellen . . .*, pp. 59–60.

20. C. Grant Loomis, "The Growth of the Saint Edmund Legend," *Harvard Studies and Notes in Philology and Literature*, XIV (1932), 83–113.

Chapter Four

1. Peter Clemoes, "The Chronology of Ælfric's Works," in *The Anglo-Saxons: Studies in some Aspects of their History and Culture*. Ed. Peter Clemoes (London, 1959), p. 240.

2. For a sound summary, see W. A. Craigie, "The English Versions (To Wyclif)," in *The Bible in Its Ancient and English Versions*. Ed. H. Wheeler Robinson (Oxford, 1940), pp. 128–45.

3. Arthur H. Abel, *Ælfric and the West-Saxon Gospels*. Unpubl. diss., University of Pennsylvania, 1962.

4. H. L. Hargrove, ed., *King Alfred's Old English Version of St. Augustine's Soliloquies*. Yale Studies in English, VIII (New Haven, 1904), p. 1.

5. W. J. Sedgefield, ed., *King Alfred's Old English Version of Boethius' De Consolatione Philosophiae* (Oxford, 1899), p. 1.

6. Quoted in Flora Ross Amos, *Early Theories of Translation* (New York, 1920), p. 55.

7. An interesting study of the way Ælfric referred to his work is Ann E. Nichols, "*Awendan*: A Note on Ælfric's Vocabulary," *Journal of English and Germanic Philology*, LXIII (1964), 7–13.

8. The most thorough study is Charles R. Davis, *Biblical Translations in Ælfric's Catholic Homilies*. Unpubl. diss., New York University, 1949. (An abridgment of this dissertation was published by N.Y.U., 1949.)

9. The subject is reviewed by Abel, *Ælfric and the West-Saxon Gospels*. (See Note 3.)

10. Davis, *Biblical Translations in Ælfric's Catholic Homilies*, abridgment, p. 6.

11. *Ibid.*, pp. 1–4. See also Max Förster, "Ælfric's s.g. Hiob-Uebersetzung," *Anglia*, XV (1893), 473–77.

12. Marguerite-Marie Dubois, *Ælfric: Sermonnaire, Docteur, et Grammairien* (Paris, 1943), p. 90.

13. Dubois, *Ælfric,* pp. 93–94.

14. The subject is reviewed and discussed in Josef Raith, "Ælfric's Share in the Old English Pentateuch," *Review of English Studies,* NS III (1952), 305–24.

15. Clemoes, "The Chronology of Ælfric's Works," p. 225.

Chapter Five

1. They are listed in the foreword to Zupitza's edition.

2. See books cited in Chapter 1, Note 23.

3. On the history of grammar, see J. E. Sandys, *A History of Classical Scholarship* I (Cambridge, 1903), 88–102.

4. A useful survey of early grammars is provided by Jackson J. Campbell, "Knowledge of Rhetorical Figures in Anglo-Saxon England," *Journal of English and Germanic Philology,* LXVI (1967), 5–10.

5. See Lawrence K. Shook, *Ælfric's Latin Grammar: A Study in Old English Grammatical Terminology.* Unpubl. diss., Harvard University, 1939, pp. 17–24.

6. *Ibid.,* pp. 20–21.

7. See, in addition to Shook, Edna R. Williams, "Ælfric's Grammatical Terminology," *Publications of the Modern Language Association,* LXXIII (1958), 453–62.

8. Marguerite-Marie Dubois, *Ælfric: Sermonnaire, Docteur et Grammairien* (Paris, 1943), p. 279.

9. They are listed in the Introduction to the best edition, G. N. Garmonsway, ed., *Ælfric's Colloquy* (London, 1939), p. 1.

10. G. N. Garmonsway, "The Development of the Colloquy," in *The Anglo-Saxons: Studies in some Aspects of their History and Culture,* ed. Peter Clemoes (London, 1959), p. 254, n. 2.

11. *Ælfric's Colloquy,* p. 10.

12. *Early Scholastic Colloquies.* Ed. W. H. Stevenson. Anecdota Oxoniensia, Medieval and Modern Series, pt. XV (Oxford, 1929). The background of the *Colloquy* has been studied by J. Zupitza, "Die ursprüngliche Gestalt von Ælfrics Colloquium," *Zeitschrift für deutsches Altertum,* XXXI (1887), 32–45; E. Schröder, "Colloquium Ælfrici," *Zeitschrift für deutsches Altertum,* XLI (1897), 283–90; and Garmonsway, "The Development of the Colloquy" (see Note 10, above).

13. "The Development of the Colloquy," pp. 258–60.

14. Eric Colledge, "An Allusion to Augustine in Ælfric's 'Colloquy,'" *Review of English Studies,* NS XII (1961), 180–81.

Chapter Six

1. R. W. Chambers, *The Continuity of English Prose from Alfred to More* (London, 1932).

2. See Charles S. Baldwin, *Medieval Rhetoric and Poetics* (New York, 1928), pp. 51–73.

3. Quoted by Baldwin, p. 65.

4. For example, see George Saintsbury, *History of English Prose Rhythm* (London, 1922), pp. 41–42.

5. G. H. Gerould, "Abbot Ælfric's Rhythmical Prose," *Modern Philology,* XXII (1925), 353–66.

6. *Ibid.,* p. 361.

7. Dorothy Bethurum, "The Form of Ælfric's *Lives of Saints,*" *Studies in Philology,* XXIX (1932), 515–33.

8. See Otto Funke, "Studien zur alliterierenden und rhythmischen Prosa in der älteren altenglischen Homiletic," *Anglia,* LXXX (1962), 9–36.

9. Angus McIntosh, "Wulfstan's Prose," *Proceedings of the British Academy,* XXXV (1949), 109–42; John C. Pope, "Introduction" to *Homilies of Ælfric.* Ed. John C. Pope. Vol. I. Early English Text Society 259 (London, 1967), pp. 105–36; Peter Clemoes, "Ælfric," in *Continuations and Beginnings: Studies in Old English Literature.* Ed. E. G. Stanley (London, 1966), pp. 176–209.

10. Peter Clemoes, "The Chronology of Ælfric's Works," in *The Anglo-Saxons: Studies in some Aspects of their History and Culture.* Ed. Peter Clemoes (London, 1959), p. 223. n. 3.

11. Clemoes, "Ælfric," p. 206.

12. Angus McIntosh, "Wulfstan's Prose," pp. 123–24.

13. I have departed here from the typography of both Thorpe and the rest of the quotations in this volume by spacing between "half-lines," in order to illustrate their structure more clearly.

14. "Wulfstan's Prose," p. 120.

15. *Homilies of Ælfric,* pp. 118–19.

16. Arthur Brandeis, *Die Alliteration in Ælfrics metrischen Homilien* (Vienna, 1897).

17. *Homilies of Ælfric,* p. 124.

18. *Homilies of Ælfric,* p. 128. The Schipper study is Jakob Schipper, *Grundriss der englischen Metrik* (Vienna, 1895), pp. 39–43.

19. Clemoes, "The Chronology of Ælfric's Works," p. 222.

20. *Homilies of Ælfric,* pp. 125–27.

Selected Bibliography

PRIMARY SOURCES

Almost all of Ælfric's works have been printed, but the editions are of uneven quality and some are difficult to obtain. This situation is being partially remedied both by new editions and by the reissue of some of the older editions. The first volume of Pope's edition of the previously unprinted homilies has appeared (see below) and a new edition of *Catholic Homilies* I is being prepared by Peter Clemoes for the Early English Text Society. The principal manuscripts are listed in the *Cambridge Bibliography of English Literature*. Ed. F. W. Bateson (Cambridge, 1941), I. 89–92, and in more detail, in N. R. Ker, *Catalogue of Manuscripts Containing Anglo-Saxon* (Oxford, 1957). The following list gives the best editions currently available in the order of their publication.

The Homilies of the Anglo-Saxon Church. The First Part containing the Sermones Catholici or Homilies of Ælfric. Ed. Benjamin Thorpe. 2 volumes. London: Ælfric Society, 1844–1846. No "second part" ever appeared. A translation is provided.

The Anglo-Saxon Version of the Hexameron of St. Basil and the Saxon Remains of St. Basil's Admonitio ad Filium Spiritualem. Ed. H. W. Norman. Second edition. London: J. R. Smith, 1849. Still the only edition of the *Admonitio*, but superseded by Crawford's edition (see below) for the *Hexameron*. Translation.

"Vita S. Æthelwoldi, Episcopi Wintoniensis, Auctore Ælfrico," in *Chronicon Monasterii de Abingdon*. Ed. J. Stevenson, Rolls Series 1858, Vol. II, pp. 255–66. In Latin. No translation, but translated by S. H. Gem, *An Anglo-Saxon Abbot* (Edinburgh: T. and T. Clark, 1912), pp. 166–80.

Old English Homilies, First Series. Ed. R. Morris. Early English Text Society OS 29 and 34. London: N. Trübner, 1867–1868. Ælfric's *De XII Abusivis* appears in two versions, pp. 107–19 and 299–304. The first version is translated.

Ælfrics Grammatik und Glossar. Ed. J. Zupitza. Sammlung englischer Denkmaler in kritischen Ausgaben. Berlin: Weidmann, 1880. Reprinted Darmstadt: Wissenschaftliche Buchgesellschaft, 1967, with a new preface by H. Gneuss.

"Ælfric's Version of Alcuini Interrogationes Sigeuulfi in Genesin." Ed.

G. E. Maclean. *Anglia,* VI (1883), 425–73, and VII (1884), 1–59. No translation.

Angelsächsische Homilien und Heiligenleben, Ed. B. Assmann. Bibliothek der angelsächsischen Prosa III. Kassel: G. H. Wigand, 1889. Reprinted Darmstadt: Wissenschaftliche Buchgesellschaft, 1964, with a supplementary introduction in English by Peter Clemoes. Items I–IX are by Ælfric. No translation.

Ælfric's Lives of Saints. Ed. W. W. Skeat. Early English Text Society OS 76, 82, 94, and 114. London: N. Trübner, 1881–1900. Translation provided.

"Excerpta ex Institutionibus Monasticis Æthelwoldi Episcopi Wintoniensis Compilata in Usum Fratrum Egneshamnensium per Ælfricum Abbatem." Ed. Mary Bateson. In *Compotus Rolls of the Obedientiaries of St. Swithun's Priory, Winchester.* Ed. G. W. Kitchin. London: Hampshire, 1892, pp. 171–98. Ælfric's letter to the monks of Eynsham; no translation.

Twelfth-Century Homilies in M. S. Bodley 343. Ed. A. O. Belfour, Early English Text Society OS 137. London: Oxford University Press, 1909. Items I–IV, VII–IX, XIII and XIV are by Ælfric. Translation provided.

Texte und Untersuchungen zur altenglischen Literatur und Kirchengeschichte. Ed. Rudolf Brotanek. Halle: M. Niemeyer, 1913. Item I (pp. 3 ff.) is by Ælfric. No translation.

Die Hirtenbriefe Ælfrics. Ed. Bernhard Fehr. Bibliothek der angelsächsischen Prosa, IX. Hamburg: H. Grand, 1914. Re-issued, Darmstadt: Wissenschaftliche Buchgesellschaft, 1966, with a supplement by Peter Clemoes. Contains Ælfric's pastoral letters, both English and Latin, and two Latin tracts on the seven ecclesiastical orders and the Ten Commandments. German translation provided.

Exameron Anglice. Ed. S. J. Crawford. Bibliothek der angelsächsischen Prosa, X. Hamburg: H. Grand, 1921. English translation provided.

The Old English Version of the Heptateuch. Ed. S. J. Crawford. Early English Text Society 160. London: Oxford University Press, 1922. Also contains "On the Old and New Testaments" *(Letter to Sigeweard)* and the Preface to Genesis. Only the *Letter to Sigeweard* is translated.

Ælfric's De Temporibus Anni. Ed. H. Henel. Early English Text Society 213. London: Oxford University Press, 1942. No translation.

Ælfric's Colloquy. Ed. G. N. Garmonsway. Methuen's Old English Library. 2nd edition, London: Methuen. 1947.

Ælfric's First Series of Catholic Homilies. British Museum Royal 7C. XII, fols., 4–218. Ed. Norman Eliason and Peter Clemoes. EEMF XIII. Copenhagen: Rosenkilde and Bagger, 1966. Facsimile.

Homilies of Ælfric: A Supplementary Collection. Ed. John C. Pope. Vol. I. Early English Text Society 259. London: Oxford University Press, 1967. No translation.

SECONDARY SOURCES

I. Books

BARRETT, CHARLES R. *Studies in the Word-Order of Ælfric's Catholic Homilies and Lives of Saints.* Occasional Papers, No. III, Department of Anglo-Saxon, Cambridge University, 1953. A useful stylistic study.

DUBOIS, MARGUERITE-MARIE. *Ælfric: Sermonnaire, Docteur et Grammairien.* Paris: E. Droz, 1943. Lengthy and often useful, though not always reliable in detail.

GEM, S. H. *An Anglo-Saxon Abbot: Ælfric of Eynsham.* Edinburgh: T. and T. Clark, 1912. A popular treatment, intended to present Ælfric and his times as relevant to England on the eve of World War I. Useful mainly for its translations of the Latin works.

JOST, KARL. *Wulfstanstudien.* Schweizer anglistische Arbeiten, XXIII. Bern: 1950. Contains much useful material on Ælfric's language. See, especially, pp. 159–76.

POPE, JOHN C. "Introduction" to *Homilies of Ælfric: A Supplementary Collection.* Early English Text Society 259. London: Oxford University Press, 1967. This book is listed above, but special attention should be called to the 190-page introduction, a major contribution to Ælfric studies.

SISAM, KENNETH. *Studies in the History of Old English Literature.* Oxford: Oxford University Press, 1953. "MSS Bodley 340 and 342: Ælfric's *Catholic Homilies,*" pp. 148–98, and "The Order of Ælfric's Early Books," pp. 298–301.

WHITE, CAROLINE L. *Ælfric: A New Study of His Life and Writings.* Yale Studies in English, II. New Haven, Conn.: Yale University Press, 1898. Old, but not completely superseded. Closely based upon Dietrich (1855–1856).

II. Essays and articles

BETHURUM, DOROTHY. "The Connection of the Katherine Group with Old English Prose," *Journal of English and Germanic Philology,* XXXIV (1935), 553–64. Important study of Ælfric's influence on Middle English literature.

————. "The Form of Ælfric's *Lives of Saints,*" *Studies in Philology,* XXIX (1932), 515–33. A reply to Gerould (1925), this article finds the major inspiration of Ælfric's rhythmical prose to be Old English alliterative verse.

CLEMOES, PETER. "Ælfric." *Continuations and Beginnings: Studies in Old English Literature.* Ed. E. G. Stanley. London: Nelson, 1966, pp. 176–209. Graceful, scholarly appreciation.

————. "The Chronology of Ælfric's Works," in *The Anglo-Saxons: Studies in some Aspects of their History and Culture Presented to Bruce*

Dickins. Ed. Peter Clemoes. London: Bowes and Bowes, 1959, pp. 212–47. An indispensable guide to Ælfric's canon and its chronology.

————. "The Old English Benedictine Office, CCCC MS 190, and The Relationships Between Ælfric and Wulfstan: A Reconsideration," *Anglia,* LXXVIII (1960), 281–83. A reply to Bernhard Fehr, "Das Benediktiner-Offizium und die Beziehungen zwischen Ælfric und Wulfstan," *Englische Studien,* XLVI (1913), 338 and 344–45. Clemoes points out that there is no evidence that Ælfric made the extract from Hrabanus Maurus referred to.

CROSS, JAMES E. "Ælfric and the Medieval Homiliary—Objection and Contribution," *Scripta Minora: Kungl. Humanistiska Vetenskapssamfundet i Lund.* 1961–1962. Supplements Smetana (1959) by pointing out several other sources for the *Catholic Homilies* in sermons found in the homiliary of Paul the Deacon.

————. "Bundles for Burning—A Theme in Two of Ælfric's Catholic Homilies—With Other Sources," *Anglia,* LXXXI (1963), 335–46. Continues the study of sources.

DIETRICH, EDWARD. "Abt Ælfrik: Zur Literatur-Geschichte der angelsächsischen Kirche," Niedner's *Zeitschrift für historische Theologie,* XXV (1855), 487–595; XXVI (1856), 163–256. The pioneer work in modern Ælfric studies; still not completely superseded.

FÖRSTER, MAX. *Ueber die Quellen von Ælfric's Homiliae Catholicae.* I: Legenden. Berlin, 1892. Still of value for the sources. The exegetical homilies are added in *Anglia,* XVI (1894), 1–61.

FUNKE, OTTO. "Some Remarks on Late Old English Word-Order with Special Reference to Ælfric and the Maldon Poem," *Englische Studien,* XXXVII (1956), 99–104. Supplements Barrett (1953).

————. "Studien zur alliterierenden und rhythmischen Prosa in der älteren altenglischen Homiletic," *Anglia,* LXXX (1962), 9–36. Good study of rhythmical styles before Ælfric.

GARMONSWAY, G. N. "The Development of the Colloquy," in *The Anglo-Saxons: Studies in some Aspects of their History and Culture Presented to Bruce Dickins.* Ed. Peter Clemoes. London: Bowes and Bowes, 1959, pp. 248–61. Supplements the useful introduction to Garmonsway's edition of the *Colloquy.*

GEROULD, GORDON H. "Abbot Ælfric's Rhythmical Prose," *Modern Philology,* XXII (1925), 353–66. Finds Ælfric's prose to be closely modeled on Latin "rhymed prose." See Bethurum (1932).

————. "Ælfric's Lives of St. Martin of Tours," *Journal of English and Germanic Philology,* XXIV (1925), 206–10. Good study of Ælfric's methods of adaptation.

HALVERSON, H. O. "Doctrinal Terms in Ælfric's Homilies," *University of Iowa Studies,* I. 1 (1932). Study of Ælfric's contribution to this area of the Old English vocabulary.

JOST, KARL. "The Legal Maxims in Ælfric's Homilies," *Englische Studien,* XXXVI (1955), 204–205. Brief but interesting note.

———. "Unechte Ælfrictexte," *Anglia,* LI (1927), 177–219. Examines Ælfric's contribution to the "Pentateuch." See Raith (1952).

KISBYE, TORBEN. "Zur pronominalen Anrede bei Ælfric," *Archiv,* CCI (1964), 423–35. Useful contribution to the study of Ælfric's style.

LADD, C. A. "The 'Rubens' Manuscript and 'Archbishop Ælfric's Vocabulary,'" *Review of English Studies,* XI (1960), 353–64. Study in attribution.

LOOMIS, C. GRANT. "Further Sources of Ælfric's Saints' Lives," *Harvard Studies and Notes in Philology and Literature,* XIII (1931), 1–8. Supplements Ott (1892).

MCINTOSH, ANGUS. "Wulfstan's Prose," Sir Israel Gollancz Memorial Lecture. *Proceedings of the British Academy,* XXXV (1949), 109–42, and separately. Also contains a precise and accurate description of Ælfric's style and a contrast of it with Wulfstan's.

MEISSNER, PAUL. "Studien zum Wortschatz Ælfrics," *Archiv,* CLXV (1934), 11–19; CLXVI (1935), 30–39. Notes on Ælfric's vocabulary.

NEEDHAM, GEOFFREY. "Additions and Alteration in Cotton MS Julius E VII," *Review of English Studies,* IX (1958), 160–64. Useful study of the principal MS of *Lives of Saints.*

NICHOLS, ANN E. "*Awendan:* A Note on Ælfric's Vocabulary," *Journal of English and Germanic Philology,* LXIII (1964), 7–13.

OTT, J. H. *Ueber die Quellen der Heiligenleben in Ælfric's Lives of Saints.* Halle, 1892. Still useful. See also Loomis (1931).

PRINS, A. A. "Some Remarks on Ælfric's *Lives of Saints* and His Translations from the Old Testament," *Neophilologus,* XXV (1940), 112–22. Considers the question of the number of items originally in *LS* and concludes that Judges and Esther, or perhaps Judith, must have once been part of the set.

RAITH, JOSEF, "Ælfric's Share in the Old English Pentateuch," *Review of English Studies,* NS III (1952), 305–24. Valuable review of the problem.

RAYNES, ENID M. "MS Boulogne-sur-Mer 63 and Ælfric," *Medium Aevum,* XXVI (1957), 65–73. Offers evidence that the MS is a "commonplace book" made by Ælfric.

SCHELP, HANSPETER, "Die Deutungstradition in Ælfrics Homiliae Catholicae," *Archiv,* CXCVI (1960), 273–95. Studies Ælfric's methods of interpretation.

SMETANA, CYRIL J. "Ælfric and the Early Medieval Homiliary," *Traditio,* XV (1959), 163–204. Demonstrates that Ælfric. in the *Catholic Homilies,* drew heavily upon a version of the Homiliary of Paul the Deacon. A very important study of Ælfric's sources and methods.

———. "Ælfric and the Homiliary of Haymo of Halberstadt," *Traditio,* XVII (1961), 457–69. Supplements Smetana (1959). The Haymo referred to is actually Haymo of Auxerre (See Pope, p. 157, n. 1).

WHITELOCK, DOROTHY, "Two Notes on Ælfric and Wulfstan," *Modern Language Review,* XXXVIII (1943), 124. The first note concerns the date of Ælfric's death.

WILLARD, RUDOLPH, "The Punctuation and Capitalization of Ælfric's Homily for the First Sunday in Lent," *Studies in English* (University of Texas), XXIX (1950), 1–32. Specialized but valuable study.

WILLIAMS, EDNA R. "Ælfric's Grammatical Terminology," *Publications of the Modern Language Association,* LXXIII (1958), 453–62. Study of Ælfric's coinages.

WOOLF, ROSEMARY. "Saints' Lives," in *Continuations and Beginnings: Studies in Old English Literature.* Ed. E. G. Stanley. London: Nelson, 1966, pp. 37–66. Places Ælfric in the tradition of Old English hagiography.

Index

DATE DUE

AGELESS SOUL

THE LIFELONG JOURNEY TOWARD MEANING AND JOY

THOMAS MOORE

THORNDIKE PRESS
A part of Gale, a Cengage Company

Farmington Hills, Mich • San Francisco • New York • Waterville, Maine
Meriden, Conn • Mason, Ohio • Chicago

LIBRARY OF CONGRESS CIP DATA ON FILE.
CATALOGUING IN PUBLICATION FOR THIS BOOK
IS AVAILABLE FROM THE LIBRARY OF CONGRESS

ISBN-13: 978-1-4328-4686-2 (hardcover)
ISBN-10: 1-4328-4686-8 (hardcover)

Published in 2018 by arrangement with Macmillan Publishing Group, LLC/St. Martin's Press

Printed in the United States of America
1 2 3 4 5 6 7 22 21 20 19 18

To James Hillman,
buddy (his word) and guide

CONTENTS

ACKNOWLEDGMENTS

While writing a book I keep my ears open to all useful ideas, even the slightest, that come up when I'm with friends, colleagues, and family members. They usually don't realize that I've just filed a mental index card when they said something stimulating. I am grateful beyond words to the following people. They fed me generously when I needed a fresh thought and a new direction. My friends: Robert Sim, Patrice Pinette, Gary Pinette, Carol Renwick, Hugh Renwick, Judith Jackson, Joel Laski, John Van Ness, Liz Thomas, Pat Toomay, and Mike Barringer. My colleagues (also friends): Todd Shuster, Denise Barack, Nancy Slonim Aronie, George Nickelsburg, and Hugh Van Dusen. New acquaintances: Burt Bacharach, Kristan Altimus, and Carl Shuster. The loves of my life: Ajeet and Abe. My soul-partner: Hari Kirin. I'm also

9

profoundly grateful to George Witte and Sally Richardson at St. Martin's Press.

INTRODUCTION

In a lovely quiet section of a large American city, a young architecture student was preparing a Zen garden for a new season after a long winter. As he worked, an old monk sat on a bench across the road watching him. The young man raked up the leaves that had covered the ground and spruced up plantings and bushes. He gathered the leaves into a large tarp and tied it up and pulled it far off to the side.

He looked over toward the monk, whom he knew was a well-known teacher of Japanese garden design. The monk stood up.

"A very nice garden," the monk said.

"Yes," the student responded. "So you approve?"

"One thing is missing," the monk said. The student helped the aged monk walk over into the garden. The old man went right up to the tarp, pulled on the rope, and let the leaves pour into the garden and blow in the wind. Then he looked at the newly disheveled space and smiled.

"Beautiful!" he said.

Wabi-Sabi is the Japanese aesthetic in which imperfection, age, brokenness, and a run-down appearance are considered beautiful. This is not strange to the modern eye, which also appreciates furniture that has dents, scratches, and layers of fading paint. A weathered barn isn't entirely unlike a person who has had a full life, and Wabi-Sabi is a good place to begin discussing the two basic aspects of a human being: the passing of time and ageless mysteries.

We, too, may develop dents and scratches, and we, too, may be beautiful nevertheless. As we go through both the satisfying and the unsettling experiences of our unfolding lives, it helps to keep in mind a simple phrase: "the beauty of imperfection." Age offers good things and bad things. And so we need to appreciate the value of an imperfect life.

A Zen master might say: "Aging happens." Our task is to be there for the aging, no matter how it shows itself, rather than fight it. Fighting anything makes it into an enemy and then it looks worse than it is. Keep working against aging, and before long you will have lost the battle.

The secret to aging is to face the loss of youthful beauty and strength, and from there use all the resources we have to be creative, positive, and optimistic. Whenever I use the word *optimism,* I think of the Roman goddess Ops and the abundance she gives to humankind. She was the sister and wife of Saturn, the very archetype of old age. Abundance herself, Ops is there to make our aging wealthy and pleasurable in the deepest ways.

As a psychotherapist, I can help people best by encouraging them to be where they are. I don't mean accepting a bad situation that needs correcting, like an abusive marriage, and I'm not talking about surrender or resignation. But if a person fights his situation without knowing what it's all about, he is bound to lose in the end.

For example, I worked with a woman who kept saying she wanted out of her marriage, which she felt was intolerable. But year after year she did nothing about it. She told me how friends and family members tried to convince her to leave, which only kept her frozen in place. I felt she needed to really be in the situation before she could leave it. I made a point not to speak in favor of ending the marriage, but rather to help her know where she was. Eventually, she stopped complaining and evading and simply got a divorce. Later she told me how happy she was with her decision, and she thanked me for helping her. Yet all I did was accompany her in her long and painful decision making, as though I were breathing in sync with her every breath.

It's similar with getting older. If you fight it and complain about its downside, you may be miserable for the rest of your life, because aging is one thing that doesn't get better. If you can be with it now, then you will be equally at peace when you're five years older. If you can just be with what is, you have a good starting point and a base. Then you can do other things to improve your situation. Don't get lost longing for a past golden age, and don't yearn for a different future. Let the leaves spill out over your ideals, and then see the full beauty of your life.

In all my work, following a long line of teachers, I look for the deep stories, the mythologies, and the eternal, archetypal themes that lie beneath the surface of ordinary experiences. We are not people simply dominated by time with its unwanted effects. We are ageless people, too, participating in a mysterious and wonderful process in which our eternal, unchanging selves

— I prefer to call it our soul — become more visible over time. This is the key sign that you are aging and not merely spending time — gradually you discover your original self, your own pristine way of being.

Aging is an activity. It is something you do, not something that happens. When you age — active verb — you are proactive. If you really age, you become a better person. If you simply grow old, passively, you get worse. Chances are, you will be unhappy as you continue the fruitless fight against time.

We tend to see time as a line that inevitably moves along monotonously like a conveyor belt in a factory. But life isn't so mechanical. Ralph Waldo Emerson once wrote a simple line that could change the way you look at aging:

The soul's advances are not made by gradation, such as can be represented by motion in a straight line, but rather by ascension of state, such as can be represented by metamorphosis, — from the egg to the worm, from the worm to the fly.*

Ascension of state. I imagine this ascen-

*Ralph Waldo Emerson, "Oversoul," *The Portable Emerson,* eds. Carl Bode and Malcolm Cowley (New York: Penguin, 1981), 214.

sion as a series of plateaus, initiations, and passages. Life is not a straight line but an array of steps moving from one level to the next, each level possibly lasting years. Often the ascension to a new level will be inspired by an extraordinary event, like a sickness, the ending of a relationship, the loss of a job, or a change of place.

Notice that Emerson could be speaking of a butterfly emerging from its worm state, a theme in the ancient Greeks' use of the word *psyche* for both *soul* and *butterfly.* We start out small and not too pretty, and we emerge in our older years with the beauty and wings of a butterfly.

By "ascension of state," I think Emerson means that we go through a series of phases or plateaus. When I look at my growth over the years, I focus on special events: leaving home for religious boarding school, ending my experiment with monastic life, being fired from a university position, marriage, divorce, the birth of my daughter, success with books, surgeries. These events mark the steps, but each one occupied a long period in which I grew up and aged. My soul emerged over several distinct, well-defined periods.

One more point about the structure of aging: As you move from one phase to another, you don't completely leave behind the phases that have occurred before. They don't go away; they are always available. This makes for a sometimes complicated life, but it also adds richness and resources. You can tap into the experiences you had when you were a child, a young person, or a middle-aged man or woman. Your youth is available and accessible. Even your personality, or more deeply, your very soul, is made up of many ages and many degrees of maturity. You are a layered being. You are many ages at the same time. Crossing through all these layers is a corresponding law: There is something in you that is not touched by the brush of time.

What Does It Mean to Age?

When I use the word *aging,* I mean becoming more of a person and more you over time. I keep an image in my mind of cheese and wine. Some get better with the simple passage of time. We set them aside to rest until they are ready. Time improves them, as an inner and invisible alchemy transforms them and gives them taste and flavor.

Human beings age in a similar way. If you let life shape you, then as time goes by you will become a richer, more interesting person. That is aging in the style of cheese

17

and wine. In that sense, your very purpose in life is to age, to become what you are; essentially, to unfold and let your inborn nature be revealed. You let your ageless self, your soul, peek out from behind the more anxious, active self, trying hard to be successful through planning and hard work.

Notice, too, that in this way of thinking, aging in the deep sense may happen anywhere along the way. You may be thirty-five and have an experience, learn some facts, or encounter a fascinating person who helps you evolve a step further. You age, in my meaning of the word, in those moments. Your soul ages. You take a step further toward being alive, engaged, and connected with the world. Even infants age. Some toddlers are quite aged. Some old people haven't gotten far in the aging process.

Growing Older Without Aging

Some people grow older in years, but their interactions with the world remain immature. They remain focused on themselves. Empathy and community elude them. They can't open their hearts to another person. They may hold on to anger and other difficult emotions that took hold early in life. They have experiences but don't grow up. They have birthdays but don't age.

18

As a writer, I sometimes run into people who don't want to bother with the difficult process of aging. An aspiring or even published author will ask me to look at her work. I read some of the words and feel that they haven't matured yet as ideas or craft. This happened recently, and I told the woman that she might benefit from reading some books on style and even grammar. I think she was insulted. She told me she was attending a workshop where they promised not to talk about the basics and to emphasize exciting ways to get published.

Sure enough, I looked at the workshop website and found the statement: "We will not be dealing with the dull basics but will stress techniques for creating a brilliant writing career." I felt that the ad was against aging. In whatever work you are doing, you need to develop the skills. You can't just skip over them and dive into fantasies of glory and success. To use Emerson's language, you don't go from one state to another without a challenging initiation. You have to do your homework.

I'm aware that those last words come from an old person's perspective and I know from my own experience that a younger, adventurous writer might want to shoot straight for the glory. I can only hope that my embrace of experience isn't so heavy that it would turn off a young person. Ideally, you can offer your insight without wounding youthful enthusiasm.

The Art of Being Affected

To age well it isn't enough to have experiences; you have to be affected by them. If you go through life without being touched, you may be continuously unconscious, never thinking about what is happening. You are protected or numb or simply not intelligent enough to understand what is happening to you. Some seem to prefer the carefree feeling of an empty head to the weight of being a real person.

Those who can say yes to life and engage the world grow up at every step, from youth to old age. You may be six months old when something happens to bring out your personhood. You may be ninety-nine when you make a leap into serious living — the possibility for aging never ends. You may think you're too old to grow up, but there is no time limit on aging. But if you never age, that is a problem. So is getting stuck at any period in your life. I like to keep at hand a saying from the profound Greek philosopher Herakleitos: *"Panta rhei,"* or "Everything flows."

I'll never forget the woman in her late sixties who rushed into my therapy room one day to tell me that she had had enough. She had been raised in a rigid religious family and never felt good about herself. No matter how hard she tried to be good, she felt she was a sinner. She realized, too, that she was hard on her husband, complaining about the slightest fun thing he did. She had been strictly against drinking, dancing, sports, and just having a good time.

"But it's over," she said that day. "I've seen the light again, and it's a different color. I'm not going to hide any longer and I'm not going to be my husband's conscience. I'm going to live and let live."

That day, I believe, this woman started to age in a positive way. She made a decision that some people make in late adolescence: not to be ruled by a narrow family outlook. She grew into her adulthood, choosing to no longer be controlled by the hard teachings laid on her when she was a child. "I've been a five-year-old all my life," she said. "It's time to be an adult."

This move out of the family mythology is one of the most crucial in the process of aging. Many adults haven't achieved it yet, and they suffer the consequences. To all appearances they grow up, but in their emotional lives they may be six or twelve or twenty-three years old.

People in their sixties and seventies may finally decide to shake the anxious, over-whelming, and burdensome influence of their parents. For years they have numbed themselves to the possibility of growing up. But once they understand what has been going on, they abandon that old pattern passionately. They get a taste of what it is to be themselves and they feel reborn.

The Joy of Aging

Let us be realistic about the downside of growing older, but positive about the joy of aging. If you find aging sad or frightening or even disgusting, maybe your imagination of it needs some tweaking. You could find meaning where before you saw only despair. You could probe more deeply and grasp the Zen parable of the leaves — bad times can make the good times beautiful. You become a real person, someone with individual judg-ment, a particular outlook on life and a set of values to believe in.

When you open yourself to a transforma-tive experience, whether it seems positive or negative, your soul blossoms. It is born in you again and again. Soul refers to our mysterious depth and substance, what remains after medicine and psychology have analyzed and explained us. It is a profound sense of self, far beyond what they call ego, and it helps us connect with others. The soul offers a strong sense of identity and individuality, but at the same time it includes a felt awareness of being part of humanity. In some mysterious way we and others share an experience of what it is to be human, and we do this so deeply that, according to many traditional accounts, we share one soul.

Some people have no such expansive sense of self and can't connect positively with others. They are more like machines than persons. These days, when our experts almost always offer mechanical explanations for experience, people easily develop a mechanical view of themselves. So for them, when they have a real experience, even a deep-seated interpretation of an experience, they feel they're entering life fresh.

I've received several notes from readers telling me that they discovered that they have a soul, but only after learning about it. They needed a word for what they sensed intuitively. They needed to know that for centuries people have humanized culture by speaking of the soul. Once they discover this soul, they live differently and have a far different understanding of themselves.

Soul is not a technical or scientific term. It's an ancient one, rooted in the idea of breathing and being alive. When people die, suddenly something is missing, a source of life and personality, and that missing element has been called soul. It lies deeper than personality, ego, consciousness, and the knowable. Because it is so vast and so profound, it requires both a spiritual and a psychological mind-set to appreciate it.

If you don't nurture your soul, you are not aging. You may feel like a cog in the mechanics of society. You may be active, but your activity doesn't generate a deep awareness and connection with the world around you. When you really age, you are engaged, and from that deeper taste of being a participant, your life finds purpose and meaning, gifts of soul. Now aging is a joyful experience, because you want to be open to learning and experiences as you feel the seeds of your self sprouting and blossoming in your evolving life.

■ ■ ■ ■

PART ONE:
RITES OF PASSAGE

■ ■ ■ ■

1
THE FIRST TASTE OF AGING

In adolescence, individuals start to perceive their age more in social and psychological terms and, indeed, frequently report feeling significantly older than their chronological age. This process continues in early and middle adulthood, yet the subjective experience of age now starts to take the opposite direction and individuals report feeling younger than their chronological age.*

The first taste of getting old can be unsettling. You have been cruising along without giving much thought to age. But then you notice an unfamiliar stiffness and soreness after exercise. You can't stand up from a

*Manfred Diehl, Hans-Werner Wahl, Allyson F. Brothers, Martina Gabrian, "Subjective Aging and Awareness of Aging: Toward a New Understanding of the Aging Self," *Annual Review of Gerontology & Geriatrics* 35, no. 1 (April 2015), 1–28.

crouch as you used to. You see some wrinkles and a new crease. People treat you differently, offering to help you and asking about your health, saying how wonderful you look in a way that says: "You look good — for your age!"

Each decade feels different. When I turned thirty, I didn't know I was young. I never thought about age. When I became forty, I felt a jolt for the first time and became aware that I was older than some of my friends. A faint scent of aging. When I turned fifty, I could no longer deny that I was getting older. I began receiving mail for the senior citizen at my address. But I was in good shape and didn't notice many physical indications. Sixty was not an easy birthday. I was in Ireland, and a neighbor was celebrating his fortieth at the same time. I felt ancient in comparison and began to wish that I had been born twenty years later. Your comfort with age is delicate and easily upended.

When I consider aging, I think of my friend James Hillman, who was one of the most remarkable people I've ever met. He began his life as a writer and then became a psychoanalyst, basing his work largely on the psychoanalytic pioneer C. G. Jung — for years he was the head of the training program at the Jung Institute in Zürich.

But James went his own way in a community that honored every word Jung wrote, making revisions to Jung where he thought fit. He was an original thinker, always turning old and familiar ideas upside down, and he was passionate about bringing soul to every aspect of life. He didn't want to define therapy as just having to do with an individual's deep process. In his later years he was especially interested in the soul of the world, and he wrote eloquently about transportation, politics, city planning, racism, architecture, and gender issues.

When James turned sixty, he threw a big party to celebrate the big turn in his life. He told me privately that at sixty he wanted to enter old age consciously, and not let the years slip past. On a small outdoor stage in the round at his house in rural Connecticut he put on a talent show accompanied by a smoky outdoor roast, and several of his friends performed. He himself did a lively tap dance.

But after the party, to all appearances, he didn't change much. He kept his vigor and was active and productive. I felt that the hoopla he created was premature in some ways, and yet for him sixty was an important marker. Maybe the party was an unconscious way of keeping old age at bay.

In my mid-sixties something happened that forced me to think seriously about aging. I was on a book tour in San Francisco, walking up and down the steep hills, when I felt an unusual pain in my back. I went on to Seattle and again felt the pain and became dizzy even on a flat street. I stood at a corner amid heavy car and pedestrian traffic and held on to a post for a few minutes, my head spinning. I thought it might be pneumonia, which I had contracted on two previous tours. When I got home, my doctor suspected a heart problem and scheduled a stress test.

It turned out that I had considerable blockage in one of the main arteries. Having them cleared out with tiny boring tools and receiving two stents wasn't painful, but I found it difficult to recover emotionally. As soon as I got home from the hospital and lay back on a comfortable reclining chair, I felt Saturn place his buttocks on my chest. I went into a mild depression. My wife says that I became a different person, softened and more relaxed. I certainly felt older.

Even now, ten years later, it seems that those days of recovery were a turning point in which I really began to feel my age. The slope tipped in a downward direction. But the depression didn't last long. Besides, I felt so good after the treatment that I also gained back some youth. In the years since then I have had an active and productive life, both in my career and with my family.

I took up golf as a way to get more exercise, and I found the game relaxing and fun. This game that many find silly or only for the upper crust helped me relax, get more play in my life, and develop new friendships in a light and happy context. While playing at down-home local courses, I met a variety of people from all backgrounds and enjoyed many deep and moving conversations. The game also put me in a meditative state, and sometimes I'd come off the course with a story in my mind. I collected and published eighteen of these stories, each making a certain subtle point about human nature.

As we'll see, sensing your old age and your youth at the same time is a signal that you're aging well. After my surgery I felt both older and younger and enjoyed the benefits of each. In part, my new peace of heart came from entering the new flow of aging, in contrast to any attempt to stay inappropriately young. Any traces of the ambitious hero seemed to fall away.

Now seventy-six, I notice when someone

in her early fifties or even forties complains about growing old. I'd love to be fifty-five again, when my daughter was four. I liked telling her, when she asked my age, that I was "two nickels," or five-five. I felt good and was able to do anything physically. I had no worries about my heart or other things that might be falling apart. But I understand that an awareness of aging comes in steps and phases. You get glimpses, and those hints accumulate into a loss of youth. Professional psychology calls it "subjective aging." I think of it as the aging of the soul.

Fleeting Youth

We say that youth is fleeting. By that we usually mean that our youth goes by fast and it's gone before we know it. But in mythology, stories full of insights into what is eternal and essential in human life, young people are fragile and often live short lives. It isn't just that the years go by fast; there is something about youth that is brief and vulnerable. The well-known phrase "eternal youth" means that when we are young, we may feel that youth will last forever. So then, as we notice signs of growing older, the shock is strong. The shiny glass sphere of eternal youth develops a crack.

In Greek mythology young people often come to a quick end, and that myth stirs whenever we hear about a young person whose life has been cut short. Icarus is well-known for putting on wings crafted by Daedalus to fly up high into the sky, only to have those wings melted by the hot sun. He falls, plummeting into the sea. Phaethon was a young man whose ambition was to drive the chariot of his father that made the sun rise each morning. He tried but came down in a fiery crash. We idolize movie actors who die young, after being "stars," and some of us mourn young people close to us who lived short lives.

Lessons in the ageless soul are sometimes bitter. My daughter lost a friend not long ago, a gifted, bright young man in her Sikh community. He fell off a mountain cliff while on a simple hour-long hike. It has been two years since the accident, and the community is still in shock. A promising young man losing his life throws his community into deep and painful wonder about the nature of things.

We have to find our way toward appreciating the ageless soul, the meaning of a life that wasn't allowed to reach full maturity, to say nothing about old age. We are forced to consider that the life of the soul may be complete and full without the usual span of time that includes getting old. Aging, in the sense of becoming a whole person, is not the same as growing old.

We can learn several lessons from the mythological stories about young men. One is to keep our ambitions even and moderate. Peaking too high can cause a painful crash. This could mean, psychologically, that youth and old age should be joined together as long as possible, the mature element in us keeping the valuable immature part from reaching too high and the spirited youth keeping us ever on the adventure, not giving up because we're getting old.

When I was a music student in my early twenties I had a professor who was something of an Icarus. Donald Martin Jenni had been a musical prodigy and was also remarkably gifted in languages. When I met him, he was working on a degree in world literature by reading all the assigned texts in their original languages. I remember the time when he was reading *War and Peace* in Russian. One story is told of how he stepped in at the last minute to be the translator for a Vietnamese speaker who was visiting the college. He was also a musical genius with an ear beyond normal human limits. I sometimes wonder if the reason I didn't pursue my career in music — I was a composition major — was that I was discouraged by having such a genius for a teacher. I knew I could never equal him.

Don embodied one of those soaring boys of myth. His gifts and talents were remarkable. But for the most part he didn't show signs, not to me at least, of reaching too high. For all his abilities, he also had the discipline to study hard and balance his genius with hard work. In style he was somewhat aloof and some would say arrogant, but I found him remarkably even and humble. I was his friend for six years, but I couldn't keep up with him. I was a mere mortal and he was born on Mount Olympus.

From reports I heard, in later life Don kept his even profile, though he continued to astonish with his talents. His students loved him as a professor, and he made significant contributions to education and to his art. I mention him as an outstanding example of someone who was filled from birth with the spirit of youth yet able to suffuse that creative spirit with qualities of the mature man. You can do the same.

You do it not by surrendering your adventurous spirit in the name of maturity, but by taking your vision seriously and doing the hard work required to keep it alive and effective. Don's soaring imagination inspired him to study hard, do research, and prepare for challenging concerts.

You may not be a genius and yet still enjoy a strong youthful spirit. You need to enrich that youthful spirit, as early as you can, with a corresponding seriousness and willingness to engage the world, be close to people, and do the hard, sometimes routine, and uninteresting work. When the first taste of aging appears, you can worry about it, if you want, but welcome it as well. Understand that it has much to give you and can be a way of providing the other half of life, the one you've neglected by indulging in your youth.

At that first taste of old age, you may realize for the first time, in your own body and soul, that the youth you've taken for granted is fleeting. You didn't know this when youth reigned, but now you'll never forget it. That first taste is a turning point with no going back. Now you will probably appreciate your youth more than ever, but don't give up. You can keep your youth forever.

I was at a neighborhood party, standing in line for a potluck dinner, deep in thought about this theme, when the man in front of me introduced himself. I noticed that he had gray hair at his temples, and his wife looked younger than he did. I told him that I was writing a book on aging. Immediately he frowned and said, "I'm forty-five and just recently came to the realization that I'm getting old. I decided that I have to do some things right now so that when I get old I'll be in good shape. I have to eat right and exercise and enjoy my youth while I have it."

The line at the food table stopped as this unsettled man described his problem with aging. It wasn't the best occasion to mention that he might be fighting age too vigorously. Clearly he was upset at the perceived loss of his youth and was anxiously doing his best to combat it.

Often we try to head off age by doing what society tells us will keep us young. But it might be better to welcome age and honor youth at the same time. My dinner mate was trying to be clever and block the aging process. He spoke in favor of youth but wanted to frustrate aging. I kept hoping to hear him say something good about getting older. Had he forgotten that youth has its downside as well?

At the same party, I had a long talk with my old friend Gary. He and I see life much in the same way and often compare notes and laugh at the human condition. He's interested in what we're going to do as a society when the system of work and money we have collapses because we have not taken care of the planet or the majority of people on it. "Yes," I said. "I'm writing about aging as a personal matter, but it's the same issue with society. We're not preparing for our old age, and we're not aging well in my sense of the term. We're not growing up properly and dealing with our problems intelligently. We're just assuming that the future will automatically turn out all right."

"Denial," Gary said.

"Heads in the sand."

"Tragic."

Gary said he had to get home, and as he reached for his coat he gave me some good book titles on the cultural issue of dealing with a decaying system. I decided to stay focused on the individual's problems with aging, hoping that some movement forward there might help society.

The Stages of Aging

Growing old catches up with you gradually and in stages. The first taste is the beginning of a process that moves along in a series of plateaus. First, you notice a few

AGELESS SOUL

k or run as far as
ried, but the full
oesn't fall flat on
r other signs. In
itive to the theme
ely. You begin to
st time, about the
tart counting the
ou can tell when
for you when you
e these that you

ely, and as many
at constitutes old
re to culture and
ny are saying that
and today many
be the real begin-
me call old-old age.
g in different ways,
more complicated
ets a special subjec-
e or she approaches
g of being younger
period in one's life
he circumstance to

t writing this book,
a group of psychia-
host referred to me,

with the intention of giving me some honor, I'm sure, as one of the elders in my field. I wasn't expecting the word *elder*. This was the first time anyone used it to refer to me, and I felt shock. It was my first taste of old-old age. I reacted by making an anxious-sounding humorous remark that only made matters worse.

I thought I had dealt quite well with getting older, and yet this uncomfortable moment, sparked by a single positive, uncontroversial word indicates that I have more work to do. I wonder if it will ever end: Will I always have a new experience of entering yet another stage of growing old? My friend Dr. Joel Elkes — I'll say more about him later — told me that he couldn't wait for his one hundredth birthday to pass so that he could get on with his life and not focus on age so much. When my father celebrated his one hundredth birthday, he seemed to really enjoy his party, but I could see that immediately afterward he was happy to go back to his ordinary life. Aging is a fact of life. You might want to honor it and reflect on it, but you don't need to be obsessed with it.

Phases in Aging

Although there are countless ways we could determine stages in the aging process, for my purposes I see the following five phases as basic:

1. Feeling immortal
2. First taste of aging
3. Settling into maturity
4. Shifting toward old age
5. Letting things take their course

For about a quarter of a century you don't think much about age and don't imagine the end. The first taste is something of a shock, as literal youth is left behind. The next phase is a gradual process that takes years, as you create structures for your life and become somebody else. Fourth, you slowly realize how many ways you are no longer young and have to adjust to many changes. Lastly, you can put on old age like a tailored coat. Then you identify yourself as an elder. The final phase is quasi-mystical: You forget about age, deal with your physical problems matter-of-factly, and let yourself be free of judgment and other limitations. You may develop a more mystical approach to life and aging and worry less about what other people think.

A colleague of mine is in his mid-forties. Recently he told me how he noticed a sign of getting older: He has to hold printed words away from his body at an arm's length to read them. He told the story as if some minor tragedy had taken place. In fact, it was a first-taste experience, one that jars you out of youthfulness into a larger sense of time and some awareness of the arc of your life. This momentous change in your life, your awareness of aging, may be nothing more than adjusting your prescription or buying a pair of reading glasses. At a deep level, these moments, however trivial they may appear, are true rites of passage.

For the Greeks, Hermes is our companion on life's journey, and he helps us grow up mainly through surprise. Mythologically, the feeling of shock you get each time you become aware of getting older could be a gift from Hermes, a step into your destiny, and that sensation of shock can help you age with some awareness and control.

You need at least a small shock so that you can feel the impact and not let it drift by. A shock is a small wakening, and it's true that without these shocks we might remain unconscious and let the years pass by without reflection and without a constructive response.

In those apparently insignificant turning points when you really feel age taking over, it's tempting to indulge in the sad reality of aging; however, this might be the best time to appreciate the youthfulness you have. The first taste is a pricking of the psyche into awareness that life is afoot, that something is going on. You have reached a telling moment, an early awareness of aging. Now you can begin to think of your life as taking a longer and greater arc and imagine that some significant changes are just getting under way.

This first taste may be a shock because, before, you comfortably assumed that you would be eternally young. As we have seen, that is part of the archetype of youth: You imagine that it will last forever. When you feel old age arriving, you sense that something is different. It sparks a process of serious change in orientation. The spark may feel like a jolt of electricity and may unsettle you. But you don't have to give everything of yourself to it. Take serious note of it and then go on enjoying your youth. Stretch out that youthfulness as long as you can — to the very end, if possible.

Recently I was sitting in a dentist's chair about to have an implant to replace a baby tooth I had enjoyed for seventy-odd years.

The dentist said it was the oldest tooth he had ever seen, and that news didn't make me happy, especially in the presence of a much younger man. He had been a little late for the appointment, and before drilling into my jaw he pointed to a bandage on his cheek.

"I had a cancer removed from there this morning," he said with some frustration. "I'm forty-six years old. I'm too young for this. Now I have to stay out of the sun and use sunblock." First taste of aging, I said to myself. An initiation. A deep change. It takes some getting used to.

I'm speaking as though the first taste of aging automatically takes place in your forties. But I have an early memory of my aunt one day going into a fit of crying. The family tried to console her, but it took a long time for her to pull out of it. She was overcome by the awareness that she was getting old. She was sixteen.

When my daughter was born and I was in the birthing room with her mother, I remember holding her when she was only minutes old and thinking that already she was getting old and would face challenges and sickness and, of course, death. I didn't intend or try to have these thoughts. They simply came to me. A father's first glance at the full arc of his daughter's life.

At that moment, for me, thoughts of my infant daughter's inevitable aging made me cherish the beauty and joy of that moment, minutes after her birth. I packed those thoughts and sensations away and I find that, twenty-five years later, I can still draw on that joy.

One thing my daughter and I like to do now is watch an old home movie in which she is a little girl taking a bath in the large tub in our then-beautiful, oversized bathroom. Her feet are crossed and lying on the edge of the pearly white tub. I am looking out the window at the view we had at that time. She asks me what my favorite animal is, and talks in the funny dialect of a four-year-old girl.

I loved that little girl so much that to watch us enjoying an ordinary day in the bathtub gives me endless pleasure. It allows us to visit an Eden-like moment in the past. I love her as much now, but being able to keep those other moments in mind — her birth and that bath — reminds me and restores me to the timelessness of a father's love. If that moment at the bath is not a soulful one, then I have never seen such a thing.

My thoughts at the birth of my daughter

also pictured life as complete from the beginning. Today we tend to see everything in a linear, horizontal fashion. We think of a human being on a numerical chart going from left to right, from zero to around one hundred. But my thoughts didn't put my daughter at zero. At that precious moment of birth she was all her ages at once.

Because we think in a linear way today, we are tempted to treat children as though they are nothing, zero, and old people as though they are beyond counting, and therefore also worthless. We fear growing old, when, from a more subtle point of view, we were old from the very beginning. We're just discovering our age, or putting it into practice. In this way of picturing it, aging is a fulfillment of who we are, not a wearing out.

Still, that first taste of aging stings. As long as you are identified by your youth, you never have to think seriously about getting older. But a taste of aging marks the beginning of a passage out of youth, a passage most of us would rather not enter. People around the world have recognized the importance of this particular passage, from youth to adulthood, and have invented strong rituals to help navigate the transition.

We have our own rituals, like getting a driver's license, voting for the first time, and graduating from high school. Any of these experiences give you the clear sensation that you've taken a big step, turned a corner, and entered into unknown territory.

We could use such rituals throughout life, because the passage into our maturity and old age happens in many stages and many different experiences may mark the transitions. Illness, a new job, a new relationship, the passing of a close relative or friend, or even an important event in society may take you to yet another place in your journey. Notice that each of them may well involve some pain.

This sting is an important part of growing up, not necessarily growing old. If we are not stung into awareness of our limitations, our personalities will be lopsided. We'll identify only with youth and we will not have the benefits of the archetype of the old person, with his or her wisdom and weight. You probably know people who are too young emotionally. They haven't grown up and matured. They don't take life seriously. They don't know how to be in the world, hold a serious job, or engage with people gracefully.

Every advance in life involves a sting. It

wakes you up and encourages you to pay attention. If you avoid the sting or explain it away or numb yourself to it, you don't age, and that is a tragedy.

A Tale of Two Plumbers

As I was writing the last few paragraphs, two plumbers came to my house to repair our ductless heating system. One, the older but not old-old man, introduced himself and offered to check out the condenser. His younger partner didn't say a word — no greeting, no conversation. I noticed that he was looking into rooms he had no business with. He was just being nosy, while still saying nothing. The older one asked if he could check out our bedroom, while the younger, silent one walked into our bathroom. I hoped my wife wasn't getting dressed, since it was early in the morning. He looked around and remained silent, which was not surprising, since he had no reason to be in the bathroom.

When the two plumbers left, I felt like calling the owner of the business and telling him I didn't want that young man in my house again. He felt threatening, although he may only have been immature. What was his problem? I thought that maybe he hadn't been stung into old age. He was indulging his eternal youth without the benefit of social graces, responsibility, and a sense of boundaries. I'd like to think that the older one would teach the young man how to act in an adult world, but even though he was more mature, he didn't appear to have the capacity to be an elder. He wasn't yet able to guide the young. I realized that two eternal youths, not yet initiated into adulthood and of different ages, had visited my house.

Maybe our world in general is suffering from a widespread failure in dealing with prolonged youthfulness. We fear old age, and we don't seem able to enter it with grace and so we remain young in shallow ways. We need to age. We need to move naturally away from actual persistent youthfulness to a more complex and enriched personality made up of both age and youth. Aging allows us to be in this world solidly, as mature people, able to relate and motivated to make our contributions.

Aging is not just adding years to our total on earth. It is a process of humanization, of becoming more spiritually and culturally complex. It allows us to get down to business and make life worthwhile. Over the years, it is also a blending of valuable experience with youthful hope and ambition. It is the process by which a person's natural gifts and potential get worked into something real and subtle. Jung called it "individuation." Keats called it "soul-making." I think of it as the creative working through of the raw material of a personality.

As I said, the first taste of age begins as a slight reminder, such as a few wrinkles or gray hairs, and grows into concern about sickness and loss of mobility. Like any anxiety, the worry escalates quickly and before long we feel that life is over. For some, aging is an anxiety disorder and can dominate their emotions. We need to find ways to calm that anxiety, preferably at the first taste of aging, before it blooms into a real disturbance.

We can deal with this anxiety individually by living a day at a time, being present to what the day has to offer. If there is no sickness or any other problem, we can enjoy the day. Some people project themselves into a debilitating future and live in the anxiety of imagined woes to come. As I said in the introduction, the first rule in dealing with aging is to be with what is, even when it's bad. Sometimes we get a touch of masochism — the odd tendency of humans to enjoy pain — and prefer worry to enjoyment.

Another principle at play here is the simple idea that youth and age need to be present and together always, affecting each other so we don't fall into the exaggerated innocence and naïveté of isolated youthfulness or the despair and grouchiness of plain old age.

The First Taste Never Ends

The sensation that you're getting old doesn't end. Even as an older person you may wake up one day and suddenly realize you're not young anymore. At sixty you wish you were fifty, and at seventy you wish you were sixty. Yes, you've had this sensation of aging many times before, but it keeps coming. It's outside of time, archetypal, one of those timeless reminders of what life is all about.

The sensation of growing old is deeper than you thought. It's a discovery of your mortality, of the very laws of life. You have to come to grips with it, or you will be, as we like to say, in denial. You will be cut off from the all-important realization that as young as you are, you are getting older.

This is the law of life. You are born, you live your life, and you age. It's an illusion to think that you can enjoy your life and not grow old. If you can step outside that illusion, you may be able to enjoy aging, especially if you see signs that life has taught you something and not only are you getting older, but you're getting better. ✓

One curious aspect of growing older has to do with sexuality. Your experience may be different from mine, but when I see a beautiful young woman, now that I'm seventy-six, I can appreciate her attractiveness objectively, but I find that I'm not interested. I used to be. But I find older women, women in their sixties and seventies, more attractive. I used to wonder about that. When you get older do you want to be with a woman your age? Yes, I do. I find my wife incredibly attractive in her sixties. I look at young college students, and I go back to what I was doing.

I find older women attractive, but for myself I'm quite envious of men with flat bellies and dark hair. I look at photos of myself now and see my head aflame with white hair on my head and in my beard, and I'm shocked. I look like a male version of the Bride of Frankenstein. For a while I thought of dyeing my hair dark brown, but now it's really too late. I'd just look foolish. So I'm trying to be content with neon white. Do you see how my own aging can send me off into brief flights of insanity?

Aging can be so unsettling that we succumb to wild fantasies, as though we were suddenly taken over by a psychological complex. In this way, aging can occasionally be akin to jealousy. Our thoughts get away from us and emotions take over. We lose our ability to sort things out and keep our emotions in place.

I've always been intrigued by the three sisters in Greek mythology known as the Graeae. They are so old, the story says, that they can't remember their youth. They share one eye and one tooth among them, and the hero Perseus, preparing to confront the Gorgon, steals the eye and barters some advice. Jung describes them as images of the dark, negative mother.

Here's another way to regard old age: It has its own effective vision, even if it is limited, and its own means for nourishment, also restricted. Like Perseus, at times we may need the older point of view to deal with the terrible side of life on this planet. There are times when we need to feel older than old just to tolerate and survive the horrors we witness or hear about.

But aging is also a beautiful thing. You are moving toward your apotheosis, the thrilling fulfillment of it all. There is nothing to be worried about. The body has to fall apart. You need an invitation to depart. You have to give up this physical existence. How else can you explode into self-realization?

I don't know what death is all about or what happens. No one does. But I do know that I have lived a life that constantly becomes more interesting and more meaningful. I have grown to love life and in particular the life that is in me. Nature has brought me here and I trust that nature will take care of me in my final years and after.

I'm happy to have reminders that I'm getting old. If I weren't getting old, I'd be worried. This is like the river, as the Taoist says, that flows and finds its own way. All I have to do is float and go with the current. I don't have to dig out the banks of the river of life that flows in me. If we didn't try so hard to do it right, we might enjoy the process of aging.

When I was the father of a young child, I wished I could spare my daughter the realization that life involves aging and death. Yet, as a student of religions, I knew that the Buddha only became the Buddha when he was let out of his protective shell and allowed to see suffering and death. It was then that he began his career of teaching and creating a model community.

The Buddha's discovery of suffering

humanity was his first taste of aging, and it was good for the world that he had it. The Buddha is yet another archetype of human advancement. If we could all feel the suffering of humanity we would become the persons we are destined to be. But we typically protect ourselves from this transformative knowledge. We pretend to be children in a nursery kept at a distance from the real world.

What is the deepest secret to the lives and careers of Jesus and the Buddha? Both were experts at compassion, a word that means "to feel with." They could feel with the suffering of others and from that experience they could develop a way of life that might minimize suffering. We admire both figures, but generally we decline the invitation to follow their example.

If the Buddha remained in his protected environment, he might have been happier, but he wouldn't have become the Buddha. Similarly, if we agree to remain ignorant of life's challenges, we will forever be cut off from our deepest selves. That is why taking on aging is so important. We have to be with what is, not what we wish the situation could be.

To mature as a person requires that we break through the curtains of protection that have kept us from feeling the world's suffering. Maybe that is the essential secret of aging. We age with soul when we stop living an unreal, safe, and impractical life of denial, when we feel the corruption at the heart of humanity and resolve to do something about it.

Aging can be penetrating and powerful, but to take advantage of these benefits, we have to dare to approach the Gorgon with the understanding of an unimaginable old figure within. Sometimes, to deal with the fear of age, we may have to go deep, deep into the sense of being old and put it on like a coat or carry it like a pair of antique magic glasses: the eye of the Graeae.

2
OLD BODIES, YOUNG SOULS

My imagination is a monastery and I am
its monk.
— John Keats to Percy Bysshe Shelley,
six months before Keats's death
at twenty-six

Recently we moved our things from our old
house into the new one, and I spent two
weeks carrying boxes of books back and
forth — one of the downsides of being an
independent scholar and writer. "I'm tired
and sore," I said to my wife. "Well, you're
seventy-six. What do you expect?" she replied.

For just a few seconds I felt that time had
shifted under my feet. I'm seventy-six? I had
forgotten, because I always feel like I am
forty. All the intervening years have slipped
past, and I remain stuck in that Shangri-la
of early midlife.

Some people reading this would say that

I'm in denial. I won't accept the fact that I'm getting old. But it's more complicated than that. I identify with my fortieth year. I don't care what the calendar says. I have a strong youthful component in me, and often that person in his forties seems to inhabit my body. Even when I look in the mirror, I sometimes manage to see more of the forty-year-old man than the one who is seventy-six. I've always been a strong believer in illusions.

My father was similar in this respect. He died at one hundred, but he seemed even then like a person in his mid-fifties. He once told me that he had trouble growing up, and that little confession stuck with me. I've had trouble growing up as well, and when I look back on my life I'm embarrassed at how immature I have been at times — the price of enjoying eternal youth.

People speak highly of a fountain of youth, but they seem to forget that youth has its downside. As a young person, you can do anything physically, but you may be quite ignorant about how to live your life, and you will make many mistakes. We are all different about this: Some people seem to be mature in their younger years, while others, like me, suffer a long, extended adolescence.

Yet it's strange when I'm offering therapy

to others and I feel like someone who is two or three hundred years old. I feel knowing, experienced, and sometimes even insightful. I know this could be a dangerous illusion, but I do think that there is a deep-seated old man in me as well. When the youthful element is not too extravagant or out of hand, the older self can blossom.

Puer and Senex

My friend James Hillman began his career as a wandering youth, spending years in France, Ireland, and India, with trips to Greece, Egypt, and Italy. I met him in person in the mid-seventies, when he decided to return to the United States. Our friendship took off quickly, and because I was so enamored of his approach to psychology, I watched closely, as our friendship developed, to see how he lived.

I saw a sometimes startling combination of youth and age in him. There were times I wished he would take himself more seriously, and other times when I felt he was acting like an old man. I consider him the equal of Plato or any major intellectual genius, and yet I noticed that he didn't put himself on the world scene as he could have. He seemed to lack a certain gravitas. He would say that eternal youth was strong in him, and I would take that as a diagnosis.

Early in his career James wrote extensively about the interaction of youth and old age in a person, or even in an institution or in society. He used the old Latin terms for these two spirits that can dominate life: *puer* (boy) and *senex* (old man or old woman). Our English words *puerile* and *senile* come from these Latin roots. The English words are not complementary, but the Latin are neutral, simply referring to youth and old age.

Hillman thought it was important to realize that age is relative, something we imagine that is not as literal as we think. Or another way to put it: We all have a young person and an old person deep in our makeup. You may feel the youth suddenly come to the foreground, full of energy and ideas, and then the old person may rise up, wanting more order and tradition.

A young manager in a business may enter his role full of youthful enthusiasm and the spirit of adventure, but soon he may become so identified with the system that he begins to act like an old man, insisting on rules and traditions. The spirit of maturity gradually overtakes the initial adventurous young idealist. Sometimes puer and senex work this way: They keep moving back and forth, one dominant for a while, and then the other.

On the other hand, some people who create a business never lose their youthfulness. The owner of a company may be full of adventure and creativity, while his younger managers may insist on staying with the old ways and formalities and authority. The point is, age may have less to do with how many years a person has been alive and more do to with how that person lives.

The biographers behind *Becoming Steve Jobs,* Brent Schlender and Rick Tetzeli, describe the computer genius as "a singular freethinker whose ideas would often run against the conventional wisdom of any community in which he operated."* They show how he tempered in some ways as he gained experience and got older, but he never lost his sometimes outrageous youthful spirit.

For Hillman, himself an odd mixture of rebellious youth and the old curmudgeon, appreciating the imaginal nature of aging is crucial. We talk about old people in conflict with the young, but we don't realize that within us all there may be a young rebel

*Brent Schlender and Rick Tetzeli, *Becoming Steve Jobs* (New York: Crown Business, 2015), 40.

and an old traditionalist. They are not just personality traits but ghostly presences that can haunt us and inspire our actions. Not just two complexes among many, they are defining points of view that seriously affect everything we do. Sometimes we identify with one or the other. Sometimes we sense the presence and impact of either of them on our lives.

Once, when I was in my mid-forties, I applied for a teaching job at a nearby university. I had an appointment with the dean of faculty for an interview. I had just moved from a Texas school, where it was customary to dress formally for such a meeting. So I put on a suit and tie — it was a warm mid-July in Massachusetts — and went to my interview. I was surprised to find the dean dressed in shorts, running shoes, and a polo shirt. He looked me up and down as though I were an exotic bird that had flown in from a South American jungle, only much more drab in appearance. The meeting went well, and I was hired.

It turned out that the dean was one of those people who don't begin looking old until late in life. He had a youthful spirit, yet he was excellent at managing an academic program and showed few signs of immaturity. Whenever I was with him I felt the boundary sensation where youth and age touch, a creative, responsible liminal condition that I could only aspire to. In other words, as far as I could see, the spirit of youth and spirit of maturity were on good terms in his psyche.

The spirit of youth and spirit of maturity play a major role in our experience of aging. If the spirit of youth has been strong throughout life, it may well continue into old age and keep you feeling young. On the other hand, if the spirit of youth is weak or missing, age may be entirely in the domain of the elderly spirit, the senex, and then it can be a painful burden, not because of the advancing years but because of the excessive weight of the elderly spirit on the psyche.

The Unexpected Revival of Youth

If a youthful spirit is present, as you age you may actually become young in unexpected ways. I worked with a man in his eighties who found this to be true. After his wife died, he thought that his life would be a gradual decline toward the end. Instead, his dreams began to portray his early life as a college teacher. At first, we didn't know for sure what these dreams implied. But as they continued, and as he began to get ideas for new projects, it was clear that in spirit he was back in that early time in life of starting a new career.

It was as though now in his eighties he was in the same place, or in a very similar place to that early time in his life. He had a similar spirit of adventure and he was actually experimenting with a new identity. It was a return of his youth, in spirit if not in body. He was being defined not by the settling tendency of old age but by the reinventing spirit of youth.

I've seen this unexpected development in other people, too. Do we all have an opportunity in old age to go back to an early creative and defining period in our own history and start over? Is the return of youth a natural occurrence that we ignore simply because we don't expect it?

In short, you stay young in soul by not becoming a fossil in your life. You keep abreast of the world as it advances. You stay fresh in your understanding and values. You say yes to life's invitations. You keep your heart active by loving the world rather than hating it. Chronic hatred is a good way to get fixated in a crusty old age.

You can also stay young by avoiding old habits of thought and behavior. You try new things and resist the comfort of the old ways. Yes, you can enjoy old traditions, but you don't let them become dominant. You don't stay with old forms on principle. You mix the old with the new.

When people think of keeping their youth as they age, they often think too physically, materially, and literally. They get facelifts but not personality lifts. They sink unthinkingly into old age without doing anything to have a youthful presence in everything they do. They try to look young without being young.

It might be better to stay young from the inside out. For some people physical condition often follows their emotional attitude. If the spirit of youth is strong in you, you may see it in your body. I have no doubt that my father looked young, even at one hundred, because of his youthful spirit. So for those people who are trying so hard to look young, I'd suggest instead reviving a deep kind of youthfulness, an aspect of character, and an approach to life.

You can delve more deeply and become aware of the spirit of youth that has been in you from the beginning. You don't have to make yourself young, because you are young inside. That youthfulness needs only to be freed. From what I've seen in the older people I've counseled, the resurrecting of youth in our older years may simply happen. You don't have to manufacture it, but you do have to welcome it, receive it, and allow it to influence how you live.

I often suggest welcoming the invitations that life offers you. These are not always external matters, like moving or getting a new job. They may be internal, like noticing signals of some new youthful urge that wants you to take a risk or go out on an adventure.

For example, these days I'm thinking of traveling less to teach and speak and instead staying home and creating online courses. I will be successful only if I can conjure up the youthful identity needed for a new adventure. The next appearance of your youth may be in something small and ordinary. If you're open to these apparently mundane charges of puer vitality, you stay young in your soul, and that is ultimately what counts.

I feel that I've had the puer spirit in me most of my life. As I said, I was slow to grow up. Once, my mother visited me, looked around at my rented house and rented furniture, and said, "Tom, when are you going to have your own furniture?"

I was just turning fifty and wasn't worried about living in a rented house and not having my own furniture. I wasn't making much money, but I had enough to pay the rent and enjoy modest pleasures. During those years I also had many flying dreams, which are often part of the puer psychology. In particular, I dreamed of planes either trying to get off the ground or flying low in a big city among the skyscrapers and landing on city streets.

I now see those dreams reflecting my efforts to keep my spirit free while dealing with the demands of ordinary life. Eventually, I started to make some money, just at the time I got married, had a child, and became more serious about my writing. Interestingly, the airplane dreams ended. I've never had one since then.

I recall a key moment in my early forties when I was leading a dream group for student psychotherapists in my house. One evening I presented one of my dreams, in which as usual I was on a large jet plane trying to get off the ground. My father also was on the plane.

From my perspective now I can see that at that time in my life my work was too limited in scope. Later my books would sell around the world and my spirit would soar. Back then I couldn't get off the ground, and I knew all along that my father had to settle for a career that was too small for him. As I see it now, he gave in to the limitations of his educational background, when he could have soared free of them and found even more joy in his work.

My father's struggle to find his place in the work environment was "on the plane" with me. Apparently I had inherited this pattern and it was keeping me grounded and stuck. My father had a happy life, as far as I could see, but there was some resignation in it, or at least a willingness to accept limitations. Once I started to soar, he was interested and supported me, and yet I felt a bigger gulf between us. My boundaries were expanding, but he was content to do his job. This interesting dynamic brought us both closer and farther apart, but it didn't affect our love. I have loved that man every day of my life.

When I first got a taste of the writer's life, I could sense the landing gear of the plane touching ground. For me, growing up and out of a puer condition that was more child-like than adventurous felt liberating, even though I now had to deal with the practical details of ordinary life. As that particular spirit of the child left me, I aged, and that aging lifted the burden of having a low estimation of my abilities and prospects. In those days I believed that several of my friends were real writers, and I left it to them to do greater work. That diminished estimation of myself changed, and in that shift came significant and fruitful aging. Today I'm happy and grateful to take on the role of a serious writer, and I embrace the international reach of my books.

One conversation with a close friend when I was in my forties stands out. It should be clear by now that I have idolized James Hillman from our first meeting. A friend suggested that my work might one day be more effective than Hillman's. I laughed at the thought. "Never," I said. "I don't have a tiny portion of Hillman's genius."

I've thought of that conversation many times since. I'm not concerned about the literal issue. I still know that Hillman's genius and writing style are unmatched. But I do feel that I have now claimed my own genius, the creative spirit that works in its own way. You can sense the youthfulness and lack of self-discovery in those statements from my forties. Finding and valuing my own spark aged me in the best sense.

Now I like feeling older and wouldn't go back to those puer years for anything. Still, I think that the young spirit in general, so familiar to me, colors my old age. Maybe it's more accurate to say that I still have some of the puer spirit in me, though it has transformed. It is not the child puer that inspires me today but the puer frustration at the intransigent self-destructiveness of the world. I want a more idealistic society.

I'm suggesting that the figures of the soul can go through change and grow up, and that is part of aging. You can watch how the spirit that drives you shifts from one period of life to another. An earlier puer spirit kept me childish, but the later one serves my aging.

It may also be important to remember that the soul is the playground or Olympus on which many different spirits play out in your life. The puer spirit of youth is only one among many, and it will thrive only if it isn't dominant. Renaissance health writers said we should avoid the "monarchy" of a single indwelling spirit. For example, Saturn's depressiveness and deep thought may be valuable in itself, but if it dominates you, you become a depressed person. That is not our goal.

Some people seem to feel that to age well they have to surrender to it and act like an elderly person, even though that persona depresses them. It isn't so. You can age well only if you retain much of your youthful enthusiasm and imagination, even as you adapt to aging. As I have been saying in many ways: To age well you have to be profoundly old and profoundly young.

When I was talking with my mother in my rented house with the rented furniture, I was in the proper state of being for who I was at that time. I was identified with the young innocent, but identification can be a way of defending against that very spirit. The paradox was that I looked like a typical puer, but it was only later, when I anchored my work in a serious role in society, that my puer spirit soared. Then I didn't have to dream about flying any longer.

Notice this pattern: My youthful spirit allowed me to write fresh ideas that caught on, but at the same time these writings connected me more directly to the world and grounded my life. Youth and age sometimes work together to make a complete life.

With this somewhat feeble attempt to analyze myself, I'm trying to show how deep this pattern of youth and age lies in your soul and how it influences the shape of your life. You can be adventurous and stable at the same time, a condition fueled by two fundamental orientations: one a sometimes subtle spirit of innovation and creativity, and the other a new seriousness about your place in the world.

The Inner Pilot

People with a young psychology often dream of flying and may enjoy high-risk adventure, extreme creative experiments, and novelties of all kinds. They want freedom from limitations and shackles and want to create from scratch. They may also appear fragile and tender and so are often the object of love and care from others. People often fall in love with young men of this type, wanting to save them from their follies and care for them in their times of weakness.

My flying dreams began early in my life. I'd be in a room, flying by moving my arms and then floating to the ceiling. The feeling was exhilarating, and I was disappointed each time the dream would end. Later the dreams shifted to those I've already mentioned: commercial jets trying to take off or taxiing on busy city streets. Then, about ten years ago, the flying dreams ended, never to return.

People are also attracted to women who have a young soul, who tend to be androgynous in style and appearance, the type we can call Artemis, after the Greek goddess of personal integrity, whose job was to protect young girls. Katharine Hepburn, the popular actress of the classic Hollywood era, had the sassy, independent, charming beauty that dares you to get close. A classic photograph shows a smiling, aging Hepburn standing next to a sign at the front of her house saying "Private Property" and another sign below it, "Keep Out!" This is not just of anecdotal interest; the photo betrays something of Hepburn's soul, her need to be her own person, an interesting aspect of her lifelong young female spirit.

But the mythic boy or young woman, one of Artemis's girls, has a downside. He or she is not dependable or stable or grounded. He may be highly sensitive, rebellious, and generally immature. The inwardly young person doesn't have tradition behind him and generally dislikes authority. He makes up life as he goes along and therefore tends to be narcissistic. He can be both lovable and annoying.

Because of these qualities, when a person with a strong boyish psychology runs up against people who cling to their maturity, he finds it difficult to be civil and to compromise. There are many battles between the two kinds of people, and those fights engage the spirit in each of them, not their ego-centered selves. These people may not be aware of what the struggle is all about, since the strong spirits in them hide beneath the surface.

If you are this kind of person, as I am, you need a relationship with the boy in you as though he were another person, not someone you are but someone who dwells in you. He has a separateness, and you can make some progress with him if you allow him his independent existence. It doesn't do to identify fully with him. You need to be more complex, while at the same time giving him some space in your life.

Throughout my life the boy figure has been a constant companion. I feel him in my tendency to expect people to be good and treat me well. I get really upset when I am belittled and deceived. Often I don't understand why people don't rush to my latest idea for changing the world. I have many plays, novels, and screenplays that I've never completed — another sign of the boy at work. I also sense him strongly when I can't seem to deal well with seriously mature types.

An example: Once, a group of business-men with whom I was meeting posed a question: Suppose you inherited one hundred thousand dollars. How would you invest it? One after the other, these experienced and serious men offered their smart financial schemes. When it came to me, I said I'd use it to get along for three or four years and do my writing. Not a bad idea, but very boyish. The wise old men smiled at my naïveté.

I no longer imagine investing money in creating time to write. Writing is now part of my work life, and I'm paid for it. Today my youthful spirit has to keep me fresh and creative, and it has to save me from rehashing the same old material.

You can diagnose yourself emotionally and determine whether you are losing touch with the youth that is in you. If you find yourself preoccupied with growing old or acting like an old person too often or fighting off youth in yourself or in other people, you can search for a youthfulness that you used to have. You can help resurrect it, or simply allow it to come alive. There is nothing as tragic as neglecting some youthful figure in yourself just waiting to be accepted.

The Girl of the Psyche

Let's go back to Artemis, the virgin goddess known by the Romans as Diana, who stays in the woods, seldom goes to town, is surrounded by her young female attendants and has young men in her court as well. She's been called a puella figure, parallel to puer — puella is Latin for girl.

Artemis is an important aspect of the psyche in both men and women, but most notably in women. She is the spirit in a person that doesn't want to be identified through a relationship with another. She doesn't want marriage, she tries to keep her integrity as a person intact, and she may be strong in her own defense. Artemis is a volatile, aggressive figure, at least when she is protecting herself. She can also be vulnerable and tender. To the Greeks she was the protector of young girls — nine-year-olds went through a tough rite of passage in her name — and of women in childbirth.

Whether you are thinking about the girl psyche in men or the more literal girl in women, she offers joy in life and a tender openness to experience. She often has a high degree of innocence and vulnerability to male society and to men themselves. Daphne was one of the Artemis girls who didn't want to get married and had to protect herself from the attentions of Apollo, the god of medicine, and from music and culture in general. Ultimately her father changed her into a tree to keep her innocent. There is something in us, especially in the girl aspect of the soul, which prefers to be in nature rather than to be caught up in Apollo's brilliant ideas, refined music, and polite society.

I want to say the same about Artemis as I did for the puer. It's a spirit that for all its complexities can keep you young as you age. Honor the spirit in you that is not identified with your spouse or partner. Stay natural and don't give everything to culture, no matter how good it is. Protect your personal integrity, even if you have to be aggressive to do so.

Many people confuse the Artemis and Daphne spirits for personal anger and neurotic aggression. But there is a goddess behind your frustrating attempts not to be overeducated, treated medically, and made part of society. There is something deep in that part of you that doesn't want to give everything to being a couple and getting married. That spirit, having both boy and girl qualities, helps keep you young.

Youth Through Osmosis

Of course, there are other methods for getting back in touch with your youth. You can do things you used to do, at least those activities that are still possible and comfortable. You can reflect on old photographs from your youth and visit places associated with it. You can pick up projects you left off in your youth and do them with today's awareness and intelligence.

C. G. Jung, who was good at healing his psyche in concrete ways, tells the story of how in adulthood he went back to his eleventh year, where he felt his current emotional troubles had their roots, and actually played with toys from that period in his life. He said it was embarrassing and difficult for him to do this, but it helped.

Here is Jung's description of that process: "As soon as I was through eating, I began playing, and continued to do so until the patients arrived; and if I was finished with my work early enough in the evening, I went back to building. In the course of this activity my thoughts clarified, and I was able to grasp the fantasies whose presence in myself I dimly felt."*

Notice that Jung was not just going back in time to understand his current behavior. He was trying to revive the spirit he had then, the way he looked at the world, and even ways he resolved difficult problems.

*C. G. Jung, *Memories, Dreams, Reflections,* ed. Aniela Jaffé, trans. Richard and Clara Winston (New York: Pantheon Books, 1963), 174.

He went back into the past to resurrect an aspect of his youth for the present. He also uses a powerful phrase: "My thoughts clarified." That, too, is a lesson for us all. By going back to particular moments in our past, our current thoughts can clarify. Maybe we can get out of the muddle we are in, unaware that the roots of the problem go back to a particular time in the past.

One caution: You can't revive the mythic boy without evoking his shadow. Sometimes people misunderstand this point about the shadow aspect of the soul. They accept that there is a dark side to everything, but they think you have to conquer it and be free of it. The fact is, you have to allow some shadow to accompany any manifestation of the soul, including the spirit of youth. You can't have that young person present without his foolishness and immaturity to some degree. What is required is not muscle to fight the shadow, but an expansion of self to allow for it.

We've seen this principle at work in all aspects of aging: You take life as given, not as you imagine it perfectly. Although this is difficult to understand, the shadow has as much to give you as the bright side does. This is also true of youth. As you allow yourself to stay young, you keep some of the immaturity, foolish adventure, and narcissism. Eternal youth is not perfect, and yet it can still be of benefit.

When I was a boy I spent many summers on my uncle's farm in upstate New York. My parents would come for a week or two and then bring me home to Detroit. In my memory, farm life was a mixture of hard work and lazy storytelling. My father had many skills and, when he visited, he would often spend his time painting, fixing, and wallpapering the farmhouse. Then my uncle would try to teach him the tricks of bringing in loose hay from the fields. I noticed that my father's vacation on the farm was all work.

One summer my dad, who loved golf, set up a small putting green on the lawn in front of the house. He made some holes and brought out his putter and golf balls and played his rounds while the uncles and others watched. At first they spoke about the game being silly and a waste of time and gave the usual comment, "Why would grown people chase a tiny ball into a hole in the ground?"

But my father persisted and left the clubs available on the lawn when he left off playing. Soon the uncles and aunts were hitting the golf balls from hole to hole and my father was teaching them how to hold the club. In no time they all became addicted to the game.

In this little scenario we see many aspects of youth and maturity playing out. The senex criticism of youthful play, the cultural emphasis on work, and finally the irrepressible appeal of a youthful and useless game. Notice that my father did not succumb to criticism of his folly. He remained faithful to it, which is a good way to avoid the shadow of youth, and not to give up in the face of judgment. He took his youthful play seriously and triumphed.

In women the youthful figure who appears now and then can be either the young boy, the puer, who is androgynous and applicable to either gender, or the puella. You see the puella in men sometimes — a wonderful openness to life, tender emotional sensitivity, and a shyness, perhaps, that covers over a wealth of vitality and desire.

These youthful figures of the soul are a fountain of youth, a source of green immaturity and open-eyed wonder that would keep us hopeful. Without them you succumb to old age, completely and literally, and get depressed. With the spirit of youth in you, you won't be weighed down so much by the heaviness of the years and the complaints of the body. It's a matter of steady deliteralizing, a refusal to take aging as physical deterioration. You continue living a soulful life, where the nonphysical and the invisible keep you young and allow you to become old at the same time.

In an interview late in life, Igor Stravinsky, then in his eighties, was asked if it was different being a composer in old age. Was it more difficult to find inspiration? He smiled in his characteristic way and said that they, the reporters, were looking at him as an old man, but he didn't experience himself that way. So the question had no meaning for him.

He offers a good lesson: Don't accept the typical, limiting view of others who may see you as older than you sense yourself to be. Be true to your soul's age, not the numbers or the sight of weakness and ill health. To the soul these are meaningless.

Allow me to indulge in some thoughts about Stravinsky, since he has made an appearance. As a classical musician, I've been devoted to him for fifty years. To my mind, if there are two composers in history who embody complete and utter genius, they are Johann Sebastian Bach and Igor Stravinsky.

One of the great stories about Stravinsky is the one about the debut of his *Rite of*

Spring in Paris in 1913. With its dissonance and strong rhythmic pulse, it created a riot in the audience. Then, his next major piece was almost sweet, *The Pulcinella Suite,* like a French Enlightenment wig-and-breeches entertainment. People didn't know what to expect from him. In his style he moved from one historical period to another, refusing to be stuck in time. This is the man who couldn't understand reporters asking him what it was like to be old.

The deep, mythic, youthful side of the soul is the true fountain of youth that many have sought. Stay in touch with your soul's youthfulness, and you won't feel the full burden of aging. The trouble for many as they get older is that they take age too literally. Yes, they may be eighty-five years old according to the calendar, but the condition of their soul may be more like forty. Wouldn't it be wonderful if we could all respond as Stravinsky did: "I don't know what it means to be old."

3
THE PASSAGES OF LIFE

Although I favor the old idea that we human beings are born with a soul, full of the essentials and the seeds of a personality, still we start out raw. It's amazing how much we have to learn from others, and keep learning into old age. Most of us become wiser and more capable as the years go by, and we develop a strong personality and a degree of individuality, but it takes hard work, persistence, and intelligence.

To a large extent we learn and become more subtle, complex people through experience and even through our mistakes. We get stung by life — a failed job, a sickness, a lost relationship — and in that pain we can become more aware and more prepared for challenges to come. Emotional pain can be a catalyst to thought and character. It can wake us up, if only for a moment.

But as a psychotherapist who has worked deeply with people for over forty years, I can say with confidence that we all develop at our own rate. Those who have had traumatic experiences in childhood, like sexual or physical abuse, may find it difficult to face the passages of adulthood. They tend to get stuck in a place of memory. The images of the trauma remain potent and flare up whenever trouble brews. Many of us have had milder challenges, but even they get in the way of the steady progress toward being a deep-seated, sensitive, aware, and mature person. We all seem to be in different stages or places on our individual journeys, and many reach old age not quite prepared.

Let me emphasize here one of the main ideas in this book: In order to enjoy and thrive in our older years, with a positive outlook and creativity in all areas of life, we have to ripen at every stage in life. Even children have to face the hard work of aging, going through phases and facing the terrifying guardians at the gate of yet another advancement, on their way toward old age. They have to figure out how to deal with bullies and demanding friends, how to get along in spite of their parents' imperfections, how to survive a culture that often doesn't know what to do with kids. I remember as a child thinking, "When I become an adult, I'm going to remember what it's like to be a child and treat children with understanding."

We age all along, and how we arrive at actual old age depends in great measure on how we have dealt with turning points and passages all though life. Therefore, aging is not just about the older years but about the whole of life. It's not just about older people but young ones, too, who have a choice of whether to live fully or shy away from life's challenges. It's important to keep moving, unfolding your deep potential, becoming a real individual, loving life more and more, and arriving at old age prepared and ready for more of the same.

The task is to advise and guide younger people as they try to stay on track toward becoming who they are essentially. As we'll see, the life work of the older person is to be an elder and to leave a legacy for the future. But you can do this effectively only if you have aged well at every stage of life.

Let me return to the passage in Ralph Waldo Emerson's essay "The Oversoul" that has guided me for many years. I will quote it now at some length so it may guide you as well:

The soul knows only the soul; the web of

events is the flowing robe in which she is clothed. After its own law and not by arithmetic is the rate of its progress to be computed. The soul's advances are not made by gradation, such as can be represented by motion in a straight line but rather by ascension of state, such as can be represented by metamorphosis, — from the egg to the worm, from the worm to the fly.*

This passage is full of insight. Don't be put off by Emerson's nineteenth-century writing style. Read a few words at a time. For example, modern psychology would change overnight if it took to heart the line about events being clothed in the soul. That means that the experiences we have, life on the surface, make sense in relation to the soul that is contained within them. It isn't enough to change life patterns. You have to see and touch the soul matters enfolded within them.

Then Emerson goes on to say that we don't develop along a straight line from infancy to old age. Instead, we go through phases, one plateau after another. The shift

*Ralph Waldo Emerson, *The Portable Emerson,* eds. Carl Bode and Malcolm Cowley (New York: Penguin Books, 1981), 214.

from one to the next is less like a stream constantly flowing and more like a river filled with locks, where boats have to pause and be lifted or lowered to another level. Emerson calls the process an "ascension of state." He doesn't use the metaphor of steady growth, as we do, but emphasizes moments of transformation. You may be going along in your familiar life when something makes you realize that you have a higher calling. I've met many people who suddenly quit their jobs to care more directly for their souls.

But the movement from one level to another doesn't happen automatically. You have to cooperate and experience the transformation from worm to butterfly. The passage isn't usually an easy one. You have to face yourself and allow a significant change to happen. For example, it may not be easy for a graduating college student to leave the safety and comforts of school to enter a life of work and production. This is an ascension of state, a progress through metamorphosis that has its rewards but may still be difficult. Some prefer to remain eternal students. Some prefer never to grow up.

The Freezing Point

Most of us reach a point in life where we get stuck. The river of life is frozen in a winter of uncertainty and anxiety. I see it in the faces of friends and of people I meet in my travels. I see worry around their eyes, the sadness of a dead spot on their lips, the disillusionment of life not working out as hoped in the stoop of their shoulders.

So many people are gifted and skilled and bright, and yet something in them, if not in the whole of their lives, has come to a standstill. You look at them and almost everything you see is attractive and lively, and yet there is a portion that doesn't move, that seems to be petrified with fear or self-doubt.

Often this cold, frozen portion is so potent that it holds back the whole of life, and the person never accomplishes what he wanted and always feels frustrated and jealous of people around him who haven't succumbed to doubt. These lives are not complete disasters; they can be successful to a point. Maybe that is why the people haven't been able to get past the frozen portion: They aren't disturbed by it enough to make a significant move. They can get along fairly happily, and so they don't make the further effort needed to break up the ice jam. They seem partially resigned, and resignation is one of the unhappiest solutions to a life problem.

The suppression of even a small portion of creative potential can generate anger. The sadness I see in certain people who have a portion of their soul on ice is often ringed with a slightly seething anger that never explodes but is always there with its frigidity. Anger can be useful, but in this state it only serves to keep the vital piece of life dormant. It interferes with relationships and spoils happiness.

When I encounter a piece of deadness in an otherwise lively personality, I often do something. I encourage my friends to take some risks. I assure them of the talent I see in them. An example is the friend who is a writer who hasn't gone past his feelings of inadequacy. He has low expectations of himself and is therefore always disappointed, envious, and, yes, resigned. I try to jump-start the process of reflection and renewal in these people.

I'm not saying that I have succeeded in this while others have failed. I have my own icy areas that I wish would thaw. For example, I sometimes wish I had a more public voice and made a direct impact on politics and government. I'm aware that I come from a family that enjoyed its humility and preferred to be in the background. That family trait hangs around in a closet of my memory, holding me back and keeping me quiet. It needs processing. On the other hand, my quiet way has its own power and helps me do my job of persuading people to waken their souls and stop being resigned.

Resignation is shutting down, perhaps being so discouraged that instead of fighting a longer fight, you just give up. I meet many resigned people, and their lack of energy and zest for life is palpable. You sense it in the atmosphere around them.

Henry David Thoreau's often-quoted passage in *Walden,* explaining why he went to the pond, places resignation in context: "I did not wish to live what was not life, living is so dear; nor did I wish to practice resignation, unless it was quite necessary. I wanted to live deep and suck out all the marrow of life."

The Trusting Ego

Aging with soul requires that we navigate the many passages that life presents to us. Sometimes it seems that there is a plan for you alone, that each challenge is just what you need to become who you are. But people often decline the invitation. The status quo is too comfortable, and so they don't age. They just pile up years. They get old without having aged, and their lives look more like tragedies and unfulfilled promise.

You can imagine the whole of life as a long series of passages. We always seem to be going through something. But as we look over our history we will likely see special turning points or problems that helped us grow up. As I reflect on my own life, immediately I notice about a dozen turning points that were crucial. In each case I could have declined the invitation to move along, as when I decided to leave monastic life after thirteen years. I'll tell that story later, along with most of the other passages that I went through.

I don't see myself as a terribly decisive person or heroic in temperament. Just the opposite, I'm quiet and introverted. Yet there is something in me that all along was willing to change and take the next step. In some cases, my willingness looked foolhardy to my friends and me, but blindly I went ahead. If there is one major mythic, archetypal figure at work in me, it is Parsifal, the young knight at King Arthur's Round Table who was inordinately close to his mother and acted like a young fool most of the time. Yet he played his role and in the end found the Holy Grail. He's my hero.

I'm not suggesting that anyone be heroic in this aging process. I don't believe you need a strong ego and willpower. But I do think you need to love life and trust it cautiously. You have to be a close observer to see how life works and then realize that you have two choices: life or death. You can follow the life principle, by which you move forward and accept the invitations life brings to you for more vitality. Or you can opt for the death principle, which means remaining in place, avoiding new ideas and new experiments in living. The way of death — I mean soul death, not literal dying — is safer and in some ways more comfortable. It's predictable and you don't have to be bothered with change. But death is death. You don't feel alive and your life has no basis for meaning and purpose.

The Process of Aging

Now let me be more precise about rites of passage and the process of becoming a person of depth and substance, which I consider a prerequisite for aging as opposed to just growing old. Notice that word: *process.* Aging is a process by which you become somebody real and alive. The process is always going on, but at times it becomes especially intense. You may elect not to be in process. You can step aside and vegetate for a while, or forever if you are really afraid.

As a therapist I've watched people as they contact me for counseling. They usually express an eagerness to work at their lives and understand themselves better. Often they have a specific issue that is driving them crazy or giving them pain. Some don't know how to be in therapy, and so I teach them through experience what it's all about.

Now, many latch on to the work and enter into it. They are generous and thoughtful in giving it a good try. Others seem to stiff-arm the process. They keep it at a distance, even as they show up for appointments. I understand that they are afraid to reveal themselves or admit to weakness or open up cans of worms. I don't judge them at all. I hope they will find some form of therapy that allows them to enter into the process.

Those who do enter the process are often surprised how long it can take. I don't try to speed it up, because I don't think I'm in charge of the timing. A person who was regularly beaten as a child isn't going to get through the memory of that trauma over-night. I urge patience. Most of my clients stay with it for a decent period of time and make some progress, if that's the right word.

Sometimes a person will pull out at a particularly challenging moment, and I'm tempted to object. I see that they are facing a big challenge, and I think they can make a big difference in their lives by being patient. Recently a man came to me presenting some ordinary conflicts in his marriage. But through dream work we quickly discovered some important childhood pressures that seemed to remain in his soul. He also bore physical symptoms of these burdens. Just when I thought we were moving close to the heart of the matter, he told me he wanted to end the therapy.

I try to avoid a God complex during this work, so I don't pretend to know what is best for this man. He made his choice, and I will honor it. I can't help thinking he chickened out, but who knows? He may go on to find some other form of therapy, but he left the process he was in, and now he may well stop aging and just keep growing old. I hope and pray that he will have to face some key issues so that he can ascend to a new plateau.

Aging requires courage. It's an active decision. You live your life onward. You say yes to life's invitations. You read the signs. You take it all on. You don't back off. You don't make excuses. You don't run for safety.

Everyone has issues from past experience that need sorting through. I see them as the basic stuff for making a life and a personality. Alchemy refers to the accumulated matter of our experiences in Latin as *prima materia,* or raw material. But to work this material requires both courage and insight. Many people avoid it because it stirs up too many emotions.

Let me give you an example of how this works.

Let's call her Brenda. Brenda is a professional woman. On the surface she looks fully in control of her life. She's been successful and possesses considerable psychological understanding. Her problem is that she continually lets people take advantage of her. From our conversation, though, it appears more likely that she needs to have people beholden to her, too. She takes care of them, pays their way, and then she wishes they didn't burden her. She has little time for herself and feels overwhelmed and mildly depressed.

I ask about her parents. I don't reduce all adult problems to the influence of parents, but it helps to take note of childhood patterns that persist into adulthood. "My father always tells me what to do," she says.

She's about fifty.

"As long as I can remember, he has known what is best for me and he refuses to discuss how I might feel or how we might relate better to each other. He doesn't like that kind of intimate talk."

"Do you still see him occasionally?"

"I see him several times a week. I ask him for advice."

I don't want to reduce adult conflicts to past relationships with parents, but it is interesting how many people in their mature years still act out old patterns with their parents. The complexity of the relationship may be lost on them, because it seems subtle in comparison to what it was in childhood. But it's still present and significant.

We discuss both childhood patterns and the adult relationship, and I listen carefully to many stories from both periods. But listening isn't always enough. I am acutely aware of the dynamic between us, and sometimes I sense the conflict in me: I don't want to upset my client to the point where she can't explore her emotions, and yet I know that the story has to go deeper. So I take a risk and confront her.

"Do you still like being a little child with your father?"

"I'm not being a child. It's my father. He

can't seem to get out of his role. He's the one treating me like a three-year-old."

"But how could he do that unless you were playing your part in that little drama? You don't want his protection and approval?"

She stops, puts her head down and thinks. "It looks that way, doesn't it? I turn to him the same way I did as a child. I complain, but I do it anyway."

We are making one small movement into her deep, basic, and unrecognized emotions. She is seeing something she hasn't noticed before. That is how processing your life takes place, often one small step at a time. But soon the small steps will add up and reach a tipping point. A significant change may appear. It happens all the time in a therapeutic setting, and it can happen in ordinary life, if the process goes on.

This small discovery of a debilitating pattern ages this woman. She gets freed, if only slightly, from a pattern that has kept her a child and immature in her choices. She grows up and is now more her own age. You might say that her soul age is now more in line with her physical age. She is no longer a child in an adult body. Well, not completely. She has many more discoveries to make, and this one will have to be rediscovered again and again until the change in her is deeply set.

The problem with aging is not just that we resist growing older physically but that we don't want to grow up emotionally, intellectually, and spiritually. We don't concern ourselves with whether or not our soul expands. But if we were to age in soul as well as body, we would embrace our maturity and no longer have such a conflict between time and personal character. Congruence of soul and body would make aging easier.

Critical Points of Passage

Most journeys, from sailing trips to hikes in the woods, run into crises that test the character of the traveler. Homer's *Odyssey* is all about such critical points along the path. They are not just obstacles but ordeals. If you can pass the test, you have been changed in a good way and are no longer the same person. The ordeal transforms you and truly ages you.

Remember that if you don't come through the ordeal transformed, you will remain in a fixed, undeveloped state, unaged in my sense of the word. We all need to go through an aging passage with some regularity in order to be mature enough to have an identity and be creative in the world. If we lack those two things, our soul is weak or even absent. We are hollow and we try to fill up that void with useless addictions and empty behaviors. The absence of an identity leads to purposelessness and existential depression, while the failure to be creative generates depression and anger. To age is crucial.

Marriage Is a Rite of Passage

A common passage most of us go through is marriage. I would guess that most people would find it difficult to articulate just what marriage is and what it's about. It's an expression of life, a shared life, a committed relationship. But it's also an initiation into a new state of life. Marriages often have trouble because the spouses think of it as a state, the marriage state, rather than a passage. Marriage can be difficult because we are each asked to be a very different kind of person from the ones we were before marriage. We are asked to think differently about life, now not about "me" but about "us." The movement from *me* to *us* is epic, a fundamental shift in one's reality.

It may take a long time to make the change, to go from *me* to *us*. The challenges are great, full of unknowns. There is often the struggle to remain true to oneself and open to the other, and there is the challenge to surrender partially to another person's worldview and way of life. It's a simple fact that marriage is rarely a union of sames. Almost always it's a coming together of fundamental differences. No wonder it sometimes takes decades for the spouses to be transformed enough to enter deeply into a married state.

Many people get stuck in the middle of no-man's-land, where they are half-married and half–not married. They experience this painful condition as being married but wanting not to be married, or being married to one person and wanting to be with someone else.

If a married person is forever trying to suppress his or her desire not to be married, then the marriage may never be fully satisfying, and he or she may never fully embrace the marriage. So we have a condition like the one I'm describing, where a person doesn't fully embrace the life that he or she is given. He or she resists life and therefore doesn't really age. Time goes by but the person's life doesn't deepen. It is stuck in an empty place where time doesn't have the traction of maturing. In that case marriage is not a soul-making enterprise.

I've seen many examples of marital impasse like this. For instance, one woman, Joanie, married a man she liked but didn't love and had a child. She told me that she knew she married this man because he came from a wealthy family, and he could give her security and a comfortable life. She had come from a family that was not well-off, and security and comfort meant a lot to her. She and her husband were friends, and she thought that she could live without love, which she felt in most cases is not very real. But over time she discovered that the marriage felt more and more empty. She had been wrong: Even for her, love was essential.

But love is one of the main experiences that allows you to age, to feel that life is in gear and matters. When she came to see me, Joanie was unhappy with her life. She felt the emotional distance in her marriage and was gradually coming to realize that love is important. She didn't want to get divorced, because that would be a serious failure. No one in her family had ever been divorced, and she didn't want to hurt her son. She was in the kind of impasse that afflicts many people, where they feel stuck and unable to make a good move.

In a relationship impasse, which I see quite commonly in therapy, I try not to get caught up in the person's game of considering one solution after another. That approach only makes the impasse more palpable and maddening. Instead, I explore the stories of the person's life, stories from the marriage, fears and wishes, dreams, hopes for life.

My approach to therapy in general has five main elements:

1. Story: Listen closely to the stories of life.
2. Dreams: Track dreams to see the soul stuff and time line.
3. Perspective: Express your own perspective, e.g., don't judge where the client judges himself.
4. Face the demons: Deal with issues that arise within yourself.
5. Spirituality: Be open to questions of ultimate meaning and mystery — the spiritual dimension.

The purpose of therapy is not to come to a rational, logical solution to a problem, but to explore it in different ways so that eventually a new perspective arises and a solution appears out of the intense reflection of therapy.

Therapy can help the aging process by allowing a person to reengage with life and get past impasses. For example, a man or woman may be able to either be truly married or get a divorce. Other areas of life may require similar movement, such as getting out of a stale job or career, or moving to a different location.

I have found that on a surface level people may want a change, like Joanie's divorce. But change is terrifying, and so they come up with excellent reasons for not changing. Sometimes the reasoning is so smooth and convincing that it takes me a while to see what is going on. They are delaying and defending with all the intelligence they can muster. They both want a change in life and are deathly afraid of it.

Joanie decided that divorce was her only option, and although it took a long time to get through the process of separation, eventually she found herself single and facing a new, promising life to which she felt connected and dedicated. This was after years of struggle and unhappiness. Those years were productive internally, at least toward the end, but now she was fully in her life and able to fulfill herself. She entered back into aging. Time and vitality once more came together.

The Passage to Old Age

Another passage we should consider is the first taste not of aging but of old age. It's one thing to age at different times of your life and another to really be approaching old age. I found that turning seventy was a true initiation into old age. I began to see myself differently, partly because of the way people treated me. They began to relate to me as an old person. Inwardly I didn't feel old, but I had to adjust to a world that seemed to want me to be old.

Then it took at least five years to settle into being an old person. I still haven't done this completely, because I believe I am a young seventy-six. But I know that it is time to adopt a different role in life, even if I do what I can to maintain my youth. In other words, I still feel young but I'm willing to be the old person in society. I don't want to be old in my marriage, and I don't feel my age there. The old person comes out more in public life, where people tend to respond conventionally.

Still, entering old age, whenever that occurs, is a rite of passage as significant as any earlier shift in identity. It asks you to rearrange your thinking and bearing and adopt the role of a truly older person. You will likely think of people you knew who were old, some of them appearing to be of an advanced age, and now here you are at that place in life.

Recently I was watching a movie with my wife, and a woman appeared who looked very old and was treated as an elderly person. That was the point of the story. Then someone in the movie mentioned her age, and it was my age. For a few seconds I had to make the new connections. I knew I didn't have to be as elderly as she was in appearance and style, but I did have to come to terms once again with old age.

You don't go through a passage once and for all. You have repeated experiences that stun you briefly, cause you to rethink your life and your identity, and be in the world in a different way. Each moment of passage turns the wheel a little, forcing you toward a new realization. Each moment, however insignificant, adds to the total impact of aging you appropriately. Your job is to accept that turn of time and fate and at the same time enjoy the youthfulness in you that is not overcome by being old. You can't have the youth if you refuse the passage of time. Inner youth and calendar aging are two sides of a coin, one supported by the other.

Passages are not always easy. You may decide it is too much for you and settle for being stuck in a comfortable phase. In my profession I meet many writers who seem to me not quite ready. They want immediate success and appear desperate to have their work recognized and praised. They ask me to help them, but I know they won't hear me if I say that they need to grow into the role of writer. It doesn't happen automatically. You have to do the work, go through certain initiations, and personally grow up. Yes, they may be successful. Some immature writers win the lottery. But they may never enjoy the deep joy and sense of fulfillment that really good creative work offers. Of course, I can't say "grow up," but I wish I could.

Going through a narrows in your life progress, an uncomfortable period in which change is demanded, seems essential for all people as we age. It may be difficult to see the growth taking place when the pain is prominent. A personal philosophy of aging, an approach that you have thought through and prepared for, may help you see the positive potential in difficult challenges. It may help you to understand life as a blend of pain and pleasure, good times and bad, so you won't collapse in despair when life narrows and presses and forces you to adapt. Real aging commences when you accept the challenge and dare to endure yet another passage.

■ ■ ■ ■

PART TWO:
BECOMING A DEEPER
PERSON AS YOU AGE

■ ■ ■ ■

You could never find your way to the soul,
no matter how many roads you traveled,
so profound is its meaning.

— HERAKLEITOS

4
MELANCHOLY:
A WAY TO HAPPINESS

So you're sad about aging. You're moving closer to the end of life. Your body is not as strong and flexible as it once was. Your friends are dying. You're worried about your health. Your memory is slipping. What's to like about this aspect of old age? Well, melancholy is as natural a mood as longing and delight, and if you can't find your way to appreciating it, it's likely you won't know happiness when you see it, either.

As you grow older, sadness is a natural part of the process. You don't have to medicate it or make efforts to be artificially happy to overcome it. In fact, if you accept this existential, natural sadness, it may not be overwhelming but instead only one strand of mood among others. When you can live out the emotions and moods that float in or rush toward you, you may feel more alive, less defensive, and more present.

I recommend that you avoid referring to this sadness, so appropriate and natural, as depression. The word *depression* is a clinical term that today automatically calls for an allopathic response, usually a pill. Worse, it makes you think that your melancholy at the passing of years is a sickness, something to cure and get rid of.

There are alternatives to using the word depression. One is to be specific about what your feeling is. If you're sad, call it sadness. If you're wistful, call it wistfulness. If you're angry, show it in your voice and speak clearly about it. So many of our emotional problems would lighten if we could be more specific about what we're going through.

The other alternative is to use the much older term that you don't hear much any longer: melancholy. Melancholy is not clinical. You don't go to a doctor or pharmacist complaining of melancholy. You don't see a sign posted somewhere listing the warning signs of melancholy. It can be a bitter form of sadness and a loss of vitality, but it isn't a sickness.

There is a centuries-old tradition connecting growing old with melancholy. The word itself has medieval roots: *Melanis* means black and *choly* is one of the classical humors or personality traits. Writers of this period in history often refer to melancholy as "black bile." It's not nice, but it's natural.

The black humor of melancholy is not an illness but a condition, either a personality trait or a mood created by the situation. It can also be the result of a certain lifestyle. Marsilio Ficino, the Renaissance magus I often rely upon, wrote a three-volume work called *De Vita,* or *On Life.* The first volume is *On a Healthy Life,* and there he offers suggestions for dealing with black bile. After mentioning many foods and good music, he says, "I encourage you to gaze on sparkling waters and things that are green or red. I recommend walking through gardens and groves and along rivers and beautiful meadows. I also suggest horseback riding, hiking, calm sailing, and variety of all kinds: pleasant jobs, varied and carefree work, and the constant company of agreeable people."

Simple, ordinary activities can improve your health and ease the black bile of melancholy that afflicts many older people. Take that walk in the woods, look for a sparkling lake or river, and don't spend much time with negative people. Today we've lost the wisdom of a Renaissance doctor like Ficino. We don't realize how important it is to rely on nature for our health and mood, to think about the kind of people we have around us, and to understand the value of gardens and trees. By the way, when Ficino advises a walk near sparkling water, the sparkle is important. Not just any old water will do. Time your walk so you can catch the sparkle.

If you're feeling sad about the passing of years, you shouldn't repress this feeling. Tell someone how you feel. Then go on and fill your life with inspiring experiences that counter the melancholy. If you were clinically depressed, I'd recommend getting to the roots of the depression. But this is melancholy. It's all right to be comforted and cheered up by positive experiences in nature and among friendly people.

Since melancholy is a natural part of life, even if it is a personality trait, you can let it be. Not repressing it helps keep its natural boundaries and limits. You can give in to it too much, and then it becomes a problem. The whole idea is to accept sadness as one emotion among many. It need not dominate or become the emotional standard of your life. You can see it as connected to everything else that is happening, and in that way it will stay within bounds.

My friend Hillman always spoke for his anger and let it out when it wanted expression. Look at a photograph of him and you'll likely catch a glimpse of his anger, even if he's smiling. Look at the way he sits: He's ready for the fight. I'd have to say that for myself, I speak for my sadness. I have a melancholic streak. It doesn't interfere with my happiness or sense of humor, but it's there, feeding my imagination the way anger fed Hillman's.

Recently I saw a photo of myself and was taken aback at first. Look at those sad eyes, I said to myself. Sometimes I wonder if it comes from almost dying at four years old in a boating accident.

We are all like cows, constantly chewing on memories of the past, trying to make sense of them and trying to arrive at some peace. Just recently I said to my wife, "A week doesn't go by when I don't think about almost losing my life in a lake, and my grandfather giving up his life for mine." It's true, I frequently call up that memory from when I was only four years old, and I wonder about the meaning of it all. I wonder if it is responsible for the fear I sometimes feel. Certainly it affects me as I try to enjoy rowing on a lake today or as I try to swim in a relaxed way. When I am doing what I consider to be relaxed swimming, other people watching me must think of it as panic.

But I also wonder what this dangerous and frightening experience gave me. Sometimes I think it set my course on a serious life of study and reflection. The nearness of death has a way of focusing your attention. It also echoes the experience of shamans who often come out of an early sickness or wounding to become a spiritual leader. I don't mean that I am a shaman, except in the sense that we all have a shaman's potential to see through the skin of life to the mysteries beneath and above.

My father's father, my grandfather, would sometimes take me out on a small lake to go fishing out of a little rowboat. One time we ventured into a big lake, and apparently strong winds came up and capsized the boat.

My grandfather did everything he could to keep me from succumbing to the rough waves, holding me desperately onto the inverted bottom of the capsized boat. He drowned and I was rescued in time. He was certainly not the kind of man favored by many today; he was not politically correct and endowed with a strong feminine side. He was an unpolished but sensitive man, the salt of the earth. But he gave his life for me. What about his capacity to be so generous? Maybe I also learned on that day not to judge all men as representatives of the much-maligned patriarchy, but to stand up for men by refusing to blame all social ills on them as a class.

The accident also put me in touch with death. I was four years old and came back to consciousness lying in a huge bed with sheets and blankets stretched tightly across my body. I heard someone refer to an undertaker, and so naturally I assumed I was dead. I couldn't move because of the tight sheets, and the voices in the room were all hushed and somber. I was like one of those young people anthropologists write about, who in rites of passage is buried under leaves and mourned as if dead, only to rise to a new kind of life in the community. My initiation at four years old got me ready for a long life dedicated to the spirit.

That accident early in life aged me. After it I wasn't like the other children in the family. Of course, a certain boyish gravitas was part of my character and identity, but I believe that my acquaintance with death gave me a seriousness that was unusual. Nine years later I left home with the thought of becoming a priest.

I don't think I'll ever come to a conclusion about the meaning and implications of the accident, but reflecting on it for seventy years has been an important part of my aging, my blossoming into my own self. The story of the accident is a portion of the raw material that life has given me over the course of seventy years of experience. It stands out as important. I think about it often and wonder how it affected me. That sheer wonder is my soul work, processing my life.

I also wonder if my light but constant sadness is a leftover from the sharp homesickness I felt upon leaving home at thirteen to attend a seminary boarding school. Is it just my disposition? Whatever its origins, melancholy works for me. It keeps me quiet, a state that pleases me. If I reject or try too hard to control my melancholy, I think I'd lose my passion and my joy. Melancholy is a route to happiness.

The poet Wallace Stevens wrote: "The death of one god is the death of them all." I think this wise precept applies to emotions, too. Suppress your sadness, and the whole of your emotional life will suffer. Emotions come as a package; you can't choose which among them is pleasing and acceptable to you and dismiss the rest.

Born Under Saturn

Early Renaissance books said that black bile has its own benefits. We have to remember that, in the very nature of things, black is beautiful. First, it gives you weight, gravitas. Many people don't feel the seriousness of their lives. They bounce through life, taking it too lightly. Melancholy forces you to stop and think. One traditional image of black bile, often referred to as the saturnine humor, is an old man holding his head in his hands. Rodin's famous *The Thinker* is an example. This gesture, a kind of mudra or spiritual and expressive posture, shows what the person suffering melancholy needs to do. He should stop and reflect on life and thus achieve a level of gravitas.

Melancholy helps the saturnine spirit, necessary for a good life, to seep gradually into the personality and into attitudes and actions. You may begin to feel your own authority, instead of letting others decide your life. You may trust your own knowledge, intuitions, and experience more as you take charge of your life. In *The Book of Life,* Ficino says that the ancients made images of Saturn out of sapphire, showing him as an old man sitting on a throne or a dragon, clothed in a dark robe, his head covered with a dark linen cloth, raising his hands above his head, and holding a sickle or some fish.

Here we have a few hints about melancholy. It can put us on the throne of our own lives, ruling them rather than passively suffering them. The old man has a cloth over his head. In Renaissance times people were encouraged to stay in enclosed places and to wear wide-brimmed hats so as not to be in emotional sunshine all the time. Saturn is a far-out planet, signaling quiet and removal. If we were to follow Ficino's advice when we feel the melancholy of old age, we might cover our heads in some way, find good retreats from the world, and assume more authority over our lives.

But we can get too much of this heavy spirit and sometimes have to counter it. Ficino advises wearing white clothes, listening to lively music, and spending as much time as possible in the open air. My thought is that we could do both at the same time: accept the melancholy, really get into it, and also find ways to temper it with more lively and juicy activities.

I feel the melancholy of age almost every day. I wish I could live forever. I don't like the idea of death at all. It forces me to accommodate it in some way, and I don't like that. Life can be difficult, but it's beautiful.

What's the alternative, anyway? To make it even more frustrating, we don't know anything about death. We can only hope for an afterlife. Many intelligent people would say that afterlife is an illusion meant to comfort us.

Woody Allen famously wrote: "I'm not afraid of death. I just don't want to be there when it happens." That's my feeling exactly, although I'd extended it to becoming what they call old-old. I can appreciate it in principle, but I don't have any free time for it.

Hillman once looked me in the eye and said, as if he were throwing down a gauntlet, "I'm a materialist about death. I think it's the end." He and I were very close friends, but he never liked the monk in me. I felt that he was speaking to that monk when he proclaimed his materialism, the man who spent much of his life arguing against a materialist way of life.

There are good reasons to be melancholic as you grow older. My wife tells me that she feels melancholy at night, and this sensation is part of her aging. We are opposites in almost every way, so I feel my melancholy in the morning, when I wonder how many mornings I have left. Your melancholy is your own, and there are no rules about it.

I feel it, as I already confessed, when I see men who have a lush head of naturally colored hair. I remember having hair like that — thick and dark and silky. This is only a passing sensation, but it's enough to introduce melancholy into my life. I wish I had my youth, my brown hair, endless mornings.

As I search for a way to get rid of this nagging melancholy, I realize that I have to come to terms with it. It won't go away. It's part of growing older, and there is no good alternative. I have to feel the melancholy, let it seep into me, let it transform me into a genuine older person who is not always trying to make it otherwise. Age conquers. You can't win. Let it be. Be older. Stand passionless in the exact age you are. No excuses, no denials, no sneaking away.

I'm giving a weekend workshop and an older woman sitting in the front row, who has shown her vitality and lively mind, proclaims, "Aging is not for wimps." Her main complaint is that she has lost most of her close friends and will continue to lose the rest as she gets older. When she makes her proclamation with feeling, I remember my father at one hundred talking about all the friends he had and who went before him. It's sad.

Yet the other side of this sad reality is the fact that you are alive. You have the gift of old age. You have new friends and opportunities for experience that were not granted to the friends who have passed. There is still reason for some sober joy. You could also find deep pleasure being in tune with your fate, with the number of years the universe has given you. You don't need to slip off into sadness and indulge in it.

In all ways and not only in aging, being exactly who you are, with your personality, history, abilities, weaknesses, knowledge, and ignorance, is the key to living without heavy neuroses. Notice how most people find subtle ways to discount their natures and their experiences. They may hide, tell little lies about themselves, pretend to be someone else, and use humor to keep from being seen. You don't have to do that, and one good way to deal with melancholic old age is to let people see you.

There is an old saying in philosophy: To be is to be perceived. To have your being, your life and vitality, you need to be seen. When you are seen for exactly who you are, you have your being. Your being seen pushes you forward into existence. You feel your life, your presence. When you hide out of shame, you are not present, not even to yourself. You are diminished.

So a good strategy for getting older is to let yourself be seen. Be public with your age. Don't hide. Don't excuse. Let people see you for who you are, even if your dark brown hair has turned smoky gray.

A few years ago a big crowd of people jammed into a basement room in our small public library to hear the poet Donald Hall read and speak. He was in his eighties, and as I heard him and saw how important his presence was to the people gathered, I reconsidered a resolve I had made not to be in the public arena after I turn eighty. My thought was to hide my age and not appear weak or feeble. But Donald Hall's generous presence in that homespun situation emboldened me to imagine doing my usual thing, giving talks and teaching, as long as I am able. Why not be seen at eighty?

There is much talk these days about the importance of the gaze, how we need to see this world in all its particulars intensely. But we also need to be seen. We need to be the object of a gaze. In this process of becoming a real person we need others. It's a community process. And we need the community to see us for who we are, in all our splendor and imperfection.

Let your melancholic mood be seen, too.

It can give you fuller existence and presence. Without it you are only partially there, because that melancholy is part of who you are. We don't invent ourselves. We are invented. We have to show what we have come to be, not who we want to be. And by showing ourselves, we become who we are.

Melancholy Should Be Dark

When you say you are melancholic, there may be other complicit thoughts circling around: *I should be cheerful. There's something wrong with me. People won't like me.* We tend to pathologize melancholy, thinking of it as a problem rather than a legitimate mood. But you have to wonder about people who are always cheerful. No one has good reason to be perpetually in the sunshine. In fact, in my opinion constant and impenetrable happiness is a mood disorder.

In melancholy you may discover things about yourself or your world that are not visible in a cheery atmosphere. The dark tone may help you realize that some things have to change, that you're not happy in your current environment, that certain relationships are not good for you, that your creativity is dormant. The gray mood is like a filter that allows you to see things that are blotted out by the sunshine, and that new awareness may be helpful. Your melancholy may serve you well.

The *Tao Te Ching* says, "Happiness is rooted in misery." In that spirit you could say that cheerfulness is rooted in melancholy. Not only do both moods demand a place in anyone's life, but melancholy is also the mother of happiness, the root and base of it. If you can allow melancholy its place, you have a better chance to be deeply happy.

Let me explain that further. What people sometimes call happiness is simply an effort to avoid sadness. Or to put it in slightly more psychological terms, happiness can sometimes be a defense against unhappiness. We don't want to be unhappy or show sadness, and so we paint a picture of cheerfulness that is not real or at least doesn't go deep. This false happiness isn't really satisfying, but it may feel better, momentarily anyway, than appearing sad.

The Taoist passage goes on with another insight that applies here:

The sage is sharp but not cutting,
Pointed but not piercing,
Straightforward but not unrestrained,
Brilliant but not blinding.

We could add: "Melancholic but not depressed."

Often, when you reveal your genuine mood, it isn't as pronounced as when you try to hide it. The *Tao Te Ching* suggests expressing your mood, but not to an extreme. This is a subtle and interesting technique for showing your emotions without letting them get away from you. It's yang and yin: expression of what you're actually feeling but with a toning down.

The first stage of dealing with melancholy may be to realize you don't have to fight it or cure it. You can speak for it by letting people know about it and know that you accept it. You may also design your life around your melancholy, instead of using your life decisions to maintain a false sense of cheer. You may decline invitations to parties and gatherings, becoming, at least temporarily, something of a loner. I don't mean that you should surrender to the melancholy and become a misanthrope. I'm talking about acknowledging the melancholy for a while until it is woven securely into life. You may have to work at it for a period of time.

Writing about my melancholy in this book is a therapeutic strategy for me. As I said before, I have an abiding, mysterious, and complicated sadness. I feel that I can write about aging positively and yet confess that I find it sad. I also find it creative and fulfilling. Whenever we speak of emotions, it helps to keep all of them in mind. I can confess to their pain and yet feel an overall happiness about aging and becoming a real person, an essential aspect of growing old. This is what I mean by aging with soul: You grow older with a full range of emotions that sometimes contradict one another. A soulful person can hold such a varied emotional array without being overwhelmed. This is an essential art, a skill you can't do without.

Remember the lines from the *Tao Te Ching:* The sage, who is you trying to be your best, is pointed but not piercing. Piercing would be going too far, but don't merely react by being soft. Be pointed. It's similar with melancholy. You can be sad in a natural, accepting way without being depressed and seeding the world around you with your depression. It isn't easy to be around a depressed person, but a melancholic can be soothing.

I have had two or three friends in my life who were up and down emotionally, cheerful some days and melancholic the others. I liked both moods but preferred the quiet of melancholy. There seemed to be more room for friendship in times of sadness than in outgoing cheerfulness. This is not to say that sadness is better than cheerfulness, but only to notice value in not being "up" all the time.

Another lesson to take from the *Tao Te Ching* is to move in the direction of the mood that is pressing, whether it's sadness, anger, or desire, but don't take it to extremes. When you honor the mood that is gripping you, by speaking for it and allowing it some play, you can adjust your life to it, at least moderately. If you are angry, let that anger give an edge to how you speak and what you do, but don't let it get out of hand.

For example, you can take the Ficino path and dress in tune with the melancholy: dark clothes, brooding hat, scarves, and veils. Take solitary walks, listen to contemplative music, and have a good black-and-white photograph of nature nearby. You can sleep longer, move slowly, and talk less. These activities help you stay in tune with your melancholic mood. They honor it without succumbing to it fully.

The Art of Being Melancholy

Most of us are not happy about getting older. We long for the old days and wish for the bodies we used to have, and we miss friends, lovers, family members, and co-workers. The sadness we feel is natural and understandable. It's also incurable. It's part of life experience.

Arnold Palmer, the great golfer, played his last Masters Tournament in 2004. He said, "It was a tough week, ending my career as a competitive player there, knowing that I wouldn't go out and try to win one more. Yep, it's hell to get old."*

But it doesn't have to get the better of us. There are things you can do about it. You don't have to simply accept it as it is given and surrender to it. You never have to surrender completely to a feeling. There is an art to dealing with emotions, and art itself can help.

In some ways Arnie was as effective in his retirement as in his career. He brought the game of golf to a high level of distinction and cultivated young players who didn't know him at the peak of his career.

You could learn to enjoy melancholic music and painting. If you're feeling sad, listen to Samuel Barber's famous "Adagio for Strings" or J. S. Bach's "Air on a G String," or the many melancholic country songs. A song that touches me with both

*Golf Magazine, January 2007, 25.

sadness and romance is Eric Clapton's "Wonderful Tonight." Willie Nelson's "September Song" is another popular song that links melancholy with love, as is Leonard Cohen's "Suzanne." But music is personal, and you have to find just the right songs or pieces that can accompany your sadness without contradicting it.

The visual arts can also carry your emotions deeper into the realm of imagination, where they are less troublesome. The image takes some of the raw power of the feeling away by giving it shape and even a hint of meaning. The really difficult feelings are those that come at us strong and without reason. An image doesn't explain the emotion, but it wraps it in something intelligible and graspable.

A visual example would be the movie *The Truman Show,* about a man whose entire life is part of a reality TV show. He doesn't know that everything he does is being watched by millions of people on television. Everything in his life is a set and all the characters he meets follow a script. In the end he discovers a door to the real sky, through which he can escape and finally live his own life.

This film could help many people find hope for discovering their own lives and stop living the way of life their society approves and encourages. It might deepen their understanding of the importance of being yourself and the feeling of emptiness that many have when they follow the crowd. Some films can help you see important patterns that are usually invisible and that interfere with the joy of life.

We live with visual art for years and sometimes for a lifetime. We breathe in its lessons and insights. That's why we listen to a song or piece of music again and again, to let it get into us and do its good work. When you're sad, art can give image to your feeling and make it digestible and loftier than it otherwise might be. It relieves heavy feelings by giving them some distance without suppressing them.

It's even better to create your own artwork or compose and play music. Just simple singing can relieve your heaviness. Just let your voice out and create a song all by itself. That kind of singing can heal. As you gradually get your troubling emotions out of yourself and into an external form — a painting, a song, or a poem — you can feel some relief. You can see it and hear it and no longer feel forced to carry it in yourself. Art can make the feeling bearable and eventually even creative.

Aging takes you away from an active life to one that is more contemplative and expressive. Melancholy is not just sadness; it contains some of the quiet and contemplative qualities that can be useful or may actually be needed. In melancholy you may withdraw from your active life to just sit and feel things. You may not have the lightness of spirit needed to stay engaged with the turbulence of life.

Melancholy and Genius

The art historian Erwin Panofsky explored the idea of melancholy in art from the Middle Ages to the Renaissance. He charted the movement from where it was understood as an illness to when it was recognized as a sign of artistic genius. You can use your common sense to arrive at a similar conclusion. Think of people you know who are always cheerful. Maybe you see a lack of maturity. Perhaps they don't recognize the difficult challenges of life or that sometimes it makes sense to be miserable.

If you can accept melancholy as one part of your experience, without succumbing to it entirely, you can become a thoughtful person who has something to say. And that is the basis of the art of living. You have to have reflected on life, including its downside, before you can start crafting a life that is subtle and wise. This rule applies to aging. Your genius will emerge once you stop trying to be cheerful at all times and start appreciating the pains and labors of a fully lived life.

Along with excessive cheerfulness, sentimentality can also get in the way of artful aging. You enshrine youth and simply make too much of it. It, too, has its own pains and struggles. I come close to sentimentality when I talk about missing my dark, full head of hair. If I go too far in that direction, I may overlook the beauty of aging. The only way is to accept the melancholic necessities of a generous life and go forth as a changed person, one who is acquainted with sorrow.

This poignant phrase from Handel's *Messiah,* taken from Isaiah and referring to Jesus, makes the point: "He was a man of sorrows and acquainted with grief." Those who are acquainted with grief can go on to resurrect and live a joyful life. Their acquaintance with grief will make them appear more trustworthy and maybe even more attractive.

In the end you arrive at a paradox. Accepting melancholy, without letting it reach depression, is an effective path to a joyful old age. Accepting is neither wallowing in it nor avoiding it. You speak for it without glorifying or romanticizing it. You let it be without worrying excessively about it. You certainly don't become heroic in an effort to keep it at a distance.

Of course it's sad to grow old, and pangs of melancholy may well accompany you from early on in your slow drift into old age. It may sting and slow you down and diminish your joy. But it can also deepen your life, give you perspective, and sharpen your understanding. It is one of those bittersweet gifts that are so common and that we have to get used to as we learn more about what it is to be a human being.

5

PROCESSING LIFE EXPERIENCES

I'm sitting with a client, a sixty-five-year-old man who is a therapist himself. I've been impressed with his understanding of human nature and the absence of conflict in his life at the moment. He seems to have resolved many issues of his past and is quite comfortable with himself. He has many close friends and is interested in science, the arts, and the spiritual life. As I listen to him talk about his role in his family — his children, of course, are grown and married — I admire the calmness of his soul and the richness of his life. I'd like to be his friend, though I know that it isn't easy to be relaxed in a friendship when you are also the therapist.

We spend most of our formal time together focused on his dreams, which hint at how he might deal with some of the issues that are current in his life. But there is no bloodshed, fright, paranoia, construction, or wandering that is the stuff of many people's dreams. Even his deep inner life appears calm and in order. Not much is happening.

One day he presents me a dream in which he is teaching a group of young people, when a member of "the board" appears and tells him that the board doesn't approve of what he's teaching. They've decided to let him go, and he feels sad to leave his students behind. He loved being a teacher, but there is nothing he can do if the board doesn't support him.

We talk about the dream for a while, and I feel unusually at a loss for meaning. With this man and with most of my clients I usually arrive at a point where the dream elucidates some aspect of life. I don't mean that we solve the dream or apply it in a final and obvious way. But this time I have no idea what the dream might be saying, how it might connect to my client's life, or what general theme or truth it might convey.

I did know that my client had a history of getting into trouble with organizations like churches, schools, and other groups. He was a quiet gadfly, taking positions that were not popular among establishment people. He was a reluctant rebel, I thought, who lost his job more than once because of his public stands.

But now he is retired and has no organizations in his life to answer to. There is no board to give him any grief. He is free and easy and doesn't have to answer to anyone. So what could the dream be about?

I don't believe that dreams are meaningless. We are the ones who have the problem of not grasping the meaning. I said to myself: This session is going to feel worthless to this man, who, retired, doesn't have the money to spend on a therapist who can't help him. I felt challenged.

But then I thought of the man's life story, where the theme of taking unpopular positions and being threatened by a board kept coming up. Maybe he is not living this pattern now in retirement. Maybe he is still trying to work it out as a piece of his past. Maybe the pure emotion in being rejected still floats in his system, not yet settled, still causing some discomfort.

As I think this through, another thought comes to me, one that is more typical of a dream image. I have been too literal about the board. Everyone has a board in his mind that he has to answer to and that he or she sometimes fails and disappoints. That board doesn't let us feel satisfaction about what we have done. I wonder if my friend is sad about all the rejections life has given him, as if they were one overall punishment.

In later sessions we had the opportunity to move more directly into the feelings my client had of being a failure. They were not dominant in him. He was generally a happy and content person. But even in the midst of comfort he might have some unfinished material from his past. That is how I felt about his "board," a leftover from his early days that was still gnawing at his present happiness. We were able to sort out the personal history and arrive at a place of deeper contentment.

Digesting Past Experiences

Aging with soul means becoming who you are essentially. You keep going over your experiences in a spirit of wonder, telling your stories again and again. You get to know more about yourself and you act from that knowledge. As you tell your stories, you sink further into your fate and you find your identity. None of this is superficial. Identity has nothing to do with ego; it emerges gradually from deep in the soul.

My friend who dreamed of answering to "the board" may have to reflect on his experiences on a college campus the way I continue to think about my near-death accident in a boat with my grandfather. It isn't obvious to either of us what those past experiences mean or how and why they continue to impact us. But clearly they are asking for something. All we can do is remember, consider, explore, and take them seriously. This is what older people do when they are sitting quietly.

The Essential Raw Material

Some events need working through more than others. I see this principle lived out in therapy. In every life a few events give a person's overall experience a certain direction or tone. For some people it's a parent's emotional issue, a traumatic event, abuse of one kind or another, a helpful relative or teacher, a serious illness, an accident, or a big move to another geographical area. The possibilities are many, but everyone can tell a life story and see significant turning points or influences that leave a mark.

Working through these events, especially the unsettling ones, is a big part of aging, in the sense that I am using the word. If we do nothing with them, they tend to block the flow of life and interfere with the aging and maturing process. These thoughts and dreams keep coming up in conversation, begging for attention.

In my therapy practice I've worked with a

number of women in their late forties and early fifties who had particular difficulty getting their lives on track. They couldn't secure a settled relationship or satisfying work. The one issue they all shared was their parents' failure to enjoy happy lives together.

Typically the fathers didn't know how to be in a close relationship with another person and expressed their frustration in overbearing efforts to control everyone in the family, therefore not only depriving their children of love but also making them the victims of empty authority and chronic anger. The mothers were often appeasers, not standing up for their daughters or retreating into the materialism of a proper and comfortable home.

I generalize, but this description summarizes many life stories I have heard. You could say that it's a picture of modern Western life. We're not good at the dynamics of marriage, and those difficulties pass down to the children, who eventually discover the effect bad parenting has had on them. In their middle age they feel the impact painfully. The parents' difficulty in being married is part of the child's life story and sometimes prevents the child from aging well.

It's clear that we need to reassess the very institution of marriage and attitudes toward parenting. Today these important roles are largely carried out unconsciously, and so a great deal of shadow material creeps into them, presenting obstacles to children. As adults these children still have to deal with the impact of unconscious marrying and parenting. It would be better to be aware of the deep issues and be more conscious.

Some people like to divide life into halves, the first half of life having its own tasks, and the second half turning in a different direction. I prefer to imagine a whole life unfolding in multiple phases.

Perhaps I'm influenced by my own experience, a life full of surprises and many turning points. I had a long period of apprenticeship: leaving home at thirteen and embarking on a unique and very engaged life in a monastery. People are often intrigued by this part of my story, though it doesn't feel quite as remarkable to me, probably because it wasn't so unusual in the 1950s. I wandered for a few years, looking for a personal path, and then found focus through my doctoral studies in religion. These were obviously an outgrowth of my monastic life, but they also expanded my outlook and brought me to my ultimate life's work: writing about the soul. My doctoral studies at Syracuse University opened worlds to me, and then my later apprenticeship to James Hillman and his community completed that education, adding depth psychology to spirituality.

By fifty, I was ready to "graduate." I was married, for the second time, and had a daughter and a successful book, *Care of the Soul.* My life changed radically, if rather late. Most of my colleagues had children and success in work much earlier in life. I detect five or six significant turning points in the arc of my life.

The first fifty years had clear segments: general childhood unconsciousness, with a taste of death; the move into a bigger and more intense world of spirituality and study; a period of uncertainty and wandering; further study and experience bringing soul and spirit, or psychology and spirituality, together; and finally, a productive, fulfilling life as a husband, father, and public spiritual leader.

Fifty was the fulfillment of many experiments. I was able to transform a happy childhood into happy parenting, and an early wish to be a priest into an odd and unexpected secular priesthood as a spiritual writer and teacher. The women in therapy I mentioned turned fifty feeling that it was time to find a solid base in work and a relationship. But their troubled childhoods kept getting in the way. They had to work hard with their raw material before they could make the turn and age well.

One of my clients keeps remembering one scene from when she was about twelve, when her father screamed at the top of his lungs at her for breaking one of his annoying, minor rules. This impatient, unaccepting, and unreasonable father shouting his wrath is one of the first scenes that defined her place in life. As an adult she has made progress, through several different forms of therapy, by finding her own "rules," and not caving in to many father figures in her life. But the work isn't done, and she still struggles with the old pattern. Being a truly aged self, for this woman, would mean learning how to be in a relationship with a man where this pattern was far in the background. You can never expect complete resolution or perfection.

We all have raw material that needs working through. When I use that phrase "working through," I have in mind the alchemy that Jung studied so extensively and used to elucidate many life processes that can bring us to a happy old age. Alchemy refers to the process of becoming an aged or ripened person as The Work. This Work isn't a demanding ego effort to make sense of life and do it properly. No, it is going through the processes, the initiations, and rites of passage that we need in order to become mature persons, and consciously employing various methods of reflection that can release us from old inhibiting habits.

Alchemy is the process of becoming the person you are equipped to be, and finding the golden self that is hidden beneath all obstacles. Alchemy is a process the way a chemistry experiment is a careful work on the properties and possibilities of various materials. In this case, life itself processes you with the promise of making you a real and unique person.

How to Deal with Specific Raw Material

Reflection is a rich word. It means "to bend back." So when we reflect on the past, we bend back to see what has happened. It is also what happens in a mirror. We see what is in front of the mirror reflected back to us. We see ourselves from a different perspective, appreciating the many facets of the self.

When we reflect on experiences in our lives, we bend back, placing ourselves back in time. The past is our rich storehouse of images and narratives that make the present meaningful and possible. We are sometimes afraid of it because of the pain it has caused, but we are stronger than we think and can carry that past into the future, making the present multilayered.

How do you bend back and reflect? By having real conversations with people, for a start. Many of our encounters are small and protective because of our fear of the past. Having an open conversation, where we tell our stories without excessive censoring, is a form of reflection, and it's an effective one because we hear the story and make it public. You can easily tell the difference between revealing yourself in a story about your life and hiding details that you fear would show too much.

You can also reflect by simply thinking about old times again and again. You can make a point to meet with a close friend or family member with the purpose of saying something about your life that is revealing. The revelation is a first step toward acknowledging what has happened to you. It may even be a discovery. You may begin the story in a familiar way and then mention details that you had forgotten or repressed. Owning your past allows you to feel the weight of your own experience. You can go on from there more as yourself than if you are hiding and disowning elements of your identity.

A person will say, "I've never told anyone this before." This is a special moment. A revelation is pending, and that revelation may be helpful to the one making it. He or she is letting down a barrier so that something new may happen. Although it may not seem that way at the moment, such an opening up is a kind of reflection. The breakthrough allows you to reflect on events that you've kept hidden. That is a step forward.

As I mentioned, Jung used the imagery of alchemy for the process of soul-making or working through your raw material. The material itself was called, in the Latin of the alchemists, *prima materia.* Prima means "first," but it can also mean "primal" or "raw." We usually say "raw material."

The alchemist accumulated actual raw material, various substances that he put into the glass vessel, where it could be mixed with other material, heated, and observed. That is exactly what we do with our memories and other thoughts. We bring them out of hiding and put them in a container where they can be seen. An open conversation is such a container. It allows us to keep putting material into the collection for processing, and it allows us to look at it all closely — reflection. Other containers might be formal psychotherapy, a family reunion, or writing in a diary.

Psychotherapy is a particularly intense form of conversation where you focus on the material of the soul: memories, ideas, emotions, relationships, successes, and failures. It all goes into the pot of reflection, where it can be seen, heated up with intense analysis, and transformed. We need containers that hold the material of our lives, allow us to observe it, and encourage emotional heat and transformation.

In therapy, the first problem may be one of creating the vessel. One day, a woman came to see me; she was quite eager to find out what therapy could do for her. At the first session she walked into the room, sat down, and did nothing. She didn't say a word. I asked a number of questions, which only elicited some grunts or stillborn one-word answers. Nothing happened. After an hour there was no material in the vessel. She never came back.

Maybe another therapist could have handled that situation better than I did, but I felt that the woman was at a point where she just couldn't open up. Without any material, there wasn't much we could do. I can imagine my wife getting her to make drawings or paintings or do yoga postures to pry loose some of the material, but I didn't have those resources. Besides, it didn't seem right for me to take the role of encouraging a confession. In fact, I felt that the material was the plain fact that this person was not ready to look into her soul. Or maybe I was not the right person to help her do so. I honored that material by not forcing anything different. The therapy became the place where nothing could happen.

Today it seems that many people are not interested in living a reflective life. Modern life is dedicated to action or planning for action. We may evaluate what we have done, so that our future action will be better. But this is not reflection, it is not truly bending back into the past. It is using the past for a better future.

Reflection does its job without serving as an evaluation or plan. In itself it deepens our state of being. We become more thoughtful people through reflection, and that transformation is part of aging.

For a short while when I was living in the monastery, as a community we would meet after an event and talk about it, under the leadership of a young but wise prior. Our purpose was not to evaluate it with the hope of doing it better next time, but simply to see what came up in our reflections. We thought our community would benefit from sheer conversation centered on a common experience.

Reflection fosters being rather than doing, and aging has to do with who you are more than with what you do. If you keep having plain experiences without thinking back on them, you develop your external life but not your interior life. With reflection, you draw closer to your emotions and to the meaning of events.

I understand that people differ on the scale from active to reflective. I happen to be on the far end of reflective myself, and I admire people who make more of an active contribution to society. But since the culture as a whole is given to action and doesn't understand reflection, I put the accent there.

A reflective person develops an interior life, but what do we mean by that? Interiority is the capacity to hold an emotion without acting on it, to feel its layers and meaning and tone, to connect it with other experiences and to appreciate its value. It's the ability to think things through to their depth.

When you have an interior life, you are somebody. You are more than a cardboard personality. You're complex, layered, and sophisticated in a genuine way. I've used these words before to describe what it is to age with soul. Developing your interiority is the same as aging well.

Ultimately you become like two persons — one that people see and the other less visible but equally important. A hidden self doesn't have to be a bad thing. It may be a quiet interior life that doesn't show itself often. This hidden interior can make you interesting and give you dimension.

One of my closest friends — we met around 1980 — is Pat Toomay, a former professional football player. When I'm out with him, people often notice his Super Bowl ring and are excited about this active side of his life. But Pat and I met because of our common interest in European Renaissance magic. When you discover this very different side of Pat, you realize that he is a very intelligent person with an amazing depth of knowledge and understanding. These are two of Pat's "selves," quite different from each other: one prominent in the world of sports and entertainment and the other less visible but now the primary source of Pat's life work in his more mature years.

Some people go through a depressive collapse or at least a flattening of energy when their public life ends. But Pat's intellectual inner self went into high gear when he retired from football. He is a good model for aging well, because he has an inner life that began to flourish as he got older. This is the pattern I'm looking for: As you get older, your life becomes more active than ever in certain ways, and aging means an increase of vitality, not a decrease. But this works best when the inner life has a base and can become more important as the years go by.

Pat is a reflective person, not only when writing about his experiences in football, but also when thinking about the big questions of myth, symbol, religion, and art. People often endlessly discuss the externals: politics, entertainment, and the weather. There may be some reflection in these conversations, but they could be more substantial if they included the bigger questions of meaning, history, and social justice. We could all become philosophers as we get older and start thinking more and doing less.

It's difficult for a person to age with soul if the intellectual life is stagnant. But just think of things we talk about, the books we read, the movies we watch. They are mainly external and unconsciously play out the issues in our lives, especially those that have little reflection: sexuality, violence, power, love, and intimacy.

The older years offer a perfect time to reflect more often, more deeply and more seriously on these important aspects of life. Of course, we need to begin this kind of reflection in our youth, but it can reach its depth in old age. Being part of a culture that has lost its interest in profound ideas and intense reflection on experience makes aging more difficult.

Discovering the Kernel of Your Existence

I had a dream recently in which I was in Ireland in a shop talking with an Irishman. I asked him how old he thought I was. "I'd say thirty," he said. "Well, I'm seventy-six," I said. He didn't seem interested in my information and just asked me to join him in some project he was involved with.

I thought it was interesting to have a dream about aging just when I'm writing a book on the subject.

The first striking thing about the dream is

the notion that to the Irishman I'm thirty years old. He sees my younger self and is not interested in the fact that I'm seventy-six. I first visited Ireland when I was nineteen and still in monastic life. I studied philosophy in Northern Ireland from ages nineteen to twenty-one.

In Ireland I discovered the ways of a new culture that coincidentally was the homeland of my ancestors. I met Irish cousins and quickly grew to love the country and to feel at home there. I also began to think philosophically and was introduced to existentialism, a big step toward a different view of religion.

This was one of the first intense experiences I had of aging, leaving some of my youth behind, discovering new worlds, and learning how to think. I can recall experiences before my trip to Ireland that helped me age, but none were quite as powerful. In another chapter I describe in some detail my friendship with Thomas MacGreevy, an important mentor who was part of my Ireland experience.

During that first stay in Ireland I also began reading many writers, especially James Joyce and Samuel Beckett, who steered me away from an innocent view of religion, another aging process. Why did the

Irishman in the dream think I was thirty rather than twenty? Maybe because I have grown some since those early days and yet still retain some of my "twenties in Ireland" youthfulness. Certainly, the dream is saying that I am younger in some ways than my literal seventy-six years.

The dream also invites me to reflect on my feelings about Ireland. At fifty I began to travel to Ireland regularly. One year I brought my family to live in Dublin for a year and put our children into Irish schools. It was not an easy year, and we all agreed that the family aged considerably during that time. We all loved and still love Ireland, but the experience of being in a different culture had its challenges.

There is also the fact that I come from an Irish family, completely Irish on my mother's side. My wife is fully Irish in background, as well, and soon after we all arrived in Ireland we discovered a big, warm, and talented family of relatives who are still important in our lives today.

I often travel to Ireland by myself now, and I know I'm looking for and experiencing something important and quite deep for me. When I'm there, I often just walk the streets of Dublin, taking in all the sights that by now are very familiar to me. I seem to be looking for lost parts of my self, and I wish I had even closer ties to Ireland. I wish my grandparents, instead of my great-grandparents, had been born there so I could now be an Irish citizen. What is that wish, except some desire to be more closely connected to that important part of my identity? I'm looking for a past, perhaps a lost sense of myself, which seems essential.

Years ago a therapist advised me not to confuse the Ireland of my dreams with the actual place — this isn't my first dream of Ireland. In that sense maybe there is a part of me that is Irish in not so literal a way. One memory makes this clear to me.

After publishing *Care of the Soul* I had many opportunities to create a new life and new work. People asked me to set up training programs and create study guides and courses, maybe a center somewhere for people to visit. But I kept thinking of Samuel Beckett and James Joyce. I wanted to be a writer, not the founder of a school. I was clear about that. And so I created the life of a fairly isolated author. I traveled a lot, but I didn't found anything. I have lived like a writer in the fashion of my Irish idols.

These thoughts about my life in relation to Ireland are an example of how reflection can contribute to aging with soul. I am bending back to Ireland. As I continue to think about my Irish roots and experiences and about Ireland as the home of my ancestors, I develop an identity. I become someone with an ancient past and a broad level of belonging. Because of this Irish connection I am more of a person, more layered and deeply established. Every contact with Ireland has aged me by bringing out my interesting complexity and giving me a colorful and potent background. By becoming a richer personality, I am aged. I have not just gone through life on a single, thin plane of reality.

I have found that I have to actually visit Ireland to know the place and the people before I can fruitfully reflect on my Irishness. I feel at home there, and that sense of home gives me a base even when I am at my other home in New Hampshire. There, the longing for Ireland fills me with fantasies of the place and of being there, which are another form of reflection. When I am in the United States I am thinking about Ireland, and when I'm in Ireland I feel my American soul with greater intensity.

In spite of my love of Ireland, I choose to live in New Hampshire. I love this home, too, and largely because of my knowledge of American history and culture, I am dedicated to the well-being of America, as well. I count among my neighbors Emily Dickinson, Ralph Waldo Emerson, Henry David Thoreau, and Walt Whitman, and among my compatriots Louis Armstrong, Benjamin Franklin, Thomas Jefferson, Anne Sexton, Alvin Ailey, Woody Allen, Joyce Carol Oates, Oprah Winfrey, Susan B. Anthony, all of whom let their talents shine and dedicated themselves to the American vision.

Reflecting on these creative Americans has inspired me to make my own contribution to the positive, utopian vision of what humanity can be. The more I feel part of this movement, the more mature I become, the more I age in soul. Anyone can do this — age by becoming a visionary and advocate for the human experiment.

I have an Irish soul and an American soul, and the two seem to coexist fruitfully. One of the things I look for in Ireland is an "old country." I love the old buildings, the many ruins, and the traditional ways that pepper the very modern culture there. It sounds as though I am looking for age itself, not growing older as much as gaining an awareness of the old, old self that resides deep in my soul.

Developing a Clearer, Deeper Sense of Self

Aging with soul is the process of becoming a full, rich, and interesting person. It happens over time and requires your active participation. It isn't automatic. Often when we use the word *aging* we give the impression that aging just happens in spite of our wishes or our participation. But when you look closely and see that to age means to become somebody, then you understand that the process can't go on without your involvement. You age yourself. You do things that make you an interesting, evolved, and ripened person.

Here are some guidelines for being proactive as you age with soul:

1. Accept promising invitations from life for greater and deeper experiences. It's easy to excuse yourself when the opportunity arises to try new things. It might be traveling to unfamiliar places, developing new skills, trying a new job or career, or cultivating new friendships and relationships.

2. Reflect on your experience so far through open and probing conversations. Use your friendships for

meaningful talk. Reviewing your experience in a probing manner can give you depth and complexity.

3. Look far into your past to see where you have come from and what your heritage has to offer you. I wrote about my Irishness. You may reflect on your European, African, or Asian roots. This kind of reflection helps you know what you're made of and what kind of person you can become as you age.

4. Use travel as way to discover who you are and what you are capable of. Travel does not have to be unconscious, or merely for entertainment value. It can have a purpose, a personal point for your development. You may choose where to travel by knowing how pieces of your self are scattered around the world. For example, I find many parts of myself that I'd like to embody in England, and I discover other different parts of myself in Italy, a place I also love.

5. Read authors who allow you to hold a mirror up to yourself and give you ideas on who you might become. Learn skills in the arts and crafts,

for instance, that surprise you with hidden talents and pleasures. Much of the self lies undiscovered unless you experiment and allow yourself to open up outward. Experimentation is an important part of aging well. If you hide in inactivity you may never know who you are and will never have a self to become as the years go by.

Processing your life is being an alchemist to your own experience. You observe it closely, watching it change, noticing hidden colorings and smells. You remember sensually. You help all your experiences focus on your current life and identity. They are the raw stuff of your soul. Out of them emerges a person the world has never seen before. This process is called aging.

6
THE MATURING OF SEXUALITY

Aphrodite found Anchises all alone and
saw how beautiful the gods had made him.
The daughter of Zeus stood before him
looking like a young maiden. Desire took
over him. "You must be a goddess," he
said. "No," she replied, "I'm human." And
she filled his heart with delicious longing.
— Homeric Hymn to Aphrodite

Some of the warm memories from my early
teenage years are going out to the car on
cold snowy winter mornings in Michigan
when my father volunteered to drive me to
school. We would scrape off the ice, the car
running quietly all the while, and then crawl
into the warm interior. We'd sit still a moment and then my father would sit back and
work his way toward a conversation about
sex. I knew that he had read books on sex
education, and always wanted to be a good
and enlightened parent. I was embarrassed

and couldn't wait for the car to get rolling toward school.

The trouble was that my father was a plumber, more formally a sanitary engineer. And so the lesson on sex was always about sperm and eggs and the body's plumbing. I appreciated my dad's good intentions, but his approach didn't answer my questions. The cold facts didn't match my very warm fantasies and preoccupations. Now, in memory, I treasure those frigid moments with him, even if the sex education wasn't what I wanted.

In almost every field today the preference is to talk like an engineer, whether you're discussing a social problem or difficulty in a relationship. We live in a technological age when hardware and hardwiring are our favorite metaphors. We apply the same mechanical language to sexuality, and so when we try to figure out elderly sex, naturally we focus on the breakdown of organs and bodies. A more positive outlook comes when we instead consider sexuality as an experience of the whole person, not only regarding emotions and relationships, but considering the search for meaning, as well.

Sexuality in Aging

It's difficult to draw meaningful conclusions about sexuality in aging because everyone is different and their situations are different. Some people age quickly and seem to lose their interest in sex. In others libido either remains strong or gets better. Some have no intimate partners, and some don't want them. Some people get sick or physically weak and don't think as much about sex.

Studies show a decline in interest in sex as people get older, but also indicate that almost half of men and a smaller percentage of women over seventy still want a good sexual experience. About the same number say that sex at seventy-plus is as good or better than ever. Obviously, it's a mistake to think that older people are not interested in or capable of sex. Some want sex, but medications, surgeries, or lack of a partner get in the way.

But there is also a psychological barrier. Some older people think it isn't seemly to want sex at their age. Younger people don't help when they show their surprise or even disgust at an older person's interest in sex. So it appears that our general attitude toward sex plays an important role in how we deal with sexuality as we get older.

What Is Sexuality For?

In general, society is confused about sex. We have graphic sexuality everywhere in our movies and on the Internet. Yet our churches and political leaders often advocate purity and restraint. We are split between fascination and fear, graphic sexuality and moral outrage, Puritanism in the sense of strict moral control and lasciviousness. Such a splitting of values and passions is always a sign of confusion and the failure to deal adequately with the issue at hand.

Therefore, somehow we have to work toward keeping sexual restraint and freedom much closer together, so that we might have comfortable limits on sex in the media, for example, without being prudish about it. It doesn't work well to have one group urging for sexual excess and some other populations pressing for moral control. This is a concrete example of the split I mentioned.

A good starting point would be to find ways to be more relaxed about sexuality and about our judgments and worries, but for that we need a deeper understanding of what sex is all about. Most people would probably say that sex is for having children, expressing love, and satisfying a biological urge. But sex has less tangible qualities and purposes that tie it in with other aspects of daily life.

For example, sex may begin in our noticing the beauty of another person. Beauty wakes you up to the possibility of a relationship. The person may not be beautiful to everyone or match cultural standards of beauty, but you notice their beauty and desire stirs. So we can generalize: sexuality has something to do with beauty, and maybe beauty has something to do with sexuality.

Plotinus, the second-century Greek philosopher whose work is all about the soul, refers constantly to beauty. He makes this provocative statement: "The soul is always an Aphrodite." For the ancient Greeks, Aphrodite was the goddess of beauty and sexuality. I take this to mean that sexuality is essential to the life of the soul, and that erotic life is equally important. Beauty is a given.

Obviously I have to explain myself because today we don't see sex in such exalted terms, and we use the word erotic to mean something dark. For the Greeks, Eros was a god, known as the great creator who holds the world together by a cosmic loving embrace. This eros has to do with loving life, the world, and everything in it, and wanting to be connected and involved. We can feel eros for our garden or toward our work and, of course, for a person. In that case, eros may lead to sexuality.

The Catholic visionary scientist and priest Pierre Teilhard de Chardin wrote similarly about love: "If there were no internal propensity to unite, even at a prodigiously rudimentary level — indeed in the molecule itself — it would be physically impossible for love to appear higher up, with us, in hominized form. . . . Driven by the forces of love, the fragments of the world seek each other so that the world may come into being." This cosmic or personal theory of eros echoes the Greek mythologists and brings this rich idea into modern life. Our erotic feelings are a high version of the same energy that holds the elements together. They are noble and creative.

I'm making this connection between the erotic and the sexual because, especially as we get older, we may satisfy our sexual desire through a broader erotic lifestyle. I don't mean that we should have less sex in our lives, but that we can extend our sexuality to include pleasure in the beauty of the world.

When I work with people's sexual dreams, I often get the sense that what is being asked for is not more sexual experiences but more delight in being alive. Lust for a person is surrounded by a lust for life. As you get older you may or may not have the same amount of sex, but you can expand your sexuality to become a significant part of your lifestyle.

You can do more sensual things, like gardening, painting, taking nature walks, and eating with imagination. These don't take the place of sexual experience, but they extend it, making you a more erotic person. If you were to study Plotinus, you might appreciate how living more erotically is the same as bringing soul into your life.

Follow the chain: sexuality to an erotic life to becoming more soul-oriented. An erotic life puts an emphasis on pleasure, desire, connection, contact, involvement, and deep fulfillment, not just among people, but with the things of the world, as well. Throughout your life, even in your younger years, you might tap into your sexuality to become a more loving person, more connected to the physical world, and capable of seeing the beautiful in unusual places. You may appreciate beauty in a person that other people pass over as ordinary, and you could use your sexual experiences as the starting point for a more erotic life in general. I'm not talking about sublimating your physical sex, but rather expanding and deepening it.

In this way, as you get older you naturally become more sexual, not less. Besides, as you live more erotically, your interest in sex may increase. There is nothing worse for an older person's sex life than to be vaguely depressed, angry at the world, and resigned to falling apart. It would help a person's sex life to be more alive and living from a deeper, more pleasurable place.

The important role of beauty could also inspire you to pay attention to how you look. Making even small efforts to be beautiful is a way to keep your sexuality and eroticism alive and to have more soul in your life. After my mother had a stroke and subsequent brain surgery — she was eighty-seven — my teenage daughter visited her in the hospital. My mother wouldn't see her until she had primped her own hair, put on some handsome but simple clothes, and applied some makeup. For some people this preparation might seem vain, but my mother had no vanity in her. She just knew intuitively how beauty serves the soul, and she wanted more than anything to have a soul connection with her granddaughter.

Life as Foreplay

As we age and deepen our thoughts and values, we may discover that flawed bodies have a beauty that transcends the perfection of youth, that movements of the heart can be more sexual than physical positions. In fact, elderly sex may be the most fulfilling and exciting of all, precisely because it transcends ego, power, and control. In a certain way, it may be fortunate when physical sex breaks down and the soul comes into the foreground. Sometimes disappointments to the ego can crack an opening to the deep soul of a person.

Although it has other important purposes, sex is of course largely about a relationship. Even if your focus is on physical pleasures, you can do the pleasuring and receive it as part of your love for your partner. You can treat your partner as a love object without turning him or her into just an object. Lovers give each other their bodies and imaginations in the greater context of expressing love.

It helps if the sexual component has a foundation in love and friendship. Whether or not elderly sex is better than young sex in your case, the important thing is to age into your sexuality, allowing it to become more subtle and complex, more easily con-

nected to the emotions of love and together-
ness, and in these ways more satisfying and
fun.

Old friends of mine, Joel and Lloyd, are
gay and have been in a long-term three-way
relationship for years. They are among the
most creative, bright, warm, and sensitive
people I know. In a recent letter to me, Joel
hints that it isn't always easy to sustain such
a relationship, but he offers some insight.
"Lloyd and I cemented our relationship in
friendship four years before we had romance. Similar interests excited and continue to excite us. Our meeting in a high
school play meant that we both love acting
and the theater. When we discovered we
shared an irreverent sense of humor, things
really started taking off. Then, after a few
years as buddies, we noticed what one
another looked like."

Notice the foundation of the romantic and
sexual relationship: interests, humor, friendship, and then romance. This pattern echoes
the Kama Sutra, which begins with suggestions on how to live your everyday life effectively, and then goes on to sexuality.
Notice especially in these brief quotes from
Joel the love and joy he feels in spite of both
usual and not-so-common complications.

Joel goes on to speak about their trio:

171

"Lloyd has been asked about jealousy because of John. There's been none as far as I can tell. Even when I divide my attention between Lloyd and John, each gets my attention. And one more thing: From the beginning, we've been in it for the long run. These principles apply also to our life with John. The good outweighs the bad by several tons."

To be in it for the long run helps with relationships, even with older people for whom the "long run" may be not all that long. Time, in this case, is a quality rather than a quantity. If your orientation is serious, you can accomplish almost anything. It also helps to accept the bad with the good — a sign of maturity.

Joel's situation is not the norm. I understand that. But this is another aspect of the life of the soul: It doesn't always fit within conventional boundaries. If you want to live a soulful life, responsive to impulses and directives you feel deep within, you may well find yourself in "creative" arrangements. That may be the reason why we don't have a terribly soulful society: We choose standardization and compliance over listening to our hearts and living from love of both self and other. Some people, like Joel, follow their hearts and create original lives.

When the love is strong and the people involved are mature, generous, and forgiving, problems can fade into the background or are at least manageable. Attraction takes its cue from the life lived between people. Relationships often get into trouble because there isn't the vital everyday rich experience to give them grounding.

These values could help any older person make sense of his or her sexuality. You may have to explore solutions that aren't the standard fare of society. You may have to be original and imaginative as you weave your erotic values into ordinary life.

As you get older, you may find your sexuality becoming richer and more satisfying not through big orgasms, but through a more intense and pleasurable life. Think of sex as bridging lovemaking and life-making. If for some reason age has set some limits on your lovemaking, that doesn't mean it has to restrict your joy in life and the deep pleasures you can find everywhere.

I can appreciate a broader definition of sex because of my early monastic experience when I lived with a vow of celibacy. I had no sexual experience until I was twenty-six. That is not only a long time, it's the time of life when desire is strong. But I never felt repressed. I think the reason for my comfort was the intense community life I enjoyed then. The thought would come to me, when I had just had a good time with the many close friends I lived with, that the real joy in community made it possible to be celibate.

I'm suggesting that our sexual needs can be satisfied in many ways. It helps to have a broad vision of what sex is all about and of how to make life in every way sensual and joyous. These are not two different realms: lovemaking and a sensuous lifestyle; one is an extension of the other.

The Dignity of Pleasure

Pleasure is a worthy sexual goal as you get older. Today people may think of pleasure as superficial. Many men and women grew up in religious households where pleasure was considered indecent. I was always taught to be pure, to work hard, and to control myself. No one told me to pursue pleasure as a worthy goal in life. Of the hundreds of sermons I heard in my younger days, not one was about pleasure or showed positivity regarding it. Of course, it was good to have fun, and I learned from my parents to dance and play sports. But pleasure itself always had the ring of vanity and excess.

I changed my whole orientation to life when I discovered the Greek philosopher Epicurus, who taught the value of pleasure and its specific importance to the soul. From him we get the word *epicurean,* which often implies excess. But Epicurus was interested in simple, lasting pleasures like friendship and ordinary good food. He was modestly sensual. Read his writings and you'd never guess that his name would later be used for hedonism. One of his sayings gives a clear idea of what he means by pleasure: "Pleasure is freedom from bodily pain and mental anguish." Another word Epicureans often use is *tranquility.* The idea is to be comfortable and emotionally at ease.

Over the centuries, many writers who put soul at the center of their work were Epicureans who considered pleasure one of the basic elements of a soul-centered life: not wild and untamed pleasures or superficial entertainments, but the deep pleasures of family, friendship, good food, and happy times — no physical pain and no emotional disturbance.

Epicurean sexuality would have this quality of deep pleasure. It combines the pleasures of relationships with the simple sensuousness of physical contact. Put the two together — emotional connection and sensual touch — and you have Epicurean sexuality.

You can easily see how this kind of sexuality would be just right for people getting older. It isn't necessary to be as driven and excitable as when you were young in order to settle into a kind of sex that is more deeply moving and enjoyable. You can now experience a different kind of sexual expression that reaches calmly and deeply into the heart.

If an older person were to ask me what is the secret to a satisfying sex life, I wouldn't hesitate to tell him: Become an epicurean.

Sexuality Means Vitality

Over the years of practicing deep psychotherapy, I've paid close attention to the many sexual dreams people have presented. You might think they have to do primarily with the sexual experiences of the dreamer, but more often the conversation drifts toward longing and desire in general, the need to be connected in the world, and the feeling of vitality that often accompanies both erotic desire and experiences.

I've come to the conclusion that sexuality itself is largely about the great desires of life and the quest to feel fully alive. People will say that after a special sexual experience they feel good about life in general. A single experience suddenly opens into the whole of life.

This connection between sex and overall vitality offers a good reason to be positive about your sexuality as you get older, because the pattern goes in the opposite direction, as well: You can bring a general lust for life to your sex life. If you experience joy in living, naturally you will bring a good attitude toward sex, the ritualizing of vitality, and a celebration of life.

Sex with soul is generous, loving, ethical, relaxed, patient, imaginative, and sensual. It is not dominating, coercing, proving yourself, or surrendering. It offers an opportunity for souls to commingle in the context of pleasure. It is also oriented toward the world, spilling out into daily life.

As you get older, sex could become better, not worse.

Myth and Romance

For centuries "gods and goddesses" have represented the deepest patterns that shape our lives. The Greek goddess Aphrodite, almost identical to the Roman Venus, portrays the deep power and meaning in sexual pleasure. If you want to learn about deeper levels of sexuality, read stories and prayers sung to the goddess.

The Homeric Hymn to Aphrodite says that she "wakens the yearning for pleasure." In my way of thinking, good sex is not just about two people loving each other and doing the right things, but about evoking Aphrodite, making her spirit present, letting her create the arousal. You look at your lover. If all you see is an ordinary person, you may not feel the yearning. But if you glimpse Venus in your partner, desire will come to life.

You can look at your lover in different ways. You may have the eyes of a no-nonsense objective person and fail to see Venus, or you can have the romantic eyes of someone who loves and sees more than the person. These eyes allow to you see past any actual imperfections to the perfect goddess waiting there to be seen. Soulful sex starts with this romantic vision.

To invoke Venus you must allow yourself to be in a special state, not entirely conscious and in control. It may help to keep the light low. You drift into a place similar to dream, a light dream state. From there you look at your partner and touch, speak, and feel your emotions. In that condition you make love to a person transformed by your love and desire.

You are in the realm of myth, maybe not completely, but enough to give you an experience that is deeply romantic. This doesn't take away from your personal relationship, because the very point is to give each other a taste of otherworldly sex. By enjoying your partner sexually and romantically, you find your way even deeper into that person.

I'm aware, once again, that what I'm saying goes against the spirit of the times. We're supposed to get rid of fantasies, take away our projections, and get over our illusions. An alternative is to use your illusions to get to a special place that can eventually lead to knowing the real person.

A romantic favors imagination over fact and often sees value in dark, rejected elements. Romantic movies celebrate the thief and the misfit. The romantic also lives in a magical, enchanted world, where there are invisible rules that contradict the laws of nature, or at least stretch them. Above all, the romantic wants to live more by love than by logic, leading from the heart rather than the mind.

If this language sounds strange to you, read the Homeric Hymns or the poetry of D. H. Lawrence or Greek tragedies or *The Odyssey*. Lawrence writes: "What's the good of a man unless there's the glimpse of a god in him? And what's the good of a woman unless she's a glimpse of a goddess of some sort?" In a famous line at the beginning of *The Hero with a Thousand Faces* Joseph Campbell writes: "The latest incarnation of Oedipus, the continued romance of Beauty and the Beast, stand this afternoon on the corner of Forty-second Street and Fifth Avenue, waiting for the traffic light to change."* Many a man or woman has seen Aphrodite standing at the office cooler.

To live mythically today you have to let your practical mind slip into the background. Allow some fantasy. See past the literal and the pragmatic. But take it seriously. Stand apart from the crowd and be a romantic.

To invoke Venus, we pay attention to the surroundings and do what we can to evoke her. It doesn't take much. You don't have to be physically perfect or even above average. A single physical attribute — a smile, a curl of hair, a bicep, some soft clothing, a shade of color, an aroma, a few appreciative words — any of these can summon Venus, and it makes no difference how old you are.

*Joseph Campbell, *The Hero with a Thousand Faces* (New York: Pantheon Books, 1949), 4.

Transcendent Sexuality

From the soul point of view, sex is not just the expression of love and desire; it is also a genuine ritual that allows us to be in touch with the realm of the holy and mysterious. Sex can also take you out of normal time and space and allow you to drift to a level where you move deep in your thoughts, feelings and sensations. At times, it may even feel like a mystical experience. In this kind of sex we are ageless, neither young nor old, or both. At times you may feel that you are young again, in your twenties.

You may have to develop this "soul" appreciation for sex and approach it with the intention of making it deep and meaningful. You may have to learn this lesson that sex is not just for the young and not just physical, that you can go so deep into sensations and emotions, that you get lost, in a positive way, the way a religious person loses herself in meditation. You might even understand sex as a kind of meditation that serves a relationship and at the same time puts you in touch with the great mystery of life.

Sex is a dreamy experience. You don't have to be so aware and conscious. You may fall off into a kind of sensual reverie where you may not hear the sounds of life in the world around you, as in deep meditation. This is meditating in the style of Aphrodite — sensual, drifting, physical, and emotional.

Sex can go even further to touch the souls of the people involved. Your deeper self, expressed in subtle ways, does things, says things, and feels things that are at least partially hidden to consciousness. Much goes on that is not intended or understood. You prepare for sex by tapping into your depth, allowing your deeper self, your soul, to make an appearance. You can do this at any time in life, but in the older years it may be easier, because you know yourself better and are not preoccupied with many neurotic issues that a young person has to deal with. You may trust yourself and your partner more, thereby allowing your deeper self to be present.

Quiet Sex

Older people may find new pleasure in "quiet sex." Linn Sandberg, who studies sexuality in later life, has shown that older people prefer "intimacy and touch" to more energetic forms of sexual expression. The men she studied confessed that they became more skillful sexually and more considerate as they got older. Before, they simply didn't know enough about how to be a good sexual partner and were influenced by what they heard from other men. They distanced themselves from people who saw sex as dominating and self-absorbed.

By "quiet sex" I don't mean not making noise, but rather quieting any need to prove yourself, conquer, dominate, or make too much of sex. As you age, sex may become less impassioned, not because of limitations, but because it is maturing. It is a more integral part of life. It no longer breaks out as an exaggeration but stays close to other values and other aspects of living. It gives joy and erotic delight. It no longer upturns everything, but rather intensifies it.

You may discover the joys of quiet sex — emotions more settled, a more relaxed way of going about it, perhaps years of loving — and maybe struggle to give meaning to the sexual relationship. Your sexuality may change over time as you age and temper your passions rather than repressing them. Your sexuality may not be so goal-driven but instead focused on steady, calm pleasuring.

I knew a man in his late seventies, Bruce, who was happily married and yet developed an infatuation with a neighbor in her sixties. "Why did this happen to me now?" he exclaimed in our first session. "I thought I was free of this awful complexity of love and desire." He was an erudite man who had spent his life as an editor of a small-town newspaper. "I don't want it, and yet it is delicious."

A perfect and traditional description of Eros, I thought. In antiquity he was called "The Bittersweet."

"I love my wife. She would be upset if she knew I had these feelings. I don't want them, even if they bring me to life."

Those last few words struck me. This new woman has brought him to life. It must have been in his deadness that he saw her and recognized a route to vitality. Not consciously, of course, but somewhere deep inside.

"People will laugh at me. An old guy, pathetic in every respect, balding and paunchy and shuffling. What does she see in me?"

"Your soul is quite handsome, I guess." I spoke to affirm his experience.

"What can I do?"

The Zen master in me came to the foreground. "Why don't we try just being exactly with what is?"

"I know: I love my wife, I'm swept away by this other woman, I'm in a quandary, I want out but don't think I should escape."

"That's pretty good," I said. "That is what is."

This man's experience is not rare. Sexual attraction is not just for the young, and, in fact, people who have aged well may be especially susceptible to complicated connections. They are open to experience, comfortable with their emotions, and moved by desire.

You may not have such an obvious experience of your sexuality when you thought it was all behind you. But you can still benefit by understanding, as I have been saying, that sex is not all about making love. It also includes such sexual qualities as pleasure, joy, intimacy, connectedness, and sensuality in general. To be open with people, capable of closeness, having fun, engaging in real conversation — these, too, can be an expression of your sexuality in a broader sense. The secret is that these experiences can satisfy your sexual desire enough so you don't have to ruin your life experimenting with a new partner.

I thought Bruce would find his way. He acknowledged the love that had smitten him. He was fully aware of the complexity of his feelings and wishes. He loved his wife but found the new person "delicious." The scenario played out for a few months, and then Bruce decided that his wife merited all his attention. Without any drama, quieting his heart, he let go of his newfound love. But he did make changes in his life that I thought were inspired by his erotic experience. He didn't work so hard and he made a point to enjoy the simple things more.

Human sexuality is an activity of the soul. It is deep, emotional, relational, and connected with meaning. As you get older, you may discover this deeper dimension of your sexuality and actually find more pleasure in sex rather than less. Aging can be a maturing and ripening of sexuality by making it less literal, certainly less driven, and not so unconscious. It can be a matter of the heart and not just the body.

Aged Sex

A twenty-something university student, Carol Ann, once told me that she liked having sex with single older professors because they were thoughtful and attentive. She still had sex, she said, with the young male students just for their wildness and stamina. She wanted that mindless and potent sex in her life. But she'd never want a lasting relationship with one of the young bulls.

"It's like you're using them as studs," I said.

"Maybe," she said, "but they're using me, too. They're not expecting a relationship or meaningful sex from me."

I learned a lot about sexuality from Carol Ann. She had a fairly active sex life, but she was discriminating and had limits. When I knew her, in her mid-twenties, sex was the main thing in her life, but it wasn't the only thing. Men were attracted to her because they could sense her sensuality and open lifestyle immediately. It took them longer to discover that she was a thoughtful woman who knew what she wanted and had high aspirations. That she consciously sought out partners among both young and older men shows that her sexuality was complex and in many ways rich.

Carol Ann's story could encourage older people who believe that their sexuality is behind them, in the past. Carol Ann, a vibrant and sophisticated young woman, might want one of them as a partner. She's looking for a mature person who enjoys sex but who is not full of raging, irrepressible, and long-lasting hormones. Of course, there are many men comparable to Carol Ann looking for mature women, as well.

What we really need is Viagra for the soul. We could use an intensification of personal integrity, generosity in relationship, and the capacity for intimacy. These are the qualities most often lacking in sex, and they are the very qualities that an older person might have.

Aging Sexually

Then how do you age sexually?

1. As much as possible, you work out conflicts that have roots in your early life. Sex embraces the whole of your life and is especially influenced by childhood experiences. You get images and narratives from many parts of your life that add up to a developing picture of what your sexuality is. There may be a lot of wounding in that picture that is in need of reflection and working out.

2. You take a proactive position in response to the opportunities and challenges life presents to you as a unique person. Sex is both the symbol of and the harbinger of life. It offers vitality in all spheres. Although it has several specific purposes, at the same time it affects everything you do. Aging means taking life on and being transformed and matured. This is especially true

of your sexuality. Hide out from life and your sexuality will suffer.

3. Many of us have sexual wounds of various kinds, so you do your best at being a loving and sensuous person. Wounds to the psyche are both the occasion of some suffering and limitation and also a positive force for depth and character. It all depends on how you deal with the wounds. Don't let them darken your mood or swamp your other emotions. Give them some of what they are asking for, but don't surrender to them.

4. Your sexuality matures as it generates an erotic style of life. An erotic life is one that enjoys deep pleasures such as friendship and intellectual curiosity. It is not conditioned only by anger, frustration, depression, and fear. The mature sexual person is in love with life and seeks vitality and connection at every turn.

5. You are less driven, less compulsive sexually, and make better choices that keep your sexuality in line with other values. In youth we tend to make rash decisions about partners and our willingness to enter sexual

situations. The aged person usually understands his emotions better and knows not to follow them blindly and impulsively.

6. You understand that sex has real depth of meaning, and so you don't take it lightly. You feel the weight of sexual decisions and consider the whole of your life. This is not a burden for the aged person but an opportunity to avoid the entanglements that siphon off energy and make life too complicated and unnecessarily difficult. The best sex doesn't contradict your values.

7. You reconcile your sexuality with your spirituality. You can give your sex life some of the qualities of your spiritual practice and thinking, and you can enjoy the kind of religious life or spirituality that is not against sex, even in subtle ways. Both sides benefit from intermingling. Spirituality without sex is empty; sex without spirituality is too small.

You age sexually when you bring your long-cultivated rich personality to a relationship and you relax and allow the other to be close and present in all his or her own differences. Sex is not about blending but about coupling — two different worlds, not colliding, but enjoying each other.

■ ■ ■ ■

PART THREE:
IMAGINE AGING
DIFFERENTLY

■ ■ ■ ■

Medicine is useless if it doesn't get rid of diseases of the body, and philosophy is useless if it doesn't get rid of diseases of the soul. — *EPICURUS*

7
ILLNESS AS AN INITIATION

One way to imagine human life is to see it as adding up experiences and memories, counting the years, and arriving at the end with a full vat of personal history. Personal growth is a similarly popular metaphor. As we have already seen, it's common for people to say that they are growing, and there are centers where you can go to have growth experiences. But this metaphor is also weak in some ways. Trees grow, but we persons become more interesting, subtle, complex, and individual as we get older. At least, one hopes we do. We don't exactly grow; we go through a process of maturing that includes setbacks and reversals. James Hillman questioned the use of the growth fantasy in psychology: "Psychology's growth fantasy seems a curious leftover of the early twentieth century's colonial, industrial, and economic fascination with increase: the bigger the better."*

So, another way to imagine the passing of years is as a series of initiations or passages. Initiation means beginning, and indeed throughout a lifetime most people go through various beginnings as they enter new dimensions of who they are. A child becomes a teenager, a teen becomes a young adult, and so on.

Anthropologists have given us striking pictures of rites of passage in various nature communities, where a young person might be buried in a hollow in the earth or under leaves to indicate death to the old phase and rebirth into the new one. There may be pain and fright followed by community acceptance and celebration. It isn't easy to leave behind a phase we've come to know and enjoy.

Starting a new job may be a rite of passage. You not only learn the ropes and discover what your duties are, but you also enter an existing community of workers and a set of traditions and customs. You may adopt a new style of dress and pick up new vocabulary. It may not be easy to get through the necessary initiation, and it

*James Hillman, "Abandoning the Child," *Loose Ends* (Zürich: Spring Publications, 1975), 28.

could take a long time, even years.

One of those initiating experiences common in old age is sickness. We tend to think of illness as a physical breakdown in need of repair. But as an experience — emotional, intellectual, and relational — illness may force us to examine our lives, face our mortality, and sort out our values.

The Soul of Medicine

Several years ago I wrote a book on the soul of medicine, and in the research phase I interviewed many healthcare workers and patients. One of the things that struck me most in talking to patients was a common sentiment: Many wished that they didn't have to go through the pain and anxiety of illness, but at the same time they said it was the best thing that could have happened to them. Or, as a few summarized dramatically, they were healed by their illness.

Being sick forced them to reconsider their lives, especially the way they spent their time and how they handled their relationships. After having a taste of mortality, they felt the need to change and make life count. They sensed the preciousness of every day and saw past the minor issues in their marriages and families to the priceless value of those relationships. They felt they became better people because of their illnesses.

This is the nature of a life initiation: You go through pain and worry, you reflect as you have never reflected before, and you come out the other end a renewed person. Over time, you take note of opportunities for initiation when they appear and respond openly and courageously. In this way your fate and destiny unfold, and you become who you are capable of being.

But there is a major difference between understanding illness as physical breakdown and seeing it as an opportunity for initiation. In the first case, you are not present to the experience as a person. You are only going through the physical ordeal. Your soul is not engaged. In the second case, the illness has the positive benefit of taking you further along your life course, as you become a real person, a true individual. Illness serves as a vehicle for transformation.

If you can go through the soul experience of illness, your relationships may improve and your life will have more meaning. You will even be better prepared for the continuing drift of time, because you will have a record or habit of responding to life's invitations. You won't have to surrender to the unconsciousness of it all or try to catch up at the last minute.

When you consider the impact on the soul of any kind of illness, especially as you get older, you see its value. You don't treat it simply as an obstacle to your plans and hopes. And since many older people do experience new illnesses, this point of view is critical.

Society is not set up to care for the soul. It is largely caught up in the myth of materialism, the philosophy that treats the body as an object in need of mechanical and chemical repairs. It doesn't understand the soul of medicine and it ignores any opportunity for personal initiation when illness comes along.

Therefore, it's up to us as individuals to do what we can to glimpse the soul in illness and to pursue treatments accordingly.

Let me suggest a few things you can do to bring a deeper point of view to your illness and its treatment. Some of these will be obvious and easy, but some may seem unusual to you. You are probably not accustomed to living in a world that gives much attention to your depth.

1. My first recommendation is one many people make: Express your emotions. If you're anxious, show it. You can also put your worries

into simple, direct words and tell them to people you trust. Leaving your feelings unarticulated only pushes them down where they will work against you instead of for you. Don't hedge. Express yourself directly and clearly. People often reveal only one acceptable part of the picture, or cover their feelings over with all kinds of excuses and explanations. They put them out there but take them back at the same time.

A good soul-centered health-care worker will encourage your feelings and listen to your words. An excellent worker will give your soul many things it needs, especially a caring attitude and a depth of understanding. Many people working in medicine are afraid of feelings and have been taught questionable ideas about hiding, all, of course, for the good of the patient.

2. Tell your story. Many sick people feel a need to tell the story of the current illness, as well as stories about past physical problems and about their lives in general. These stories are of the greatest impor-

tance. A human being could be defined as a storytelling animal. Stories put many anxious experiences together in a form that offers meaning and calms and reassures.

Again, a soulless culture doesn't understand the importance of stories. Some health-care workers may be jaded and tired of stories from their older patients. That is a sad circumstance because although everyone needs to tell their stories, even children, old people have a natural need to put their experiences and memories into narrative. The rest of us play our part by listening.

You should understand that this narrative has a special quality that the simple listing of facts doesn't have: It thrives on repetition. You tell the same story over and over. Each time there may be a slight change of detail or emphasis. This is enough to warrant a retelling. Listeners need patience and need to understand that stories are essential and they have to be repeated.

3. Take time to meditate. Even if you're not a skillful meditator, you

can easily take advantage of waiting times and downtime to simply sit and let your mind go blank or just allow images to drift through. That's meditating. Breathe more deeply and calmly than usual. Sit a tad more formally — back straight, feet on the floor, hands in a gesture that is meaningful to you. If you don't know what is meaningful, use a traditional gesture or mudra. Touch your thumb to your middle finger and rest your hands on your thighs. Close your eyes, or squint.

4. Note your dreams. You may never have taken your dream life seriously. Do it now. I have been a psychotherapist for forty years and have helped people sort through their lives almost entirely through attention to their dreams. I can't tell you how useful they can be. And you don't have to be an expert. You don't even have to understand them. Just write down or record in some way everything you remember from a night of dreaming. Keep these notes in a special blank book that is private. Every once in a while, read over what you've writ-

ten. Consider your dream log as part of your treatment.

5. Pray. Prayer is not just for believers. It's a practice you can enjoy and benefit from whether you are an ardent churchgoer or an atheist. You don't have to believe in any creed or give your loyalty to any religion. As a human being you can pray naturally. Even a believer would do well to learn to pray naturally and in ordinary words. When you are getting old and are sick, you have to reach beyond modern medicine. Just open your heart and ask the universe, the Mother Goddess Nature, Gaia the earth goddess, or the Nothing you sense around you for healing and comfort.

It's a special moment when a normally secular, non-believing person feels so hopeless and ineffective that he naturally blurts out a prayer. I don't mean this in the usual sentimental sense of believers smiling smugly when someone is "converted." I mean a breakthrough from a limited, materialistic existence to a more open-ended one, where mystery must be accounted for. Illness may well inspire such a breakthrough, which can be a signal of significant aging.

6. Open your heart to your loved ones and everyone else. The best way to heal yourself is to heal the world around you. If you have blocked relationships, unblock them. Take the initiative. Don't wait for the other person. Be generous. Generosity is one of the most healing of virtues. No quid pro quo. No expectation of anything in return. Give your gift cleanly.

   Be similarly openhearted with health-care workers and others you come in contact with. Be a more open person now, as part of your healing. Speak what you usually leave unsaid: your gratitude and your praise. Engage the world in a kind and loving way. And yes, if you must, let your anger and frustration out, as well.

7. Listen to the poetry of your body. Your body is an expressive presence. You don't have to be fussy about meanings. If your belly is the problem, remember that it is traditionally the place where your anger

and strength reside. Your heart, obviously, is loving and relating. Your lungs are taking the world in; the life rhythm of in and out. Liver? Keeps your blood clean and balanced. Headaches? Your mind, thoughts, and imagination. Legs? Get you around, allow you to travel. Hands and fingers? Making and doing things.

8. Trust your intuitions. Play a central role in your treatment. Have important objects of power around you: statues, jewelry, paintings, talismans. Use music to keep you in a calm and timeless state.

9. When you go to the doctor, bring an advocate with you, preferably a friend or family member, but one who can deal with the system. Have a small recorder or notepad with you. Write down what you want to ask about and what is said. Tell your health-care provider what you are experiencing. Ask questions. Ask for more time, if you need it. Say what you want and need, how you hope to be treated, and what's important to you in that kind of relationship.

10. Allow your illness to have an impact

on you. Take its lessons to heart. Let it be a life passage rather than a problem. Study its history. Write poems about it. Have quality conversations about it.

Usually it's unclear why an illness should come along at a particular moment. It appears out of the blue — an unfamiliar lump, a pain in the back, an upset belly. My mother had a stroke that would prove fatal when, on an ordinary evening, she munched on some peanuts while enjoying the company of her sister.

We could treat illness as a mystery, giving it due honor, wondering about its timing and seriousness, praying for a good resolution. Most hospitals, not just religious ones, have a beautiful and inviting chapel because nothing calls more for prayer and meditation than a serious illness.

Whenever I pass a hospital at night and notice the lights in the windows — some bright, maybe at nurses' stations, and some dim or dark in patients' rooms — I think of all the people lying there, thinking and feeling and wondering. They are incubating their illnesses into their souls. That quiet time is important. It's an opportunity for people to take in what they're experiencing and let their imaginations wander through all sorts of thoughts and concerns. In this process they are becoming persons, making discoveries, and being transformed by their experience.

The ancient Greeks would go to a temple of the healing god Asklepios and spend the night there hoping for a dream or visitation that might cure them. They lay in the temple on beds called *kline,* from which we get *clinic.* It was said that they were incubating. In a half-awake state they might have sensed the healing presence of the god.

The patients in our hospitals are also incubating in the quiet hours, though we have forgotten the soul in illness and incubate without ritual or awareness. I imagine a hospital to be a hospice, a guesthouse, where people spend time lying in rest, not just recuperating their bodies but opening their souls to transformative discoveries.

Incubation is like an egg just being there in the warmth, ready to hatch. In the case of illness, you can incubate by lying there in the warmth of your thoughts and memories, letting the illness hatch an as-yet-undiscovered portion of your soul, your very identity. Illness is a powerful event for your inner life and for your relationships. It stirs fantasy and emotion and takes you to places inside yourself you may have never visited before.

If older people in a hospital were able to spend their rest time caring for their souls by reflecting and meditating and having important quiet conversations, their illnesses would serve them and they wouldn't have to see them only as breakdowns and calamities. We could encourage these quiet soul actions, a respite from the active, heroic treatments in an atmosphere of noise and urgency.

I once had a quiet conversation with a woman who had cancer and at that moment was receiving intravenous chemotherapy. Obviously, in extreme situations like this a person might be open to serious conversation and reflection. I felt that my presence as a representative of the soul was important to her, to give her the sense that her illness had meaning and could be an occasion for soul work. She spoke of her husband and children and her generally happy life and her wish that her family wouldn't suffer with her distress. In the time of an hour, sitting quietly in the presence of the devastating but curative drug, she covered much of her life and went through a range of feelings.

I believe that every room of every hospital needs a soul nurse (the original meaning of psychotherapist) to take the experience of illness and treatment to a deeper and much more meaningful level. That won't happen for a long time, but in the meantime each of us can do what is possible to have a meaningful, Asklepian experience of illness and healing by giving our emotions and thoughts room for reflection and conversation.

The current mechanistic philosophy that encourages us to take a pill for our moods, treats all illnesses chemically and surgically, and makes our hospitals and medical centers efficient but not beautiful and healthy affects every aspect of aging. We walk for our hearts and eat certain foods for our organs, but we are generally ignorant about the impact of soul suffering on our bodies.

Older people also worry about their future encounters with the medical world, which can be a beast to handle, and about their likely need for special care and housing. They would age much better if they could see the meaning in illness and not treat it as mere physical breakdown.

And so we have two major concerns: (1) to take care of our souls as a way to physical well-being, and (2) to transform every aspect of medical treatment into a soulful enterprise. Because illness is so often on the minds of older people, and even younger ones thinking about getting old, aging with soul in the medical arena is of the greatest importance.

The Soul Gets Sick Along with the Body

Your soul can get sick and weak and in need of special attention, and those sicknesses may translate into physical problems. Psychosomatic medicine is not a new idea. It was especially strong in the 1940s, when many imaginative psychoanalysts explored ways in which emotions "convert" into physical symptoms. For example, Thomas M. French, one of the pioneers of this approach, describes how asthma attacks can be connected to the need to confess some painful secret.*

A first step, culturally and individually, would be to get over the widespread habit of literalism and treating illness as only physical. It hasn't always been so. For millennia human beings have taken seriously the realm of deep imagination and emotion in illness. We are unconscious of this tendency in us to be only physical. We take it for granted. We assume that it is an advance

*Thomas M. French, *Psychoanalytic Interpretations* (Chicago: Quadrangle Books, 1970), 465.

over earlier ways of imagining illness.

Many medical professionals resist thinking beyond the physical because they believe, almost as a religion, their eighteenth-century philosophy that insists that a thing is real only if you can see it and touch it and measure it. Anything else is suspect.

What are the sicknesses of soul that can translate into physical problems? A big one is anxiety. If you're worried about something and can't sleep, eat nervously, and are generally unrelaxed, you may well have some belly problems or skin eruptions or some other manifestation. As we age, we might realize how important it is to deal effectively with our anxieties. Our physical health depends on it, to say nothing of our emotional well-being.

What can you do about anxiety? Express it verbally in plain, accurate terms, as openly as possible, to someone you trust. You don't have to say everything. If you have strong inhibitions about telling your story, it's important to honor them. Hold back what you have to keep to yourself, at least for the moment.

Second, do something about the cause of the anxiety. If you're worried about money, get started with a plan to make more. If you need to get divorced, start moving in that direction. You may be anxious until the problem is resolved, but at least you've taken action toward resolving it. In general, relax.

Deep relaxation is one of the healthiest things you can do. I'm not talking about avoiding your problems but about living generally in a relaxed manner. Today many people are frantic most of the time while trying to keep up with their busy lives. You can be active without giving up periods of relaxation. Find resources that work for you, even if they wouldn't relax someone else.

I do crossword puzzles, listen to music on YouTube, watch old black-and-white movies, play golf, play the piano, read cozy detective stories, and walk in the woods. Some people might think I am wasting my time doing some of these things, but to me they are relaxing and therefore important. They help me age with less anxiety.

Various forms of meditation and yoga can also help you relax throughout your body and mind. This is important because in both areas there may be tension that is unconscious. You may have to listen closely to your body, to feel any tension, before you can appreciate the role of anxiety in your illness.

I'm asking you to take relaxation seriously and go further with it than you normally think is reasonable. Notice if your muscles are tense, your mind is racing, or your emotions are frazzled. Do something about it. Take a bath. Go for a walk. Watch a movie. Meditate. Read a poem.

As a therapist, I'm alert to signs of anxiety and I do what I can to help my clients relax. I don't get caught up in their worries or sense of urgency. I breathe easily and take my time. If someone calls me in panic or extreme worry, I respond calmly. Sometimes it isn't easy to remain calm, so I make a special effort. Occasionally, a client seems to want me to be anxious with her, but I don't take the bait.

You may need a philosophy that, no matter what, you are not going to become anxious. With that philosophy you don't have to think about it when someone wants you to worry. You can cultivate a calm life that gives you a base for dealing with someone else's anxiety. I encourage therapists in training to focus on their home life and find ways to keep it calm, because home life can be a good foundation for professional activity.

Unresolved issues from the past can also find their way into our bodies and remain there for years, festering, we say, using a word that basically refers to a physical wound. People have physical tics and gestures that show their worry. They also use certain words and phrases that betray their anxiety.

It's typical for a person to say, "I'm probably taking up too much of your time," or "I'm sure you don't want to hear my worries." I'm feeling calm and open, but the other person is full of worrying thoughts. They may think they're being sensitive and altruistic, but their anxiety betrays their insecurity.

In the case of illness, we often separate body and soul, and so there is something almost ghoulish about getting sick. We are suddenly an object, a collection of organs that need to be treated with machines and chemicals. Every day men and women go into medical centers presenting themselves to be treated like the living dead, soulless, a Frankensteinian collection of body parts to be mended.

I've gone to doctors all my life, but now that I'm in my seventies I feel differently in medical settings. First, I fear that I'll be lumped in with "the elderly" and I won't be taken as seriously as younger patients. I also have a greater discomfort with huge imaging machines and the excessive use of medications. Am I a feeble old person not capable of appreciating modern science? Or am I a person just wanting to be seen as someone with a soul?

Recently I had surgery, and my story may give you some ideas for dealing with the medical establishment. My story is a positive one, full of soul. For three or four years I had a slowly developing umbilical hernia. During all that time I didn't think much about it. A doctor I liked very much told me to wait and see, at least until it grew in size. But then I read and was told by another doctor that the smaller hernias can actually be more dangerous. Gangrene is a possibility and can be life threatening.

So I decided to get the surgery soon. My local doctor said she would set it up at our nearby hospital, but I haven't had good experiences there. So I contacted a friend at a hospital in a city a two-hour drive away. He recommended a surgeon there. I wrote the CEO of the hospital and asked for his advice. He recommended the same surgeon. So I made an appointment.

The interview lasted only ten minutes, but I felt I was in good, kind hands. My wife, daughter, and stepson all went with me for the surgery, and everyone we encountered among the hospital staff treated us wonderfully as persons. The surgeon came to see me and introduced his son, who had just finished his residency in surgery. He would assist. My wife whispered to me that this was a good sign, because the surgeon would want to be at his best.

There I didn't feel like a bothersome senior citizen. Small signs of civility made all the difference. The only negative experience I had was on waking up from general anesthesia. I came to consciousness slowly, and the peace I felt was shattered when I heard loud voices in a cubicle near me. I had forgotten to arrange for music at that point. Later, I wrote the surgeon and CEO thanking them for their help, and I mentioned the problem waking up. They said they would find a solution.

You have to be proactive with your illness and its treatment. The medical establishment would like you to be compliant, do what it says, accept its pronouncements meekly. But it's your life and your sickness. You have to bring to the discussion your own insights and understandings. You might question taking so many drugs. Are they all necessary? Are they standardized and not suited to your situation? Do any of them affect you so badly that they are not worth the suffering?

One of the clearest and best books I know

on making sense of your illness is *Why People Get Sick: Exploring the Mind-Body Connection* by Darian Leader and David Corfield. They cite studies showing that life changes and health changes cluster together. They suggest determining what was going on at the onset of a serious illness and to speak of an illness not as an objective fact, but in human, relational terms.

It doesn't take much to bring soul into the medical system. In my case, it required a hospital dedicated to personal care, a surgeon with a heart, a family "business," kind and human caretakers all around, and the presence of my own family, who were treated with extraordinary respect and warmth. These are just basic human qualities, and that's all we need to transform the medical world into a realm of healing.

In the months before my heart surgery, I developed angina and had to have a stent put in a heart vessel shortly after selling a house that I had put my heart into building and enjoying. In my twenties I had appendicitis shortly after moving to Ireland after I was cut off from my family for the first time. Both of these events may have been necessary and even good from a certain point of view; nevertheless they left a painful gap in my emotional life. I'm not saying they caused my illness, but in my reflection on the time line of my health, I want to keep them in mind, humanizing and giving soul to my illnesses.

This way of responding to illness, as a human event and not merely a biological one, is another piece in the project of aging with soul. Aging is not automatic and it is not determined biologically. It has to do with our choices and our understanding of how life works. If we can maintain a human viewpoint and not succumb to the modern tendency to objectify every aspect of our lives, then we have a good chance of aging meaningfully.

8
KINDLY CURMUDGEONS

Several years ago I was walking through the Museum of Fine Arts in Boston, in the classical Greek area, when I came across an ancient vase with a remarkable scene: the young man Actaion being attacked by the dogs of Artemis. With the dogs is a young woman, Lyssa, who appears to have a dog's head sticking up out of her own head.

The story is about a young man who has been living on his father's farm. The father is Aristaeus, the mythic or archetypal founder of farming and the cultivated life. One day Actaion wanders away into the forest, where he comes upon the goddess Artemis taking a bath in a stream. If there is any goddess you shouldn't spy upon at the bath, it is Artemis, the tough virginal hunter who prizes her privacy and integrity. For punishment, she splashes some water on Actaion's head and he is slowly transformed into a deer, the very animal that he was hunting and that Artemis often hunts. His own dogs turn against him and tear him apart. They are in a frenzy, shown by the dog coming out of Lyssa's head.

I found the image of Lyssa to be mesmerizing — that dog's head emerging from the woman. I didn't have to think about it much, having seen many images of the dogs in attack mode, leaping at their former master, the apparently innocent Actaion. In some stories he climbs a tree so he can see Artemis better.

Lyssa is the goddess of anger, fury, and even rabies — the dog again. But the fact that she is a figure of myth means that she represents some necessity, some significant element in the scope of things. The dog has to pop out sometimes, rabid. And the dog serves Artemis, a lovely virginal goddess who lives in the forest and yet is known for the sting of her anger.

· People talk about the anger they see in older people as pathetic, as failure of character. But today I want to remember that Lyssa has a place both in mythology and in human psychology; she is real and important. Anger does not always involve a loss of control; it has a purpose. It belongs, even among the aged. Our job is not to judge harshly but to divine the meaning of the anger. Why is that dog sticking out of that older person's head?

The Place of Anger

There is a rule in psychology: If you repress an emotion in any of a variety of ways, that emotion may well reappear in a distorted or exaggerated form. One interesting idea that has been put forth about anger among the aged is that the young feel a need to see old age as a time of calm and emotional containment. One researcher, Kathleen Woodward, says that when we expect older people to embody wisdom, this demand is a defense against their need to be angry.* We assume that older people should be calm and wise, and so we find their anger disturbing.

I suspect that family members would

*"[G. Stanley] Hall accepts the time-honored notion that, as he puts it, there is a 'lessening of emotional intensity' in old age, in addition to a progressive abating of sexual passion that begins with senescence (26) . . . In general, throughout *Senescence,* Hall subscribes to the view that the intensity of feelings and emotions diminishes over the life course, and that this is one of the conditions of wisdom." (Kathleen Woodward, "Against Wisdom: The Social Politics of Anger and Aging," *Cultural Critique,* no. 51 (2002), 186–218.)

agree that although it's good to express your anger in general, some older people constantly bark and whine. They become curmudgeons, chronically testy and difficult. We might remember, though, that we're talking about people in a tandem: a crusty old person and an annoyed younger relative or caretaker. It's the archetypal, deep meeting of souls that defines the situation.

The curmudgeon is an inner personality that settles in many an old man or woman. It may be a compulsive presence — the older person has little control over it. It may have a history in the person's life, or it may be doing something constructive.

In James Hillman's book *The Force of Character* he tells an interesting story of an old woman on a tour of Greece who dressed down a younger one for not being more reverent in the sacred precincts. Rather than seeing it as a generational tension or as sheer personal anger, Hillman thinks the older woman wanted to save civilization in the face of the younger one's disregard of it. In arguments, sometimes one person wants to preserve basic values that he or she feels are being too easily and unconsciously set aside. Others may feel that the angry person is just being an old, impatient fool, a curmudgeon. They fail to see the greater reason for the older person's annoyance.

Hillman's response shows that an older person's anger may have a bigger, positive purpose. Even when the anger is chronic, the emotion may come from sadness at the loss of important values. We outsiders have to look closely and nonjudgmentally at the negativity to see a deeper concern. Hillman interprets the curmudgeon as an understandable and even positive characteristic.

Older people may remember certain values they learned as children and see them disregarded in the current world order. They identify with their parents and teachers, representatives of important values of the culture, and, without thinking it all through, feel compelled to speak strongly for what they perceive as right and important.

With my upbringing I never got in the habit of swearing. My dad would always use a few mild cusswords, but the family generally didn't even do that. Today, out in public, when I hear people using the "F word" several times in a sentence, often when little children are present, I get upset. But if I were to say something, I'd be laughed at for being an old curmudgeon. Once, I couldn't help myself when a young man was surrounded by children and cussing imaginatively. I said something, and he gave me the finger. Another time, an offending man said, "Sorry. I wasn't thinking." Given the choice of being a curmudgeon or changing my ways, I sometimes choose the former.

In many ways it's wise to stay current with the times. Values and tastes change. Usually they improve. I'm glad to know that today people are somewhat aware of ageism, for instance, though we have a long way to go. But some good values of the past get lost. To keep those values intact, a person like me may have to risk being a curmudgeon.

Young people are building a new world, and their attention is on the new. Eventually, they will get old and their "new" ideas will be the old ones that they will defend with considerable force, maybe as curmudgeons.

Hillman's conclusion can at least give us pause when we get annoyed at an older person's scolding: "We can all recall a drama coach, a music teacher, a shop supervisor, an old uncle coming down hard, boring in on our character with scorn and ridicule in the name of values that must be acknowledged, defended, and passed on. The scold as an instrument of tradition."*

*James Hillman, *The Force of Character and the*

I might note here that Hillman was adept at finding positive value in many human behaviors that are generally considered negative. From him I learned how jealousy, betrayal, and depression can contribute positively to a person's psyche and relationships. I suggest keeping this small but widely encountered twist in mind. When you hear negative judgments, consider the possibility that there may be something of worth there, if only you could look at it more deeply and with an open mind.

Your Anger May Have Roots

But there are other possibilities, too. Older people are not always justified in their anger. It isn't always good to be a curmudgeon.

Some people seem to have developed a negative attitude toward life all along. They may be dealing with abuse or negativity far back in their story line. They may have had a lifetime of struggle with authorities in business and government. They may never have had the chance to think deeply or enjoy sublime experiences of ideas and arts. They may have given up any sources of deep

---

Lasting Life (New York: Random House, 1999), 195.

pleasure because of their felt need to work hard to justify their lives. They may have been the victim of injustice and prejudice and have never felt free to fully enjoy the bounty of life. In the present, they may be victims of ageism.

In any case, faced with angry old people, we can try to explore their experience for signs that might explain their unhappiness. As they get older, they may find it more difficult to repress their dissatisfaction with life. But if those around them can fish for a context, they may find some understanding that will help them love the old person in spite of anger and frustration. The lack of any understanding would likely fuel the anger or keep it in place.

How to Deal with Elderly Anger

It's all about the soul of the person, which includes both character and emotion, and requires responses that go deep, remain patient, and have empathy for the human condition. People who care for the elderly may respond to their discomfort with automatic disgust. In that case, they are doing the same thing the older person is doing: not taking a moment of reflection to glimpse the source of discontent.

Anger is always a meaningful expression,

though that meaning may be deeply hidden in the hot verbiage and loud complaint of the moment. Anger can be chronic and habitual, as well, and then the meaning is so far packed away that it is sometimes impossible to detect. All a family member can do is remain patient, keep offering opportunities for reflection, and resist responding to anger with unfiltered frustration.

If you are the one getting angry and you notice that as you grow older your anger is stronger and more frequent, there are some things you can do.

1. Reflect on your anger. You can put a screen between you and your plain emotion. You can say out loud and sometimes to others: "I feel angry, but I don't know what it's all about. I'd like to do it less often, but it's difficult not to just fly off the handle." This kind of statement at least acknowledges an alternative to raw anger. You want some reflection, and you may need some help achieving it.

2. Probe your past. Look for situations, even far back in childhood, that may have made you an angry

person. A domineering parent or teacher is enough to affect you for a lifetime. Try to locate a source of frustration and tell your stories to someone you trust. Enter into a probing conversation about it. Don't expect a perfect solution to the problem, but make some progress.

3. Be strong always. Notice any habits of playing the victim or giving away your power. Sometimes anger, especially when it's chronic, comes from a degree of passivity, from holding down your own power and frustrating your wishes, desires, and plans. People who are habitually passive suppress their power, which then bursts out in the form of anger. The solution is to experiment with expressing your own needs and wishes and doing as much as you can to get them fulfilled.

4. Be in touch with your "soul power." This is the reservoir of past experiences, deep-seated talents and skills, innate creativity, and a lust for life that can be the base for a more powerful life. This source of power is not related only to the ego or the

conscious self. It is very deep, hardly touched or even known. You have to let that hidden stuff rise to the surface to give you more vitality, and that vitality itself is an early, creative form of anger. Anger arises when your deep vital force is kept underground and out of play, the repressed form of an innate vital force.

5. What, positively, does your anger want? Anger can be transmuted back into your vital force and personal soul power. Instead of acting out of frustration, you can ask yourself what it is that you are positively seeking. What do you want to accomplish? Thinking of it in these positive terms, you might give it a place in your life. It's the repression aspect that makes anger destructive and annoying to others. Ultimately, it is a matter of imagination — how you imagine your own way of being in the world, trusting it enough to have an impact and influence. These are important forms of power that, when repressed, transform into loud but flaccid, disruptive anger.

Anger as a Constructive Force

Going back to myths of old, Mars, the personified spirit of anger, had many positive gifts to offer: firmness, clarity, a creative edge, effectiveness, endurance, and vitality. The word the Romans used for the vital force in nature, *vis,* is the root of our word *violence.* To say that vis is in violence is like saying that the vital force is in anger. Or you can say Mars is a necessary force in life that, expressed freely, is a positive energy.

These associations apply to anger and even curmudgeonliness in old people. The surface expression of anger may be annoying and may appear useless, but deep within it might be the life force wanting to come forward, even in conditions of weakness. You have to look at least one level down to see signs of the life force wanting to be visible and in play.

When an old person you know is often angry, you might try to detect the life force wanting expression. If you are the one getting angry, it may help to understand anger in this deep, multifaceted and mythic way. It serves you, giving your actions some potency and warning you when the world is threatening, when something is not quite right.

My father was angry in his last days and

at the age of one hundred. Throughout his life and into his old age he was not an angry man. He had strong opinions and resisted being taken advantage of, but generally he was deeply peaceful. If he got angry at the end, I suspect it was because he lost some of his independence and dignity in a hospital setting. It isn't easy today to get through an experience of modern medicine without feeling like an object or a case. My guess is that my father's anger had good reason behind it and it served him.

When the renegade psychiatrist R. D. Laing fell to the ground with a heart attack, the story goes that he shouted out, "Don't call the doctors." It was an angry statement, but in some ways to the point. Fritz Perls, another eccentric psychiatrist, it is said, pulled the wires and tubes out of his body as he lay in the hospital. He was never one to give in to dehumanizing treatment.

We have a general bias against anger, perhaps simply because it isn't pleasant. But it may serve some good purpose, and we might be less prejudiced against it when we are dealing with older people if we understand it as a valid expression of tension. Older people need the strength to express anger toward a world that thinks poorly of them. Overall, it would help to think of anger first as a good and positive emotion. Every feeling, including anger, can be exaggerated or expressed in an extreme or negative way. Every emotion is potentially problematic. But that doesn't mean that in itself it is bad. Anger lets you know when something is wrong and that you have to step up and express your displeasure effectively. There is no age limit on this particular power of the psyche to show its outrage.

Anger Is a Secondary Emotion

Many people have no idea why they are angry, but they are aware that in an instant they can fly into a rage over a small thing. There we have two qualities of a special kind of anger: It appears in a flash and the cause may be almost nothing. Many people can trace their hidden aggression to childhood or adolescence and rough or smothering treatment from parents, relatives, and teachers.

Chronic anger is an emotion that has never found adequate expression. Some people are always seething or at the slightest frustration vent their anger, usually ineffectively and in such a way that it seems hollow. Usually it is not a response to a present irritation but, at least in part, a carryover from frustrations developed years ago. It may help to reflect on childhood or adolescent years in search of pressures that might have created frustration. Tell the stories again and again until either you get some insight or you feel a change just from acknowledging the problem.

Some think that the best way to handle this chronic anger is to vent: slam pillows, shout, scream, cry, bellow. I've never trusted therapies of venting because the emotion is usually secondary, a step away from the original frustration. Some venting may help in the context of a clarifying story, but the story alone, told enough times and with feeling, should ease the anger.

Let me use myself as an example. My mother was a wonderful and loving woman, but somewhere in her education and upbringing she learned that children should be silent and meek. She constantly told me to be quiet in public. At home she enjoyed having fun and playing games with me, but out in the company of people I was expected to sit still and do nothing. I remember one iconic episode that must have taken place when I was four or five. She was going out for an hour or so and told me to sit on the top step of our porch. Well, she was delayed and came home rather late, only to find me still sitting on the porch. She was surprised and asked me why I didn't go and play with someone. I didn't understand. I was told to sit there, not to go out and play. I was sure she would be angry if I left my post — I had seen her out of control and in a rage — but here she was, quietly expecting me to do what I wanted.

Notice how well I remember that story, and if you heard me tell it you would feel the emotion in my voice. Why? Because this is not just a story about something that happened once. It's an expression of my myth, my creation story, my tale of origins. It offers some insight into my struggles as an adult and it still plays in my memory seventy years later.

I had a blissful childhood, but as a therapist I have heard many stories from people who were profoundly hurt by their parents and other adults, who didn't tell them to be quiet but beat them and terrified them. If I feel strong emotions remembering the confusing ideals of my loving and quiet mother, imagine what is felt by people who were raised in a violent atmosphere and didn't have love and warmth to offset the confusing rules.

Now imagine that a group of people of various backgrounds — most of them, if not all, knowing too well the injunctions to behave and be still and act your age — grow old and live together in a retirement community. Each person there will have many years of experience dealing with those early demands and limitations. Add up the years of a group of old people and calculate how much anger has been stored up.

Here's another key point about anger: It doesn't come only from verbal and emotional abuse. Anger is a person's creative urge turned inside out. When for one reason or another you can't live your own life, do the work you want and need to do, express yourself fully and exactly, and be an individual in a world that wants conformity, then you will be angry. Your anger will be your creative spirit demanding a hearing after it has been stifled.

Here, too, are some hints in helping older people deal with their inner curmudgeon. Show them how to express their opinions in subtle language but with feeling. Help them find outlets for their creative urges. Give them opportunities to manifest their individuality. These are all by-products of anger, anger transformed into its creative and positive potential.

Responding to an Angry Older Person

Anger is a frustrated expression of the life force in you. Older people are acutely aware of the things they haven't done and yet wished and planned to do. An older person might ask himself, "What is my life worth? What have I done to make myself proud?" If the answers are negative, he may feel a mixture of sadness and frustration.

On reflection, much anger is understandable, even when it coalesces into the persona of a curmudgeon, where anger has transmuted into a personal style. Since the curmudgeon is a persona, a figure or a psychological complex, you can have some distance on it and you may even treat it with humor. Clean, openhearted humor is effective in warding off the destructiveness of anger.

Talking about anger offers a degree of catharsis. If you are a relative or caretaker of a curmudgeon, you can encourage memories and reveries that give the emotion images, which are a step toward finding meaning and understanding. As a therapist I rely on humor as a way of getting distance from the emotion. Humor often makes it possible to move toward images, narratives, and accurate language, all of which civilize the anger so it isn't raw and immediate.

If you are a relative or someone working with or for a curmudgeon, consult the following checklist:

1. Help the curmudgeon learn to be somebody and not feel neglected, overlooked, or forgotten.
2. Help him find ways to express himself.
3. Help her tell stories from the past, even from childhood, stories sparked by anger.
4. Make sure he can make some choices for himself and doesn't always have to follow the rules or someone else's wishes.
5. Don't take the anger personally, but try to see past it to its roots.

In many relationships we can't be just ordinary people reacting spontaneously and emotionally. For the relationship to prosper, we may have to be therapists of a sort. I don't mean, of course, playing the actual therapist with people close to us. I mean allowing a distance so you can see past immediate behavior to the deeper theme that is being expressed. Parents and teachers have to do this with children, partners with their intimate loved ones, and young people with the old.

This is a way of saying that you have to perceive a person's soul, the beauty of it and the conflicts. And with the soul you always have to think on many levels at once: You have to consider the past in the present, the person's unconscious concerns made visible in actual life, and actual behavior that symbolically represents some other issue the person is working out. Problems in relationships often come from taking everything at face value.

If you happen to be a curmudgeon, if only once in a while, don't judge yourself and feel obligated to get rid of the habit. It would be better to use your wits and find out what is trying to be expressed or where this behavior comes from. Get some distance from the strong emotions that accompany this spirit that invades you. Use your words. Find language to express your emotions that is precise and strong enough.

Sometimes anger and stubbornness have simple physical causes: certain medications, too much alcohol, not enough sleep, a preoccupying worry. Whatever the cause, a relative or caregiver need never simply react but can always look beneath the surface for a reason. We are all susceptible to misplaced anger and even to a chronic bad attitude.

After years of study and experience, I like to summarize my remedy for such behavior in a simple, well-worn phrase: Give people some slack. Righteous reactions help the one being reactive but don't help the person expressing their conflicts badly. It is not only the angry person, the curmudgeon, who has to get some distance from emotions; the relative and the caretaker, too, are well advised not to respond with raw feeling. Think things through and create some space for reflection.

If you have to deal with curmudgeonliness regularly, get some help and some time off. The role of therapist can be rewarding, but — ask any professional — you need breaks. Days off. Time between sessions. You always have to take care of yourself in extra measure when you are caring for someone else. This is especially true when anger is in the air. The temptation to react is strong. You need some space around you and inside you.

Think of anger as a creative force. Like any emotional expression it can be excessive, off the mark, and rooted in bad experiences in the misty past. Your job, as the angry one or the one nearby, is to resist the temptation to react with your own raw emotion and instead see what the anger is trying to say. Don't confuse the emotion with the person. You need some distance and a bigger field of vision.

As we get older, former angers come into view and new indignities generate new angers. Anger is often like an inverted lotus: On the surface lie muddy, not-so-beautiful roots. Under water lie beautiful blossoms. You need to develop an amphibious eye to appreciate the full meaning of such an unusual flower. You can assume that anger always wants something, that it is expressing displeasure for some good reason. It is often covered with complex disguises and excuses, but at its core it wants to serve life.

9
PLAY, WORK, RETIRE

> To God everything is good and right, but humans experience some things as good and others bad.
>
> — Herakleitos

Think about the scope of your life for a minute and you may realize how it is largely all about work. Today, education, even in the early years, aims at preparing new citizens for jobs that require technical knowledge and skills. Many would like to see the school day lengthened, recesses and vacations shortened, the arts curtailed, and even play and sport turned into opportunities to make a living. In other words, the delicate dance of work and play in a life is leaning heavily toward more work.

The entire theme of a work life tends to be a burden. As a young person you look for a job in a difficult market, you try to get the training and experience you need, you put in long hours so that you're noticed and have a chance for advancement, and you may really work hard in labor that is exhausting. Many people say that they can get up in the morning and go to work only because they'll be with coworkers who have become friends.

But after a lifetime of working hard to make a living, retirement is also a problem. How do you survive? How do you spend your time? How do you maintain a sense of purpose in life? Until now work has been your main source of meaning. Your psyche has been tilted in that direction. If the job goes away, what is left?

These questions are depressive. No wonder older people feel discouraged. But the problem is not aging or even getting older. The problem is that people have put their trust in an activity that does well only for youth. Getting older may make it all crumble and dissolve.

The answer is to avoid ceding work such a central and rigid place in life. There are other things that can give a sense of purpose and bring joy, things that don't involve strenuous physical activity, endurance, and advancement. These are things of the soul that are lasting, ageless. And they are the things you can focus on when your career is subsiding.

We use the word *retirement* for what we do when we end the cycle of career and job. But that word implies that work is the end-all of a life, the main source of meaning and pleasure. You work, and then you don't work. You stop working and have no positive word for what comes next. Retirement is a negative concept. It means "after work, then what?" In fact, you may well have been preparing for a renewal after work from having traveled, studied, read, or from being involved in avocations and many other activities outside of work. The approaching freedom from your career can be a positive development, and it would be helpful to use hopeful language for it.

Retirement leads to relaxing, free, alternative, creative, individual, reward, and discovery time. If you feel lost because you have gone to work for decades and miss the structures and activities you know so well, then you have a partial view of your capacities. You can now discover what else there is to do with your life.

Retirement brings out the contrast between soul and self. Your career has been all about the self: gaining prestige, making money, feeling successful, winning goals. The deeper soul is not so heroic. It lives on a different set of values that are so important that I want to present them as a checklist:

1. Beauty
2. Contemplation
3. Deeply felt experiences
4. Meaningful relationships
5. Knowledge
6. A sense of home
7. Art
8. Spiritual peace
9. Community
10. Relaxation and comfort

I would like to see these values included in every retirement community's mission statement and given to the children of parents who are getting old. Earlier in life you may have had a different set of values, such as making money, working hard, raising children, developing a house, going to school, or striving for independence. The older person is in a different place and is becoming more of a contemplative than a maker and doer. Of course, some people continue to work hard into old age, but even they would benefit from a gradual introduction of the soul values.

The time to begin preparing for retirement is the day you begin your career. This is an example of what I mean by aging at every stage in your life. You age in your twenties by being a multifaceted person who is not identified by your job, no matter now important or rewarding it may be. You continually expand your participation in life and decide not to hide out in safe, chosen areas such as a career or a home.

Suppose you've made this error and surrendered to your career early in life. Now you have some work to do, as you retire, to examine yourself and find those elements that want attention and development. Yes, you have them, even if they have been hidden behind the façade of your career. Or, you can just open your eyes to the world in front of you and discover areas that waken your desire.

A dear friend of mine, Hugh Van Dusen, an editor at Harper-Collins for sixty years, retired recently. Hugh is a soft-spoken, kind, and sophisticated man. He began his career with an interest in theology, philosophy, and cultural studies, first with Torchbooks and then with Harper Perennial. I met Hugh in the 1980s, and in 1990 he was my editor for *Care of the Soul.* We worked together on a number of books over the span of ten years and grew close.

Over the years Hugh has made oil paintings; some of them hung in his office in Manhattan. I'm always attracted to paintings by amateur artists who are trying to discover the building blocks of a meaningful life. Hugh's paintings appealed to me. There was originality in them, and his use of color was fresh. One day he showed me more paintings at his apartment in New York, and again I was struck by both their simplicity and their sophistication. By that time, too, Hugh was doing some quilting, and again I enjoyed seeing how his imagination worked, especially in a homespun craft that you rarely see men practicing.

Now, almost twenty years later, Hugh has retired from his Manhattan work life and is eager to have more time to paint and quilt and enjoy time with his wife. He has aged very well because he has lived into life by keeping his mind alive, making some difficult decisions, and expanding his life work. For him retirement means making what were formerly avocations into vocations, or at least giving more time and attention to arts that represent a world that is rather different from the business environment of a major publishing house.

Of course, books and paintings and even quilts are not unrelated, but the arts give Hugh a way to retire that shifts his focus, and that is so much better than wondering what to do with time on your hands. I'm not suggesting a life in art as a retirement strategy. It is far more than that. It's a way of aging all along by living an interesting and creative life and by following urges toward self-expression. These can lead you to mixing realms of practical business activities with the realm of dream, which is what the arts can evoke.

So the point is not just to age by having many different things to do, but specifically to connect the outer world and the inner one in your way of life, and this can best be done by pursuing an active career while at the same time giving art a serious place in your life. Art is the realm of mystery, image, and depth, even when the art is something as simple as quilting. Having images from art around you is like living with animals — they give something essential and mysterious but difficult to pinpoint.

From my perspective, Hugh Van Dusen's serious work with painting and quilting aged him with the lessons he learned directly from the art while also preparing him for the retirement aspect of growing older. It isn't just that he had something to do, but that he had a way of making beauty while being reflective. Quilt making and painting are forms of meditation.

I feel similarly about two activities in my life: music and writing fiction. I studied music seriously in my early college years, but I never pursued it professionally. Playing the piano almost every day and studying musical scores frequently has kept me tied to the mystery realm of dream. Music takes you to another level of reality, and musicians have something in common with shamans in that respect. Shamans use music as an aid to their spirit travels, while musicians can use a shaman's vision and purpose to deepen their understanding of music.

I sometimes wonder about all the years of effort I put into my studies in music composition. I've never used those skills professionally, and yet my understanding of music has enriched my life immeasurably. In retrospect I realize that I went to music school for my soul, not to make money. Music saturates me and affects everything I do. It is especially valuable as I get older, not just because I have time for it. I don't have any more time because my career hasn't slowed yet. But temperamentally aging has me in a place where music is more important than ever. It feeds the part of me that is now in its ascendancy as I feel different and reflect on my life more and think constantly about eternal things.

Playful Work and Serious Play

We often separate and even oppose play and work, but from a depth point of view they are usually mates. The effort to secure a job may feel like a game. You do everything you can to make it happen, and then you win or lose. Once in a job, you may struggle with a competitor over deals and accounts and customers, and the entire contest may be like a sporting event. You can see the game or play elements if you look closely, and you'll notice that they take nothing away from the seriousness.

In one of the most basic books written about the play element in culture, *Homo Ludens,* which means "The Human at Play," Johan Huizinga stresses contest as one of the essentials of play. In work we are often battling other companies or employees in a race toward success. From a certain point of view, it is all a game, a serious game that has some of the fun and excitement of play. Politics, too, is full of play. People enjoy debates so much because there is a strong play element in them, and we are usually happy to discuss who won, as though it were a football game.

Even religion has play in its rituals. People

dress up in unusual clothes and go through theatrical actions and movements, all to win the ultimate game, life itself. Marriage and making a home have a play side, as well, which we see in children when they "play house." It's difficult to imagine anything without some play and game aspect.

One reason why play is not just something we do but is an aspect of everything we do is that play is the primary activity of the human soul. It has many of the main values of the soul: pleasure, poetry, symbolism, layers of meaning, drama, and a quality of "as if," like the theater. Our surface lives may look serious, but beneath the surface you find hints of play and games. Pleasure, too, is a giveaway. Pleasure is what the soul seeks, even in serious business.

As head of a small business, you may imagine yourself as being among the chief players, as we say in commerce on the international stage. You win and lose contracts, and you learn to play the game.

It isn't enough to notice the play element in the serious things you do. You can also play those things up, making the most of the qualities of play as you go about your serious work. Then, when you get older and retire from serious work, you have all that play intelligence available to you. You might understand that the opportunity to play more doesn't mean that your life is any less serious. It simply has more soul.

I meet retired people on the golf course or tennis court and see that they are now able to really be serious about their game. And in that game they are still working out the raw material of their souls in the terms of the game, whereas they used to play the game within the camouflage of a job and career. A game is always a soul activity, as long as you do it largely for the play rather than for a practical, financial, or egotistical reason — if you really play.

Work without play is a burden. Play helps relieve some of the weight of labor. You can love and enjoy your work, as long as it consists of both serious purpose and play. In this sense, as you grow older you are becoming more of a person through work infused with play. You are doing your necessary soul work, working through many issues that need resolution or at least processing. But if you work without play, that soul work is neglected, and your work doesn't age you well. You get older as the years pass, but you don't get better as a person.

Say you've been a carpenter all your life. The play element there may be like a child's pleasure in using building blocks or making an igloo or a fort in snow. Building can be fun. You can bring that fun into your serious work as a carpenter, and then, as you get older, you may restore more of the play aspect. You may want to try building in a way you've always thought about but have never had the freedom to try. I knew a man who built the house he lives in and in which he raised his children. As an older man now, a house project is too big, but he is taking great pleasure in building a small Japanese teahouse on his property. In this case, it's difficult to draw a line between work and play.

Aging with soul is not just passing time but becoming somebody real and interesting. When your work has enough play in it, you become absorbed and imaginative and creative. You are engaged with what you do and are therefore affected by it deeply. You work from a place deep inside you, and the pleasures and rewards are equally deep.

When I was a college student, just having left monastic life, I got a job rolling coins at a machine that sorted quarters, nickels, and dimes. My task was to wrap these coins, as quickly as I could, in paper rolls. I did this for eight hours at a time and at the end of my shift I swept up loose money, amounting to hundreds, perhaps thousands, of dollars, off the floor. In my memory this is the least soulful job I ever had. And yet, I did learn a lot about myself and about the world of labor from that brief experience.

That meaningless little job aged me, and I still think back to it as a way of sorting out values in my current life. For one thing, I don't complain if my job of being a writer asks for some mundane activity, like counting words and pages. I remember what it was like to wrap coins for eight hours a day. I also have empathy for people who make a living at such numbing, playless forms of labor.

These days when there is no rain or snow on the ground I hit tennis balls with my old friend Robert on Sundays. He was born in England and lived in Germany for a while before becoming a Waldorf teacher in the United States. Robert is very thoughtful, so I asked him what he thought about his own old age and retirement. Robert is sixty-seven.

"I think about this often," he says. "It's important to me. If my health is good I have plans to do many things when I stop teaching."

Let me stop quoting Robert here. Notice that health is the first concern, and health is always a matter of fate and is mysterious.

We don't know what to expect for certain, and we have to leave room for fate to knock us down and interfere with our plans. But we, like Robert, still plan with hope.

He went on: "I'd like to continue teaching in different parts of the world for just a few weeks at a time. I want to travel and study. I also have to take care of my soul." As a Waldorf teacher, Robert uses the word soul quite naturally. "I mean my relationships especially: my wife and children and their families. I'd also like to focus on languages and music. I still want to help young people find themselves and learn the basics of a good life."

Robert is an extraordinary person, and I notice that when I first ask him about retirement, he looks quite serious. The whole discussion is important to him, as it is for most people I have interviewed. Robert wants to continue to give meaning to his life through service, but he has concerns about his family and he has some plans for himself.

I felt that his statement is a good model for anyone thinking about retirement. Informally but clearly, he sets up a hierarchy of values: health, family, service, personal desires. He has thought it through. His plan is clear but flexible.

Notice that this serious conversation takes place in the context of tennis. Just as when you need to have a serious talk with a friend about a relationship, you might do it over lunch — food evokes the soul, so you might play a game with a friend when you want to accomplish some serious soul work.

Play has another advantage. It has its own time frame and gives us a taste of what it's like to step outside the rush of ordinary time. There is something eternal and time-less about a game. In the middle of a game we can sense the ageless soul that is not caught in the fast, purposeful time of daily activities. Sometimes it's enough to be reminded of that ageless element and know that what we do in ordinary time is not the whole story.

The retirement years — I use this term loosely to apply also to people who don't formally retire but go through significant change in their work lives — are a good time to reflect and process such memories of labor past. That kind of sorting helps firm up your identity and your values. So it's good to bring up those memories in conver-sation, to work them through once more. You could make your own list of priorities and then fill in the details.

The Soul in Retirement

There are many attitudes toward retirement today and many ways of doing it. Some people go the traditional route and take their gold watch, figuratively speaking, and leave their jobs behind. Others feel that they do the kind of work that doesn't lend itself to retirement at all. Still others officially retire, in their own minds at least, and yet continue to work almost as much as they did mid-career and at a variety of activities.

When my father, the plumber and plumbing instructor, retired, he liked to give talks in schools about how water plays a role in everyday life. But with this my father was doing what he did all his life: taking every opportunity to expose children and young adults to life's beauty and fascination. In retirement he wanted to use his experience and knowledge to give back to his community and help the children grow up.

In researching this book I had a long conversation with my literary agent's father, Carl Shuster. His experience offers similar lessons for anyone looking for "soulful retirement."

Carl is a retired lawyer. He decided to spend most of his freed-up time in the Berkshires of western Massachusetts and only occasionally returns to his city law office.

He now says that retirement is the best part of life, especially the gift of being able to do what you want. He feels strongly, as many older people do, that giving back is part of everyone's life. Carl does it by supporting and enabling a program in which musicians, especially young ones, perform in people's houses.

Carl has found a way to resolve any conflict between senex and puer, the old and the young, by now focusing on young people and helping them to be successful. You don't have to be a psychoanalyst to see that at the same time he is bringing together in himself the world of the old man and the world of youth, an essential accomplishment for anyone getting older.

He is aware that his program helps create community, as friends bond over these home concerts. The events enrich people's lives and give the musicians both experience and a little money. Any money the program raises goes directly to the musicians.

Carl refers to music as "spirituality without doctrine." He is Jewish and feels that though music is related to religion, it is more primal and relevant to human beings as a whole. Music takes him to a peak experience that is in the region of religion but is free of its problems and limitations.

For Carl, this discovery of home professional music led him to relationships that for him are akin to that of father and child. He finds the young musicians are excellent people, hardworking and devoted. He loves them, he says. And the classical music brings a light of new understanding to older people, especially when it is experienced up close, allowing you to follow the lives of musicians you have met and come to know.

When he goes to Florida to get away from winter, Carl meets many people who spend time in the Berkshires and know of the home music program. He feels as if he is part of a web of people who share the transcendent power of music, especially when it comes to appreciating the personal connection with young musicians who inspire them all. Now Carl plans on getting involved in broader continuing education for seniors, and he feels that there are no limits to what he can do as a freed-up retired person.

"Retired" doesn't really mean retired; in many cases it means liberated, free to pursue activities that were out of reach when a career was dominating life. It might be better if people who are finished with their careers say that they are in the "liberated phase of life." Now they can follow their hearts' desires and truly pursue the longings of their souls.

Again that interesting pattern shows up: The work life had soul from the play element in it — the law is full of play and game, especially in the courtroom. Now, in retirement, Carl turns to music and to musicians, the players. From hidden play to public playing. From play in serious activities to serious play.

We could think about this dynamic as we retire and get older. At that time of life it makes sense to lean more toward play as a way of focusing more on the soul. It can be serious play — those young musicians are dead serious about their art and their careers — but all the while they are playing music.

My own idea of retirement is perhaps unusual. As a writer I hope to be able to write until the end. I was watching closely when I visited my friend Hillman shortly before he died. He was lying in a hospital bed in the living room of his country house, a morphine drip draped over him, and yet he was working on a project right up to the end. One day he told me, "I feel liberated. I'm not nervous about how the elections will turn out. The news isn't so crucial, and so I have more energy for other things."

I do have my own personal goals, some rather selfish. I'd like to learn the Sanskrit language. I've known quite a few words over the years because of my interest in the religions of India, and I have found them particularly beautiful: *samsara, dukkha, dharma.* I know Greek and Latin fairly well, having studied them when I was young. They are sacred languages, too, because they have allowed me to be close to the original inspiration in the Gospels and the stories of the gods and goddesses. *Anima, vis, puer* in Latin, and *metanoia, psyche, kenosis* in Greek. It seems to me that learning a sacred language is the perfect thing to do in old age, perhaps to prepare for the eternal, however it may show itself. Maybe the eternal languages are the languages of eternity.

But like my father and like Carl Shuster, I feel a need and a calling to give back after having received so much. I want to help the young perceive the beauty of life and the world and other people. I'd like to inspire them to keep learning and discovering beautiful words and great images and unlikely animals and insects. I'd like to help them find ways to deal with life's painful emotions and entanglements and make the most of personal limitations. I'd like to give them hope and insight and a capacity for deep pleasure, especially the kind offered by the best in classical music and thoughtful painting and marvelous architecture. I know these are my biases and the narrow tastes of my age and generation. The young can find their own parallels.

The post-career years are a time for new discoveries and old resolutions. They are free time, when you have nothing to accomplish and everything to experience and express. Like my friend Hugh, you can forget about custom and expectation and paint your seascapes and quilt your oven mats and bedspreads. What could be more important? This is life in all its simple glory, and in old age you can indulge in it.

This is a time for alchemy: observing the glass vessel of memory and turning over events again and again, releasing their beauty and sadness and eternal meaning. This is what is called soul-making. It rounds off the process of becoming a person and, in fact, may be the most important part. There's much to do in old age that is not frenetic and purposeful and time-bound and heroic and demanded.

Retirement means that you retire, go to bed, and dream. Your attention turns inward and you feel a host of emotions: longing, wish, remorse, satisfaction, desire, regret, resolution, guilt, and, one hopes, a speck of hope. You live it all over again in imagination or memory and bring it closer to the heart and, again one hopes, gain a little insight and understanding and even forgiveness. This retirement is an essential process of turning events into processed memory, like food your soul can live on.

I like to think of retirement as a time to "re-tire." You put new wheels on and move in a different direction with fresh impetus and a new motor compulsion to live it all to the end. You stop working in career fashion and play more and discover the paradoxical playful seriousness of life and find out what really matters and wish you had retired much earlier, maybe at the beginning.

There was a famous and much-loved song in the Middle Ages, "My End Is My Beginning." It's a song for retirement. You go back to the beginning, sorting through your experiences and decisions. You turn them over as if you are polishing river stones. Your storytelling polishes the stones, as do your feelings of pleasure and regret, your new ideas about how you could have handled things.

That is how you feel now, so mindful of

your early years and how you began and how much you didn't know and how you might do it differently, even though you know that to get here to retirement you would have to do the same thing. You are what you have been. You are your choices. Change them, and you are a different person. So you learn to accept who you have been and understand that all the mistakes were part of the puzzle and make you the person you are. It can be a bitter lesson.

If your life has been a mess, you have to take all that unsavory material and transform it into gold. That's alchemy, too. It isn't an easy process, but it's possible, if you don't feel sorry for yourself and love life and your process.

Old age can be bitter. At least it has its bitter moments. It doesn't have to turn you into a bitter person, but often it does. You need redemption, which comes if you accept your fate and don't demand that life be different from what it is. If you have had sorrow, that sorrow is the stuff of your life. It's what you've been given to make your own gold. I've known many people who feel that they can't make anything of their lives because their fathers were failures. But there's no logic in that position. You can live your own life and let go of your father's problems. Let him have them, and let him seek redemption. It isn't your job.

We return to the theme of anger. Sometimes the best thing you can do for yourself and your relationships is live from your anger. See it as a necessary fuel. You don't have to indulge in it and be violent or crude. Be angry in a moderated manner, if that seems appropriate. Let your anger make you firm, unyielding, clear, edgy, forceful. You don't have to explode. Exploding anger isn't usually effective. It can be, when the situation is dire. But it usually isn't.

Anger clarifies and gives the necessary distance. It helps you make decisions you already know have to be made. Retirement is the opportunity to clarify your life. No more need for artificial relationships. No more holding back to safeguard your income. No more niceness to keep the peace.

Work and Retirement: Two Sides of a Coin

Retirement is not the end of a period characterized by a career; it is the beginning of a new phase that is perhaps the most important of all. As they enter this phase, men and women may feel confused. They may have worked all their lives, if not formally then at least at home or in some form. They have found meaning in this work and have learned to adjust to it. Now they're supposed to give it up and enjoy doing nothing.

They may think about things they've always wanted to do and now have the time to do them. They travel, take up hobbies, learn some skills, or even stay busy at an avocation. My father collected stamps all his life, and when he retired he turned his hobby into a real business. But if, as I have been saying, the later years are for the soul, then maybe you have to make retirement a more serious period of life. Maybe dabbling in skills, no matter how useful and enjoyable, isn't enough.

When you make your plan for retirement, consider your deepest self and how you can add significantly to your life now. If you plan to travel, you could go to places that have deep meaning for you. If you volunteer, make it something that speaks to your soul. If you want a new hobby, consider an activity that has substance and will open up new life for you. Popular ideas on retirement focus either on money or superficial activities, but now is the time to make life more meaningful, not less.

I want to study Sanskrit because I know how much my early years learning Latin and Greek added to my writing. I've worked with Sanskrit words frequently, but I've never studied the language. I know that my career may be in decline now as I get older, but I still may have many years of writing ahead of me. Yet, when I think of learning Sanskrit, I see myself doing it leisurely, very differently from when I was a driven young student. In your older years nature slows you down, and I like the idea of doing that slow dance with nature, taking my cue from a less agile body.

As you get older and move toward retirement, you could retire in a more general sense of the word. Retire not just from your job and career, but also from your habit of hurrying through life and trying to advance your ego. You could go into retirement mode in general, not to give up on your life but to do it differently, maybe more substantially and more profoundly, giving you deeper pleasures and satisfactions. Retire from doing too much, moving too fast, not giving yourself time to reflect and enjoy some beauty. Retire from spending time at things that don't matter. Retire from aspects of society that are without soul.

Writer John Lahr is quite passionate about doing something in retirement: "I want to feel the earth before I'm returned to it. I want the sun in my face. While my legs are still moving and my eyesight is good enough I want an adventure. I want to go fishing."*

Redefining retirement takes the yawn out of it and reframes it as a new adventure. You're leaving something old to begin something new. But you don't need to do the new thing just because it's new. Now you have an opportunity to connect your activity with your soul. You can do what is most meaningful, and that may be in contrast to the work you are retiring from, which was possibly a compromise between who you are essentially and your financial needs.

You can now retire from the hero's story, where you needed to slay dragons and win princesses, all the while engaging in other exhausting ordeals. You can listen to what your soul wants and ease into a different style. Now you can find meaning in less demanding ways and yet be fully engaged. But you don't have to prove yourself or achieve the impossible.

I certainly don't mean being passive and still in later years. People are different in this way. Some like to sit in a chair and others become more active than ever. Gloria

*John Lahr, "Hooker Heaven," *Esquire,* June/July 2016, 89–140.

Steinem wrote in her essay "Doing Sixty": "Age is supposed to create more serenity, calm, and detachment from the world, right? Well, I'm finding just the reverse."*

When I talk to friends who have retired, I don't hear them distancing themselves from life; just the opposite. They are more engaged than ever, but they are engaged with things that matter to them and to the world. However, I do sense a calm and quieting of whatever anxious motive kept them working hard for decades.

The idea of retiring fits in well with the Taoist ideal of achieving much without doing, or doing what you need to do without the old qualities of effort and anxiety. This philosophy, known as *wu wei,* is the ideal I've set for my older years. Do a lot without trying so hard. Or, more radically, accomplish great things without any effort. Accomplish everything by doing nothing.

*Gloria Steinem, *Doing Sixty and Seventy* (San Francisco: Elders Academy Press, 2006).

■ ■ ■ ■

PART FOUR:
OPEN YOUR HEART
TO THE FUTURE

■ ■ ■ ■

There is no difference between being alive or dead, awake or sleeping, young or old. One becomes the other in a surprising, sudden shift. — *HERAKLEITOS*

10
Being Fulfilled as an Elder

I tell myself that I must see something in the mirror besides my wrinkled veneer if I am to have any calm; that I will have to make my peace with the loss of smooth skin, and find satisfaction in the gaining of something to take its place. Something, yes, that should always have been in me. Or something that has always been in me but has never seen the light of day.

— Peggy Freydberg*

Many people say they are looking for the fountain of youth, but you never hear anyone in search of the fountain of old age. Yet real aging, not just getting older, is a rare gift. We fight it because it has many undeniable liabilities. But if we were to ripen in character and personality as we get older, we might discover precious benefits

*Peggy Freydberg, *Poems from the Pond,* ed. Laurie David (Los Angeles: Hybrid Nation, 2015).

in aging.

A person who really has matured, to the point that he or she naturally becomes a source of wisdom, is referred to as an elder. It's a term of distinction. It's true, in a soulless age, when people give their attention mainly to superficial values, that the nobility of the elder often goes unnoticed, and society suffers from losing that essential source of wisdom and inspiration.

One of the key stories of my life, which I've told in several of my books, began when I was nineteen. I had been in the Servite religious order for six years and had just completed the novitiate, a year of intense focus on the spiritual life. I was heading for the next phase in my long journey toward the priesthood — the study of philosophy in Northern Ireland. On the way to Ireland, aboard the *Queen Mary,* the idea came to me to find a piece of Irish art and bring it home with me after my two years there.

As soon as I got settled, I wrote to the public relations office of the National Gallery in Dublin, asking for advice. Soon a letter arrived from the director of the Gallery himself, Thomas MacGreevy, a distinguished poet and man of letters. He asked me to come to Dublin and visit him.

Let me pause here for a moment. Notice

this special talent of the elder to break protocol and instead make a friendly gesture that could turn into friendship, as it did in my case. Thomas was obviously ready to make a new friend whom he could guide like a father, as he had done many times in his life.

At the Gallery I was invited into his private back office, a small room with a fireplace. Thomas sat on the couch in front of the fire with a shawl over his shoulders, wearing his usual suit and bow tie. He began to tell me about his friendships with famous writers — W. B. Yeats, D. H. Lawrence, T. S. Eliot, James Joyce, and Samuel Beckett, in particular, and the painter Jack Butler Yeats. Thomas is especially known for helping Joyce's wife, Nora, and his daughter, Lucia. He was sixty-seven, I think, when I met him, somewhat formal in his manner, and yet warm and relaxed.

I visited him in the National Gallery many times, and sometimes we'd take a walk along Merrion Square and over to the landmark Shelbourne Hotel for high tea. Thomas never stopped talking about poetry, painting, and the complex lives of the artists he knew. He also liked to give me advice, the highly educated old man advising the foggy-headed youth.

One rainy day on our walk, a disheveled man approached us and stood there without a hat or umbrella, his hair matted to his head and water dripping from his nose. He stood still on that wet street and recited Thomas's poem "Red Hugh O'Donnell." I was stunned, and tears came to Thomas's eyes as he thanked the man and we all walked on. I never forgot that brief encounter, an affirmation of Thomas's work from an ordinary Dublin citizen.

At that time Thomas was a close friend of the Irish writer Samuel Beckett, who was living in Paris. I had already become a devotee of Beckett, so I paid close attention to the stories Thomas told of him. I remember him saying once that although Beckett's plays are dark and sparse, he himself was an affable and congenial man. One day Thomas told me that "Sam" had asked if I would accompany the two of them to Venice for the Biennale. I might have fainted at the prospect — there is no famous artist I would rather have spent some time with than Beckett — but my prior, the head of our community, would not allow me to go, and I wasn't ready to leave the order then.

I continued meeting with Thomas, listening to more stories of his famous literary friends. He also gave me bits of advice. "Be sure to spend some time in a country where you don't know the language," he said. "When you write, do it with some style and grace but keep it simple and flowing." "Be loyal to your friends, no matter what. They are your most precious gifts."

When I returned to the United States, we exchanged a few letters. He died not much later. In one beautiful letter he wrote: "I hope that when you are my age, and your apostolate is almost over, a young man will come into your life, just as my Thomas did, bless him, and give you new life."

I've often wondered what made Thomas MacGreevy give me his valuable time and attention. For one thing, he had been an *anam cara,* a soul companion, to others all his life. He was such a friend to one of the best American poets, Wallace Stevens. As you can see, if you read the letters they exchanged, to Stevens Thomas was not an elder, but a true soul friend. Stevens wrote to another friend, "He [Thomas MacGreevy] is, in any event, a blessed creature, sustained by a habit of almost medieval faith, and I, like the God bless you with which he winds up his letters, which for me are so extraordinary all around."

From what I know of his tendency to help other artists, I would imagine that he was poised to respond to me in a similar way, even though I had yet to emerge from my childhood cocoon. In any case, he is a good model for us all, men and women, as we grow older. We could find real pleasure in aging by making an effort to be the elder to young people who come into contact with us.

The Elder as Friend

The MacGreevy model of mentoring, if I can call it that, has some special features. When you read about his relationships with Joyce and Beckett, you discover that he "befriended" them. He wasn't a distant or formal mentor, but an intimate who helped them deal with life. In my case, he just invited me to visit him at work and treated me with respect and careful attention. He didn't look down on me, although I was young and ignorant. He enjoyed being with me, and I with him.

For centuries books on the soul have highlighted the importance of friendship. It seems an obvious part of life, but it doesn't always get the attention it deserves. Often people move in and out of friendships casually and unconsciously. MacGreevy made it a way of life. It was his style, his modus operandi that gave his life meaning.

Some commentators lament that he didn't become a great poet. He wrote excellent poetry and translations of poems, but he seemed to find purpose in helping gifted people find their way. Here's a lesson for us as we age and become elders. We can find meaning, that elusive substance that people talk about so much, by befriending others intimately. We can also intensify this kind of friendship by offering quiet guidance, the way MacGreevy did.

I would say to young, untested counselors and therapists: Contact that elder deep inside you, in some ways your opposite, given that you are young, and become a mature friend to your client. Don't worry about friendship appearing in the relationship that you may have been taught should be distant and formal. Let friendship rise up and enter the scene, for healing and wisdom can flourish there. It's the spirit of friendship, anyway, that's important, not necessarily literal friendship.

Friendship arrives in degrees. Some friends are so close that there seems to be no barrier between you and them. Others are "good friends," but not so intimate. Others you may refer to as your friends, but they are actually more like acquaintances.

As I think back on my friend Thomas, I

wonder if he was just sitting around waiting for me to appear. He seemed ready and alert. By the way, we were never buddies. He retained the role of an experienced, worldly, well-placed gentleman, a father figure, and yet he was warm and spoke affectionately of our friendship. That, too, was a special gift he enjoyed: He could be formal and affectionate, older but not out of reach, wise but tolerant of my lack of knowledge.

Enjoying the Role of Elder

As you get older, you could find meaning and joy by being a Thomas MacGreevy. You could be ready in your role of elder to befriend a young person and offer him or her some guidance. But to do this well, you have to make being an active elder part of your identity, an aspect of your philosophy of life and part of your character. One commentator said of MacGreevy: "It wasn't like him to go off to a room alone and write a poem. He'd rather join a group and have a conversation."

You can imagine the role of elder in many ways. You could be the all-knowing, powerful senior in the community. Or you could be a friendly, gregarious person who acts from your heart, as part of the group rather than its leader. You have to be careful not to imagine old age as stereotypically rigid and solitary.

In English we speak of "making friends." You don't necessarily fall into friendship; you have to do some work and be creative. As an elder you become a person who can make friends everywhere you go, and not just your own friends. You help other people make friends, as well.

An elder also, presumably, has wisdom to offer. I find that older people often don't appreciate the value of their experiences or of things they have learned along the way. I once participated in a conference for doctors, an excellent program called the Osler Symposia. In one session a retired physician told the story of his life, focusing on a few events that were challenging and even life threatening. It was a simple but effective idea on the part of the symposium planners: ask an elder to tell the story of his experience. Other doctors present told me later how much these stories meant to them. I appreciated that there were no facts or figures, only personal stories, wisdom based on the older doctor's experience.

An elder also teaches by his willingness to confess to mistakes, failures, and close calls. My father once told me about a woman who was trying to seduce him. "That would be fun," he told me, "but not worth it. My marriage gives me more satisfaction than any fling could provide." I knew that he was trying to give me a life lesson, but he usually tried to give the lesson without making it look like a lesson. MacGreevy, too, offered some lessons on the sly, such as when he walked me through the National Gallery while quietly showing me how to look at art.

The Role of Grandparents

We should also distinguish between the male and female elder, the father or mother or grandfather or grandmother or some other archetypal image of the elderly. For many people, their souls are sustained more by the spirit of their grandparents than that of their parents. In many of us, the combination is powerful. It would help if grandparents understood how important they are to children and that they play a mentor role, as well.

The grandparents may be able to give their love and attention more abundantly and without the emotional complexity of the parents. Through life the child soul needs more acceptance and praise than is reasonable, and the grandparents can fill in what the parents can't do. As in the case of mother and father, other people can evoke the grandparent figure and supply some of the needed love.

The grandparents offer their own kind of guidance and wisdom. We see this mythically in the great vision of Black Elk, the Sioux holy man whose visions early in his life made him a leader of his people. In his vision one of the grandfathers said to him, "Your grandfathers all over the world are having a council and they have called you here to teach you. . . . I knew that these were not old men, but the Powers of the World."

Black Elk always said we should see in a sacred manner, that is, not literally but deep into the interior of nature. He listened to his grandfathers speaking in a mythical manner, through the natural world and through animals and in his visions. We could do the same, understanding that in some way life itself has a grandparent, an elder visage, and a voice, and it is there to guide us.

The grandparents are closer to the eternal; their youth goes back into a time difficult for the young to imagine, and their future is closer to the timeless. They have had many experiences and hold many secrets. They are perfectly suited to be spiritual guides.

Elder Writers

Yet another elder guidance is to be found in books, where those who are our elders and who have gone before us have much to teach us. We read their words on paper or on a screen, but we are hearing them speak. A voice speaking to us from within is part of the experience of reading, and so we need not treat books as though they were distant and abstract ideas derived from our ancestors but as though we were hearing their voices as they thought. Books are a medium for hearing voices that have much to teach us.

As a writer I feel this elder role strongly and hope that my voice sounds through the words on paper. My life's work has meaning only because readers in the future will "hear" me thinking and talking in an internal way and always in dialogue with them. I have them in mind lovingly and hope they will be able to receive my attentions as an elder.

The task of us elders is to be prepared to notice the person who comes into our field of vision in need of guidance or simply at a point in life when they could use some modeling and support. Older people may well feel empty if they wait for meaningful experiences to come to them. They have to prepare themselves and actively respond to invitations to mentorship, just as my friend Thomas was ready like a hair trigger for me. He broke the convention of a formal, distant institutional response and instead offered his friendship.

Elders Can Heal

John O'Donohue describes the special friendship of *anam cara* as a profound connection that is not dependent on the literal, natural laws of nature. "With your anam cara you waken the eternal. . . . Fear changes into courage, emptiness becomes plenitude, and distance becomes intimacy."*

These are the conditions you need to be an elder and to benefit yourself and others in the process: the courage to be creative and unconventional, the willingness to allow empty moments when life can happen, and an intimate way of living rather than the usual distancing that is so much a part of modern life.

In general, neurotic suffering can be healed through service and reaching out beyond yourself. In particular, you can deal

*John O'Donahue, *Anam Cara: Spiritual Wisdom from the Celtic World* (London: Bantam Books, 1999), 31.

with some of the sadness of old age by being available, by shaping conventional ways
to your own inspirations. You can transform
the meaning of elder from someone who
happens to have more years stacked up than
others, to someone who has come to a point
where he or she can forget about dry conventions and be creative and assertive with
life for the benefit of those in search of guidance.

My wife once dreamed that she was in the
house of her spiritual teacher Yogi Bhajan.
His wife was there, only the wife in this case
was my wife's former husband's grandmother, in real life an elderly woman who
had trouble getting the care she needed. We
talked about this fascinating arrangement: a
very strong Indian patriarchal teacher and
his consort, an old-old woman in need of
care. First, we wondered about spiritual
people lacking a strong elder woman spirit
to match the heavy father teacher. But we
also discussed the dream as my wife's need
for a healthier wise old woman to match the
fatherly teachings she received in her training.

All of us, men and women and young and
old, need the strong spirit of the old-old
woman. She may be wise, supportive, mystical, or hardworking. In any individual

person she is not really a type but an individual figure, an inner spirit. For you, she will have unique qualities that you need. Your task is to get to know her and experiment with her gifts. Although she is timeless, she can help you age. With her assistance, you age from within, from your soul, and not just in comparison with other people or in your body.

As many women try to deal with aging by trying to look younger, they could also invoke the spirit of the female elder. They could try looking older and beautiful, appreciating the beauty of an older face and body. Then they would be young without denying their age. The paradox holds: You can only look younger by first being the age you are. Then you can make efforts to call back the youthfulness you love. Denial of your age doesn't make you young.

Think of youth and age as yin and yang. You can move quietly and smoothly from one to the other, keeping both in mind as desirable and attainable. Develop the capacity to evoke your youthfulness with subtlety and to appreciate the beauty of your age. The two go together to make a beautiful person. They don't have to be in perfect balance, only represented in appropriate and effective ways and degrees.

Single men and women who are getting older sometimes say that they feel alone and needy, asking for too much support from their friends. It may be helpful to remember that dependency and independence work in tandem, too, much like youth and age. They, too, need mutual representation like yin and yang. In fact, you can only be truly independent if you know how to be dependent. You know how to rely on others without losing your power or your independence. Dependency is an art, nothing to be ashamed of. You may discover that it takes more strength of character to be vulnerable than to be in control.

One of the primary complaints of aging men and women is that they don't want to be a burden on their children, or on anyone else for that matter. But in avoiding dependency they may become more of a burden. It might be better to just face the facts. You can find effective ways to keep your spirit of independence, but sooner or later your ability to do it all yourself is going to decrease.

The sense of being an elder rather than elderly may help offset the need to rely on others for help. You can receive help and yet maintain your dignity and worth. You may be dependent for many things, but you are still an elder who is worthy of respect and a joy to know.

How to Be an Elder

I've always found the word *elder* a little strange. I've never had the ambition to become one, and I've never known for sure what one is. Yet many people I run into speak of elders with a hushed reverence, and recently a friend told me that the main point in growing older is to become one.

On reflection I can see that becoming an elder could be a good way to feel positive about growing old and doing some real good in the process. Elder means that being older is an honor and carries with it a particular role of quiet leadership and teaching. I've described my experience of an elder enriching my life, and based on that experience and a few others, I'd like to list some ways a person can take on this positive and needed role.

1. The first requirement is to be comfortable with your years. An elder is someone who is older. How you define the required age is relative. Some people can be elders in their fifties, perhaps, and others more convincingly in their seventies and eighties. My father was an elder in

his nineties, and my friend Dr. Joel Elkes in his one hundreds. Whatever your age, you accept it and speak forthrightly and calmly about it.

Many people try to avoid being public with their age. They may be coy and only hint at the number or always qualify it so it doesn't sound bad. An elder is first of all a man or woman who can sit easily with his or her age. If you hedge about your age, it means that you are not comfortable with yourself. Not acting your age is a little bit neurotic. You have some hidden agenda or game going on in the privacy of your mind. You are not clear and clean with the way you present yourself. In that condition, it's quite difficult to be an elder.

If you are not being up front about your age, maybe you want to remain close to your friends who are younger. You may be so attached to your youth that you can't bear the thought of losing it. You may live an artificial life and not be able to deal with the natural process of getting older. These are only possibilities to help you reflect on your own reasons for denying your age.

2. Have confidence in your education and experience to the point you may guide and educate others. It takes some strength of character to acknowledge your own genuine wisdom. Today it appears that many people assume the role of wise counselor, perhaps by writing books or generating a following, when they haven't done their homework and are not ready for the position. So I'm not talking about a false sense of ability and capacity. On the other hand, some people just don't recognize the knowledge they have accumulated over the years and how much they have to offer young people. Here the issue is not so much knowledge and experience as the ability to lead.

Thomas MacGreevy never said to me, "I'd like to give you some lessons in life." He took on the role of elder without a thought, full of confidence and joy. That act requires character and the ability to know yourself without falling into either too high an opinion of yourself or false humility.

Normally you develop this capacity for honest leadership over many years. The apprenticeship for the elder begins very young and continues over a lifetime. Then the role of elder is like a flowering of the personality and a completion of one's life mission. That's what Mac-Greevy told me: He thought his active life was over, but then I came along as a potential student for his personal school of guidance.

3. The elder has to love young people. But some older people are so jealous and envious of youth that they feel angry in the presence of the young. They complain and judge and criticize as a way of expressing their own failure to deal with old age. They need a catharsis, a cleansing and clearing up of their struggle with age and their anger at youth. They have to learn to love being older and in that way they will learn to love themselves. Self-hatred often transforms into anger at someone else. The older person's task is to live naturally, allow time to do its work, and to be the product of nature — old but not angry, experi-

enced and ready to teach.

4. The elder uses any knowledge and wisdom he or she has to benefit others, especially the young. Remember my father's desire to teach middle-school students about a city's water supply. When he stood in front of those children, he was using his technical knowledge of plumbing and water treatment, but he was also an old man talking about his life and inspiring young people to make something of themselves.

There is direct learning, understanding the technology of water treatment, and indirect learning, seeing how an old man has found joy in his life's work. An elder would be wise to keep both kinds of learning in mind. You can teach technical skills, but as an older person you can also teach life lessons and offer inspiration.

One of the problems my father encountered as he tried to be an elder to very young people was the attitude of the teachers and administrators of schools. When he approached many schools and church groups, he was turned away by some administrators who told him they didn't have room on their schedules. They probably saw him as a crank trying to do something for his own life. But my father had a lifelong habit of teaching the young whenever the occasion presented itself. He loved children and young adults and would automatically help them at every opportunity. He was a thoughtful man who lived by the philosophy that young people benefit from exposure to older people. It was from him that I first learned what a real elder is, though he never used the word.

5. Cultivate your power to inspire.

The word *inspire* means "to breathe into," so when you inspire you breathe into another person a reason to work hard and be creative and engage the world meaningfully. You take your own good breath and give it to someone else, much as when a person gives artificial respiration, only less literally.

Inspiration is magical, not just because it has a wondrous effect but because of the way it works. You don't usually inspire someone rationally, but you can find powerful words or gestures, maybe your example, that will light a fire in the other person. You can be a muse and a guiding spirit. People may see your age and look to you to get through difficult times or to come up with fresh ideas. When a student referred to me as an elder in my field, at first I was taken aback. I often forget how old I am. But since then I have tried to take on the role purposefully. Sometimes people informally anoint us with our role and task.

An Elder's Shadow

Everything has a shadow side, including the role of elder. A path to glimpsing this dark aspect of being an elder is Jung's idea of the animus. After reading Jung by way of James Hillman, I would describe the animus as an element in us that is analogous to soul. But whereas soul is concerned with love and images and poetics and reverie, animus tends to be the rational, intuitive, critical, and reflective power in us or in our activity.

Jung was especially interested in a weak and undeveloped animus that appears in a person full of opinions but not many real ideas. This animus may show itself in prejudices, faulty thinking, bad logic, borrowed judgments, and the pose of a thinker or expert without much to back it up. Hillman offers more ways in which the shadowy animus might damage some deep movement of the soul: "We hear animus voices driving us from it by spiritualizing the experience into abstractions, extracting its meaning, carrying it into actions, dogmatizing it into general principles, or using it to prove something."*

In all of these ways an older person might take on the role of elder in a way that is not so noble or effective. You probably know people who use their age to make empty pronouncements and judgments or try to lead when they don't have the stuff for leadership. Sometimes older people think that merely having more years piled up gives them wisdom. They don't realize that aging goes on all life long, building a thoughtful, patient person into a real leader and source of wisdom. The role of elder may sometimes be a mere shell lacking the substance that a

*James Hillman, *Anima: An Anatomy of a Personified Notion* (Dallas: Spring Publications, 1985), 181–83.

full life would have given.

In public life you sometimes see the press treating an old person as an elder, when it is clear that man or woman hasn't done the work involved in becoming an elder. All you get are shallow opinions and self-serving judgments.

If you find that you are being treated as an elder and sense the emptiness in you, your secret knowledge that you aren't really the elder people are looking for, you can convert the shadow elder into a more effective wise old person by admitting your ignorance where applicable and becoming better informed to make good judgments and offer good counsel.

Of course, being a "shadow" means that nothing you do will ever be perfect. So expect that when you slide into the elder role you may well become somewhat opinionated and inflated. You may be too critical and make too much of your role as advisor. All you can do is accept those shadow trimmings to your elder status, try to minimize their impact, and take on the challenging task of being a source of wisdom in a world hungry for it.

The Joy of Elderhood

Being an elder not only helps other people find guidance and wisdom, but it also gives the older person added reason for living. It may be the final act of a generous and thoughtful life. It is service taken to the last moment and done with a special authority and dedication.

It helps if the older person consciously adopts the role of elder. I can say from my own experience that at a certain point people will begin to treat you as an elder and look for benefits you may be able to give them. That is your cue to make a shift. You are no longer part of the crowd. Now you have to step up and assume a new place in your community. For you it is yet another rite of passage, an ascension of state, a transformation of you and your life to a level at which you can enjoy new pleasures and feel new obligations.

You may have to dress differently, speak with more authority, acknowledge your age and experience explicitly and accept opportunities for leadership that you otherwise may turn down out of tiredness or lack of interest. I might like to stay home and take it easy after a lifetime of writing and traveling, but I know that I am elected to be an elder, and so I have more work to do.

Older people have to become familiar with the requirements and opportunities of time. Getting older is all about time, not just the minutes and hours counted by a clock, but the qualities of time. You can say to yourself, "I am getting older. It's time to think about how I will use my time and make my life meaningful."

For some, being an elder is a major decision because their influence may be extensive and public. But the rest of us are elders in a small way, advising our grandchildren and neighbors and being available for the input from experience. The world would benefit from older people making a conscious decision to play the role of elder in the settings appropriate to them. Eventually they will learn the art of being an elder and come to enjoy it and make solid contributions.

11
Legacy: The Future of Your Life Experiment

Like many people, my wife and I would like to keep a neat home and to organize all the paraphernalia of our work as an artist and a writer. In terms of neatness, we both fall short of perfection. On a scale of 1 to 10, we're about 7.5. In spite of our spiritual work, we're both soulful people, and the soul is a pack rat and loves disarray. But my reason for keeping stuff is my feeling of connection to those who will probably come after me.

I know that I should tread lightly on this earth, but I keep thinking about my grandchildren and my great-grandchildren. I love them already and want them all to have copies of my books, even if in their time I am forgotten or deemed irrelevant. And so I keep books and papers and souvenirs and vases and Buddhas and mementos. Why I keep old extension cords and dried-up pens, I don't know.

Part of living a soulful life is to be in relation to people who are not here physically: those who have gone before and those who have yet to appear. This expansion of time puts you in touch with your eternal, ageless self. One good way to grow old effectively is to live from another place in you, one that isn't so connected to your present time but stretches it out both backward and forward into what are called "the mists of time."

My devotion to my great-great-great-grandchildren helps me deal with the shortness of my life. I know that death is not the end of my relationships and me. But it helps to work on that widening of my time span. I make concrete provisions for my future loved ones and feel their presence, just as I continue to work on my relationships with those who preceded me.

Expand Your Sense of Time

I've never been satisfied with the mantra so common among spiritual people today: "Live in the moment." Sometimes spiritual teachers try to get people to do something that is not natural to them and that they don't really enjoy, and people often succumb. It takes effort to be in the moment, and in my experience, the effort isn't worth all the praise it gets. I'd rather live more in the past and in the future. I'd prefer to expand the time frame in which I live rather than contract it into a moment.

C. G. Jung, a good model for doing something concrete to make life more meaningful, built a stone tower as a retreat on Lake Zurich, making a point not to install electricity or running water. He wanted to intensify his sense of time. In his diaries he makes some valuable points about his experience, explaining that he wanted to be close to water, the primal substance, and live in a maternal, womb-like structure. "In the Tower at Bollingen it is as if one lived in many centuries simultaneously. The place will outlive me, and in its location and style it points backward to things of long ago. There is very little about it to suggest the present."

So there is Jung disparaging the present. I appreciate his desire to expand the time frame in which he lived his life, and I'd like to push into the future, as well as the past. I'd like a relationship to future generations now. One way I've done this is to remember the people who will one day live in my house. In most of the houses I've lived in with my family, I've buried a time capsule with a message and photographs. Maybe the next owners found them right away, or maybe it will take several generations for them to surface, if they ever do.

Living into the future, leaving all sorts of legacies, takes faith and the ability to put yourself into an imaginal space, your conception of what the future will be. It is that kind of imagining that helps you enjoy the aging process and discover that it is truly an adventure.

When my father was in his late seventies, he left me a letter with practical information on what to do when he died, but it also contained his reflections on life and the feelings he was experiencing as he wrote to his next generation. This letter is a precious relic that I will leave for my children and theirs. It was typical of my father to think compassionately of others, and I wasn't surprised at the power of his words to his children and grandchildren.

A word about letters: In this day of email and instant messaging, letters have gone the way of telephone booths. But letters are even more effective now. You can still sit down and write a letter by hand or print it out on a computer. You can write with some style and formality and say some important things. Don't assume that your children and friends know what you have to say. Put it in words, special words, on good paper with care for the appearance. Sign it with a flourish and put it away properly. Use a wax-sealed envelope if you like. You may want to present it now and ask the recipient to keep it for a later time. Be dramatic. These are your thoughts, a gift for the future.

These are simple ways to relate to the future: Leave a time capsule and write letters to be read at another time. Teach anything worthwhile that you know and in which you have some skills. Pass on wisdom. Let your personal style be seen and appreciated.

Leaving and Receiving a Legacy

Legacy works in two directions: one is to leave something of value for future generations and the other is to receive and appreciate what has been left behind for you. When people tell me that I should live in the present moment, I confess that I feel more at home in the fifteenth century. It was an especially creative time period in many parts of the world, and I admire the work left behind by that special generation: its art, writings, ideas, and even forms of dress. I travel to Europe largely to enjoy the old world that is still there, and in Ireland and England I like to visit fifteenth-century castles and churches for that purpose.

Personally, I find that I can more easily think of leaving a legacy for the future when I appreciate what the past has left for me. And that expansion of time helps me be positive about growing older. I'm not so enamored by the present and can enjoy what it feels like to be out of step with the young impulsive world. A portion of my cherished eccentricity is being out of step with the times, at home in another world and another era.

As a writer and teacher, I find that my old ways and ancient ideas appeal to young people, if I can avoid being apologetic about them and can find exciting ways to present them. It's all right with me if I'm something of a curiosity. It actually helps me be prepared to give something to young people, to leave a legacy with style.

A legacy can be substantial and concrete, like a large house or a thriving company. Or it can be quite subtle. Painter and sculptor Anne Truitt describes her visit to her alma mater, Bryn Mawr College, and dwells on a quiet moment in the cloister: "There, across the grass, brilliant green brightened by rain, beyond the jet of the circular fountain in the center of the court, I saw a student. Her back was propped up against the granite wall. She was writing, utterly intent. Not to disturb her, I departed by a far door, leaving her as if leaving myself in place, linked to her in silent continuity."*

The deeply involved student reminded Truitt of herself when she was in college, and the care she took to protect the student's privacy was her small gift, both to the student and to herself. She had such empathy for the student, based on the thought that she was looking at herself years ago, that she gave the student precious privacy.

Such regard for a younger person helps the older one age well by maintaining a slight yet meaningful connection and identification with the young. As in this small event, the student and the mature woman share an identity. I don't have to wonder if Anne Truitt is a real artist. She exhibits the sensitivity of someone who can see herself in another and treat the other graciously because of that identification.

A Spiritual Lineage

Centuries ago artists and writers had a practice of honoring a certain historical line of figures who shaped them. They referred

*Anne Truitt, *Prospect* (New York: Scribner, 1996), 216.

to their own list of inspirers and muses as *prisca theologia* — a spiritual lineage.

For example, a fifteenth-century writer might make a list of important figures who contributed to his thought and way of life. It might vary from Plato to St. Augustine to an Arab scholar to a more recent teacher. My own line would start with Euripides and go to Plato and Ovid, Thomas More and Emily Dickinson, through Bach and Glenn Gould, and then on to Jung and Hillman. I'd have to fill in this list with at least a dozen other names.

I try to honor my lineage by placing their books on a special shelf. Jung's collected writings are right over my shoulder as I work every day. Hillman's are on the shelf above. Books that are not terribly meaningful to me but are occasionally useful are down in the basement.

I have a bronze statue of Thomas More in my private study, as well as old photographs of Emily Dickinson and her hometown of Amherst, Massachusetts, and picture books of Glenn Gould. I love these ancestors of mine and give them as much honor as I can. I feel that this practice prepares me to connect to the future. I write with affection and concern for future readers, and I want to leave them as much of my way of looking at life as I can. I don't think this is narcissistic, but rather simply a good way to age, to enjoy growing older and having more to pass on to generations. Anyone can do this. It requires opening your heart to the future, moving, as T. S. Eliot says, "into another intensity."

In psychotherapy people often talk about the ancestors and parents who hurt them in childhood, but I make a point to ask about parents and great-grandparents in a positive way, wondering how they contributed to good aspects of the life of my client, or at least find a few who were positive with their influence. Some psychologists say we shouldn't keep blaming parents for what goes wrong in adult lives. I agree, but I don't want to forget about parents altogether. My strategy is to encourage stories about family members that have had both good and bad impact on the adult.

People who come to therapy are sometimes suffering more from the narrow range of their lives than from a more obvious problem. Their imaginations don't have enough room to breathe. Often I try to help them expand their way of looking at life. I ask for stories about their grandparents and ancestors, about the places where they grew up, and especially about ways they have served other people. Just opening up into a bigger world can relieve symptoms.

If you listen closely to what I'm saying, you'll see that I'm suggesting that we notice the good that our ancestors have given us and that we appreciate their legacy. Seeing their value helps us see ours.

A simple example: Recently in her first session of therapy a woman in her early seventies told me of her depression about getting older and the sense she had that the years had passed unnoticed. Suddenly she found herself an older woman and was full of regrets for not having done the things she had always dreamed of. She felt she had not been in charge of her life but had let others decide what she should do, and most of that advice was to work hard and make money.

Hearing that her sense of timing was off, out of the blue I said to her, "Tell me about your father."

"Listen," she said. "I've been in therapy multiple times. I've gone over my parents' lives until I'm sick of them."

I didn't take her words literally but saw them as resistance. So I pressed on.

"I understand that someone who's been in therapy before may have talked a great deal about childhood and parents. But often that conversation is an attempt to explain and understand the son or daughter's psychology. I'd just like to hear what kind of person your father was. I just want to know his story."

So she talked about her father, and I encouraged her to elaborate on her stories. I didn't want a parental explanation for her current problems but only to get her life story extending back into her history and forward into her longings and wishes. I wanted to begin the therapy by extending the sense of who she was. I thought this stretching of time would itself be therapeutic and would invite her deep soul into the picture. I was taking a lesson from Jung, who went to great pains and expense to build a tower that would house the fullness of his psyche. We were building an extended space in story. Our ultimate goal was to catch a glimpse of the ageless soul.

When people tell the stories of their parents and grandparents and other relatives, they tend to give more complex portraits of these people. When you're trying to explain why you are so unhappy now, you may reduce your parents to a single, negative layer. But when you just tell stories of people important to you, you may feel lighter and have some appreciation for their struggles.

When people are in a storytelling mode, they are more inclined to find the good in people. Or if the family situation was really bad, which is sometimes the case, at least they see the complexities involved and are less judgmental. A story either includes important details of family dynamics or it hints at complexities that make the situation more layered. You can't come to simplistic conclusions when the story is subtle.

I don't want to give the impression that all stories are equal and good. Often within a family certain stories are told again and again because they keep the situation stable, perhaps at the expense of one of the members. It's easy to blame the father for not being sensitive, and it's common to blame mothers for all emotional problems. Almost always the situation is more complicated.

I see my role as a therapist as an opportunity to help people tell their stories effectively. I listen closely and encourage going into details that make the situation more subtle. Often, when the story leaves familiar ground, free of the usual blaming and excusing, insights pour in, and the insights are precious, because they change the imagination of how life has proceeded, maybe for years.

A good therapist doesn't accept the story that is usually told. He or she presses for further details and often comes up with a revised story. Revisionist history is part of every individual's sense of self, as well as a nation's way of interpreting its past. It's a sign of good aging.

It isn't easy to honor our ancestors. We can feel the impact of their problems on us. We forget that we are all weak and make mistakes. But if we could see the good our foremothers and forefathers have left us, we might be better able to face the future. We need something solid to rest on as we face an always uncertain future.

Everyone Has a Legacy

Why would you be concerned about your own legacy's impact on future generations? The obvious answer is that you want your life to amount to something, to count. You want to show something for the years of struggle and creative effort. You also want to make a contribution. Your legacy doesn't have to be a bolstering of your ego but rather an expression of generosity and desire for connection.

I think of my mother, who was a housewife and parent. She left no grand or remarkable legacy, and yet she was a woman of unusual devotion and love. I see her impact on my daughter, who is ever grateful for her grandmother's support and attention. When I consider the particular direction of my work, especially its emphasis on the intimate and soulful aspects of life, or my devotion to my clients in therapy, I'm aware of my mother's influence, her legacy. I honor her gifts to me by speaking highly of her and keeping her photographs and letters.

She had a lovely Rose of Sharon tree next to her summer house for years, so whenever we move to a new place, I plant a Rose of Sharon in her honor. We did this recently, and my wife asked if I wanted white or colored flowers. I knew immediately that my mother would want white ones. Now, every morning when I look at our little bush at the side of house, I'm reminded of my very personal *prisca theologia*, my spiritual lineage through my mother, an anima lineage that is full of soul.

Relating to Future Generations

While it's natural and admirable to want a legacy, you don't have to be intentional about it. You can live your life fully, accepting its challenges and opportunities, and automatically leave something for those who will follow you. It's sometimes said that a good teacher is someone who has developed to a point where he is worth taking from. It's similar with a legacy. If you have lived a rich life in a spirit of generosity, you will leave a rich legacy without making too much of it.

Still, it's worth thinking about future generations. Should my generation leave a natural world that is depleted and sick? Should we leave our children a world full of conflicts abroad and at home? Obviously not. Individually we can make our contribution to a peaceful world, but we can also leave our wisdom, our discoveries, and our creative work in ways that will help future generations benefit from them and treasure them.

As people get older they sometimes ask themselves: Has my life been worth anything? Will I be forgotten? You could say with spiritual detachment that we shouldn't be worried about our reputation after we die. We should just let it go and melt into the vast sea of life. But the worry that my life won't be valued persists and upsets some people. I don't think it's an idle or neurotic thought. I suggest taking it seriously and letting it motivate you to do something for future generations.

In a sense, leaving a legacy is the opposite

of remembering, and yet the two are closely connected. There's a simple practice that often stirs me into deep thoughts about legacy. I will be playing golf and arrive at the next hole or tee box and see a bench anchored into the ground, often facing the fairway, on which there is a small brass plaque commemorating someone who used to play golf there and whom friends, a spouse, or family members want to remember. But the remembrance is also a gift to all golfers in the years ahead who arrive at that hole and can sit down for a moment's rest. It's a simple ritual that demonstrates the connection between remembering and leaving a legacy. I hope people leave some legacies in my name.

In this simple example you see the presence of the heart in legacy. The legacy shows that a person has cared and has been thoughtful enough to think fondly of those who are coming and who will need some support and someone to take care of them.

The poet Maya Angelou once wrote: "I've learned that people will forget what you said, people will forget what you did, but people will never forget how you made them feel." Thus, legacy is a matter of the heart. It's not an idea but a feeling connected to largely invisible people. It's a special way of loving, and if there is anything that could make growing old more pleasurable, it would be to discover new ways to love.

A simple gift for the future opens your heart wide to include those who have not yet appeared. It's a spiritual action based on hope and forethought and kindness. In a way, it extends the range of your relationships far into the future and makes you a bigger person. It also helps you deal with your own aging, because it makes special sense as your attention shifts from the active present to the reflective future. It also extends your role as elder to embrace those who are yet to come.

In some cases a strong legacy will be created when we put an end to some atrocious cycle of behavior, such as using violence for social change. On the positive side, our legacy may be a new, enlightened, compassionate way of dealing with obstacles, leaving an example for later generations to be inspired by and to follow.

Can we open our hearts to people we don't know and who will replace us in this mysterious pageant of generations? Can I look at my achievements and get past any ego needs to open the heart to others? In this sense, cultivating a legacy can be part of your maturing, expanding beyond self-interest.

Legacy can also be part of a great vision for your life. You want to be happy, you want your family members and friends to be safe and healthy, and you want your country to thrive. But what about the grand scope of galaxies and universes? Do you want to make your contribution to the building of a world?

In this great vision, your legacy may be so small as to be insignificant, and yet it is precisely our small contributions that add up to the rich complexifying of life, of its development into something glorious. Our small lives meet up with a grand vision of creation itself to evoke one of the greatest paradoxes of all: How our lives can be meaningful in the context of a vast world.

To leave a legacy, therefore, we have to take our lives seriously — one of the main themes of this book. We have to build our vision so we don't feel swamped and eradicated by the vastness of the world in which we play out our destiny. We have to become big enough in our sense of self to realize how significant we are in the midst of our insignificance.

People often say that they are looking for meaning, whereas meaning may be fully accessible in the present moment. Living our vision, cultivating our compassion, daring to be on the side of life rather than its repression — these are all sources of meaning. If you want to leave a legacy, all you have to do is live a meaningful and generous life.

Legacy Is a Way to Age Well

One of the bitter sorrows of aging is the thought that this short life hasn't been worth much. But the feeling that you are leaving a legacy for others can give your life value. Many people, realizing the importance of legacy, make symbolic gestures that put a legacy into motion. They may bequeath a rare forest to posterity, or build an inspiring monument, or buy a brick at a school monument. In my rural area of New England, people sometimes donate a park, a beach, or a pond to common use.

In 1993, Elizabeth Marshall Thomas published a bestselling book, *The Hidden Life of Dogs,* and with the proceeds purchased beautiful Cunningham Pond in Peterborough, New Hampshire, and donated it to the town. She stipulated that there be a beach for humans and one for dogs. I've enjoyed that beach frequently with family members and particularly appreciate watching dogs having a wonderful time playing on their own beach. While there, you will sometimes hear the story of Liz Thomas and feel the generosity in her legacy.

The very sentiment that you should care for future generations helps humanize you and gives your life depth and breadth. It's a sure move beyond the narcissism of the times, which is rooted in anxiety about meaning in life. You pay excessive attention to yourself because you're worried about the value of that self. But once you realize that you become more of a self by caring for others, you can link your own peace of mind with your legacy. By leaving something for others, you become a bigger and deeper person.

As you age, the question about your worth may become more pressing. Time is short. What can you do to make your life count? Have you done enough in the past? What will people say and think about you?

People often criticize those who have a large sense of themselves. They can't distinguish between narcissism and a great self. We need big people, people who see their mission in life in global terms. Of course, many people have a self-image that is empty and unrealistic, but many also are the real thing. They see life in big terms and take it on in grand style.

If you don't think consciously of your legacy, you may fall into one of the bitterest conditions of old age: regret. You may regret not having done things you could have done and having done things you wish you hadn't. But regret is a fruitless and empty emotion. It isn't grounded in the soul. In this sense it is like guilt, which is only feeling bad, without any real determination to change or repent.

Similarly, regret also goes only halfway toward change. The better option for guilt is to really acknowledge responsibility, to truly be guilty rather than just feel the emotion. When regret matures, it becomes remorse. Remorse touches the soul and makes a difference. It is not just a floating feeling that gives the impression of change. It's a realization that affects you as a person and your choices in life. An even better option is to make life count day by day, to think of life in large terms, and to do whatever you can to make your contribution now. No room for regret.

You can't leave a legacy if you are full of regret, which has a way of stopping the natural movement of your life. You wish yourself out of who and where you are. You become fixated on the thing regretted, frozen in an emotion that has no life in it.

When regret dominates, you can't age positively; you only grow old.

. Regret is an attempt to feel remorse, but it doesn't quite get there. If you find yourself full of regrets, you might consider how to transform that regret into remorse. You may have to feel it more directly and do something in response. Re-morse (like morsel) means "to keep biting." Remorse gets its teeth into you and you can't ignore it. It demands a response.

I once met a woman at a book signing who told me her story of regret. As a teenager she had entered a Catholic convent and become a nun. For many years she lived that strict and celibate life before she finally left. But now her emotional life had a large stain on it, her regret at making the decision to enter the convent and give up an active sex life during her prime years. The older she became, the stronger was the regret. It lingered and made her life miserable.

I wondered if that regret could change into remorse, if she might look more closely either at whatever weakness of character or loose emotion led her into a life she didn't want or what might lie behind her inability to shake the painful regret. She couldn't accept her fate or her formative decision. She couldn't live with the life she had; instead she allowed her regret to keep her at a distance from her deeper reality. Maybe she still didn't value her sexuality. Maybe she found it easier to pity herself than to go at life in an entirely different, more proactive spirit. We didn't have an opportunity for a lengthy conversation, so I can only surmise.

Redeeming One's Life

Feeling that you have a valuable legacy to leave the world, your family, or particular people makes old age more bearable. It can give you a taste of immortality. Your influence will go on, at least for a while, after your passing. You can feel that life has been worth living because you have something to pass on.

A legacy might make up for omissions and misdeeds, any suffering you have caused, or any other negativity in your past. This is no small matter because it isn't enough to say you're sorry. You have to do something to redeem yourself after you have made a mess of things. Leaving a noteworthy legacy restores the purpose and value of your life.

I think of a certain aspect of my legacy whenever a book I publish doesn't sell as well as I had hoped. I'm inspired once again to write for future generations, hoping that one day someone will come along and appreciate what I am trying to do with my writing. I keep those future readers in mind and try not to be swayed by the vagaries of current opinion and taste.

Specifically, I know that the spirit of my time favors quantified studies and hard, factual solutions to problems. In this context my emphasis on the soul and on the religious and magical traditions may appear anachronistic, even irrelevant. So I place my hope in a future generation when our current attitude, which I consider materialistic and mechanistic, will change and favor the humanities and spiritualities. I'm already fond of those people of the future and hope that my words will speak to them as my legacy to their generation.

A legacy can activate your heart and expand your vision. You can see in my thoughts about it that a legacy is not a simple thing. Subjectively, it may include some conflict and worry, as well as good wishes and love. It may seem delusional, wishing that people of the future will love you. Let's call it an illusion, which is more generous.

As my love for future generations grows, I feel more a part of the cycles of life, and I don't worry so much about the shortness of my days. My aging is a gift to the natural cycle and to a better future. And this attempt at generosity expresses a deep-seated spirituality. People often talk about the spiritual as though it were all about learning how to meditate and purify your lifestyle. A more challenging aspect might be working out the limitations of your life in relation to future generations. Developing your legacy could be one of your most significant spiritual achievements.

Finally, legacy is also a source of joy and a feeling of fulfillment, valuable qualities as you age. Legacy completes the process of a life work, a process that has several stages:

1. Educating yourself and developing talents and skills
2. Looking for a job that employs those abilities
3. Developing a career
4. Dealing with endings and turning points in the career
5. Achieving success in your own way
6. Shifting into the older years with an emphasis on service
7. Creating a legacy for future generations

This scheme is only a skeleton of what it could be, but it shows the flow of a creative life from start to finish. It is more than a diagram, because you may feel the dynamics in your life as you move from one phase to another. The sense of leaving a legacy can fit into the rhythm by offering not just an ending but a feeling of completion. The arc is whole and has its natural ending in the legacy.

Even though our culture may be moving away from a work-oriented source of meaning, you can still leave your legacy if you have enjoyed a more relaxed kind of life. One would hope that when the work ethic eases, we will want to be more creative and perhaps even more concerned about the world we leave to our children.

Legacy is largely a way of imagining the time and effort you put into your life's work. Some people have such a standing in culture and history that their legacies are grand, but most of us live ordinary lives and can imagine only slivers of influence reaching into the future. The point is, legacy is not about the size of our impact on those who will come after us, but only the fact of having been significant to someone.

It gives me joy each time I can publicly honor the men and women whose wisdom and creative work have so affected me: Thomas I. Nugent, Gregory O'Brien, Rene

Dosogne, Elizabeth Foster, Thomas MacGreevy, and James Hillman. My very personal spiritual lineage. My list could be much longer, of course. You might write down the names of your more intimate lineage and decide to help the legacies of those on your list by acknowledging their contributions.

As we do the work of aging, we need community and collaboration. It is never a solitary task. And we can prepare for our old age by taking part in the aging of others around us. Our community includes future generations, and all it takes is a serious effort of imagination to feel close to those people to come.

12
TRANSFORMING LONELINESS

I don't believe in aging. I believe in forever altering one's aspect to the sun. Hence my optimism.
— Virginia Woolf, Journal, October 1932

One of the main principles in the psychotherapy I have practiced for over thirty years is a simple one I got from James Hillman: "Go with the symptom." In a world where we are always trying to overcome and conquer problems, it is like magic, helping us find relief from heavy emotional strain and opening up into new areas of life. In part, its magic comes from being so different from common sense. Almost always, in the face of pain we ask, "How can I get rid of this?" But our magic principle is quite different: "How can I go further into this problem and find myself on the other side, relieved and happier?"

Hillman liked to quote a line from the

poet Wallace Stevens on this point: "The way through the world is more difficult to find than the way beyond it." Can you take an unpleasant matter, say loneliness, and instead of trying to avoid it, go into it and find relief after you've come to know it?

Let me explain how this dynamic of going into or with the symptom helps with loneliness.

If you are lonely and try to get rid of the loneliness by forcing yourself to be around people, in effect you are repressing an emotion. You are repressing it by fleeing from it, going to an opposite place where you will be far away from it. But Freud's basic principle still stands: The return of the repressed. You try to shake yourself free of a condition, and it comes back, maybe stronger than ever. You drag yourself to a social occasion, and then when you return home you are lonelier than you were before.

Going away from the symptom is fleeing from yourself, from the state your soul is in. It might be better to acknowledge your loneliness and then give it some attention. You don't have to surrender to it or wallow in it. I used to tell people that I didn't call my book *Wallowing in the Soul;* I titled it *Care of the Soul.* So, you might care for yourself in your loneliness, but you don't try to get rid of the feeling.

You also go into your symptom, your loneliness in this case, because it shows you not only what gives you discomfort and pain, but also points to what you need. This is a germ idea I've cited many times, and it comes from a good friend and superb psychologist, Patricia Berry. If you're feeling lonely, instead of trying to be more social and engaged with people, you might explore possibilities for solitude that work for you and are not uncomfortable.

Your loneliness could be telling you that you need to be alone more or at least appreciate times when you are not among people. Or, more deeply, you may need to be more of an individual and not part of the crowd. Loneliness may take us into the space needed to reflect on the things that matter instead of being occupied all the time. Loneliness may be a hint at a cure for the incessant activity people engage in that is often empty and pointless.

Physical Loneliness in Old Age

Some feelings of loneliness are due to circumstances, of course. You may have had an active life, and suddenly, in old age, your family is scattered and busy with their lives, your friends have moved away or died, or you find yourself in a community of old people where friendships like those of the past are difficult to find.

The question then is: How do you deal with this physical aloneness?

My father was ninety-one when my mother died, and he lived alone in his house for several years afterward. He seemed quite happy with his independence. Naturally, he missed his wife. Once, he told me that every morning he'd gaze at a photograph of her that he kept in his bedroom and have a conversation with her. He also continued to work with the stamp collection that he had begun seventy-five years ago, when he was in his teens. It kept him busy with work that he loved, and connected to people around the world, and it even made him a little money. Neighbors liked him and would bring hot food and groceries to him regularly. Despite living alone, he didn't seem to feel lonely.

But then he started falling. He'd be rushed to the hospital and then returned home. It became clear that he couldn't continue living in his house, enjoying his beloved independence. My brother helped him find an assisted-living situation near my brother's house. Every time I saw him there, I noticed sadness in his eyes. He was always a good joiner. He could make friends easily and get involved in activities. He did some of that in his new surroundings, but he obviously missed his independence. At this point he couldn't even find much enthusiasm for his stamps. The one thing that seemed to motivate him was giving support to his grandson, who was in a long recovery from a serious accident.

What I thought I saw in my father's face was not loneliness from being alone, but from having lost his world and his life's work. He had always been a bit stoic about life's tragedies and requirements. He was the one in our large extended family who people would turn to for funeral arrangements, wills, probates, and emotional support when bad things happened. He never complained about his situation. He knew that he couldn't live independently any longer. But life in his room in the institution was not the life he had enjoyed at home.

He seemed to lose his passion for stamps, but not for life. At his one-hundredth-birthday party he laughed heartily and carried on many conversations with the different sorts of people who had come to celebrate him. But once the party was over, he went back to his room. I pushed him there that day in a wheelchair and saw both his usual sense of fun and his loneliness.

Loneliness and Being Alone

Loneliness and being alone are two different things. You can feel lonely in a crowd and not lonely in your solitude. If we follow our rule of thumb, "Go with the symptom," we might cure our loneliness by being alone. Our painful feelings give us a hint and a direction about what we need. But how does that work? How does it make sense?

It may be important to feel your own life and to have a strong sense of self. And it may be difficult to do that when surrounded by a gaggle of people. There is too much going on. There are too many people to consider. You can't hear yourself and know what is going on with you. You get lonely for your own life.

Aging is full of transitions where you miss your former life, which is a way of losing touch with who you have been and who you feel you are. The emotion may seem to be loneliness because that is the obvious possibility. But it could also be the loss of a familiar world, with certain people, places, and experiences.

When I left the monastery, I remember being quite lonely. I rented an apartment on the Near North Side of Chicago, an area

I didn't know. I would walk the streets returning home from DePaul University and notice people having dinner together in lighted dining rooms as I passed. I felt pangs that I assumed came from being alone, but in fact I enjoyed living alone at that time. What I missed was my old community and friends I had known for many years. I missed a lifestyle that I enjoyed and valued, and I didn't know at all where I was headed. The "loneliness" I felt was really the loss of a familiar world and the security and familiarity I knew there.

I didn't have myself or my world, and that loss was disturbing. The scenes I saw in the lighted windows were people enjoying their own familiar world. I had a lot of people in my life then, but I didn't have my own world, and I didn't know who I was. Loneliness is often far less literal than it might appear to be.

The reverse may be true, too. You may be too closely connected to the past, to family, friends, and places that meant a great deal to you in former years. Now it may be time for a fresh approach. By missing the past, you may not put much emotion into the present and future. Your loneliness may be a way to keep from accepting the present and future.

Liz Thomas told me that she was living in the home she had shared with her husband for many years. The place reeked of memories of a life that was gone. Now she wanted a new life and a new home, a place free of the memories and supportive of new adventures. People around her might have assumed that she liked to be reminded of the past, but she wanted to move on.

Again we see the wisdom of yin and yang, or any dynamic opposite principles that don't annihilate each other but work in tandem, first one strong and then the other. W. B. Yeats imagined them as gyres spinning in and out of each other, sometimes fully interpenetrating and at other times quite separate.

The past and the future may shuttle back and forth, much of the time offering their distinct rewards.

As we age we go through passages that demand flexibility and resilience. We lose, we gain, and we lose again. The theme I keep repeating in this book is that aging is not watching time go by but being open to life and being transformed time after time by specific invitations. The many transformations amount to a life lived rather than watched. Or, as Thoreau says in *Walden:* "I went to the woods because I wished to live deliberately, to front only the essential facts of life and see if I could not learn what it had to teach, and not, when I came to die, discover that I had not lived." If life ages you, it is because you have welcomed it and opened yourself to its alchemy, the steady transformations it can work on the chemistry of your soul.

Again I ask you to hear the word *age* not as we often do, as the passing of time, but as the way we speak of certain wines and cheeses that "age" well over time. They get better and even take on special value from having aged. Human beings can age in a similar way, becoming more real and richer in flavor from having been changed by experience. But to age in this way you have to allow experience to affect you and shift your perspective and make you more aware and more sophisticated as a person. For example, you have to follow through on your loneliness and turn it into individuality.

There is an unconsciousness in people that itself is unconscious. We don't realize that we are unconscious about things that really matter. We are not aware that we go through life often not thinking about things that need to be considered and processed.

In day-to-day activities we react rather than reflect.

The capacity to reflect well and deeply on daily life is an achievement. You might expect to be better at it as you get older because experience has taught you some things. To reflect well you have to be comfortable with a degree of solitude, because reflection requires some quiet and aloneness.

What we call loneliness may simply be the quality of being alone with yourself, undisturbed and open to your thoughts. Externally, you may be doing nothing, while internally you are abuzz with memories and ideas. You may need tolerance for that kind of solitude with your reflections. It can age you well and give you character.

Good Conditions for Reflection

It's odd even to advocate for reflection. Doing so would seem to be a matter of course. Naturally you need to reflect in order to be a mature person. But we live in a highly extroverted society that interprets life in terms of external events and objects. Our capacity for reflection is diminishing day by day. We used to talk about "sound bites" of news coming to us in increasingly abbreviated form, but now even sound bites seem too long for people to digest.

Reflection doesn't have to be done in pure quiet but can be evoked in deep and pleasurable conversation, relaxing, reading, and even while listening to television or an online analysis of world events and cultural developments. Reflection is not the same as entertainment, but sometimes the two overlap, such as in a thoughtful movie that prompts looking inward. Personally, I find biographies and memoirs good resources as I reflect on the direction my life has taken and where I want to go next.

Let's say that the first stage of reflection, for the ordinary person, is reading or listening to someone else offer an understanding of events. You listen or read and make those ideas your own in your own way. You probably don't buy the whole point of view the other is presenting, but you may take some ideas that are useful to you.

The second stage of reflection is conversation. You make a point to speak with people who have something worthwhile to say and with whom you enjoy speaking. Pleasure is an important ingredient. Again, you don't accept everything the other person presents, but in the exchange you clarify your own thoughts and pick up some new ones.

A third stage of reflection is to find some

effective mode in which you can express yourself. It could be writing of various forms — journals, poems, essays, fiction. You could make videos or audio programs of your ideas, and you may or may not make them available to others. You can work out your ideas as you craft your writing or speaking, even in the most ordinary ways. A letter to a friend, a loved one, or a family member can be the occasion for reflection. If you want a model for this, look at the letters of famous writers like Emily Dickinson or Virginia Woolf. They took letter writing seriously. For them it was the occasion for serious reflection.

For over three years now I have written a tweet on Twitter every morning. Each fewer than 140 characters, these short messages to about five thousand followers have allowed me to reflect on various matters at the beginning of each day. The practice has been painless and rewarding.

But let me repeat: Reflection is essential. Keep in mind the famous quote from Socrates first spoken at his trial: "The unexamined life is not worth living." Or, closer to the original Greek: "The untested life is not for humans." We need to be provoked into thinking about what has happened to us. Maybe that is the purpose of life's setbacks and failures. As Keats says, "A world of pain and troubles is necessary to school an intelligence and make it a soul." Is it the pain itself that helps, or is it the reflection that comes from being tested?

One of the key points in this book is the simple idea that you truly age, in a positive and desirable sense of the word, when you have been struck by events and are transformed even in small ways. You become what you are capable of. You are educated by life. You make an advance in your personality and character. You grow. You mature. You ripen as a person.

The Aging of Burt Bacharach

So, I was in the thick of writing this book and teaching a course for an environmentalist program called the Viridis Graduate Institute, created and run by my old friend Lori Pye. One of the students informed me that she was a friend of the famous composer Burt Bacharach and that Burt would like to talk with me about aging. He was eighty-six.

Before I recount my conversation with him, let me tell you that Burt is known all over the world for the hit songs that he wrote, many with his lyricist partner Hal David: "Close to You," "Alfie," "What the

World Needs Now," "Arthur's Theme" and the musical *Promises, Promises*. In 2012 he was awarded the Gershwin Prize from the Library of Congress at the White House, and he has received three Academy Awards and six Grammy Awards.

We talked by phone and the conversation threw me at every turn. First, I called and he was busy. He asked me to phone back. I called again, and he answered. He said, "Tell me your questions." I had hoped just to have a conversation, but I knew that Burt thought of me as one in a long line of interviewers. I know the drill well myself. I've been interviewed by strangers for thirty years, though surely not as much as Burt has.

I thought, this may be difficult. How will we get to a deep conversation? But in the next sentence he began to talk openly and thoughtfully about himself and the things that matter to him. He had had a successful but challenging life. He told me that he was too caught up in his music in his early years and wasn't as available to people as he could have been. He had obviously changed. Something had happened to him. He spoke lovingly about his former wife, Angie Dickinson, his wife, Jane, his sons, Christopher and Oliver, and his daughter Raleigh. He reflected sadly on his daughter Nikki, who suffered from Asperger's syndrome when little was known about it and eventually committed suicide.

Here was a man to whom life had given exceptional talent and wonderful success, as well as much pain and loss. I heard both strains of emotion in his voice and was struck by his openness and the transparency of his feelings. He had good reason to be lonely, and I thought I heard that in his tone, as well. But he wasn't a lonely person. He wasn't identified with his loneliness. It was a part of him that you could sense immediately, but it wasn't the whole of him.

There is an important lesson about loneliness. It is part of life and can be respected and spoken for. But it doesn't have to take over. You don't have to be a lonely old person. You can be an older person who gets lonely sometimes. The difference is vast.

In most psychological matters it is better to accept the emotion or condition and give it a place in your life. Repression in any form doesn't work. What I felt talking to Burt Bacharach was a maturing of emotion, and that is what aging at its best is all about. He had many feelings, some wistful and some painful, others positive and hopeful. In the background of all of it was a deep satisfaction over his creativity and accomplishments.

The reflective quality of Burt's attitude at eighty-six is another essential ingredient. He isn't letting age end his creative life. He still gives concerts, still writes music, and still has a regimen in daily life that includes physical fitness.

Burt teaches us that you can be swept away in some activity in your youth to the point that you make mistakes in relationships and have much to give you feelings of remorse. But as you mature, you can reach a point where your remorse doesn't undo your hope and happiness. In fact, it gives happiness a coloring of pain and wistfulness that only deepens it. Happiness is a worthy goal, but it has to be deepened and made more complex with many other emotions, some of them painful.

Burt's amazing creativity at eighty-six shows another remedy for loneliness. We may pull back from life just because it seems customary in old age, or because we don't want to be seen as old, or because our abilities aren't as strong as before. There are many good reasons to choose not to live, but usually they stem from fear. You don't want to be seen as weak. If you can live on strongly, it isn't likely that loneliness will be an issue.

The Cure for Loneliness

Since I was a child, I have had a strong need for solitude. Maybe the ideal situation for me was the arrangement in monastic life, where I had a private room that no one else could enter and time for quiet alone. But for most of my life I've also had a partner in some way. I've been married now for twenty-five years and have to deal with my need for solitude. Otherwise I suffer the opposite of loneliness. I don't know if we have a word for that condition.

But to my surprise, as a lover of solitude, I get lonely when my wife and children are gone. Beforehand, I look forward to some solitude and enjoy it for several days, but then some loneliness creeps in. I rather appreciate it, because it lets me know that I'm a human being, normal. I can get lonely. I'm not self-sufficient. It also reminds me not to overvalue what I sometimes wish for, that prized solitude. One day I may find myself alone, and I may discover the depths of loneliness.

What if we assume that loneliness is not just about not having people around you, relating to you? What if you are lonely for yourself? For the person you were and the people who made up your life. For the projects you were involved with and for the work life you always wished you could escape and that you now miss. Loneliness is the emotion connected to becoming a unique person and learning that ultimately you are alone, in spite of the many people who share your planet and your city and your home.

Relationships can be a distraction from the existential fact that you can't give your life to anyone else. If you go into a relationship to cure your loneliness, then what is the relationship but a narcissistic manipulation, using someone to solve your problem? As odd as it may sound, I don't think loneliness is caused by not having people in your life, and it's not cured by developing new relationships.

In a column in *Publishers Weekly* reflecting on books about loneliness, Olivia Laing says: "The strange, almost magical thing about these books is that in examining loneliness they also serve as an antidote to it. Loneliness is by its nature a profoundly isolating experience. But if a novel or memoir succeeds in mapping its icy regions, then it can alleviate something of the acute pain of feeling islanded, cut off from the world at large."*

*Olivia Laing, "10 Books About Loneliness," *Pub-*

A novel can alleviate loneliness. Not a person and not a crowd of people. In her book *The Lonely City,* Laing says that imagination can work to resist the pain of loneliness. Again, imagination, not people. This could be our clue to responding effectively to the loneliness in older people. They may need imagination more than relationships, just as a person living in a city teeming with people can be lonely and in need of something other than people.

But how can this be? Isn't it obvious that lonely people need family, friends, and society? Consider the lonely city syndrome: people surrounded by people and utterly alone in their experience of it all. Lonely people may first need a different way of imagining loneliness. Second, they may need the kind of connection with people that enlivens them. A group of lonely people may not solve the problem of loneliness. Third, they may need an intimate connection with themselves. You come into a group lonely. What you need is to enter a community when you're not lonely.

---

lishers Weekly Tip Sheet, February 26, 2016, http://www.publishersweekly.com/ pw/by-topic/ industry-news/tip-sheet/article/ 69506-10-books-about-loneliness.html.

I want to spell this out further, but first let's consider that loneliness may sometimes be alienation from oneself or some aspect of your soul. The short story writer John Cheever is sometimes brought up as a particularly vivid example of loneliness, but when you hear his story you see that not accepting his gay self made him lonely for who he actually was. If you don't welcome an obvious part of your nature, it's understandable that you might be lonely, and having many people in your life is not going to solve the problem.

People who live in a crowded city might be less lonely if they befriended the city. Our relationships are not all human, and our intimacy with our homes, neighborhoods, and all those things that give life to the city could temper our loneliness, because they can make us feel alive. It isn't just companionship that overcomes loneliness but anything that is life giving. To put it another way, the world itself has a soul, *anima mundi,* and can give us ties that make life worth living. That is what is at stake in loneliness, not just companionship.

There may come a time when you can't be out in the city as much as usual, but even then caretakers, friends, and relatives might keep in mind how important it is to have even the slightest experience of the city, if only by looking out windows and having special foods brought in. If you live in a town or in the countryside, the situation is similar, only the experiences will be different.

I don't mean to make little of people and their friendships and community. Of course, they, too, can give us vitality. But then it is mutual, and we have to be alive to begin with. As I said before, it doesn't work to turn to people as our only source of vitality, as a defense against feeling alone. That would be a recipe for loneliness. A lonely person in a crowd may not be less lonely.

Some people seem to be lonely because they can't accept their aging self. They wish they were younger and sometimes even try to be a different age. You can bring a youthful spirit into old age, as I described in the first chapter, but to deny your age is to create a split within yourself, and that is one source of deep loneliness. It may be difficult to correct this source of loneliness, because most people wouldn't make a connection between denying your age and feeling alone.

Let me remind you of the paradox at work here. If you accept that a person is not a solid unified block but has many distinct aspects or even personalities — psychological polytheism, as Hillman calls it — then you can pursue youth and take on old age at the same time. You can do two things at once. In fact, by acting this way you avoid splitting old age from youth.

The best way to deal with loneliness is to pursue vitality even in small things. This means keeping alive your curiosity, wonder, spirit of adventure, love of learning, creative character, interest in people, eccentricity, and contemplative lifestyle. You can do these things even with diminished capacity. My friend John Van Ness is making a video about his wife's dementia in which he shows how even with an advanced challenge of that sort a person can make important discoveries and stay connected to life. That he is making this video at age eighty-six adds to his persuasiveness.

The Mirror Community

A most important response to loneliness is to make sure that you are not closing off a part of yourself. The community of people in your outside world is mirrored in the many selves you are. Let me use myself as a test case.

When I ask myself what self wants to be part of my inner community, I find it difficult to discern. But I have to try. I remember recurring dreams I've had of hiding when there is a shooting. In one dream police come and subdue a woman who has freaked out and is shooting for a long time. I'm surprised to see that an ordinary man is a policeman and that he can take care of the insane woman.

The dream causes me to wonder about my own craziness and tendency toward hysteria, and then about my resistance to getting involved in resolving the crisis. I seem to be afraid of guns in my dreams. I wonder then if it's the strong male that I have not let in. All my life I've admired the quiet, soft-spoken man, the kind of person I was as a monk. I have also had trouble being active in public life and engaging in community activity. I can give talks and publish books that people read all over the world, but I have difficulty being engaged in public issues. I wonder if this is a figure I have to welcome somehow. If I start feeling lonely, I'm going to pursue this direction for sure.

You can ask yourself, as I did, who wants to become part of your inner community, a self that has been resisted or neglected? You probably have some hints as to who that is. Is there some inner character that you fear? Do you pull away from intimacy, love, creativity, anger, power? There may be a personality that embodies these qualities that could be part of your makeup, your interior community.

As you get older you may especially notice possibilities that you've kept out of sight for many years. Older people often look back and see opportunities that they let go by. You may understand now that these lost chances were due to resisting an expanding self. Usually you can try again in your older years and find ways to include more and become a larger person. Old age doesn't have to mean a diminishing of self but an increasing, multiplying sense of who you are or could be. Another tonic for loneliness.

If you are lonely, don't sink into the loneliness. Become bigger and more diverse from the inside out. Become more complex and then in new ways engage the world that needs your complexity.

■ ■ ■ ■

PART FIVE:
THE SPIRITUALITY
OF AGING

■ ■ ■ ■

You demonstrate that even in your later years you are tireless especially when you speak forcefully for what is right, and then you seem to grow young again.
— NICOLAS OF CUSA

13
FRIENDSHIP AND COMMUNITY

It's often the case that in the bodies of several friends we see one soul.
— Marsilio Ficino,
Letter to Almanno Donati

My wife tells a story about her father, Joe's, funeral. An old friend from their army days was present, and when the service was over, he went to the cemetery office and ordered a plot next to Joe. Apparently, he was overcome with feelings of friendship and wanted to somehow make it ageless. My wife was surprised at the depth of the friend's feeling. But friendship is one of the deep-seated passions that give life its meaning from the heart.

The story also reminds us how important friendship is as we get older. Sometimes it feels more important than a family connection, and there's no doubt that friendships are usually more stable than other kinds of relationships. They are also important to older people, partly because of the trend toward loneliness we just discussed, and partly because it isn't easy to face the challenges of aging without someone close by.

Friendship and Soul-Making

Let me list some of the advantages of friendship as I see them:

1. It's easy to remain an individual even though you're involved in a close relationship.
2. It's based on opening your soul to someone rather than making him or her your partner.
3. The emotional side is usually tame compared to family and romantic relationships.
4. You can more easily weave a friendship into your life than have family members and love interests close at hand.
5. A friendship doesn't change as often as other kinds of relationships do.
6. A friendship is close but has enough distance for a good balance of individuality and mutuality.
7. Friends may not see one another

often, and so the closeness doesn't feel a burden.

8. Friendship has longevity, such that those that are formed early may well last a lifetime.
9. The structure of friendship is flexible, so it doesn't have to go through difficult public changes like divorce or adoption.
10. In friendship you can love without smothering or controlling.

Friendship has its limitations and problems, but it is largely free and less complicated than other forms of relationships. Therefore, it can be good for older people. But, of course, no human relationship is simple or easy all the time. One of the skills everyone has to learn is how to be in relationship with another complicated person. And we're all complicated.

In our sense of aging, or becoming more of a person, friendship is a catalyst. While marriage, parenthood, and dating relationships are often stormy and intense forms of aging, friendship often does the job over a longer and less disruptive period.

One of the most remarkable friendships in American history was the long, productive association of Susan B. Anthony and Elizabeth Cady Stanton. They met in 1851 and worked closely together until Anthony died at eighty-six in 1902. Anthony was the strategist and organizer, and Stanton was the writer and idea person. Stanton was married and had seven children, while Anthony was single. Although they were very different in temperament and disagreed on some basic ideas, together they changed the lives of women in the United States.

"It is fifty-one years since we first met, and we have been busy through every one of them, stirring up the world to recognize the rights of women," Susan B. Anthony wrote her friend in 1902, the year of her death. They had been fueling their friendship for over fifty years by "stirring up the world" and cherishing their appreciation for each other.

The anthropologist Edith Turner says that you spark a felt sense of community by sharing a common cause, and the same could be said of friendship. Friends don't just look at one another with pleasure; they may work together to make the world better. Often they have a transcendent purpose.

Stanton always wanted to work to improve the whole lives of women and African Americans, challenging especially their religious beliefs that kept them distracted.

Anthony was afraid that being so inclusive would only turn off many women to their goal of women's suffrage. Stanton tended to be liberal and Anthony conservative. Yet they managed to support each other in an effective, fifty-year effort to change society's thinking and its values. In old age Anthony said she regretted missing an opportunity to invite Stanton to live with her permanently.

This is a story of aging together, helping each other deal with life and especially with the invitation each received to make a real difference in the lives of people. Their relationship shows how aging is not just getting older but accepting the perceived mission to stand up and do something for the world in your time. Stanton and Anthony were like facets of a single powerhouse. Over the years friendship took them to a point where today they are models of social equality in general and the nobility of women in particular.

We could imagine our own aging in this way, too, as a process of making a change in how the world works. Stanton and Anthony's example teaches us to watch out for opportunities for friendship that could be the spark that gives our lives meaning and sustains us over the years.

We might also understand the power and

importance of friendship. Knowing their story, it's difficult to imagine either Stanton or Anthony accomplishing nearly as much alone. The friendship was part of the equation, and when we look at the terribly important movement toward the women's right to vote, the abolition of slavery, and other freedoms, we can only be inspired by a friendship between two women. It looks private, but it had extraordinary public ramifications.

You could say that as the two women grew older, their friendship became more intense, or that as the friendship grew, they aged into leaders and teachers of public values. Friendship ages, in the best sense of the word. It helps you grow up, move beyond your self-absorption, and turn outward toward the needs of the world.

Notice, too, how different they were from each other. Especially in our time we need to envision friendship across political, racial, and religious or spiritual lines.

Navigating Relationship

Both friendship and community life require some sophistication in handling the problems that always appear, even in a good relationship. Intimacy may be an important aspect of living, but it is not easy. When I tell people I'm working on the theme of aging, invariably they ask me to write about the difficulties of being in a family, a marriage, or a retirement community in old age. Why are older people so difficult to live with? they ask.

Before looking at the specific issues of older people, consider the difficulties people of all ages have in getting along. Marriages, families, businesses — in all human communities we find a disconnect between ideals and realities. We imagine people enjoying these associations, but we find struggles in all of them. Here are some reasons why it is difficult to have a harmonious relationship:

1. Human beings are not moved by reasonable motives but by unsettled emotions. We call a human being homo sapiens — a knowing, intelligent, and conscious being. But, in fact, we are all unconscious. Often we have no idea why we do and say the things we do. We might be better off expecting irrational behavior and enjoying the occasional rational act.

2. We are all mysterious creatures of infinite depth, and we can never

fully know ourselves or our motives. In your interactions you may assume that the other person knows what is going on, but in fact her feelings are as mysterious to her as they are to you. Again, you might be better off assuming that the other doesn't know herself any better than you know her.

3. Much of our behavior is an expression of past and often very early childhood experiences. Childhood and life experiences don't come and go. They happen and then stay with us. The stories of childhood and family continue to play out as important themes in our very identity. The problem is, we don't know that they're in the background of our continuing adult interactions. We don't see them until someone points them out to us.

4. Many patterns from the past are raw and continue to influence us without much change. People who have been in therapy have had an opportunity to process past experiences, and that working through may help them sort out their past enough to be relatively free of its

complications. Of course, formal therapy isn't the only way to process the past, but it can be effective.

5. Human life is not rational and controlled but daimonic. Daimonic means that we have urges that come out of nowhere and can take us over. We do things we wouldn't normally choose to do and say things that just come out of our mouths. Think of a daimon, as many philosophers and psychologists have described it, as a mysterious but powerful urge toward love, anger, creative expression, or even violence. C. G. Jung used the term *complex* to name the overwhelming urges we all have that get in the way of a rational and controlled life.

These are a few "truths" about the human condition that have direct impact on our relationships, often making clear communication difficult. As we get older, we become less absorbed in the challenges of making a living and contributing to the world and feel the strength of the daimonic life in all its power. The complexes don't go away; they may even become more difficult. As you age, you may have less energy to deal with them. Old anger and longing press on us as never before.

A separate section of this book deals with the important place of anger in aging, but in this context let me point out that in sustaining friendship and community you have to beware of the temptation to "resolve" a situation through passive aggression.

You are in a conversation and some misunderstanding arises. You don't see a way out, so you say, "Well, I can see I have no place here, so I'll just go away." You sometimes hear this kind of reaction in communities of older people. But it is pure passive aggression, which means that you are trying to get your frustration and anger out without it being visible as such. Declaring your intention to leave is a way of getting back at the people involved. But instead of engaging them in your anger, you disguise it as becoming disengaged. Either way you inflict your anger on the people, but the second way is so camouflaged that the people hurt by your anger find it difficult to respond.

The elderly person may find temporary relief in venting emotion, but that doesn't improve the situation. Such passive aggression is often a sign of an immature emotional development. You have to learn how to stay engaged, show your anger, and come to a resolution. Once again, being direct and clear solves many problems.

This unsatisfactory passive aggression shows that older people are not always "aged." They haven't learned how to express themselves and how to be clear with their friends. In the end, the problem is not really old people's anger but rather anger that hasn't matured. It isn't a problem of being old, but of not having truly aged and ripened.

The Importance of Being Seen

Another problem of relationships in general that may be intensified among older people is the struggle to be somebody. One reason why so many people are fascinated by celebrities is that they have lost touch with their own value. They give weight to famous people because they lack esteem for themselves. For the same reason they may fall into a habit of putting down people close to them. Once again, the problem is not that they think their friends are lacking. They think they themselves are.

Jealousy and envy are a problem in communities of older people, and that is understandable. When a person has lost his or her work life and physical capacity, even to a small degree, the temptation to become jealous increases. This is because both jealousy and envy rise out of a need to feel one's own worth. It may pain an older person to see someone else in his community get recognition or a perk, because it immediately feeds into his deeply felt need to be special, to be the valuable person he once was.

The need to be special may seem childish because children have a similar need, though their situations are quite different. Freud called it "primary narcissism," the need to be recognized that is natural in the early years. Later it is more neurotic: An adult shouldn't still be making a scene trying to be recognized and given favors. And yet older people have an "elderly narcissism" due to the loss of respect and opportunities for reward and recognition. People generally don't realize how important it is for every person to be seen and appreciated. Affirming an older person's value in accurate and positive language could help many create a foundation for relating well. It could also be a deep solution to anger and crotchetiness.

Older people often tell stories from their past that let the world know who they were and what they achieved. It would be good for caretakers to understand this need and generously listen to the stories. Today I find myself doing this sometimes. My career as a writer peaked toward the beginning, and my really successful books came out when today's young adults were infants and toddlers. I try to rein in my desire to let people know about the past, but once in a while I mention how many people used to come to my public appearances. As an older person I know how helpful it is to have some recognition, but I also know how annoying it can be to flaunt the past.

Acknowledging another person's success is just part of being a friend. Whenever you feel that words of praise are not necessary, you should offer them anyway. If there is one universal rule about human psychology, it is that people always need and appreciate recognition. The need is beyond emotion. It has to do with the foundations of the self. When you are appreciated, your very grounding as a person becomes more stable.

Jealousy and Envy

Jealousy and envy are symptoms of something going wrong. A symptom is a sign or signal. These troublesome emotions may signal that you need a stronger sense of self. For instance, how do you maintain pride in yourself when you no longer have a job? You may do what we just discussed and tell stories about your glory years. But the stories aren't enough, and sometimes family members get tired of the old stories, which could foster pity rather than appreciation.

Jealousy is feeling pain because someone you love or appreciate is giving attention to someone else rather than you. Envy is feeling pain because someone else has something that you would like. Think about those two simple definitions: They don't make much sense because there is nothing wrong with someone else having good luck or beautiful things, and you don't want to control other people's choices of a friend or intimate, unless you think you deserve it all. The pain in both emotions is more about "me" than the object of affection. Jealousy — thinking that you deserve everything, and if you don't have it, someone with evil intention has deprived you — is especially a righteous emotion.

The masochism — pleasure in and need for pain — in jealousy, demonstrated in a person's efforts to find evidence of betrayal, shows how much ego there is in the feeling. If we go with this symptom, we can see that the jealous or envious person simply needs to receive love and attention or desirable things. The masochist doesn't love himself and doesn't feel he deserves a relationship or certain possessions. The ultimate solution is to become a person worthy of love and good fortune. When love and attention come your way, the jealousy and envy will probably weaken or vanish.

How to Love Yourself

Let's be more specific about what it means to love yourself and your life.

Most people grow up under a great deal of testing and criticism. Understandably, parents want their children to learn how to behave in a complicated world of sensitive relationships, and so they try to curb their children's wildness. They also quite naturally discipline their children the way they were disciplined. Parents are full of unconscious, unreflected assumptions about controlling a child's spontaneity, which, of course, can be a problem.

Most of us, then, carry with us voices of caution, criticism, and control that often become personal judgments. "You're a bad child. You don't do what you're told." Teachers can be equally unconscious as they criticize students harshly instead of truly guiding them. And so most of us grow up with voices of judgment in our heads. It isn't easy to love yourself; it's much easier, in fact, to find yourself lacking and highly imperfect.

Even in old age you have to counter these voices of criticism and be gentle on yourself, forgiving past mistakes and understanding why you might have done things that now embarrass you. You may not realize how long those critical voices stay in your mind. They are not tape recordings that fade but permanent images always at hand. They make it difficult to love yourself and approve your life.

But these voices of criticism can become weaker if you reflect on them and remember the full context in which they first appeared. You can tell stories about them to people you trust. When you put a face and a story to the vague voices of judgment you hear in your mind, some of their power is taken away. And when you pinpoint the source of the feelings of condemnation and criticism you hear inside you, even when you do your best, you gain some distance from them and a little relief. Keep repeating these discoveries, and the whole problem may ease.

In therapy I often hear stories of men and women who were shouted at and scolded mercilessly by parents who either had no self-awareness, were just acting unconsciously, or thought they were doing only what is right by speaking harshly to their children. We might spend considerable time, week after week, going over the memories from childhood or adolescence. We take note of how a client relates to their parents today as an adult, often with the same dynamics. Old patterns are persistent and tenacious. They feel so natural and habitual that it's difficult to imagine life without them.

Some people can't love themselves because they have been judged badly by significant adults all their lives. My attempt to help this process move forward is not to explain and understand it all. I look into my own feelings and find it in myself to love that person's soul in all its complexity. I speak from that loving and accepting place, countering years of negativity.

A friend or family member could do the same. He or she could find the genuine love they have in their hearts and express it without exaggeration or insincerity. You can love someone's deep self, even if you find certain aspects of their behavior annoying. Personally, I like to remember that a person's soul lies deeper in them than any outer behavior. Who they are is not the same as how they act.

Communitas

To put a spin on the idea of community, anthropologists sometimes use the Latin word *communitas*. With a strong background in the Latin language, I'd like to use the word, too, but with my own spin.

First, a community is not a collection of people who think alike or even have a strictly common purpose. A real community is a gathering of true individuals. If you can't speak your own mind, you aren't part of a community but a collective or maybe a mob. The joy of community doesn't come from complying with a group mentality but in the simple pleasure of being together with people who have sublime values, who want to share their talents, and who love humanity, the ultimate community that embraces the others.

The noted psychoanalyst D. W. Winnicott said that compliance is the enemy of joy. He was speaking of children, but the principle applies to adults, as well. His own words on this are strong: "Compliance carries with it a sense of futility for the individual and is associated with the idea that nothing matters and that life is not worth living."*

You may not have thought of this before, that to comply with someone else's demands, rules, or expectations sucks the life out of you. Those who work with both children and older adults might keep this in mind. Whenever you ask these people to comply, and if it's a common occurrence, you are risking taking away the joy they have simply in being their own person. Compliance is a silent enemy to community, silent because we are generally unconscious of its destructive power.

Communitas, as I use the word, refers to a gathering of people who are so varied in their makeup — multifaceted, diverse, free, and articulate — that they can be open with others, too. In other words, communitas is a deep orientation toward life that is not tightly bordered by a rigid and anxious sense of self. Communitas begins in the individual and is lived out among others. The community is inside you and therefore it is relatively easy to be with others in a way that allows their individuality. You know firsthand how important it is to be seen as an individual, with your own ideas

*D. W. Winnicott, *Playing and Reality* (New York: Routledge, 1971), 65.

and tastes.

Communitas has an outward orientation. Its gesture is an extended arm ready to shake a hand or embrace a body. It's a deep awareness of the various ways in which life presents itself, and it doesn't look for safety in sameness or in compliance.

Older people are ready to be with others. They have made the move from self to other and are now more fulfilled in being with others. But as always, if they haven't really aged but only grown in years, they may find social life uncomfortable. They are too much in the self, and the shell of individuality has not cracked, allowing them to be open to a bigger world.

I once had a client in her sixties, Eleanor, who, like many of my clients, was a therapist herself. I could see from the first session, almost from the moment when she walked in the door, that she had never fully grown up, never aged. By now I'm not surprised that many people who counsel others haven't faced life yet. There must be some subtle psychological mechanism that drives sheltered people to guide those who are in trouble. Anyway, she had little trust in me or in the process. She seemed steeled against change and against looking honestly at herself.

By the way, I don't exclude myself from that tendency of counselors to be working out their own life material. It's simply the shadow stuff that everyone has to deal with. It can grow into a serious problem, but normally it just gives defining shade to an otherwise effective career.

Eleanor continued to come week after week, and I wondered why. She couldn't open up to consider a fresh point of view. Her views on cultural values were far different from mine, but I always take such differences as a personal challenge. I try not to let my own ideas about culture get in the way. I did my best to connect with her. I hoped the best for her and wished that she would stay with me until some of her anxieties relaxed.

Week after week we talked, but I never felt that the bubble of protection that surrounded her burst. I kept waiting for something to happen, and of course I was using all my skills to help her express what was contained in her sadness. One day she told me she was going away to a retreat for professional women, and that was the last I saw of her.

This was a lonely person who had been involved only with questionable men. One had threatened her, and yet she continued a relationship with him. "I don't have a lot of choice," she said. She craved community but wasn't able to open up to other people. She wanted to tell everyone how to live.

I want to make it clear that aging with soul is not automatic. In Joseph Campbell's language, a person can refuse the call to adventure, can say no to the opportunity to proceed with life. Of course, this refusal is usually due to fear often rooted in a background filled with repression and criticism. Jung complained that our psychological thinking too often omits history, and yet our identity emerges out of many generations. We deal with the raw materials of life in families that struggle with their own particular blockages and complexes.

For example, many families today are trying to deal with the terrifying tragedy of the Holocaust, feeling it as if it happened yesterday. It's understandable that families are still reeling from the unimaginable terror that was a daily experience for grandparents and uncles and aunts and cousins. That history leaves a mark on generations that came after it. In my own family, I've seen how a morally scrupulous attitude strong at the certain time in Irish history affected us and still roams in my psyche today.

Such events inspire both fear and courage, but it is understandable that descendants of that period even today find it difficult to entrust themselves to life. I remember one afternoon in Florida, when I was visiting Dr. Joel Elkes and his wife, Sally. Joel's family was almost entirely wiped out during the Holocaust, and all his long life he felt the pain of it. He and his wife created a Holocaust library, and it was there that I spent an afternoon with him. It felt as if we were in a temple, a sacred space, and Joel went into a long, deep meditation as we felt the holy terror in the stories told in those books.

I make no judgments of Eleanor. She may need more time to learn to trust life in order to love and be loved. In the meantime, many of her actions and decisions reflect the stuckness that comes from fear. I hope that one day she will be able to live rather than build fences around her life. I hope that my hope is of some small use for her. Therapy is not a mechanical activity that either works or doesn't work. It is a mysterious engagement of people in life. It is more mutual than it might appear, as therapists themselves work out their own raw material with their clients, and as two lives intersect and move on.

Growing Older in Community

As you get older your very sense of self opens up, and the heart comes forward. The revelation of your compassion and capacity for connection brings out a part of you that may have been hidden, at least partially. In learning how to be in community you become a more defined person. You have opportunities to act on your values and let your individuality show. You get feedback that is precious. Your inner potential pours out into the world and becomes real in the midst of other people.

Those who care for the elderly might be aware of this complicated rule by which personhood is achieved in community. They might realize that older people are ready for community; it isn't a pathetic need. Communitas stirs in the hearts of people as they get older in ways that are different from the social striving of the young. In youth there is the joy of finding an adult identity shaping up through models in the community. In later years a person finds a larger identity and comfort in the midst of people, a resolving of the adult life that has taken so much energy for years. In youth community forges a self, while in old age community opens up the self to the soul.

In my practice I have noticed again and

again that older people often dream of a certain period in their lives, highlighting that time of life as needing reflection and working through. We keep talking about what happened then, sorting through the issues and seeing how they play out in life today. Then there may be a noticeable shift to another point in the past. Following the autonomous movement of the dreams, slowly we make our way through the life story.

In each case the person is dealing with a different community, and the people of that era play important roles. We get the sense of an internal dream community that has an impact on the present life community. The inner world mirrors the outer one, and vice versa. We discover how the community in play may be internal as well as external.

The older person may need to tell stories of the various families and groups he or she has known over the years and who have added to the life story. The many stories create a layered picture of life, different from the linear view we often assume. The telling is a way of sorting, a necessary step, especially in the older years, and part of the alchemy of a life, the processing of events and personalities.

Looking at a photo album can prod the

process along. You see people together from a special period in your life, and your thoughts get active as you wander your way through the memories. You see how many different communities have been part of your experience, and you gain some insight into how they made you who you are. You see a history of your life in community.

In the room at home where I write I have an old photo hanging on the wall of a great-aunt who lived in Auburn, New York. She wears a beautiful full gown and looks out at the viewer. The photo is in an unusual glass frame, my aunt's image surrounded with faded painted flowers and the glass edged with a black metal chain. It hangs there where I see it every day, reminding me of the family community of my early childhood — she died in the 1950s — and the love that I felt there.

Over a lifetime we pass through many communities, and like most items of memory they don't come and go but pile up. They are always at hand and may rise spontaneously into awareness when something happens that naturally summons them. I look at my great-aunt's photo in the antique frame and the visage of my grandfather rises into consciousness. I see some connection between what is going on in life now and what happened when I was in his community. I discover a deeper, archetypal background to my experience.

Nekyia is the word used in *The Odyssey* to describe Odysseus's experience when he sat and conversed with the dead as they appeared one by one from the underworld. One touching encounter was with his mother, who tells him how she died. He was on his long journey home from war. "It was my longing for you, your cleverness and your gentle ways, that took the sweet spirit of life from me."*

The goddess Circe had informed Odysseus that in order to complete his arduous journey and get home he would have to dare the meeting with the dead, and especially the seer Tiresias. "He will tell you the way to go, the stages of your journey, and tell you how to make your way home on the sea where the fish swarm."†

You can understand this fascinating image from myth as showing how any of us can be in the presence of the dead and live a more soulful life. We benefit from memories of those who have gone before us, who are

---

**The Odyssey of Homer,* transl. Richard Lattimore (New York: Harper & Row, 1967), 173.

†Ibid., 166.

members of communities that still exist deep in the imagination. They can inform us of the stages of our journey and how to find the desired but elusive sense of being home.

A photograph can be the occasion for such a *nekyia,* but so can a story of the past or an item connected to those who are now dead. Almost daily I think about my mother and father and close friends who have passed on and wonder about them and their lives. This kind of reflection is a form of *nekyia,* keeping the dead close, just as Odysseus did, as part of an initiation deeper into life and therefore a powerful form of aging.

You could understand aging as homecoming, arriving at that place where you belong, where your hero's journey, in which you have created a life and a self, comes to its fulfillment.

My friend John Moriarty always used a multitude of beautiful and evocative words where most writers would use one. He says in his autobiographical book *Nostos* (Homecoming), "In spite of us, a sense of final and glorious possibility keeps breaking through. In spite of us, our nostos is upon us."* He writes this in a section about go-

---

*John Moriarty, *Nostos* (Dublin: Lilliput Press, 2001), 682.

ing beyond mind, which is where we are headed as we age.

For most of our years we try to sum up the meaning of our experience and explain our troubles in rational language, especially today in the language of psychology. But John recommends that we reach a point beyond mind, beyond rational explanation. This may be a point of stillness, a sitting in wonder, a speechless expression of who we have become. Relating to the dead is a good way to achieve that mystical knowledge.

We don't have to know how it works, relating to the dead, but it's clear that it is a path to the eternal, at least a way of keeping our sights on what is beyond; paradoxically, that kind of transcendent vision makes us more human. Part of aging is becoming more of a human being, seeing human potential realized in us individually.

We can each have our own way, guided by tradition, to stay close to the dead. I do it by telling stories of relatives and old friends when the occasion presents itself. I know that in telling their stories I am giving them honor. There is something essentially human about showing respect for those who have gone before us.

Just recently I was giving a workshop on aging with soul, and I showed the group some photos of my ancestors. I had a shot of my grandfather rowing a small boat in a Michigan lake. My aunt Betty and I were with him. Then I showed the group a newspaper clipping from 1944, describing the accident I already recounted, when I was four years old and my grandfather died as he saved me from drowning.

I shifted the focus and showed by father and mother at their wedding, and then my father in his prime as a teacher, and finally my father at his one-hundredth-birthday party.

I don't usually go so public with my relatives who have passed on, but I wanted to show how I honor them simply by telling their stories and showing their photographs. It's a soulful activity that can deepen your sensibilities and help you age. These are your guides and models.

I also do my best to continue the work of those before me, and even when I cite an author like Jung or Emily Dickinson, I'm not just seeking an authority or a good idea; I'm asking the dead to nurture us with their wisdom, which today remains contained in books and memorials. Cultivating rituals of respect for the dead is a good way to age. It isn't something that might naturally occur to the young. But as we get older, we may appreciate the lives of those before us.

This honoring of the dead doesn't have to be morbid. It can be a joyous act that celebrates some good quality that we have found embodied in someone we knew or only read about. When I quote a line from one of my close ancestors, I'm letting them speak once more. I'm conjuring them up, much the way Odysseus did at the climax of his great mythic journey home.

Relating to the dead gives us a wider time frame in which to live and assures that we aren't strangers to death as we get closer to the end of our lives. We don't like to talk about it, but aging is a movement in life and is full of life toward the end of life. That is just the way it is. In youth we may feel that everything is about being born and entering into life, but very soon the awareness that life is also about making an exit grows strong.

A sense of community with all beings, human and nonhuman, alive and dead, gives us a true picture of what life is all about. If we deny that death is part of life, then we can't fully age, and that is a great problem for our era and for us individually.

As a young Catholic boy I was taught about the "communion of saints," which I would interpret as the community of holy ones inspired to live a life of love and service, the life Jesus taught and embodied. In my view, a person can be inspired to live such a life in many ways; for example, through Buddhist teachings or the wisdom of many nonreligious humanist teachers in our history. This community of fulfilled and loving people includes the dead. I think of my grandfather giving his life for mine. That act made him one of the exemplary holy ones.

It helps, as we age and look for a final feeling of fulfillment, to be part of a community where bighearted love is in play. Knowing about my grandfather's generosity, I am inspired and hope that at a crucial moment I might be as generous. One of the great mysteries of human life is that you can't go it alone. To be your best self you need others being their best.

14
THE ANGEL OF OLD AGE

All here have got their fears and cares,
Add ye your soul unto our prayers,
Be ye our angel unawares.
— Scottish Blessing

The older you get, the less you may be pre-occupied with the things of the world. You become reflective and closer to wonder. You're not focused as much on making a self, creating a career, or becoming somebody. You are naturally open to a spiritual life and to questions of meaning and purpose. Of course, this is not true of everyone. You have to have thought about your life for a long while to develop a strong spirituality in old age. You have to have aged spiritually.

Illness, which is more common as we get older, is also a catalyst for wonder and deeper questions. When your life's work is changing, too, moving toward some form of retirement, you ask yourself the deep questions you may not have considered when you were younger. As you age, you grow wings. You soar. You become more spiritual in a natural expansion of your vision.

Some older people choose to keep practicing the religion they learned as children or somewhat later in life. So today we hear about "the graying of the churches," how membership in many established religions leans toward advanced age. This is not true among some churches that appeal to the young.

At this particular time we can say that older spirituality is often linked to a church tradition, but because the churches are largely fading the situation won't last much longer unless there is a revival of formal religion. Now is the time to explore a different kind of spiritual life for older people, one that would truly nourish them and give them hope and strength.

Still, it's important for families and caretakers to know that for people of a certain age, formal religion means everything to them. The younger ones may believe that they are more up-to-date, smarter, and more informed and may not have patience with the older person's attachment to old-time religion. As someone who has studied many different religious traditions and believes that he's on the cutting edge of the new spirituality, I can say that for many the traditional approach is effective and worthy. I hope that all older people in hospitals, retirement centers, and at home with family members have the freedom and support to pursue their favorite forms of spiritual practice, including their familiar and formal religion.

But a different generation is getting older now, not the ones who used to fill churches, but searchers and experimenters. They, too, need resources and support for their spiritual lives in their mature years. They are as sincere and dedicated to the spiritual side of their lives, though their forms may be different, more scattered and more personal.

Everything I wrote in my recent book *A Religion of One's Own* applies to people getting older in these challenging times. It's all right to be a seeker and to experiment. You can find spiritual nourishment in nature, service, literature, the arts, meditation, and yoga, and in other less obvious places. The conditions are right for putting together your own traditional spiritual teachings and practices in a unique and effective way.

Lynda Sexson puts it beautifully in her book about religion, *Ordinarily Sacred:*

"Religion is not a discrete category within human experience; it is rather a quality that pervades all experience." Religion in the deepest sense of the word is not separate from life or the world. It happens everywhere and at any time, especially when we're not thinking about religion. You know it when your feelings and thoughts are taken beneath the surface into a positive and colorful darkness, the mysteries that are always deep within everything we experience.

As models of this new spiritual adventure I often cite Henry David Thoreau, Emily Dickinson, and Ralph Waldo Emerson — New England writers who were responding to a changing world much the way we are today. They probed deeply and expressed themselves beautifully and offer us fertile ideas for cultivating a spiritual life outside the formal structures of traditional religion. At the same time they valued the traditions and drew inspiration from many of them.

Letting the Spirit Arrive Naturally

A story by Gabriel García Márquez beautifully and symbolically describes how old age has its own spiritual side. It's called "A Very Old Man with Enormous Wings." It's the fantasy story of an old man with huge, dirty, smelly, and pest-infected wings, a gerontological angel. No one knows what to do with him and the people treat him with disdain. After a long period of neglect and mistreatment, one day he struggles to use his newly improved wings and flies away.

The story is richly detailed and open to many readings. To me the old man looks like aging itself being misunderstood and badly handled. The mysterious intruder is part human and part angel, capable of flight even if it is also full of imperfections. People don't understand it and are turned off by it.

It's an ancient idea that we are part human and part angel. That makes sense to me because we do in fact suffer the ravages of a body prone to illness and breakdown, and we have emotional gaps and malfunctions, and generally our minds are not very penetrating. And yet there is a part of us that yearns to know and to transcend our ignorance and our human limitations. In spite of the failings of our minds and bodies, we are capable of great things.

We have made transcendent art and music and have soared in thought through philosophy and theology. In that sense we have wings of a figurative sort. When Carl Sagan sent the music of Bach out into the universe, he was dispatching the work of an angel mind. But we all have wings of this kind that are susceptible to disease and falling apart. In old age we may overlook these wings or see that they have become weak and infested. As in the story, we need time to let them heal so that we can fly even in old age. We need to understand that as we grow older our wings can come to life and allow us to soar.

A Spirituality for the Older Years

Spirituality is not an escape from life or from self, though it often seems to be used that way. In later years it begins in the thick of life, as reflection on where we have been and what we have done. Feelings of both satisfaction and remorse come together as we recollect how events and our responses to them have made us who we are. Who we are now is the finished product, or close to it. We may have regrets or hopes or reason for self-praise. Usually all of these various emotions mix together as we consider our lives. Therefore, telling our stories, resolving some unfinished business such as damaged relationships and unfinished projects, and putting the finishing touches on an original self are the foundation for a spiritual life.

Often people think of spirituality as getting away from this world, and as a result there is something unreal and irrelevant about it. It would help to know that soul and spirit, psychology as soul work and spirituality as transcendence, go together. One without the other never works out.

By transcendence I don't mean belief in a supreme being or a supernatural world but only our own efforts to be everything we can hope to be, to be constantly moving on and upward toward a greater and more comprehensive sense of self. We start with a narrow personal life, discover love and intimacy as a first expansion of self, become a part of various communities, and maybe even develop a sense of world and universal community. We can go even further than that, imagining realities we have not yet seen or tested.

It isn't so important that you believe in God and an afterlife, as that you can imagine an intelligence in the heart of things and can entertain the thought of a life after this one. Or, you can try to be as honest as possible and see no evidence of further existence. Your very honesty may be an expression of transcendence. You refuse to be coddled with unfounded beliefs.

At the noisy breakfast nook in Peterborough, where people gather as much for conversation as for food, Liz Thomas said to me, "I don't believe in an afterlife. I'll die and be part of the atoms and molecules of the cosmos." She looked happy when she said this. But I was thinking, "I prefer to leave the matter unsettled. I like to preserve the unknown. I want to cherish my ignorance and make no pronouncements about what happens, if anything, after death." But I also felt that both of us, with our firm convictions, were doing our best to be open and honest and therefore could find joy at the prospect.

Your spirituality is the effort to keep expanding intellectually and emotionally. But the religions teach us not to be stuck with a literal, materialistic, and egotistical philosophy of life. They give us reason to take into serious account the invisible and the mysterious. For example, they treat love as a reality and speak of it allegorically, as if it were a person. They name it Eros or Aphrodite or the Holy Spirit. We tend to hear these names and think that they are creatures in the cosmos, flying around like insects, instead of imaginal realities worthy of our attention. We are then like the people in García Márquez's story, dismissive of the angel because we have lost our appreciation for the spiritual realm.

As you get older, it may be possible to let

go of the deep materialism of your times and think for yourself. You don't have to believe in anything — belief doesn't cost much. But you can open yourself to possibility. You can live in an infinitely meaningful universe. You don't have to be cajoled by modern sophisticates to have a limited view of what is real. You can let your imagination be free.

I sometimes think of contemporary life as contained in a bold, thick circle. Within the domain of this circle everyone assumes that science has all the answers and is the last word on what is real. If we can see a thing with our highly developed tools, it is real. If we can't see it, it's a delusion.

The spiritual life begins with stepping outside this circle, freeing yourself from the tight limits of its vision. You can still be intelligent and prudent, but you are free to consider many more possibilities. Maybe you have a soul, and maybe that soul is immortal in some way you can't understand now.

For me, spirituality is not a thing or a goal. It's the never-ending process of expanding your mind, imagination, and approach to life. Your ethics and sense of justice can always become more sensitive. Your degree of giving and service can always increase.

Your intelligence and wisdom about the important things can always deepen.

To transcend means to go beyond your current limits. In that sense, "God" is a motivating word, not a goal, not a thing, not even a fixed reality. God is real, though you don't have to use the word, insofar as God is an image for expansion of mind and heart without limit. As our imagination opens up, so does the world we live in. There is nothing "out there" that is not qualified by our way of imagining it, and so there can be no end to the education of the imagination.

As you get older, if you're not moving beyond your earlier understanding of life, you're not expanding. You're not really spiritual. You've become stuck on a belief. Spirituality is dynamic and existential, meaning that it's not just an idea, but a process. Therefore, as an older person you are an expanded version of the self you used to be. Spirituality in this sense is not about belief but about who you are and how you live. If you're becoming more a part of the greater world and larger life, then your spirituality is alive. This means constant change and unfolding. An unending process in which the self evolves.

Another obstacle to this kind of spirituality is simple unconsciousness. It's easy to just follow the crowd and aim for the goals that everyone seems to take for granted: financial gain, career success, possessions, prestige, comfort. You may take in whatever the media dishes out. You may not think for yourself. If you do have solid thoughts, you will probably need to opt out of the standard values around you. You may have to stand apart, not fit it so snugly; take some chances and think for yourself.

Can you live out your higher values of community, service, and social evolution? Or do you want to remain quiet in your subservience to the philosophy of the times? If the latter, don't kid yourself that you are spiritual because of your belief or your personal practices like meditation and churchgoing. Life is one whole. You are either engaged in the evolution of the human community or you are stuck in the unconsciousness of a media-driven world.

In the older years, this crushing of values turns into a crisis. There isn't much time left to live a fully meaningful life and to redeem mistakes of the past. But you can do it with a supercharged spiritual vision. You can get serious about a bigger view of what life is all about. You can give more time to learning about spiritual traditions and then putting them into practice.

A Spiritual Education for the Older Years

You don't have to reinvent the wheel. The religious and spiritual traditions of the world are teeming with great art, poetry, and teachings. You'll never exhaust what they have to offer, and these writings can be found in any bookstore and online. Read and study them, take them to heart, and use them as a base for your own spiritual adventure.

Don't worry about being superficial by trying everything. That criticism you hear often has little basis. The various traditions often counsel similar approaches. They are all different, and I don't recommend trying to reconcile them with one another. Just get started with your spiritual education. It will make your older years infinitely more meaningful and will likely inspire you to take actions that will broaden your life.

Let me be specific:

1. *Tao Te Ching.* I suggest beginning your spiritual education with this beautiful text from China that promotes naturalness and an absence of striving and effort. "Let things take their course," it says.

2. *The Odyssey.* This is a sacred story of a man's initiation into life while he is on his way home. The key word is *nostos,* or homecoming, related to nostalgia, originally homesickness. This not the usual homesickness of being away at boarding school or on a trip. This is the longing to feel at home in the world — finally. It involves encounters with deep mysteries like illness and love, and encounters with the dead. It's a soul journey where the end point is the discovery of who you are.

3. *The Book of Genesis.* Creation stories from around the world can be an important part of your spiritual life. They help you imagine both the actual natural world in its origin and development, and your own world as well. *The Book of Genesis* is a beautiful story of beginnings, but it has been read far too literally for centuries. Find a good, recent translation and commentary and include a creation story in your spiritual library. You can also get to know other creation stories. One of my favorites is from the Hopi in the

book *Finding the Center* by Dennis Tedlock.

4. *Zen Mind, Beginner's Mind.* Shunryu Suzuki brought Zen Buddhism of a special kind to the Bay Area of Northern California in 1959 and then taught many students at the San Francisco Zen Center. This book is a stellar collection of his talks. Together they present a Zen philosophy that is free from dogma and above all cathartic for a spiritual way of life. It is an important portion of the traditional resources that have shaped my own spiritual life, and I recommend it highly.

5. Several collections of spiritual poetry have sustained me over the years, such as *The Drunken Universe: An Anthology of Persian Sufi Poetry; Women in Praise of the Sacred,* edited by the deeply perceptive American poet Jane Hirshfield; and many of the poems of Emily Dickinson and D. H. Lawrence, two spiritually oriented poets.

6. Several rabbis have expanded and enriched my own spirituality, and as I get older I appreciate them more and more. The older work of

Abraham Heschel is timeless and intelligent, and the many books of Rabbi Lawrence Kushner make Jewish spirituality lively and relevant. Rabbi Harold Kushner has also been a long supporter and advisor. His books take difficult issues and treat them wisely in simple language.

7. I first read *Black Elk Speaks* in the 1970s, and it still astonishes me with its richness. I also keep Norman O. Brown's *Love's Body* close at hand. It deepens your whole approach to spiritual images and teachings.

8. C. G. Jung and James Hillman are always at my side. I see everything through their eyes, as they keep soul and spirit connected.

I have left out many excellent sources, but this is a start toward educating yourself in the spiritual realm.

Many people, as they get older, tell themselves to read now what they have put off reading for a long time, and often their lists are full of interesting materials but not the crucial and essential ones. I'm telling you to start with what really matters. If you are not familiar with the great spiritual literature of the world, then you have no option, as I see it, but to give yourself this foundation. The way you handle your old age will depend on it.

Let me also say a word about texts and translations. Many people love the familiar, old translations of the Bible and other holy texts. But for others these standard translations, and even some modern ones, act as a barrier between the reader and the important message of the text. Personally, I like an English version of the *Tao Te Ching* or the Gospels that is accurate and up-to-date but also given in smooth, easy, artful modern English. I have translated all the New Testament Gospels from Greek, so I know what you can do with a good translation. You can help your reader understand the original text both by researching the meaning of words and by expressing the original in a vernacular that is reader friendly.

Old texts especially need some background and elucidation. Find a good commentary that invites you to appreciate the depth of what is in the original. Then read meditatively, and read again and again. You don't know a spiritual text if you've read it only once. The classic words of the spiritual traditions may have been interpreted literally and moralistically in the past, but you don't have to do that. One advantage of getting older is that you may feel freer to break the rules and go your own way in a mature manner. This is not the same as a young person not having been initiated yet and breaking rules from ignorance and impetuousness.

You look for depth of insight rather than for what is true and proper. When you're faced with a decision in life, the text is there in your mind to give you a direction. For example, I cherish the line from the *Tao Te Ching:* "Yield and overcome, bend and be straight, empty and be full." These simple lines define the way I live and do therapy.

The Tao, the way life goes, is like a river flowing between its banks. If something bad happens to me, like an illness, I don't have to get anxious and worry about it. In my head and heart and I hear the words, "Bend and be straight." I don't literally give up, but neither do I fight my fate at all costs. I find strength in yielding.

The religious and spiritual literature, ritual, song, art, and architecture of the world are so teeming with beauty and truth that there is enough in them to guide and inspire you for several lifetimes. So often, though, people put up barriers and resist what the religions have to offer. They vet them in a modern way: Are they factually correct? Which one is more factually accurate than the other? Where are the proofs?

These are wrong questions. The spiritual life is fed by a special kind of poetics. The meaning of life can't be squeezed into a factoid. It requires special imagery that takes our reflections deep. Spiritual images evoke ideas and thoughts that move us on in our search for insight, and that search is lifelong and progresses step-by-step. That is why giving time to contemplating traditional stories and images can be so important in the later years. You hope you have gotten somewhere in your life and can entertain good ideas thoughtfully. In old age you should be more practiced and at a pitch where you can apply insights from everywhere in the world to your own situation. You don't sit back and ask which one is right. You sidestep the issue of whose side you are on and simply go for depth of reflection.

Let me repeat: Don't approach any spiritual teaching with the old idea of having to decide if it is factual. Most material in spiritual literature is that special kind of poetry that speaks directly to your life. You have to probe it and study it to find its spiritual message, not its factual content. Literalism is a kind of spiritual immaturity, the failure to probe and see the many dimensions of a poetic statement. Even history from a certain valuable angle is a form of poetry.

In the best of circumstances, aging means becoming less literal about life in general. You learn that anything that happens has layers of significance. Many elements of the past are present in it. The meaning of an event may be paradoxical, ironic, and allusive. That is, it may point to stories you have heard or experiences you have had. As a therapist my job is often to help people appreciate the many things going on in a single experience.

Generally we are naïve about religion. We bring great sophistication to science and culture, but we tend to see religion simplistically. In the news these days you find stories about people still looking for Noah's Ark in Turkey. That is Sherlock Holmes syndrome all over again. Holmes is clearly fictional, and yet we visit his rooms on Baker Street in London and marvel at how he lived there. I think it's beautiful to have such a place honoring a fictional character, but we don't confuse him with an historical person. In religion we encounter this confusion much of the time.

On the other hand, in our age of neuroscience and artificial intelligence, many feel that there is no room for a spiritual life. They are too sophisticated for it. They have no need for it. In this way twenty-first-century materialism is truly a kind of religion, a creed that doesn't have an opening to other points of view. It is anxious and jealous, and so people try to live in the robotic realm of pure secularism.

But this new materialism cannot foster a humane way of life. It emphasizes narcissism and egotism, where celebrities thrive and the others watch, resigned to their limited lives. We need to sprout wings, even if they are not as clean and sleek as those of an eagle. We need some loft, space, and lightness.

Personal Spirituality in the Advanced Years

While the ancient spiritual traditions offer an excellent foundation for a spiritual life in old age, they are only the base. A man or woman can do many things to create an original spiritual practice that is rich and meaningful.

Here is a list of practices that anyone can do in addition to their churchgoing or as their basic spirituality:

1. Live a more contemplative life. You can follow the signs of your health and physical condition. As your mobility and strength decrease, even slightly, you can be in tune with your aging and live more quietly and calmly. You can adopt a quieter and more reflective persona and lifestyle. You don't do this unconsciously but actually style your life to be more like that of a monk. You make the contemplative style a chosen practice and philosophy of life. One of the problems with getting older is that we feel limited by nature and by physical conditions. But you can take charge of your life by increasing the spiritual side of your very identity.

2. Explore different ways to meditate. I hear from many people who say that they are trying to be meditators but they can't stay with the program they have. They get bored or can't remain faithful to the techniques they've been taught. I hear this complaint and wonder first why people are so passive about their

spirituality, and second, why do they have such a narrow idea of what it means to meditate?

You can meditate in a thousand different ways. The main thing is to go inward, either into yourself or deep into the world around you. It's simple. Find a quiet place any-where. Get settled. Plan on sitting for a certain amount of time. It doesn't have to be long. Try to stay focused — on your breath, on sim-ply sitting, on some music or art or nature. Or just sit and don't be too distracted by wandering thoughts. But don't make a project of getting rid of the distractions. That project can be worse than the distractions themselves. Feel yourself being quieted and focused.

3. Walk in nature. The natural world is a gateway to the timeless and the infinite. We can never understand it completely, and so for us it serves as a bridge to the infinite. You don't have to be solemn. Just enjoy the walk, but do it with the intention of being pulled into the depth of the natural world. Feel wonder, ask big questions, observe closely.

4. Keep track of your dreams. I've had considerable experience working with older people on their dreams. They offer a perspective that often stretches and even contradicts the person's waking assumptions. They stretch your mind and give you a fresh perspective. Of course, to get anything from dreams it helps to know how to deal with images, a skill widely not studied among contemporary people. I've explored techniques of dreamwork in other books but the field would require a book of its own.

Dreamwork is part of the spiritual life because it is a regular practice that keeps you in touch with the mysterious dimensions of your experience. Dreams take you deep beyond your conscious awareness, and they offer insight and stir the imagination. They complete the intelligence of the ordinary world.

Because dreams provide a sense of otherness, even other selves and a mysterious collapsing of time, they play a role in the spiritual life, making it deeper and closer to the soul.

5. Serve the world. Our chapter on being an elder gives a taste of how an older person can help others. But it is also good to understand service as an essential part of the spiritual life. Just look at any of the great traditions and you will find ethics and service at their very heart. A perfect example is the life of Jesus, who spent this time teaching and healing. You find strong references to prayer in the Gospel but not much directly about meditation. Service is the main thing.

In the life of the Buddha you find a combination of meditation and service, and in the *Tao Te Ching* the emphasis is on leadership that is not heroic or overbearing. Mohammed's teaching is heavily oriented toward concrete service to people in need.

Even among the noninstitutional spiritual teachers like Emerson and Thoreau you see how involved they were in the political life of their times, such as in fighting slavery. Thoreau and his family assisted slaves going north to Canada. Emerson, though reluctant at first, became politically active in general and gave several strong speeches against slavery.

Without service and action your values remain theoretical and abstract. They may have a strong intellect but no body. Contemporary ethicists would say that a value isn't even a real value until it is tested in action.

6. Study the best spiritual ideas. For centuries study has been a central part of the spiritual life. Today you don't hear much about it, or the importance of a spiritual intelligence. Yet clearly the weakest point in contemporary spirituality is not commitment, engagement, practice, or work with teachers. What is missing is the intelligence that comes from dedicated study. The history of monasticism is largely about books, schools, and intellectual movements. The time is ripe now to go back to that portion of spirituality focused on study.

As you get older your appetite for ideas may well increase, and you can get seriously involved in study without worrying, for the most part, about your physical condition. Yes, memory can be an issue for some, but most of us have an opportunity to discover the joys of a solid self-education in spiritual matters.

One of the problems I see in this area is that it is not easy to discern which are the solid teachings and sources and who are the best teachers. People often tell me that they want inspiration. They want a teacher who will excite them. And there are plenty of those around. I don't know what to say: It's obvious to me that good solid ideas are more important than passing and ungrounded excitement.

When I write a book, like this one, I consult the challenging writings of Jung and Hillman, read classic texts in the original Greek or Latin, and look up ancient attitudes toward current ideas. I want to know the history of an idea, not just its current manifestation. That study deepens my understanding of a key idea, like faith or forgiveness. I don't want to read current writers who don't study and just speak from the top of their heads.

My favorite contemporary spiritual writers happen to be Irish: Mark Patrick Hederman and John Moriarty. And others, like Joan Chittister and David Whyte, spend time in Ireland. They are all scholars who come down from their ivory towers to speak to ordinary people. I trust John Wellwood, Jane Hirshfield, and John Tarrant, and I'm educated by Rabbi Harold Kushner and Rabbi Lawrence Kushner. Among the psychological writers I read today are Nor Hall, Robert Sardello, Patricia Berry, Rafael López-Pedraza, Mary Watkins, Adolf Guggenbühl-Craig, Ginette Paris, and Michael Kearney.

Spirituality in and of the World

The spiritual life begins with an appreciation for the soul of the world and of all beings. It can see past surfaces to the pulsing heart of things and can identify in profound empathy with the experience and the needs of other beings. Spirituality is about transcendence, not a God in the clouds, but a steady progress moving beyond a limited self and a small world. It means growing your mind so you can imagine far past what you learned as a child, to a point where you are always in a mode of discovery and wonder. You can't be spiritual if wonder is not alive in you. Traditions and practices, teachers, and workshops can support you, but ultimately you are on your own to create a unique spiritual way of life. No one can do it for you. And it may take a lifetime, so that in the older years you may finally sense the spirituality you have crafted after many experiments and probably some mistakes. Mistakes can be useful for showing us the right way.

Becoming spiritually sophisticated and adventurous is an essential part of aging, certainly aging with soul. This process may entail a difficult turning away from the values of your times, when a philosophy of materialism lies behind most of the scientific, technological, and cultural "achievements," when even religion has much materialism in it. Older people seem to be freer in certain ways than the young to choose not to participate in a soulless society. They can be eccentric and out of step with few consequences. They might take advantage of their position and be eccentric spiritually, as well, ignoring the materialism that takes the form of excessive commercialism, the veneration of science, the quantification of life, and education as training in saleable skills rather than the full maturing of a person.

I take pleasure as an old guy not spending much money on myself, getting things fixed rather than replaced, and avoiding quantitative studies in my writing, just when my editors request some numbers. I was fired from a university position to some extent because I taught the soul of the world rather than just physical life, or perhaps because I allowed eros into my teaching. Eros and the soul are partners. I'd rather write a well-proportioned sentence than cite a quantified study.

García Márquez's story about the old man with enormous wings tells of people rejecting the man's old, decrepit wings after first trying to make money off his value as a curiosity. That is often the way we treat old people, and maybe that's why we worry about getting old ourselves. We have ridiculed the elderly and know what's in store for us.

One fairy tale tells the story of a young family in which a mother, father, and child live with an old parent or grandparent. They all eat at the table in comfort but give the old person a single wooden bowl. One day the father comes upon his child working hard at something. "What are you making?" he asks. "I'm making a bowl for you for when you get old," the child says. Needless to say, that night at supper the grandparent is with the family eating off their nice dishes.

It's such an easy equation: If you honor old people today, you will probably feel good about your old age. But if you give in to your neurotic disdain for the elderly, you are setting yourself up for a painful old age.

Liz Thomas and I sat at the table in Nonie's, a favorite hangout in Peterborough, New Hampshire, on a cold November early afternoon. "The thing about getting old," she said, "is that people look at you and don't see you. You're standing there and they talk to the younger one with you. You don't exist."

In his memoir *Essays After Eighty,* Donald Hall tells a few stories of how older people can be treated as either infantile or invisible, or both. "When a woman writes to the newspaper, approving of something I have done, she calls me 'a nice old gentleman.' She intends to praise me . . . but she puts me in a box where she can rub my head and hear me purr."*

Look and notice the wings that fold invisibly but palpably on old people. That is their spirit that will allow them to soar as the years go on. They have lived lives that, year by year, have transformed them. They are less ordinary humans and more angelic beings, for all their crotchety complaints. Their

*Donald Hall, *Essays After Eighty* (New York: Houghton Mifflin Harcourt, 2014), 8.

orneriness keeps them from resting comfortably in the soulless world around them.

We should honor anyone, of any age, who has said yes to life and become a person and stands above the norm in vision and achievement. We should also feel honor for ourselves, knowing when we have failed and when we have risen above our comfort level to affirm the opportunities life has presented. This is aging: becoming, transcending, being more than anyone could have imagined we might become.

15
LIVING WITH DYING

Human beings are adrift in a universe of mysteries. There are so many things we know little or nothing about. Not just things, but the most important things. Where were we before we were born? How can we be born biologically into a life of deep emotions? How can we engage in a demanding and serious quest for meaning and yet come out of a human body after being conceived by a physical, passionate union of two ordinary people? Why are we here, what are we to do, and, perhaps the greatest mystery of all, what happens after we die?

How do you prepare for dying, how do you make sense of mortality, and how do you deal with the potential for nothingness after death? Should we believe the teachings about reincarnation, heavenly bliss, eternal judgment, passing over, and eventual reunion with loved ones? Is love truly eternal?

One of the central meanings and experiences of aging is the sense of approaching death. You can be any age and suddenly become aware of your mortality and fall into wonder and feel genuine fear and dread. And so we have to ask, is there an intelligent and positive way to think about the brevity of life and our own death?

If, from a certain point of view, aging is essentially the approach of the end, then we have to deal with this universal situation, and we may have to engage it on our own terms. Who can you rely on? Who can you really trust to give you an answer or at least a direction to move in facing your end?

One day my father phoned me to say that he had been reading my book on Jesus and wondered what I meant when I said that for Jesus heaven was a state in this life when the principle of love has been fully established. "Do you think there is no heaven after death?" he asked with considerable concern. He was in his mid-nineties and was thinking about death.

I knew that my father's faith in the Gospel was solid and deep, though he felt free to question the moral teachings of the Church.

"No," I replied. "I'm saying Jesus wasn't talking about what we mean by heaven but about the kind of life for humanity he envisioned. I'm not saying there is no heaven after death." I knew that my father had been brought up to think of the afterlife in terms of bliss, and I certainly don't know any better approach. I may express it differently, but I wasn't about to challenge my father's belief toward the end of his life.

I think we need to be open to possibilities and at the same time find inspiration and comfort in various teachings of the religions. Reincarnation and heaven make a great deal of sense, and at the same time they seem impossible. It's difficult, anyway, to come up with a real solution to this conundrum in a world divided between science's materialism and religion's illusions.

As in many crucial issues in human life, first we have to take a step outside the circle of cultural beliefs. Our so-called secular culture is full of strong beliefs and devotion to certain positions about the important things. You may have to free yourself from some of the illusions of your spiritual background, but you also have to get some distance from the religion of contemporary culture, especially limited scientific beliefs.

Once you are free of both the materialism of culture and the illusions of religion, you can begin to examine the question of death. In your openness and in the spirit of intelligent examination, you may come up with your own ideas about death and afterlife. Your images may be provisional. You may say to yourself: "I don't know. I don't have any answers. But on reflection it could be that . . ."

You could live with the hope of reunion with family members and close friends and of some form of continuation of your earthly life. This kind of hope is real, and it is comforting and inspiring to many. Or, you may want to be as realistic as possible and simply acknowledge that you have no idea about afterlife, and you can live with that unknown. But to say that there is nothing after death is a kind of pseudo-religious profession of faith. It is not open, and it offers no hope.

I have already mentioned James Hillman's pronouncement to me at a tender moment: "About death I'm a materialist. There is nothing."

I was surprised that this intelligent man who had written so much about eternal things — soul, spirit, religion — with a strong suggestion that we should always penetrate beyond the literal, would suddenly become a materialist, which is a kind of literalist. I know that he was always keen to avoid any sentimentality in his views, but still I thought he might have developed a sophisticated approach to dying, just as he had with living. This is one of the few areas where I disagree with him.

And yet — don't get me wrong, I'm not a naïve believer — I don't want to be in the camp that has too much hope or creates illusions so we don't have to face the reality of what it means to be a human being. In all things, we have to start with what is and go from there.

Let me make the basic point here as clear as I can: We can acknowledge our ignorance about death and afterlife, keeping an absolutely open mind, and at the same time find comfort and guidance in traditional teachings like reincarnation and heaven. But we have to keep saying, "This is something I can't know for certain, but I like to think in terms of reincarnation or heaven. I've believed in heaven all my life. It makes sense." Or, "I think reincarnation is a beautiful way of making sense of life and death."

Lifelong Aging and Lifelong Dying
Just as aging is a process that begins even before you are born, dying also takes your whole life. Some people talk about midlife and see it as a turning point. I prefer to see

the entire life as one of living and dying. You are going uphill and downhill at the same time, meaning that you can deal with life in both ways always. You can live and die every day of your life.

This is not a negative way of looking at things. It simply is. And if you live and die this way, you will never be depressed about dying because you've been doing it all your life. But how do you go with the dying process during your lifetime?

All the Little Deaths

One way is to accept the "little deaths" that life always brings: losses, failures, ignorance, setbacks, illness, depressions — these experiences are in a sense antilife. They halt or impede the ongoing process of living. In our society especially it's common to take a heroic stance regarding these experiences. We try to avoid them, conquer them, get past them, and eventually have a life that is free of them.

Another approach is to receive these experiences, without surrendering to them, and incorporate them into the mixture of events that make up a life. You don't have to speak and act heroically against them.

I'll mention an example from my practice. A woman in her fifties came to me very anxious because her marriage was failing. Both she and her husband had had affairs, a sign to her that the marriage was coming apart. She seemed to expect me to help her save the marriage and in talking to me she assumed that I would do everything possible toward this goal.

But I could see that the situation was quite complicated. Besides, I didn't think it would be useful for me to join with her in doing everything possible for the marriage. Maybe it was time to separate, at least. I didn't know. I don't see my job as one of saving marriages but of caring for the souls of people who may be in a marriage or leaving one. Sometimes from that point of view the breakdown of a marriage is a good thing.

Furthermore, the failure of the marriage was a taste of death, a serious ending. If death in this sense was happening, I didn't want to be the one denying it and taking only the side of life. I felt, too, that if I did take her side in protecting the marriage at all costs, I might be hastening the end of it. Marriage may have to go through a tunnel of death for its own sake. Certainly defending against the corruption of the marriage would only make the situation worse.

So, I didn't favor the destruction of the marriage, nor did I get excited about preserving it. I remained neutral, my usual position. My client was not entirely happy with me, since she expected me to feel indignant and join her in saving her marriage. Yet, for some reason she wasn't too disturbed by my neutrality. She stayed with me and observed my response closely.

Eventually things worked out quite well, and the marriage survived. I didn't tell her explicitly, but in my mind I was giving as much support to life as to death, to the marriage surviving and the marriage unraveling. I took the long view and felt that this woman was in a moment of crisis or initiation that had profound implications. If she fought the death of her marriage, she would end up fighting her own death.

Her death had risen to the surface, and she had to take care not to assume the hero's mantle and try to defeat it. She had to come to terms with it and go on living as someone acquainted with death, not afraid of it and not heroically against it. Through this experience she would become a deeper, more genuine person, someone useful to her friends and children, not superficial, not deeply defensive. You don't see this depth often in this world, because the culture is essentially heroic, death defying.

In the course of a life, death visits us

frequently in the form of endings and failures. To age well is to incorporate dying in the energetic process of your life. You deepen as a person by dying in the larger sense of the word. But this metaphorical dying is real preparation for the ending of your life. You age well when you are so familiar with the dynamics of dying that you don't freak out at signals of actual death through illness and the advancement of years. You might even welcome old age and the intimate sensation of death blowing in your ears. Because death has been part of your life, you understand that approaching death can intensify life.

Vitality with Longevity

Life is not about longevity as much as it is about intensity. If you have many, many years of tepid living, of what value is that? But if you have a few years of vitality and conviviality, you may feel that you have really lived. Life is not a quantity but a quality.

When I was teaching college students, I used to show a short film about Elisabeth Kübler-Ross. In the context of a graduate symposium, she interviewed a patient with terminal cancer. The man, fairly young, seemed to have come to terms with dying.

The graduate students thought he was denying death. But Kübler-Ross thought differently.

The man told a story about being hurt while working on a farm, but it all turned out well. He thought of that experience as he faced his cancer, and Kübler-Ross believed that his early experience had prepared him for dying. In particular, in telling his story now, he was showing where he was in relation to his dying. The young man felt he had lived a good life. It wasn't an absolute tragedy that it would be cut short by cancer.

He didn't seem as much concerned about longevity as about vitality, and that point of view made all the difference. His story has stayed with me for thirty years, and when I have to face illness or watch a friend die, I remember him and his remarkable point of view. I wouldn't say that he was courageous but that he had the fullness of life in him. He could live with both the good and the bad.

To be close to people who are dying helps us die and helps us live. Life and death are so close that one supports the other. When my friend John Moriarty was approaching death from cancer, I visited him in the hospital in Dublin a few weeks before he died. He had been through a depressing and frightening initiation between learning of his cancer and coming to grips with it. When I saw him, he was in glorious form. I could see a glow around him and feel the vitality in him, even though his cancer was now getting the best of him.

When I was about to leave his hospital room after an hour or two of intense conversation, he asked me for my blessing and I asked him for his. We did a formal brief ritual in Latin that seemed to give us both the peace we needed. I remember that blessing and his glow, and I have more courage from them to face my own little deaths in preparation for the big one.

Good, Evil, God, and Dying

In many ways dying is the most personal thing we do. If we are fortunate we will have time to reflect on our lives and assess them. We set off on a truly new adventure, and no one can join us. Of course, it may help to have loved ones nearby to help us make the transition, but they may help best by assisting us in making this important act an expression of who we have become and how we have lived. If possible, it's a good idea to ask explicitly for the kind of help we want.

Dying can be a spiritual experience, even if contemporary culture makes it a medical one. The always provocative former priest and philosopher Ivan Illich liked to say that he did not want to die from some medical condition; he wanted to die from death. It may take some effort to keep this valuable idea in mind. With all the medical issues that usually surround death, we can still respect it as a spiritual experience. If you make it only a medical matter you succumb to the materialism all around you. Death is then a failure of organs rather than a singular moment in the life of the soul.

People sometimes ask, Does the soul get sick? Does the soul die? Yes, the soul has a significant part, the major part, really, in these significant transitions. When James Hillman was told that his cancer was incurable, he felt it as a "shock to the psyche," as he said later.

Why not a shock to the system or the self? Because the soul is the most personal element in our being and yet it is also other. The soul is more "me" than any sense of "I." But it is more than me, too. You can feel a shock to your soul, so deep and fundamental that it goes beyond anything you can identify with.

So how do you die with soul?

If at all possible, you don't die alone. You make an effort to be closer to your family members and friends than ever before. You do what you can to mend hurt relationships. You take the opportunity to stop avoiding necessary confrontations. You use words like you've never used them before to make your feelings clear, especially feelings of love and friendship.

If possible, you die the way you want to die, taking into consideration what your loved ones want for you. You are both generous and in charge, both the leader and the listener. As Moriarty wrote in *Nostos,* you have to go beyond the mind and even beyond the self. He added: "Wisdom will not inhabit clear and distinct ideas." I would add: To live without avoiding the taste of death is to go beyond a clear sensation of self. You are out there as much as you are in here. You are those things and those people as much as you are this person.

To be the designer of the process of your dying, you will likely have to start a long way off, so it's a good idea to prepare and plan for years, when you first sense the possibility of your dying. Think about what is important to you. Translate your ideas about and vision for dying into certain details of the process.

Make decisions early about medical involvement, and take seriously a living will.

Let people know of your wishes for your treatment in the dying process and the care of your body. Write down important details such as the kind of spiritual care you would like, who you'd like as advocates to help you with attending professionals, especially the medical people. You may know doctors and nurses you'd like to have nearby.

Is there special music you'd like to listen to during treatments and recovery? Are there certain objects you'd like to have near you? Will you need both solitude and companionship? Is there visual art that will comfort and inspire you? Photographs or recordings? Clothes and toiletries? It may be a good time for aromatherapy and music therapy. Would noise-canceling headphones help? Movies and music to watch and listen to?

Dying is largely a spiritual process. You may want to intensify any spiritual practices you've had over your life, even old ones that you've neglected for a while. This may be a time to relax your battles over who is right theologically and which practices suit you. You could be more open to practices you've abandoned as you've tried to hone your beliefs and attachments.

Personally, I've begun carrying my mother's rosary with me when I travel, not because I'm returning to a childhood practice, but simply because it seems to hold my mother's intense spirituality, a kind of practice that I haven't followed in decades. I understand that there is some magic in keeping her rosary near me, and that's all right, too. I hope to have several of my mother and father's spiritual things with me as I face the end of my life. For all the differences in our beliefs and style, they are my models.

When Philosophers Die

Plato is famous for having said that philosophers in their deep thinking are preparing for death. They are focused on the soul rather than the body, and so at death, when the soul separates from the body, they will be at home and not be afraid. This often cited idea has some interesting implications, and if taken deeply enough, it could help us with our dying.

I've emphasized the value of reflecting on our experiences. They become meaningful memories then, even lessons as we go forward looking for a good life. The philosopher's main job is to reflect, to work ideas into insights, and to prepare for a better life. Some philosophers may be so abstract in their thinking that it takes a considerable effort from the reader to make the connection between ideas and life. But on the whole philosophy steers us away from mere practical analysis and gives our ideas some loft.

Each of us would benefit from deeper and more comprehensive reflection on experience, becoming less literal and practical in our thinking, moving closer to matters of soul, which are not separate from life and yet have enough distance to give a perspective on experiences. The materialist, the person who thinks only about practical decisions and the quantification of experience, loses everything at the thought of death. But the philosopher can see past the literal and in a number of ways appreciate that death is not the end. Moriarty says, "You don't need to be an intellectual to be a philosopher."

Therefore, if you're interested in aging with soul, you don't read just practical and technical books, you read the humanities, fiction, and nonfiction that raises and deepens your thoughts. Good literature can be part of a spiritual practice. Too often we put unnecessary boundaries around what we consider sacred. I especially like the poems of Wallace Stevens, D. H. Lawrence, and Emily Dickinson to supplement the classic sacred texts.

Literature, music, and painting, to mention only a few of the arts, nurture the soul and shift your focus to archetypal and eternal matters, the foundations of life. They prepare you for your dying, which is the ultimate encounter with the eternal, whatever your beliefs may be.

This suggestion about living with good art ties in with my previous idea that a soul-oriented person doesn't have to be materialistic in his attitude toward death. He doesn't have to come up with a solution to death, pretending to know what it's all about and how it works, but he can have an open-ended hope and trust in life.

This hope makes all the difference. But note that hope is not the same as expectation. Hope is a positive point of view tinged with joy that doesn't demand a certain outcome but trusts in the goodness of life. You don't have to argue with anyone else about what you believe about death. Such arguments are useless. But you could converse with others about your feelings about life itself, speaking philosophically and spiritually. You might receive support and get some new thoughts about death. You never have to come to any final conclusions.

The Poet-Astrologer

One of the graces of my life was my friendship with Alice O. Howell, Jungian astrologer and poet. Alice had a constant, lively imagination joined to a gift of language. She was forever in love with the British Isles and especially the island of Iona in Scotland. She had several homespun rites, including "Scottish communion" with a tiny glass of Talisker scotch whiskey and a good-bye round of hugs. Another practice was to speak often of her "Aberduffy Day," the day of her death. I heard her mention this day many times during the nearly thirty years I knew her. She was never far away from her death, and I felt that one of the big lessons she left me was this practice: to stay close to the end even as you live heartily in the moment.

We each have our Aberduffy Day, of course, and it is as important as our birthdays. Alice didn't dwell on it depressively but rather with her usual lively acceptance of life. I'm not recommending that we celebrate our last day throughout our lives, but we might keep it in mind as a transition, as yet another rite of passage.

When I use the word *transition*, I don't imply life on the other side. I don't know if there is anything there, but I do know that I can live in hope of eternal life. Hope is an odd thing. As Emily Dickinson said, it is that thing with feathers. It is not knowing what is to come or even wishing that things will work out as we imagine them. Hope is open-ended, and I suppose that is what Dickinson had in mind.

Among her words of wisdom Alice O. Howell left these:

What you would grasp
let go
only those seeds that fall
grow.

CONCLUSION: LET THINGS TAKE THEIR COURSE

The fear of death follows from the fear of life. A man who lives fully is prepared to die at any time.

— Mark Twain

In the end, the most effective way of dealing with aging is to be exactly who you are. Don't try to avoid aging by imagining how it could be otherwise. Don't think about people younger than you being better off. Don't wish for your youth back. Don't deny the negative aspects of aging. Be exactly who you are and exactly what age you are.

Being who you are works in all areas of life. You may wish, as I often do, that you had a greater talent in music. You may wish you had married that sweet person in school instead of your actual spouse. You may wish you had been born twenty years later, so you'd be younger today. All of these wishes are fruitless fantasies, helping you to avoid what is. You can't live and enter the process of becoming a real person unless you can first be who you are.

This principle applies to sickness as well. In my many conversations on aging while writing this book, one of the statements I heard often concerned a fear among people just beginning to feel old: the fear of getting sick. Illness is a great unknown that can strike at any moment and change a life.

But illness is part of life, and feeling alive requires taking all that life has to offer, including sickness. It simply is. It comes to you and not to someone else. The illness is yours and it makes you who you are as much as your various achievements do. What can you do but receive the illness as "the will of God," your fate, or even as your opportunity to add one more piece to your character.

As I sat next to my good friend James Hillman on his deathbed at home, as nurses visited and did various things for him, I never heard him complain. He never said he wished he could have avoided this challenge. He didn't say a word against the doctors who treated him. At least, I didn't hear any negativity. Maybe he needed to vent some of those emotions to others. I don't know.

434

When I sat on the edge of the bed in a Dublin hospital with my friend John Moriarty, minutes after he learned that the final treatment for his cancer had failed, he didn't complain or express any wishes for some other fate. It had taken him over a year to come to terms with his illness, but he had arrived at a place where he could make it part of his life. It simply was.

Your fate becomes part of your identity, and growing older is our common fate. It, too, is always defining who we are. People want to know how old you are, so they know more about who you are. To be truly alive, you have to live your life and be your age.

How to Tell Someone Your Age

Being your age means letting people know the number of your years. People may think you're younger than you are, and you play into this error. You may be tempted to avoid telling them the truth. You may miss out on the opportunity to begin being exactly who you are. It's not an abstract idea. You make it real by speaking for it. Today I have to say loud and clear: "I am seventy-six."

People may think you're younger than you are. If you tell them your age, they may be less interested in you, simply because of a general social bias against old age. But that's who you are. You are someone in a category that today doesn't get much appreciation. If you can acknowledge this fact, then people won't be able to manipulate you with your fears. You can't blackmail someone who isn't afraid of being blackmailed.

You can try to change the social stigma of age, but even then you have to be who you are and not let your fight against ageism turn into a personal defense against your own age. You can do many things at once: resist ageism, try to feel younger, and be exactly your own age.

You accept the exact conditions of your situation, including the years of your life, without defensively slipping into wishes and regrets that cloud the situation. You find it in yourself to be your age, with all its pitfalls, without indulging, sinking in, resigning yourself, or giving up. These are negative ways to avoid the situation. Instead, you have to find ways to own your life as it is.

The Dot at the Center

You need an attitude that is neither slightly denying nor slightly giving in. A cool, empty midpoint where, almost emotionless, you acknowledge what is happening. Once you arrive at this point, and that may take a long time, you can go on from there in more emotional and creative ways.

This discovery of a still point is a necessary achievement and a beginning. For example, in my case I have to simply say, "I am seventy-six years old." I may feel like forty sometimes, but at this key moment I have to forget forty and acknowledge my years. I have wishes to be younger, and those wishes are important in the life of my fantasy. But at this moment of acceptance, I forget them.

This focus on the reality rather than the wish is not a single moment but a permanent base, and it is part of the spirituality of aging. In *Zen Mind, Beginner's Mind,* Zen master Shunryu Suzuki expresses this idea with special clarity: "True being comes out of nothingness, moment after moment. Nothingness is always there, and from it everything appears." He calls this naturalness, or "soft and flexible mind."

As I understand him, you are natural when you base your experience on this core position where you accept your situation for what it is. You haven't embellished it with explanations and defensive qualifications. You don't say, "I'm seventy-six, but I feel younger." You say, "I'm seventy-six." This centering is not as easy as you may think.

Notice when people are talking about age how many different ways they may skirt the reality by softening the acknowledgment of their age.

One says, "I'm fifty, but today that's young." Yes, it's relatively young, but just be your age. Another: "I'm turning thirty. I'm in the prime of my life." Yes, my friend, but you are also getting older. "I just turned sixty-five, and I'm falling apart [laughing]." Yes, but Freud would say that your joke is a defense, a nervous way of trying to keep aging at a distance.

The *Tao Te Ching* says:

Life moves along by letting things take their
   course.
It does not move along if there is
   interference.

Let aging take its course. Don't interfere, even with the best of motives. Often good intentions offer the most successful distractions. Our well-meant interference stands in the way of life moving along. If life doesn't move along, like a river or stream, it is blocked, and chaos prevails. The most common problem I see among my clients in therapy is their resistance to the flow of life, my exact definition of the word neurosis.

With aging I often feel squeezed between two points of view: You should be honest and simply acknowledge how miserable it is to grow old, or you should do what you can to feel young and not succumb to old age. Neither position is soft and flexible, neither of them is natural and empty.

You can take the Zen and Taoist route and accept aging without thinking about it. Then the center of your aging world is like an empty dot: "I am seventy-six. End of story." Keep that dot in place, and then move on to consider how to keep your youth and not surrender to aging. Then you can entertain your envious thoughts about younger people and indulge your gossamer wishes. The dot will preserve your freedom and your contentment.

Here is a large painting by Kwang Jean Park, a Korean artist, which has been in our family home for several years, portraying the dot I'm talking about:

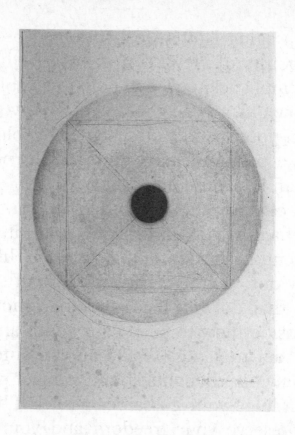

Let's call this "The Zen of Aging." Throughout life we simply want to get older without working so hard to make sense of it or make it easier. At each step, we are who we are.

Here's a principle to guide you: If you simply acknowledge your age and give no attention to all the fears and the temptations to qualify what you feel about getting old, you will have the freedom to keep your youth. And maintaining both age and youth is the deepest secret to good aging. Don't

440

slip too far into one or the other. If you don't fully and exactly acknowledge who you are as your starting point, your point zero, then you will probably compensate with an awkward attempt to stay young. Let me say it again: Keeping your youth requires that you acknowledge your exact age without any wavering.

In Kwang Jean Park's painting, notice that the dot is in a square, an image for concrete life. And there are lines connecting the corners of the square, our actual lives, to the Zen dot that is the image for nothing and the naturalness at the heart of your way of growing older. The painting guides you toward being both empty and full, centered on the profound not-doing at the heart of life and yet active in all the many ways we live under the pressure of time. You might also see that dot as the point in aging where you are today, at this minute. As long as you respect and speak for that dot, all other problems in aging will find their solution.

For decades in my own life Zen naturalness has been a principle I have tried to live by — I know, you're not supposed to try. But I've also included in my own philosophy the idea that all of our fantasies are valuable, what we consider the good and the bad. If we're afraid of aging, then we start with the Zen dot that may mark our fear and then go on to all the complexities involved in getting older. We can deal with the stories we tell ourselves and others about getting older, the memories we have of friends and relatives as they aged, and our ideas about time and identity.

Don't let this point slip by: If fear of aging or dying is the dot at the center of our emotions around aging, then that is the beginning of a solution. Don't deny your fear or distaste. Start with it. The dark element, which often lies at the very center of our lives, may be the necessary beginning point and even the heart of our progress. But don't dwell in the darkness, don't wallow, don't become attached to your fear. Acknowledge it and then let it go.

Act Your Age

In my seventies, one of the themes that floods my mind sometimes when I become aware of aging is a certain sadness that I can't plan for the future as I used to. I hear younger friends setting goals for twenty years from now, and I know I can't do that. I notice how long it takes to get a new book into print, and I'm frustrated because I don't feel that I have time to waste. My thoughts run up against the end of the years allotted to me, and I typically allow myself an advanced age.

These thoughts ask me to reset my sense of time to be in harmony with my current age. To live with life as it is. The dot, again. I may allow myself all the wishful fantasies of wanting to be younger and to have more time, because they serve a purpose. But even in the midst of those escapist thoughts I can make changes to my way of being and thinking. I can now be comfortable with limited time. Or I can do what Jung suggests: think of my life as going on for centuries, and keep doing what I do. In the end, I think both solutions amount to the same thing.

I'm reminded of a beautiful, cryptic, sad saying of the extraordinary artist Louise Bourgeois, who lived and worked until she was ninety-eight. In her last year she wrote:

Never let me be free from this burden that will never let me be free

A sense of limitation and burden need not stop you from being free to live and express creatively. Limitation is a kind of freedom. I feel that myself as I write today with more freedom and less worry about criticism than I did in my fifties. I love my forty-year-old self, but I was not as free then as I am now. Not nearly.

Louise Bourgeois didn't fall into the modern habit of rejecting classical psycho-analysis and poking fun at Freud. Throughout her life and into old age she dipped frequently into her childhood memories for inspiration and material to process. In this she offers us a good model. As we age, we can get new perspectives on our childhood and early years by sifting them through, working constantly at the basic materials. Childhood memories in all their detail are the raw material out of which we can become mature adults and even more ripened and mature old people. Those childhood memories may become sharper and more relevant as we get older, but they call for intense reflection and sorting out. The point is not to understand yourself intellectually but to actualize more of your seed material even in old age.

You don't wallow in sad memories of the past or beat yourself with regret or chastise yourself for not doing better. You allow all of those painful memories to be sucked down into the Zen hole of your current nothingness. In the emptiness you have achieved for your old age, the memories of your life lose their sting and their weight.

They become absorbed by the light nothingness of your decision to simply be.

Many of us, if not all of us, have burdens from childhood that we carry from one job to the next, one relationship to another, one decade in life to the following. We don't need to be free from this burden, but to enjoy it, sort of, as we make a more livable personality and lifestyle out of its constantly worked material.

I have met many men and women absolutely weighed down by their memories of shocking events and terrible, annihilating diatribes against them in their childhood. One wonders if they will ever be free of the burden. But here is where Bourgeois's words apply: Wish never to be free of the burden that is your special life. It is your material, precious in that it is yours alone, even if it is bitter.

So here we have another aspect of the Zen dot: Not only is it empty and natural, it is the core of our identity. Now, Hillman, whom I usually follow closely, didn't like to speak of a core identity. He wanted to keep it all multiplied and varied. Instead, I prefer to speak for both the multiplicity of the psyche and the sense of core or center. I try not to let the image of a core prevent me from appreciating the polycentric psyche.

This brings us to yet another key image from the *Tao Te Ching:*

On the hub of a wheel there are thirty
   spokes,
But the empty center makes it work.

Here the spokes are like the square and circle in the painting, and the center is the dot. You need both life and emptiness to get along. You need all your thoughts and efforts to be young, but they work only if you have an empty center.

A young woman, Kay, tells me that she had a difficult childhood, to say the least. Her parents were out of control and did countless things to undermine the young girl's confidence and sense of worth. She could do nothing right. Now those messages cling to her and as an adult she hasn't been able to accomplish any of her goals.

"I'm now in my late fifties," she says, "and I despair of ever having a life. I will end up full of regret."

Hillman says that trauma is an image, not a mere fact of history. It stays with us, and the image is the burden we carry, the thing that takes away our hope.

I've known Kay for many years, and I know her torment and her psychological and spiritual intelligence. She suffers emotionally, but she is far advanced spiritually compared to most people I know. I'm not too worried for her, though I'd love to be able to stop her suffering. Though to the passing observer she may seem pitiable, she has made a remarkable self out of painful memories. I wonder if she has ever had the courage to go to zero, the dot, the natural and soft place where there is no need for healing or change. Paradoxically, most of us look in the wrong direction for healing. We go away from ourselves instead of further into ourselves.

Notice how age is a factor in Kay's suffering. Now she wonders if she has time to work out the tragic components of her life. The fact is, she has been doing it all along. Her soul and spirit are in excellent condition, but her life has not kept up. I hope that in future years she can work out that portion of the story, and I'm rather confident that she will. She has determination, persistence and intelligence. Without these virtues, I don't know how she could go toward healing.

A big task for old age is to complete the circle of time and the flow of life. This circle is sometimes called *urobouros,* imagined as a snake biting its tale. For Jung, this was the nature of the alchemical process, the work of a lifetime to make a soul out of all that we inherit and experience. We bite our own tail. Childhood comes back to enter us through the mouth of the gaping snake. We resolve the problem of aging by returning once again to the first days, months, and years of life.

My end is my beginning. The secret to life lies in the image the alchemists and Hermeticists frequently used: the snake formed in a beautiful circle, its mouth open to receive its tail. The beginning is always present, as is every moment of life between then and now, both as a memory and as a present element in the construction of the self. The point, then, is not just to remain in touch with our youth, but to also stay connected with every moment of our lives, especially those times that seem to have forged our identity.

Age Well by Healing Split Complexes

A young woman comes to me for counseling. Suzanne is led to me because she's dissatisfied with her work life. It hasn't gelled, and she's unhappy going to the school where she is a counselor and teacher. At first, I'm so impressed with her self-knowledge and poise that I wonder where this unusually self-possessed woman has come from. She is beautiful to look at and beautiful to be with.

In our second session I hear more discordant tonalities in her story. She isn't happy at all with the way her life has gone, and I now see many loose strands of scattered emotions and plans for her future. She doesn't hold together as much as I first thought.

Suzanne is about to turn fifty, and age is pressing on her, making her feel that she has to make a change, though she has few clues of a direction to take. To me she looks much younger than nearly fifty, and I wonder what kind of youthfulness is coloring her personality. Maybe she's stuck at some point in her personal history or maybe her youth is alive in her, working for her.

The one issue I see coming to the foreground may sound simple, but I sense that it's the key to her happiness. She can't disappoint, criticize, hurt, or say no to people. She has to be sweet and understanding. We discuss how her sweetness has little depth. She tells me that sometimes harsh words fly out of her and people are hurt. They're surprised that this soft-spoken woman can suddenly turn relatively vicious.

I mention to her that this is how it often

happens: Sweetness is not real but lingers on the periphery of the emotional life, automatically and even compulsively present, and at the other extreme, harshness makes an appearance, and it is equally out of control. This split in emotions indicates an emotional complex, a situation where Suzanne doesn't own either her joy in life or her personal authority. As a result Suzanne is at the mercy of both.

Then something not terribly significant but interesting nonetheless occurs. As she is leaving I say, "I wouldn't be at all surprised if you bring me a bathroom dream soon."

Sure enough, she begins the next session wide-eyed, asking me how I knew she was going to have a bathroom dream. She acknowledges her embarrassment and then tells me the kind of excremental dream I've heard from many people who are split between their superficial sweetness and out of control harshness. Usually, the dreamer is in a bathroom stall when the toilet overflows and the dreamer has to pick up something of value lying in the filthy water around her. In this dream Suzanne comes in contact with the excrement and feels soiled and embarrassed. She doesn't want to be seen.

I see this kind of dream as an initiation

dream, a turning point where the dreamer is asked to be in close touch with her own messy and even repulsive side — Suzanne's attempts to say no and to be a stronger person. I feel that if she could now begin the process of owning all her potential, she will change. Her surface sweetness will become solid grace and good will, and her harshness will become her ability to say no when no is called for. The bathroom is the perfect venue for her transformation.

This initiation is taking place in the context of aging, turning fifty, sensing the first signs of menopause. It's the perfect time to go though a life passage and become a fuller person. Suzanne's dream, as repulsive as it may be, gives me hope that she will now start to age. If she doesn't transform, she will merely grow older. But I have strong faith in her lust for life and expect her to become a wiser and more effective person.

Over the next few months Suzanne did indeed make remarkable changes in her life and then I saw a mysterious alchemy transform her very style of relating. She gave up a fruitless job and took another that used her talents better and suited her temperament. She put herself out in the world through writing and teaching in her own original ways. As she made these changes, her tone shifted. She still had a stash of unnecessary sweetness to transmute into the gold of a wise and realistic woman, but she was making progress in that direction.

Aging with soul requires facing certain long-standing conflicts, taking the raw material of unhappiness and helping it transform into the refined material of deeper character and self-awareness. You may require a period of self-examination and courageous change.

As Suzanne and I talked about her dream, images of her parents came to her mind. She saw some of the roots of her conflict. She understood that in her own life she was working through some of her mother's unresolved issues and her father's impatience. She sorted through her many resolutions and hopes and saw that they needed grounding. In my view, Suzanne is aging, in the sense of becoming a real person, reconciling her deep, ageless soul with her personality and lifestyle.

Aging is a challenge, not an automatic activity. You go through passages, from one state to another. You become somebody. Faced with a challenge, you choose to live through the obstacle rather than avoid it. You make the decision to be in process and to participate actively.

Often the process requires meeting up once again with your unvarnished youth. It may be time to let go of half-spoken realizations and covered-over recollections, time to let it all be seen and forgiven and absorbed and laid to rest piece by piece. The head eats the tail and the snake feeds on its other end that comes full circle in the spinning of time.

Aging is a gritty process of transforming raw memories and character traits into a real and transformed self. You are no longer raw. Your conflicts have turned into qualities of character and aspects of your lifestyle. Hear the word aging differently, not as growing older but as becoming a real person and fulfilling your own destiny as you reflect on life experiences.

I'm not saying that you should live in the present moment. That is a different idea. I'm suggesting that you should acknowledge to yourself and others exactly who you are and what age you are. The number of years. Then you can deepen your aging from there. In the early traditions of the word, soul starts with the breath, where you are now, exactly as you are. No qualifications. No defensive "buts" and "ifs." It goes on to become more complex but always in relation to being who you are. You can sense your youth and cultivate it. You can wish for a different past and hope for a different future, but only if you are loyal to your age. Being your age saves you from becoming neurotic when you try to look younger.

The secret here is to make a strong distinction between what you wish and what is. Wishing can be a denial of who you are. It can distance you from your self, from your soul. Many people waste the positive advantages of being older in wishing it were not so.

That said, there is a place for wishes. Wishing you were younger can express your love of life, your preference that life would never end or at least that you wouldn't be getting closer to the end. You have to know the difference between neurotic wish as denial and beautiful wish as love of life. Behind the sadness many of us feel as we get really old is our love of life. I think it's a good thing to accept death in its inevitability, but I also think it's good to fight for life and not give in too easily.

Yes, we end with the paradox of paradoxes: You age best by embracing your age, with suitable melancholy, and at the same time choosing to live without age, ageless, with as much joy as you can muster. This requires that you understand you are not your body, you are not the sum of your experiences, and you are not as restricted by time as you may have thought. You have a soul, the river of vitality from which your life flows, a tributary of a much grander soul of the world. Your soul is there at every moment of experience in time, but it is also ageless. You have to learn to live from both places. Ficino says, "The soul is partly in time and partly in eternity." Living in relation to the eternal part is the challenge of the modern technological and calendar-driven person, and it is the best way to age with equanimity and pleasure.

INDEX

48–51, 93, 100–4, 127, 159–61,
251–52, 271, 320–21, 361, 368–75,
451

as growth enabler, 13–24, 32–38, 41–56,
450–52

guidelines for proactive, 159–61

illness in relation to, 195–218

imperfection's embrace in, 11–14, 22,
49–54, 79–84, 170–74, 177–80

legacies as relevant to, 298–324

loneliness and, 325–48

melancholy's place in, 111–35, 452

play's importance in, 246–68

processing life's experiences in, 84–88,
136–61, 445–48, 450–52

reflection's role in, 145–61, 227, 239,
248, 261–64, 332–36, 341–46,
366–68, 377–81, 383–413

sexuality and, 52, 162–90, 221n

spirituality/religion's role in, 383–413

split complexes and, 448–55

youth-old age coexisting during, 27–56,
57–83, 106–7, 345–46, 453–55

Ailey, Alvin, 158

alchemy, 96, 144–45, 147, 161, 261, 448

Allen, Woody, 121, 158

anam cara (friendship), 283

ancestors, honoring of, 305–10

Anchises (Greek mythological figure), 162

Angelou, Maya, 313

ABOUT THE AUTHOR

Thomas Moore is the *New York Times* bestselling author of *Care of the Soul,* as well as many other books on deepening soul and cultivating a mature spiritual life, three of which have received the Books for a Better Life Award. At turns he has been a monk, a musician, a university professor, and a psychotherapist. Today he lectures widely on creating a more soulful world and on spirituality. He lives in New Hampshire.

The employees of Thorndike Press hope you have enjoyed this Large Print book. All our Thorndike, Wheeler, and Kennebec Large Print titles are designed for easy reading, and all our books are made to last. Other Thorndike Press Large Print books are available at your library, through selected bookstores, or directly from us.

For information about titles, please call:
(800) 223-1244

or visit our website at:
gale.com/thorndike

To share your comments, please write:
Publisher
Thorndike Press
10 Water St., Suite 310
Waterville, ME 04901